The Public Mind and the Politics of Postmillennial U.S.-American Writing

Buchreihe der Anglia/ ANGLIA Book Series

Edited by
Andrew James Johnston, Ursula Lenker, Martin Middeke, Gabriele Rippl, Daniel Stein

Advisory Board
Laurel Brinton, Philip Durkin, Olga Fischer, Susan Irvine, Christopher A. Jones, Terttu Nevalainen, Ad Putter, James Simpson, Emily Thornbury, Derek Attridge, Elisabeth Bronfen, Ursula K. Heise, Verena Lobsien, Liliane Louvel, Christopher Morash, Susana Onega, Martin Puchner, Peter Schneck

Volume 79

The Public Mind and the Politics of Postmillennial U.S.-American Writing

Edited by
Jolene Mathieson, Marius Henderson, and Julia Lange

DE GRUYTER

ISBN 978-3-11-153372-8
e-ISBN (PDF) 978-3-11-077135-0
e-ISBN (EPUB) 978-3-11-077141-1
ISSN 0340-5435

Library of Congress Control Number: 2022936767

Bibliographic information published by the Deutsche Nationalbibliothek
The Deutsche Nationalbibliothek lists this publication in the Deutsche Nationalbibliografie; detailed bibliographic data are available on the internet at http://dnb.dnb.de.

© 2024 Walter de Gruyter GmbH, Berlin/Boston
This volume is text- and page-identical with the hardback published in 2022.

www.degruyter.com

For Susanne Rohr, Professor of American Studies at the University of Hamburg

Acknowledgements

First and foremost, we would like to thank Susanne Rohr, Professor of American Studies at the University of Hamburg. She has been a guiding light at every stage of this project, and this volume would not have been possible without her.

We would also like to thank our colleagues at the Institute of British and American Studies in Hamburg, especially Astrid Böger and Ute Berns, for their encouragement and support in the creation and editing of this volume. A special acknowledgment is reserved for our colleague and friend Jan D. Kucharzewski, who was always willing to help, whether as a proofreader, a cheerleader, or as a support in tricky research logistics. His insights have proved invaluable.

We would further like to extend our sincere gratitude to all of those who contributed to the creation of this project, including Bettina Friedl, Ulla Haselstein, Herwig Friedl, Felix Sprang, Peter Hühn, Miriam Strube, Ruth Mayer, Eva Boesenberg, and Sieglinde Lemke.

And finally, we would also like to humbly thank Hubert Zapf, who played an instrumental role in shaping this book by offering us support at every step, from conceptualization, to editing and publishing.

Table of Contents

Jolene Mathieson, Marius Henderson, and Julia Lange
The Public Mind and the Politics of Postmillennial U.S.-American Writing —— 1

Section One: **Novel Transitions in the Millennium**

Heinz Ickstadt
The Late Style of Three Postmodernist Masters: Thomas Pynchon, Don DeLillo, and Robert Coover —— 17

Hubert Zapf
Siri Hustvedt and the Transdisciplinary Knowledge of Literature —— 35

Ulfried Reichardt
Shostakovich, Totalitarianism, and Anglo-American Fiction: Powers, Barnes, and Vollmann —— 49

Joseph C. Schöpp
History is Suffering: Reading Teju Cole's *Open City* in Light of Walter Benjamin and W. G. Sebald —— 71

Christa Buschendorf
Greek Passion Revisited: Appropriations of Medea in African American Fiction —— 85

Section Two: **Realisms and Representing the Anthropocene**

Sabine Sielke
The Newly Conventional U.S.-American Novel and the (Neo-)Liberal Imagination: on Franzen, Eggers, and the Like —— 111

Thomas Claviez
Neorealism, Metonymy, and the Question of Contingency —— 129

Astrid Böger
For the Birds: Nell Zink's and Jonathan Franzen's Environmentalist Fiction —— 147

Jan D. Kucharzewski
"...the Wood for the Trees": Scale, Sentience, and Sentiment in Richard Powers' *The Overstory* —— 159

Catrin Gersdorf
Forests, Sustainability, and the Ecological Cynicism of the Anthropocene: Reading Annie Proulx's *Barkskins* —— 179

Section Three: Identity and the Poetics of Transgression

Astrid Franke
Claudia Rankine's *Citizen: An American Lyric:* Fighting Microaggression, Loneliness, and Disconnection —— 201

Andrew S. Gross
Ellen Hinsey: Poet of the Public Sphere —— 213

Kai Hopen
"In Part, Absolutely": Language, Form, and Potential in Ben Lerner's *The Topeka School* —— 229

Laura Bieger
The 1619 Project as Aesthetic and Social Practice; or, the Art of the Essay in the Digital Age —— 253

Notes on Contributors —— 279

Index —— 283

Jolene Mathieson, Marius Henderson, and Julia Lange
The Public Mind and the Politics of Postmillennial U.S.-American Writing

Abstract: The first chapter of *The Public Mind and the Politics of Postmillennial U.S.-American Writing* initially traces and recounts some of the major developments to have taken place in U.S.-American fiction in the last twenty years. Traditionally, 20th-century modes of realism and postmodernism have since been succeeded by writerly practices that, in one way or another, are relatable to neo-realism, whether it be via outright affirmation or critical experimentation and appropriation. The re-emergence of investments in notions formerly combatted by postmodernists, such as embodied "authenticity," is accompanied by an ongoing awareness toward complexity and the fundamental entanglement of writers, critics, and the reading public with pressing political concerns, and at times oppressive, social and economic discursive and structural formations. The introduction provides an overview of all three sections of this volume's collection of essays as well as of each its fourteen chapters. All contributions share said awareness toward the seemingly inextricable intertwinement of postmillennial U.S.-American writing with the reading public as well as the extratextual contexts in which it is embedded, whether this writing be novelistic or more experimental.

In his essay at the turn of the millennium, "Making the Public Mind: The Struggle for the Soul of the Sentence," the essayist and literary critic Sven Birkerts expresses his surprise that when confronted with "what seems to many an impoverished, phrase-based paradigm" in "our great age of infotainment" – instant messaging, sound bites, banners, and chyrons – U.S.-American fiction and other modes of writing had chosen not to respond with a mere stylistic mimicry of the diminished or the vacuous nor even with an updated version of mid-century minimalism, but rather, with narrative and structural complexity, with grammatical and lexical sophistication, and with social and "cultural nuance" (2001: 68).

Birkerts traces the turn in U.S.-American fiction in the last two decades of the 20th century away from the "ascetic realism" à la Ernest Hemingway and Raymond Carver to what may be understood as a 'maximalist realism,' or "maximalism" as he calls it – "a tendency toward expansive, centrifugal narrative that aspires to the complexity of contemporary life" (68). This turn, he argues, took place in tandem with two important interrelated trends. The first one is a recognition that the "great populist prejudice" (69) of equating 'American' writing and 'Americanness' with the "plainspoken tradition" (70) was no longer, if it ever had been, an apt 'realist' paradigm for confronting and negotiating the social realities of modern life. The initial attraction to ascetic realism might be explained by its appeal to the mundane and the minute in its creation of "uneasy portraits of American middle-class domesticity" (70). With its emphasis on plain English and 'plain lives,' it would seem to embody a similar democratic ideal in prose that Walt Whitman would have argued for poetry.

In its rejection of broad political themes, narrative complexity, and 'fancy language,' ascetic realism is only marginally related to what we often associate with realism: the socially conscious and political style of writing pioneered by William Dean Howells in the second half of the 19th century. Conversely, ascetic realism withholds any sense of the social, especially any feeling of interrelatedness or connectedness to the political, wider world 'out there.' It is only palatable as a 'realism' because it creates a sense of connection through individualism, through loneliness and loss perhaps, but also through a blunt matter-of-factness about simply being in the world. But herein lies the "paradox," as Birkerts puts it (we might also call it "deceit") – "For if the subject matter was, in this most reduced sense, realistic, the impetus of the mode was aesthetic" (70–71). By way of example, Birkerts points to the highly mannered style of Carver, the carefully-crafted "hyperawareness" of Amy Hempel, and the "clipped sentences" of Hemingway (ibid). While the poignant moments captured in ascetic realism might be lyrical, and for the most part, mimetic, snapshots of ordinary – mostly white, middle-class, domestic – American life, its reductionism, interiority, and pared-down poetic aestheticism obviously cannot demonstrate sustained contiguity or fidelity to the rich, messy, and often brutal political, racialized, gendered, networked reality of contemporary American life.

The failure of the ascetic, plainspoken model of realism is concomitant with the second trend discussed by Birkerts: the cultural dominance of electronic communication and digital media in all aspects of American life. "The gradual triumph of the maximalist approach" (72) by postmodern realists like, say, Thomas Pynchon, Don DeLillo, and Helen DeWitt, of the so-called neorealists like Jonathan Franzen and Dave Eggers, and the more uncategorizable realists like Siri Hustvedt, Toni Morrison, and Colson Whitehead bespeaks of a desire on the part of late 20th-century (and 21st-century) U.S.-American writers to engage with the public sphere in their fullest capacity as political actors – as public intellectuals – in an attempt "to make sense of the new situation" (69). Regardless of style or ideological bent, what these writers (and so many more of course) have in common is a willingness to comment on, negotiate, critique but also embrace and herald the *complexity* of an American culture situated in a larger, highly politicized, globalized world undergoing radical change vis-à-vis digitalization, the Internet, and the ubiquity of advanced technologies. Writing of Pynchon's influence on shaping maximalist realism, Birkerts points to how he "patented a style, an approach that could later be adapted to rendering the strange interdependence of a world liberated from its provincial boundedness" (ibid).

The effect of no longer being bounded to the provincial, to the plain, to the mundane moment, is, of course, a re-recognition, a re-confrontation of the profound, and often disturbing, political realities of so many U.S.-American lives. Twenty years after the publication of Birkerts' diagnosis of U.S.-American writing, these political realities remain, and in many cases, to detrimental effect. How, then, has U.S.-American writing and the reading public continued to respond to the rapid acceleration of production and work, the homogenization of economic markets under the hegemony of late capitalism and the increase of private debt, to systemic racism and structural inequality, to the erosion of privacy, to anti-science and anti-intellectualism in the public discourse, and to the worsening effects of climate change?

In an attempt to address this question, this volume assembles an array of American Studies scholars trained in Germany and living in Europe who examine the public mind and the politics of postmillennial U.S.-American writing from a German-inflected perspective. The individual case studies presented here mark the ways in which U.S.-American writing performs essential cultural work which addresses social, political, and environmental concerns that are of eminent importance not only in the U.S. but also on an international scale, such as the erosion of democracy in an era of pervasive "post-factual" discourse formations, digital surveillance, mass immigration, and climate change. These contributions further attest to how narrative and structural complexity, grammatical and lexical sophistication, and social nuance endure as the main literary modes of confronting 21st century political life, but also demonstrate a traceable movement away from the limitations of the postmodernist paradigm in which some of the maximalist realists discussed by Birkerts were working.

Postmodernism's profound contribution to both academic and aesthetic forms of knowledge was its recognition of the dangers of invisible metanarratives present in all discursive texts. Initially articulated as a critique of modernism's tendency towards totalizing *métarécits*, Jean-François Lyotard defined the "postmodern condition" as an "incredulity toward metanarratives" in which "narrative function is losing its functors, its great hero, its great dangers, its great voyages, its great goal. It is being dispersed in clouds of narrative language" (1984: xxxiv). Instead of continuing the dour *Kulturpessimismus* associated with the Critical Theory of the Frankfurter Schule, the post-structuralist theories regarded the abolishment of grand narratives as a vital emancipatory project: entropy became a productive catalyst of change rather than a regrettable loss of order.

While the actual extent of the mutual fertilization between continental philosophy and the first phases of postmodern U.S.-American fiction might not be as self-evident as intuition would suggest, it is also indisputable that since the 1970s writers like Robert Coover and Thomas Pynchon began to scrutinize the validity and veracity of (fictional) narratives in a manner evocative of post-structuralism, yet with a much more pronounced proclivity towards subversion, self-referentiality, and irony.

In some academic discourses, the conceptual resonances between post-structuralist theories and postmodern (meta-)fiction have engendered a casual conflation of the two movements under the leaking umbrella term of a 'postmodern relativism' marked by the "happy celebration" of "difference" and "anti-structure" (Thomassen 2014: 83) or even "outright chaos" (Szakolczai 2009: 166). According to some observers, the postmodern turn elevated critical gestures of irony and deconstruction into ends of themselves by subverting norms without offering feasible alternatives. In these readings, the utopian potentiality of Lyotard's question "Where, after the meta-narratives, can legitimacy reside?" becomes a dystopian free-for-all (un)governed by tricksters, sophists, anti-facticity, and ethical laissez-faire (Lyotard 1984: xxiv–xxv). The generation of U.S.-American writers who came into prominence during the 1990s and 2000s (among them, David Foster Wallace, Richard Powers, Jonathan Franzen, Nicole Krauss, Jennifer Egan, Siri Hustvedt) frequently express similar concerns regarding the legitimacy and relevance of postmodern gestures and attitudes in a late-capitalist mediascape that has eagerly embraced irony, snark, and self-referentiality as selling points, thus depriving these strategies of their initial subversiveness.

Many of these writers as well as the literary criticism they have spawned tend to construct a hyperbolic version of postmodern (meta)fiction as *a priori* anti-realistic, ironically self-aware, and resistant to closure. This version of postmodern fiction seems to loom much larger in critical discourses than in actual literary productions, as will be shown in the volume's first contribution by Heinz Ickstadt. More often than not postmodern metafiction can already be understood as a kind of self-aware realism rather than a mere rejection of the necessity for narrative (see e.g. Kucharzewski 2015).

But even when accounting for the degree to which postmodern literature was probably not as self-defeating as it was made out to be, contemporary neo-realist writings can be understood as an attempt of literature to step back from the ultimately anesthetizing and complacent articulations of postmodern irony that by now are thoroughly incorporated into mass media, social media, consumerism, and political discourses. But the corrective redress of neorealism has no extra-literary equivalent. While literary fiction has become increasingly aware of the epistemological entrapments of an over-pronounced rejection of organizing principles, mimetic illusions, and attempts at verisimilitude, the postmodern project of radical skepticism, irony, paranoia, and narrative refutation is currently continued by the very forces, institutions, and actors which were the original targets of both post-structuralism and postmodern fiction. Contemporary literature therefore faces the question of how to reclaim notions of sincerity, truthfulness, and authenticity while simultaneously challenging the exploding presence of anti-facticity in media and politics.

This renewed interest in and desire for signs of 'authenticity' and 'realness' in literature, it might be argued, can also find its critical corollary in what has been called 'postcritique.' In their call to move beyond a literary criticism primarily derived from post-structuralist practices of deconstruction and 'paranoid reading,' Anker and Felski posit that "the intellectual and political payoff of interrogating, demystifying, and defamiliarizing is no longer quite so self-evident" (2017: 1). Such criticism, they argue, is often driven by "a pronounced aversion toward norms and an automatic distrust of instrumentality and institutions" (17) and therefore encourages "an antagonistic and combative attitude toward the public world" (18). This self-imposed "spirit of marginality" (17), they contend, keeps "serious thought sequestered in the ivory tower, thereby working to ensure its lack of impact or influence on the public sphere" (18). We might say, then, that postcritique seeks to provide a hermeneutics of encouragement, even of reconciliation maybe, and encourages modes of critical writing which enable closure, celebrate symmetries, and work to affirm the emancipatory potential and facticity of literature in order to "forge stronger links between intellectual life and the nonacademic world" (17).

The recourse to authenticity, however, can have reactionary as well as more progressive tendencies. The authenticity claims of texts may also be indicators of the complete subsumption of life itself to economic and state-sanctioned power dynamics and should therefore be regarded as eminently biopolitical. "Googleable" author photos, book launches, reading or rather book promotion tours and online events, the presence of authors on social media, and an awareness of their association with certain cliques/social circles function as paratextual "truth signs." So while deconstructivism's overemphasis on the purely textual dimension of literature appears to have become passé, it is wise to recognize, for example, the complicity of neorealist fiction with the neoliberal status quo, both intratextually and extratextually. In her contribution, Sabine Sielke thus examines the commodification of fiction and authors, asking important questions for us as readers and as critics: What is our role in this?

Are we complicit or dare we contradict and refute the status quo in our critical work?

Authors from marginalized groups in particular have to negotiate and navigate between what Claudia Rankine has termed the "historical self," their interpellation as representatives of certain identity groups, and their more private "self self" (Rankine 2014: 14). Which of these "selves" is more marketable or can be represented in such a manner that it appears to be more authentic and readily consumed by the reading public? The renewed highlighting of the position of the author does not so evoke a position of authorial mastery over the fictional and non-fictional world as foreground their embodied situatedness in the extra-textual world. This, in turn, informs, for example, the innovative and experimental writing practices of Claudia Rankine in *Citizen: An American Lyric*, which is discussed in the volume's contribution by Astrid Franke, and of Teju Cole in *Open City*, which Joseph C. Schöpp examines in his essay. Both Rankine and Cole incorporate a number of genres in order create complex texts that move beyond traditional modes of realism to what Heather Love, in discussing Rankine, refers to as 'aesthetic' and 'political realism' (Love 2016: 420–421.) While Rankine has been skeptical regarding the ability of realism "to capture the experience of race," she "mobilizes a range of resources" – the essay, witness testimony, cultural criticism, memoir, the documentary and images – to capture "fugitive realities" (ibid: 424). The turn to political realism in the kinds of poetics practiced by Rankine as well as Cole can also be said to be less of a purely textual realism, i.e. based on the employment of linguistic codes which produce "reality effects." The reality and authenticity effects are rather "paratextual" insofar as they rely on embodied cues beyond the texts which vouchsafe for their credibility and their political import. Authenticity claims and effects also produce the feeling of intimacy – both imagined and real – between authors, texts, and readers, which also includes literary critics.

The collected essays of this volume thus present a varied spectrum of critical responses. These responses range from a certain 'postcritical' investment in optimism and positivism and the hopeful belief that writing might be conducive to a sustainable cultural ecology, as in the case of Astrid Franke's reading of Rankine's *Citizen* and Laura Bieger's luminous account of the *New York Times*' The 1619 Project, to more skeptical positions regarding the subjugation of fiction to the logic of the market, to more theoretical interventions that call into question how the social can be represented in criticism, as forcefully examined and argued in Thomas Claviez' essay. In her *Living, Thinking, Looking*, Siri Hustvedt writes that "writing is perception as encoding" and "reading is perception as translation" (2012: 133). The critics who contributed to this edited volume are foremost readers and "embodied beings" (ibid: 134), and call attention to Toril

Moi's recognition that contemporary literary criticism is less concerned with methods and methodology than with the "mood" and "mind-set" of the critic (2017: 34–35). The contributors here are committed to an open "mind-set" – open toward the dynamic intertwinements of texts, authors, readers, bodies, and contexts.

The first section of this volume, "Novel Transitions in the Millennium," comprises five chapters that critically reflect on the development of U.S.-American practices of novelistic writing in the first two decades of the 21st century. The postmillennial novels discussed in these chapters are all socially conscious and make explicit the ways in which the subject is situated in political and discursive entanglements with the world. This social awareness is marked, on one hand, by an investment in renewal and novelty, ranging from formal innovation and creative epistemological perspectives to recuperative accounts of forgotten or repressed histories. On the other hand, these novels share a sense of their indebtedness to 20th-century literary practices, discursive formations, and sets of knowledge, in some cases even harkening back to early 20th-century modernism. Hence, the novelties that are inherent in the 'novel transitions' under investigation also remain entangled with a number of aesthetic and political continuities with the past.

The volume begins with a contribution from imminent literary scholar and professor emeritus Heinz Ickstadt. As a self-confessed "aging literary historian," Ickstadt is interested in exploring the "late style" of three writers who came to prominence as innovative postmodernists in the 20th century but who have continued to write in the 21st century: Thomas Pynchon, Don DeLillo, and Robert Coover. Invoking Theodor W. Adorno's and Edward Said's reflections on "late style," Ickstadt discusses the ways in which these novelists negotiate transitory tensions between continuity and re-invention by contextualizing their work in literary history and aesthetics, in political discourses, and also in relation to their readership and its expectations and responses. In a self-reflexive gesture that soundly resonates with recent tendencies in literary criticism that pay renewed attention to the role of readership, Ickstadt also includes reflections on his own positionality as a reader and a critic.

Hubert Zapf's contribution, "Siri Hustvedt and the Transdisciplinary Knowledge of Literature," examines the multifaceted ways in which Siri Hustvedt's novels generate complex modes of transdisciplinary knowledge and shows how these works are exemplary of what he has theorized elsewhere as "cultural ecology" (see Zapf 2016). Informed by a broad spectrum of disciplines, ranging from philosophy, art history and psychoanalysis to neuroscience and medicine, the narratives and their underlying epistemologies in Hustvedt's novels generate spaces of imagination in which ostensible contradictions between epistemological stances are suspended, and traditional Western oppositions between the humanities and the natural sciences are undermined. Zapf carefully traces how these imaginative literary spaces foster relational zones of engagement and interplay, not only between different human modes of knowledge production but also between humans and nonhuman agents, objects, and materials. Hence, Hustvedt's novels engender collaborative and creative assemblages of exchange, becoming active participants in a "cultural ecology" that reaffirm the power and necessity of literature.

In his paper "Shostakovich, Totalitarianism, and Anglo-American Fiction: Powers, Barnes and Vollmann," Ulfried Reichardt explores the reasons for the renewed interest in the Soviet composer and pianist Dmitri Dmitriyevich Shostakovich in 21st-century Anglo-American fiction. Postmodern skepticism and regressive politics, Reichardt argues, provided the cultural context in which Shostakovich's complicated life and music under Soviet totalitarianism turned into a test case for questioning "not only the possibilities and limits of art" but also "the basic predicaments of our current situation." In his contrastive analysis of three novels, Reichardt examines the texts' different uses of Shostakovich's biography and oeuvre under totalitarianism to comment on our contemporary condition and the difficulties of ascribing political effectiveness to music. Whereas Richard Powers' *Orfeo* (2014) explicitly functionalizes Shostakovich to ponder the danger of surveillance in the contemporary United States, Julian Barnes' *The Noise of Time* (2006) focuses on Shostakovich's lived experience under Stalinism and the potential and limits of irony as a political and artistic strategy of survival. In contrast to Barnes' novel, in which music is largely neglected and, if at all, features as a projection screen for politically determined interpretations that obscure the sounds' immediacy, William T. Vollmann's *Europe Central* (2005) employs Shostakovich's music as a "medium for accessing experiences," putting it to use as a leitmotif that allows reflections on the composer's "doublespeak," existential conditions under war and totalitarianism and the resulting extreme moral dilemmas.

Joseph C. Schöpp's chapter, "History is Suffering: Reading Teju Cole's *Open City* in Light of Walter Benjamin and W. G. Sebald," focuses on Cole's novel of 2011. Incorporating elements of memoir, art criticism, historiography, and critical theory among other forms of writing, *Open City*, Schöpp argues, "is strictly speaking not a novel; as a plotless, free-flowing form of narration it disregards generic boundaries and oscillates between literary genres." Via intricate close readings, Schöpp demonstrates how the experimental form of Cole's text does not resemble a formalistic end in it itself but reverberates with its thematic concerns for historical reality and the political position of the immigrant as a transnational subject. Schöpp's chapter discusses how *Open City*'s open form and thematic investments draw on the likewise unconventional, genre-bending work of Walter Benjamin and W. G. Sebald. What Cole's novel shares with these 20th-century writers and thinkers is an engaged consideration of the disregarded aspects and events of the past that have been largely disavowed by hegemonic accounts of history, such as colonialism, genocide, and slavery.

In the first section's final contribution, Christa Buschendorf discusses how three novels by Black authors, W. E. B. Du Bois' *The Quest of the Silver Fleece*, Jesmyn Ward's *Salvage the Bones*, and Percival Everett's *For Her Dark Skin*, draw on, creatively appropriate, and critically rewrite the classical Greek myth of Medea. Buschendorf's chapter elucidates how the acts of rewriting in these three novels make an already complex myth, and more precisely, a highly complex and ambiguous mythological figure, even more complex and intricate "while simultaneously increasing its critical political potential." Moreover, Buschendorf demonstrates that the heightened degrees of complexity via which the Medea myth is rendered in the novels does not result in (post)modern relativism or apolitical nihilism but strikingly goes hand in hand with a sharpened socio-political critique, mainly of white supremacy and patriarchy. Whether it be via strategies of inversion and enhancement, or investments into different novelistic subgenres, modes, and styles, such as the historical novel, romance, melodrama or parody, in their rewriting of an ancient white European myth Du Bois, Ward, and Everett imaginatively and resourcefully utilize the figure of Medea in novelistically invoked visions of Black feminist and antiracist empowerment and emancipation.

In the volume's second section, titled "Realisms and the Anthropocene," two chapters which examine neorealism as a genre are juxtaposed with three chapters that also address the genre but more specifically in the context of the Anthropocene. This section thus poses a series of questions: what are the mechanics of neorealism, in which ways, if at all, can neorealism claim verisimilitude to the political realities of postmillennial life, and how, if at all, can it accommodate the profound demands of representing large-scale planetary change that in many ways is beyond human scales of comprehension?

Sabine Sielke's chapter, "The Newly Conventional U.S.-American Novel and the (Neo-)Liberal Imagination: on Franzen, Eggers, and the Like," examines the work of Jonathan Franzen and Dave Eggers, whose novels strongly draw on realist traditions, in the light of the pervasiveness of neoliberalism – not only as a structural socio-economic condition but also as discursive formation that shapes cultural imagination. Sielke introduces the trenchant notion of the "newly conventional" in order to theorize the affirmation of convention and the status quo, partially commingling with mild attempts at minor renewal, in contemporary (neo-)realist fiction. Drawing on the work of Susanne Rohr (2004), among others,

Sielke shows that the critique of the status quo only emerges in these works, if at all, in a very deflated form, no longer qua experimentalism and irony, as during postmodernism, but via a subtly showcased awareness of wide-spread accommodation and complicity with the neoliberal status quo. Critically addressing the gendered politics of the "newly conventional," the chapter ends with an insightful note on the role which literary criticism plays under the pervasive conditions of neoliberalism and on how and if criticism may sometimes fall prey to the same market dynamics to which contemporary fiction writers are exposed.

In the volume's most theoretical intervention, Thomas Claviez' chapter "Neo-realism, Metonymy, and the Question of Contingency" fundamentally calls into question key tenets of critical discourses that have thus far shaped discussions of literary realism and neorealism. The chapter demonstrates that, in terms of its epistemological principles, contemporary neorealist fiction, as espoused by Jonathan Franzen, for example, obliterates traces of a naïve belief in the transparency of language and in language's mimetic capacities. Moreover, the chapter discusses neorealism "against the grain" by exhibiting certain normative and rather totalizing assumptions which characterize prevalent approaches toward neorealism. Among these assumptions is the claim that neorealism was driven by a nostalgic yearning for the possibility of representing "reality" in writing and for a return to classical realism's investment in dialogical modes of linguistic representation and exchange along with the hopeful attachment to fantasies of non-conflictual community building and successful intersubjective recognition.

Claviez' chapter, however, dismantles these assumptions by laying bare their constitutive philosophical premises and attachments. Cogently, the chapter shows how predominant traditions in the Western history of thought, from Aristotle, via Kant and Hegel, up to contemporary proponents of dialectical theories of recognition in their most basic tropological assertions have favored metaphor over metonymy. This, he argues, has fundamentally influenced literary theory and practice, leading to the prominence of structurally metaphor-driven conceptualizations of narrative and serving to impose 'order' on the contingency of extra-textual, historical reality. The chapter attempts to temper this tendency and address its urgent ethical implications, as Claviez states: "The more we try to create order out of the contingency of historical reality, the more we by default distance ourselves from this very reality." Inviting us "to think of Realism in a new way," Claviez calls for a critical investigation of neorealism's investment in metonymy, which ultimately reverberates less imposingly and more fittingly with the contingency of the extra-textual world.

Probing the potential of neorealist fiction to effectively represent environmentalist concerns, Astrid Böger in her contribution compares the representation of human-avian interactions in Jonathan Franzen's *Freedom* (2010) and Nell

Zink's *Wallcreeper* (2014). Both novels, Böger argues, decidedly abstain from providing readers with a clear environmentalist agenda. It is precisely through their renunciation of a programmatic approach paired with a verisimitudinal aesthetic, which relies on what she finds to be "utterly relatable storylines and characters," that an understanding of the complexity of our biosphere is facilitated. While both novels functionalize birds as symbols of the strained relations between humans and the natural habitat they inevitably alter, Böger shows how they differ in their applied methods and discussions of human interventions into ecosystems.

Jan D. Kucharzewski's contribution argues that Richard Powers' *The Overstory*, an ecocritical novel revolving around the so-called "Timber Wars" of the 1990s during which protesters attempted to stop the massive deforestation of the Pacific Northwest, simultaneously serves as a critique of humanism as a cognitive bias preventing us to fully recognize non-human forms of life and as an affirmation of the novel as a mode of expression that might facilitate such recognition. In contrast to conventional critical readings which group Powers' oeuvre among neorealist writers like Jonathan Franzen, Jennifer Egan, or Jeffrey Eugenides, Kucharzewski suggests that Powers' aesthetic and political agenda cannot be squared with the neoliberal positions underwriting many neorealist texts. Instead, *The Overstory* concedes that "people see better what looks like them" and then opts for a form of neo-sentimentalism which might move its readers into recognition through false analogies. Kucharzewski deftly argues that *The Overstory* eventually reveals how verisimilitude is a purely human construct that is effective through metonymical association.

Adopting a postcritical stance à la Felski (2015), Catrin Gersdorf's luminous essay argues that Annie Proulx's *Barkskins* (2016), a realist, ecocritical novel that depicts the deforestation of North America from 1693 to 2013 in the guise of a multi-generational family saga, functions both as a critical comment on Christianity's and Western modernity's destructive and exploitative attitude towards nature as well as a sophisticated example of literature's ability to successfully depict and partake in the dialectics of "ecological cynicism" – defined by Gersdorf as "to know the truth about the destructive nature of modernity and continue the work of ecological restoration anyway; to acknowledge the ultimate ecological irrelevance of human work and insist on its cultural significance anyway." Weaving historical and philosophical analyses of the notions of sustainability and cynicism with close readings of the novel, Gersdorf demonstrates that *Barkskins* is ultimately a deeply humanist text that productively unsettles the neat dualisms of hope/despair and of human/nonhuman vis-à-vis climate change and is therewith able to provide us with valuable and veritable insights on the human condition in the Anthropocene.

The third and final section, "Identity and the Poetics of Transgression," moves away from the novelistic to more experimental writing practices that embrace the realist potentials found in prose but expand them in transgressive ways. These chapters center on the (re)emergence of an aesthetic of veracity aimed at documenting histories of (symbolic) violence and (racial) oppression in our present era of deep divisions and discontent, of illiberal tendencies, ethnonationalism, persistent antisemitism and racism, and of post-factual politics. Decidedly displacing attention from the purely personal to a larger collectivity and hence connectivity, the four papers collected here mobilize multimodal strategies – ranging from the essayistic to the aphoristic and newly journalistic – to excavate, record, and hence politically intervene in historical and current injustices on a micro- and macrosociological level.

In the first chapter of this section, Astrid Franke ponders the complex affective poetics and politics of pain in Claudia Rankine's book-length poem, to which she ascribes a transhistorically informed efficacy in registering the social and individual costs of today's racism. In a reconstruction of her own reading process, Franke elucidates the multilayered temporalities underlying Rankine's experimental, multimodal approach to conveying various forms and effects of microaggression. By drawing on intricate narratological devices and temporal structures and inserting essay-like writings and collages on sports and race, Rankine's text invites readings that transcend a narrow interpretation of its affective ethics as registering solely aggression and pain, Franke argues. *Citizen* is much rather also expressive of "a desire for intimacy, a need to reconnect in order to fight the feeling of self-alienation and loneliness."

Next, Andrew S. Gross discusses the work of poet Ellen Hinsey, arguing that her move away from confessional modes of poetic lyricism and her adoption of prosaic and more overtly political forms such as aphorisms, is a reflection of the way in which poetry can engage in the real-world politics of the 21st century and "affirm the importance of the public sphere." Hinsey's aphoristic poetics explore violence and virtue, oppression and redemption within a legalistic framework, and thereby, as Gross asserts, creates a form which moves away from the self-absorption of confessional poetry based on individual passion to one which allows for communal compassion in which justice is addressed and made possible.

Kai Hopen's chapter addresses the question to what extent Ben Lerner's loosely autofictional novelistic text, *The Topeka School*, manages to transcend its effusive preoccupation with poetics and to convincingly engage with the more recent political pasts and preconditions that led to Trump's ascent to power. Arguing that Lerner's text is "more inventorial than straightforwardly argumentative" or "classifying" in its approach, Hopen delineates how the book's underlying linguistic hyperawareness paired with its emphatic formalism and didacticism ultimately create two opposing effects. While diverting the text from the decidedly political and thus purportedly compromising its politico-analytical strength, *Topeka*'s exuberant reflections on language – including its power to mediate between private and public interests – also invite readers to ponder the protean nature and intersections of literature and politics, thereby potentially creating a more subtle exploration of the political "prehistory of the present."

In the final contribution of the volume, Laura Bieger returns us to the artform of the essay, a form she argues, that is congenial to our current political realities as it can adopt traditional modes of journalism, literature, and visual aesthetics to our contemporary media environment while also reframing history in ways that alert to us to how and why history is still very much present. She does so by drawing on the German intellectual tradition (Georg Lukács to Max Bense to Theodor Adorno) that sees the essay as a distinctive literary form and imbedding her discussion of the essay to her "larger interest in the reading public as a political actor – an actor," which she argues, "is indispensable to modern democracies" (see also Bieger 2020). By examining the hugely successful but also controversial *New York Times*' The 1619 Project, which she says to be "one of the most powerful interventions in public discourse on race and racism in the U.S. in recent years," Bieger seeks to understand how "new journalism" interjects traditional narrative modes with the personal and the moral to enact social reform. Against the backdrop of the mass protests which erupted in response to the murder of George Floyd in the summer of 2020 and the disturbing social inequalities in the U.S. that have once again been made apparent during the Covid-19 pandemic, Bieger's thorough treatment of The 1619 Project brings this volume to our most contemporary moment and argues for the transformative potential of literature in the reading public.

Works Cited

Anker, Elizabeth S. and Rita Felski (eds.). 2017. *Critique and Postcritique*. Durham: Duke University Press.

Bieger, Laura. 2020. "What Dewey Knew: The Public as Problem, Practice, and Art." Special Issue "Truth or Post-Truth?" Dustin Breitenwischer and Tobias Keiling (eds.). *European Journal of American Studies* 15.1: n. pag.

Birkerts, Sven. 2001. "The Struggle for the Soul of the Sentence." *The Wilson Quarterly* 25.4: 68–75.

Hustvedt, Siri. 2012. *Living, Thinking, Looking*. New York: Picador.

Kucharzewski, Jan D. 2015. "The Irreducible Complexity of the Analog World: Nodes, Networks, and Actants in Contemporary American Fiction." *Amerikastudien/American Studies* 60.1: 121–138.

Felski, Rita. 2015. *The Limits of Critique*. Chicago: University of Chicago Press.
Love, Heather. 2016. "Small Change: Realism, Immanence, and the Politics of the Micro." *Modern Language Quarterly* 77.3: 419–445.
Lyotard, Jean-Francois. 1979, 1984. *The Postmodern Condition: A Report on Knowledge*. Trans. Geoff Bennington and Brian Massumi. Manchester: University Press of Manchester.
Moi, Toril. 2017. "'Nothing Is Hidden': From Confusion to Clarity; or, Wittgenstein on Critique." In: Elizabeth S. Anker and Rita Felski (eds.). *Critique and Postcritique*. Durham: Duke University Press, 2017. 31–49.
Rankine, Claudia. 2014. *Citizen: An American Lyric*. Minneapolis: Graywolf Press.
Rohr, Susanne. 2004."'The Tyranny of the Probable' – Crackpot Realism and Jonathan Franzen's *The Corrections*." *Amerikastudien/American Studies* 49.1: 91–105.
Szakolczai, Árpád. 2009. "Liminality and Experience: Structuring Transitory Situations and Transformative Events." *International Political Anthropology* 2.1: 141–172.
Thomassen, Bjorn. 2014. *Liminality and the Modern: Living Through the In-Between*. New York, NY: Routledge.
Zapf, Hubert. 2016. *Literature as Cultural Ecology*. London & New York: Bloomsbury.

Section One: **Novel Transitions in the Millennium**

Heinz Ickstadt
The Late Style of Three Postmodernist Masters: Thomas Pynchon, Don DeLillo, and Robert Coover

Abstract: "Most creative careers follow a familiar arc," David Remnik remarked in his recent epitaph on Philip Roth: "the apprentice work, the burst of originality; the self-imitation; and, finally, the tailing off" (2018). In his *On Late Style: Music and Literature Against the Grain* (2006), Edward Said, building his argument almost exclusively on Adorno's discussion of Beethoven's late phase, places his emphasis differently. For Adorno, Said argues, "Lateness [...] is a kind of self-imposed exile from what is generally acceptable, coming after it, and surviving beyond it. [...] Late style is in, but oddly apart from the present." What, then, about the aging masters of postmodernism? Belatedness, apartness, yes, rebelliousness, to some extent – if, perhaps, less in terms of radical innovation than of "invention as creative repetition and reliving." In my essay, I shall discuss recent fictions of Thomas Pynchon, Don DeLillo, and Robert Coover, asking whether they, in the late phase of their writings, indeed develop a "late style" in Said's or Adorno's sense, or whether it is only a self-imitating echo of their earlier experimental radicalism.

As an aging literary historian, I have always been interested in the status of aging writers – their feeling of belatedness, even of obsolescence. At one point they believe to be on the cutting edge of literary developments, then, they suddenly discover that, somehow, they have been left behind. Inevitably, William Dean Howells comes to mind who, in the late 1880s, saw himself at the forefront of a socially conscious realism, the evolutionary conjunction of aesthetic quality, honesty, and "truthfulness." But then, early in the new century, he sadly noted, in a letter to Henry James, that he had become "comparatively a dead cult with my statues cast down and the grass growing over them in the pale moonlight" (qtd. in Crowley 1991: 91). Naturalists and bestselling popular writers had now taken front positions in the business of literature, reducing his realist novels to the size of "tea-cup tragedies" (Norris 1896, 1986: 1107).[1] James too, although never as doubtful of his literary status as Howells, may have wondered, after the

---

[1] Although Norris clearly meant Howells, he didn't mention him by name.

commercial flop of the New York Edition, whether he would ever be able to find an audience that would, like "shoals of fish," rise to the "more delicate bait" of his complex fictions of consciousness (James 1984: 654).

Does such a sense of being left behind mark the career of aging artists in general? The great writers of American modernism – with the exception, perhaps, of Gertrude Stein, who reinvented herself again and again – had apparently realized their creative potential when they were still comparatively young. Their creativity seemed spent when they reached old age or the last phase of their production. The Second World War interrupted their careers, and when they resumed writing in the fifties, neither Dos Passos, nor Hemingway, nor even Faulkner produced anything that matched the inventiveness, the innovative power of their earlier phase. The Nobel Prize to William Faulkner in 1950 and to Ernest Hemingway in 1954, made both of them living monuments of a modernist period that had already passed. "Most creative careers follow a familiar arc," David Remnick remarked in his epitaph for Philip Roth: "the apprentice work; the burst of originality; the self-imitation; and, finally, the tailing off" (2008: n. pag.).[2]

In *On Late Style: Music and Literature Against the Grain* (2006), a posthumous collection of his essays, Edward Said, building his argument almost exclusively on Theodor Adorno's discussion of Beethoven's late phase, places his emphasis differently. Adorno had taken the composer's *Missa Solemnis*, late piano sonatas, and late quartets as evidence of a late style that combined conventionality with radical innovation, rare harmonies with painful dissonances, in defiance of a contemporary audience's expectation of structural coherence. His quasi-anarchist disregard for harmony of sound and synthesis of structure represented, in Adorno's and Said's eyes, Beethoven's alienation at "a moment, when he, who is fully in command of his medium, nevertheless abandons communication with the established social order of which he is a part and achieves a contradictory, alienated relationship with it" (7). It is a moment that also anticipates negations and dissonances still to come – if only a hundred years later in Arnold Schoenberg's radical break with musical tradition. "For Adorno," Said continues, "lateness therefore is a kind of self-imposed exile from what is generally acceptable, coming after it, and surviving beyond it. [...] Late style is *in*, but oddly *apart* from the present" (15, 24).

---

2 During the last eight years of his life, Roth stopped writing altogether. See also "Interview with Don DeLillo," *The Guardian*, Nov. 5, 2018, where DeLillo refers to his and Roth's different reactions to old age.

Such a radical definition of 'late style' applies neither to the masters of American modernism nor to those of postmodernism. Since "lateness" is not necessarily congruent with "exile," Said also considers a milder version of a phenomenon that Adorno had perceived as a radical attitude of uncompromising negation concerning the dominant commercial *zeitgeist*: "Does one grow wiser with age, and are there unique qualities of perception and form that artists acquire in the late phase of their career?" Said asks (6). Even though he favors Adorno's insistence on exile and alienation, he is also aware of "wisdom" and "reconciliation" as possible aspects of late style. Belatedness, apartness, yes, rebelliousness, to some extent – if, perhaps, less in terms of radical negation (Melville's "No, in thunder") than of "invention as creative repetition and reliving" (92).

I

What, then, about those aging masters of postmodernism: Robert Coover, who, born in 1932, celebrated his 88th birthday in early February of 2020 (and, after William Gass' death in 2017, is the oldest of still writing postmodernists – since John Barth, now 90, has been silent for a long time). Don DeLillo turned 84 in November of 2020; and Thomas Pynchon, the most acclaimed of them, turned 83 in May of 2020. I shall concentrate on those three and their more recent work, not only because their names come to mind first in this connection, but also because they represent different versions of what one might consider postmodernist "late style." There is, not surprisingly, in all three cases, continuity of theme and structure: In the case of DeLillo and Pynchon, this would be a preoccupation with paranoia, plots and conspiracies, concern with the proliferation of objects and surfaces, with the power of the media, and – this applies especially to DeLillo – with the ritualization of daily life through habit and repetition, including the ritualization of language and the spoken word. Of all three, Robert Coover has been the most dedicated experimentalist: by his breaking up of narrative sequence, the reversal of narrative (causal, temporal) order, his frequent intermedial excursions into film, painting, music, and pantomime. His lifelong re-telling of stories that "make us" amounts to an aesthetic program of collective exorcism through a subversive or inversive rewriting of familiar narratives – be they religious or political, their patterns and motifs having been handed down to us in fairy tales, the bible, or the routines of popular culture.

However, I shall not start with him but with Thomas Pynchon, the youngest of the three. *Against the Day* (2006) might be considered a watershed.[3] On one hand, it reaches back to *Gravity's Rainbow* (published more than thirty years earlier), re-enacting many of its conflicts, grouping its more than one hundred protagonists along familiar oppositions ("They" vs. "us," the oppressors vs. the oppressed, capitalists vs. anarchists, paranoid order vs. anarchic contingency or entropic incoherence), setting its main characters on a transcendent yet ultimately failing search for scientific truth or religious revelation. ("Traverse" is the name of a sprawling family of wanderers, seekers, or refugees from wars and persecutions who are the novel's main protagonists.) At the same time, we, as readers, increasingly feel that, as much as Pynchon exposes us to the Mysterious, the Marvellous, or Unheard-of, we already know from his previous fictions the narrative territory which his protagonists are traversing. Whether subterraneous, trans-continental, or extraterrestrial, although surely miraculous, it is nevertheless familiar in its strangeness.

And yet, it would be difficult to maintain that *Against the Day* is little more than an ingeniously playful (if overlong) repetition of Pynchon's earlier work. When it came out, ten years after *Mason & Dixon* (1997), the large community of dedicated Pynchon-readers was elated since it seemed to confirm that the master's creativity and exuberant inventiveness, his scientific erudition and, not least, his aversion to the dark forces of global capitalism, of its henchmen and unscrupulous manipulators, was undiminished. In an amazingly short time, Pynchon-*aficionados* created an online glossary of the novel's protagonists, of its scientists and their theories (the pertinent as well as the abstruse), of obscure historical figures, events, and geographical locations. (It can still be found on the Internet as *Pynchon Wiki: Against the Day*.) *Against the Day* cuts through a period of intense national and international conflicts (military, social, intellectual), of conspiracy and diplomatic intrigue as well as of utopian, scientific, and literary fantasies between 1890 and World War I – its numerous protagonists (some historical, some purely fictional) crossing oceans, continents, and

---

[3] However, Hanjo Berressem argued years ago in his *Pynchon's Poetics* (1993) that Pynchon's late phase began with *Vineland* (1990). *Vineland* certainly stands at the end of a cycle that began with *V.* and climaxed with *Gravity's Rainbow* in which history is processual and contingent. A second cycle, begun with *Mason & Dixon* and culminating in *Against the Day*, shows an exuberant display of narrative forms issuing from a concept of history as no longer open but closed and thus as always repeating the same pattern. *Vineland* might thus be considered as marking the end as well as the beginning of two distinct phases of Pynchon's writings.

deserts in an effort to escape patriarchal surveillance or in search of a transcendent goal (be it Riemann mathematics, legendary cities, or orgasmic ecstasies).[4]

If this seems familiar, it is yet different from Pynchon's earlier books where (whether in *V.*, *The Crying of Lot 49*, or *Gravity's Rainbow*) "History" was still unfolding, still undecided – even though all vectors seemed to point toward an ending – be it salvation or catastrophe. In *Against the Day*, however, protagonists and readers do not share the same historical time/space since the readers already know the outcome of what the protagonists still experience as an uncertain and painfully open-ended present ("the moment with its possibilities").[5] What we, the readers, can recognize, however, are patterns of illusion and (self)deception marking a history propelled by the dynamics of the forces behind it: those of corporate capitalism, colonialism, technology, or rationalization – eliminating or pushing to the margins everything that resists their power or does not "fit" their purpose (a topic central to all of Pynchon's narrative endeavors). Pynchon's later novels are pervaded by the hindsight knowledge that all desire for "paradise" is ultimately based on illusion; or that, whatever paradise there might have been before the colonizing grasp of civilization, *was*, *is*, or *will be* lost forever. This echoes in Mason's and Dixon's wonder-full experience of America's untouched wilderness – which they themselves have, as they realize too late, helped destroy in the name of the Royal British Academy and its sponsor, the East India Company.

Loss of "inviolable" space, of enclaves still untouched by the acquisitive logic of civilization, is also a topic in his latest novel, *The Bleeding Edge* (2013), where Maxine Tarnow, its heroine, meditates on the vulnerability of Island Meadows, a wild life resort near Staten Island that is not at all safe from the greedy grasp of New York real estate agents and developers; or when she becomes aware that the digital virgin land of

> the Web's DeepArcher [Departure] also has developers after it. Whatever migratory visitors are still down there trusting in its inviolability will some morning all too soon be rudely surprised by the whispering descent of corporate Web crawlers itching to index and corrupt another patch of sanctuary for their own far from selfless ends. (167)

This is the Law of Entropy relentlessly at work as outlined by Claude Levy-Strauss in the last section of his *Tristes Tropiques*, his melancholic reflection

---

[4] See Heinz Ickstadt, "History, Utopia and Transcendence in the Space-Time of Pynchon's *Against the Day*" (2016).
[5] See Heinz Ickstadt, "Haunted by Ghosts of a Dream: Thomas Pynchon's *Mason & Dixon* (for Peter Freese, who knows all about Pynchon and entropy") (1999).

on civilization's inevitable destruction of "primitive" (or original) cultures. It is socio-economically reconceived and staged by Pynchon in the corporate machinations of capitalism's unrelenting drive for profit and incorporation. It is the "Inherent Vice" of civilization ("something like original sin," 351) that Pynchon explores – in different tones and modes, yet always with furious nostalgia – in all of his work,[6] most playfully in his comico-serious detective novel of the same title (2009).

Neither irony nor nostalgia are new in Pynchon's work, however. They have been there from early on – nostalgia for a lost paradise of Nature before Technology being perhaps no more yearningly (or is it parodistically?) expressed than in Geli Tripping's monologues in *Gravity's Rainbow*. The search for a transcendent signified, for a lost center of meaning, for a lost or hidden Text present in its very absence, is deeply engrained in the protagonists' consciousness as a hope for something 'other' (beyond or behind, before, or after). In the earlier novels, this had gone hand in hand with a lingering utopian expectation, the commitment of their protagonists to the deciphering of deeper meanings: of a letter (V), of a cryptogram (W.A.S.T.E.: We Await Silent Tristero's Empire), or of the deeply mysterious if technological "Text" of the Rocket. However, from *Vineland* (1990) on, such obsessions lose their urgency.

In Pynchon's earlier work, narration is thus anchored in an obsessive search for deeper meanings (that yet allow for a disturbing maximum of semantic openness and indeterminacy). In contrast, the later novels, although confronting the reader with enigmas and ambivalences in abundance, do not draw her into the enigma-solving process. While there is no lack of mysterious events and multiple conspiracies, the texts themselves, although remaining puzzling, are yet less disturbingly enigmatic. The searches lead nowhere, or the searchers get eventually tired of them. Romantic yearnings toward a Beyond are thus increasingly replaced by lateral, more pragmatic concerns: by caring for the other, or an emphasis on family and child.[7] The complexity of Pynchon's late fictions is

---

6 See also Louis Menand's review of *Mason & Dixon* (1997).

7 I am aware, however, that this has been a subdued element in Pynchon's fictions from early on: in the female figures Rachel Owlglass and Paola, or in a Black musician's slogan, "keep cool but care" (in *V.*), or in Oedipa Maas's compassion for a homeless San Francisco outcast (in *The Crying of Lot 49*). And yet, here as later in *Gravity's Rainbow*, it is fleeing or searching men like Tyrone Slothrop who are more conspicuous. It is only in the later novels that the stabilizing influence of women becomes dominant (such as Estrella and Yashmeen in *Against the Day*, Maxine Tarnow in *Bleeding Edge*) – as well as the magic protection granted especially to children. They carry hope against their elders' knowledge of inevitable loss and are blessed with a fundamental trust of life: "It's all right, Mom. We're good." (*Bleeding Edge:* 477) See also Pynchon's "Foremostly due to the dense linguistic texture Pynchon creates by drawing on the language of science and mathematics (in *Against the Day*), on that of Pop or media culture (in *Inherent Vice*), or on the new lingo of the digital and cyberspace (in *Bleeding Edge*). By now, all these have become elements of an easily recognizable Pynchon style, of a "Pynchonesque" world, in which the author as much as his readers feel at home.

Since the history of Pynchon's publications is marked by gaps – gaps often amounting to a decade – it is entirely possible that we shall see another turn in Pynchon's creativity, the exploration of yet another field of new scientific discovery, or of yet another territory of lost hope and thwarted desire. However, in repeating structures and topics of his previous fictions, Pynchon may grow aware of how difficult it has become for him to escape this world of his own creation – just as "History" always seems to follow predictable patterns of destructive exploitation. So that fiction, even when it runs counter to the forces driving the world increasingly toward closure, is also inevitably part of its endless replications.[8]

II

One could plausibly argue that DeLillo's *Underworld* (1997) marks a similar turning point in DeLillo's writing career – a sprawling novel of over 800 pages, "formless" in Tony Tanner's eyes (2000: 201–221) – compared to the tightly structured *Libra* (1988) – since seemingly compounding the material for several novels into one. It is in many ways the culmination of DeLillo's previous fiction, returning to some of its topics (e. g. the murder of President Kennedy and the Macruder film recording the moment of assassination) and the ritualization of everyday life apparent in repetitive patterns of behavior and articulation. The novel is also a fictional record of almost fifty years of the Cold War and its paranoid fantasies, of the enormous amount of waste it produced: the wasteful pro-

---

word" to George Orwell's *Nineteen Eighty-Four* where he expresses his faith in childhood emphatically (2003).

[8] In all of Pynchon's novels the "Counterforce" is notoriously weak, eventually succumbing to the unrelenting forces of capitalist greed or technological progress. New in *Mason & Dixon* is the sensuous delight taken in the linguistic re-creation of a 'new' world together with the melancholic knowledge of its unattainability: of a world that has become fantastically "Subjunctive" because the rational and technological Indicative has won the day. In *Against the Day*, fiction's "Subjunctive" appears to be the only counterforce available – as precarious as is the hope Pynchon places on the trust and confidence of children.

duction of consumer goods, the enormous production of industrial waste, of nuclear waste, of image and linguistic waste, as well as of wasted human lives.

DeLillo's narrative strategies resemble those of an anthropologist/archeologist who, in his effort to understand a past culture, digs through the various layers of its underworld of junk. The question whether waste can be recycled and creatively reused, is essential here – as is the question whether an abundance of objects and material facts can be brought under a controlling form, a narrative order. DeLillo deals with this thematically as well as structurally. To call the novel "formless" is to overlook his evident desire to impose pattern and design on the overwhelming mass of information that this book incorporates. The gap between structure and the materiality of things seems to confirm his statement that art is both *in* history and *outside* of it – history understood here both as form-giving narrative and as the unstructured mass of mere data, facts, things, the raw material of reality, the terrors of life and death which create the need for order of any kind, be it narrative design or ritual control of daily life.

The same gap between form and materiality marks DeLillo's use of language – the split existing between the name of the thing (as well as the whole system of naming) and the thing named. DeLillo is fascinated with language and its various subsystems (in the sciences, in mathematics, in the language of the digital world) – often highly abstract and self-referential special languages, strange and meaningless to those who cannot speak them, yet also suggestive, mysterious, even magical. However, there is also his yearning to take language away from abstraction and arbitrariness in order to get "a grip" on things (47, 55, 63, 522, 759, 808, 825). There is, for instance, the linguistic exercise the novel's young protagonist goes through when he follows the advice of his Jesuit teacher who wants to make him more aware of the things surrounding him, "to invigorate the senses" by patiently and meticulously naming the things he sees: "You didn't see the thing because you don't know how to look. And you don't know how to look because you don't know the names" (540–41).

This longing to tie language to body and to earth as well as to an original magic of the referential sign that would make the thing present in the word that names it, has occupied DeLillo from early on (topically in *The Names*.)[9] But after *Underworld* he takes this desire into a slightly different direction: to find, by abstraction, a new language precisely to counter the culture's incessant push toward ever increasing abstraction; to find a language closer to the body's more immediate perception of the things to which it is related by its own materiality. It is to deconstruct familiar ways of seeing and naming in order "to see

---

[9] See Heinz Ickstadt, "The Narrative World of Don DeLillo" (2001: 375–391).

the depths of things so easy to miss in the shallow habit of seeing" (*Point Omega* 2010: 16).

After *Underworld*, DeLillo's novels become more condensed, more lyrical, more focused on language as an instrument to heighten perception by "suspending our usual sense of time," of getting into "the moment" (*The Body Artist* 2001: 75). What Laura Bieger, in an illuminating essay on *Point Omega*, calls the new "lyricality" and narrative "brevity" of these late novels – from *The Body Artist* (2001), via *Cosmopolis* (2003), *Falling Man* (2006), to *Point Omega* (2010) and *Zero K* (2016) – is part of a deepening awareness of the body's concrete materiality, its beauty as well as its inevitable dying (2010: 3–4) – "[e]xtinction was a current theme of his," is said of Richard Elster, the protagonist of *Point Omega* (page number).[10] It goes together with an off-centered use of language. As when, in *The Body Artist*, the protagonist Lauren, emotionally struggling to cope with the unexpected suicide of her husband, meets a man in her house, who has possibly fled from an asylum, and who talks to her in a strangely distorted way: "shadow-inching through a sentence, showing a word in its facets and aspects, words like moons in particular phases" (48). She suspects him of living "in a kind of time that had no narrative quality" (65). ("Body Time" is the name of the piece that Lauren, the body artist, performs toward the end of the book.)

The attempt to create a narrative form outside a narrative time frame is perhaps the main characteristic of DeLillo's late phase and its most innovative element. The possibilities of film to break through that frame via the speeding up or slowing down of motion and time make the filmic medium especially attractive to him. "[T]o feel time passing, to be alive to what is happening in the smallest registers of motion" (*Point Omega*: 7). Bieger reads DeLillo's slow-motion narrative as an effort to undermine the logic of a narrative emplotment that, by definition, points towards an ending. The slowing down of time is therefore also a slowing down of the approach of death, or, on another ontological level, a breaking through "the nausea of News and Traffic" (*Point Omega*: 22) to the "deep time of geology," to a transcendent timeless Now ("Time that precedes us and survives us" [ibid: 56]), intrinsic to the very materiality of things, taking us outside the consciousness of self into a state of objectness, "a radically altered plane of time" (15).

---

10 This thematic dominance of "death" and "extinction" may also be the result of 9/11, an event that clearly traumatized DeLillo. He dealt with its impact directly in *Falling Man* and indirectly in *Point Omega* and *Zero K*. – evident as an almost baroque awareness of death's constant presence. See also DeLillo's essay "In the Ruins of the Future" (2001). But perhaps this consciousness of death (and the need to confront it) is part of what Said called a growing "wiser with age" and thus characteristic of the late phase.

Suspending the frame of conventional narrative structure (causal and temporal sequence, 'plausible' characters, structural coherence) is thus the only recognizable narrative strategy in *Point Omega* – substituting cohesion for coherence, as Laura Bieger argues. There is a frame tale titled "Anonymity 1 and 2" (marked September 3 and 4, respectively) where an anonymous observer watches with unceasing fascination an installation at the MOMA: Hitchcock's *Psycho* – its ninety minutes slowed-down to 24-hour frame-sequence: "He was mesmerized by this, the depths that were possible in the slowing of motion, the things to see, the depths of things so easy to miss in the shallow habit of seeing" (16–17). The four main chapters framed by these two episodes in the museum are located somewhere in a Californian desert where Richard Elster, now 73 and a former consultant to the Pentagon during the Iraq war, owns a house to which he has invited Jimmy, a filmmaker who hopes to make a film with Elster talking about war and human existence.

There is much talk about Time and Extinction but no film is made. Elster's daughter suddenly appears and through her we learn that Elster and Jimmy were the two visitors whom the anonymous observer saw enter the gallery and briefly watch "24-Hour-Psycho" on September 3. "He told me it was like watching the universe die over of about seven billion years" (59). Elster's reaction to the film installation is continued in the landscape he chooses as his everyday environment, a landscape out of time in geological Time where timeless chaos may point toward an apocalyptic ending when everything falls apart – or to a new convergence: to Teilhard de Chardin's evolutionary "Omega Point," a vision of fulfillment in a future out of Time.[11] However, when Elster's daughter disappears as suddenly as she has come – has she committed suicide? has she been murdered? (as the context of *Psycho* might suggest), has she gone back to New York? – Elster collapses, talks stop, and theories fall apart. On September 4, the anonymous observer sees a woman enter the gallery – but this encounter, too, like everything else, remains inconclusive, just as the reader's speculation that the woman might be Elster's daughter can never be more than that. Plotlines are suggested, structural echoes connect the frame tale and the main story only loosely – they constitute no more than a structural surface of connectedness.

---

11 In Teilhard de Chardin's evolutionary theology, Omega Point is the singular final point of a still evolving universe when all divergent forces converge in lasting harmony. In *Zero K*, which, in many ways, could be taken as a sequence to *Point Omega*, one of the believers in "The Convergence" (the millionaire adherents of a "faith-based technology" striving for immortality) declares that "one of our objectives is to establish a consciousness that blends with the environment" (64) – the environment being a desert somewhere in Uzbekistan. Elster seems to be doing the same in his talks with Jimmy.

What creates the book's cohesion is the slowing down of Time in the film installation of the frame tale which is echoed throughout in DeLillo's language-in-slow-motion. (Bieger associates this with lyrical brevity, but it is most obviously connected with the medium of film.[12])

"Apocalypse is inherent in the structure of time," says one of the figures in DeLillo's most recent novel *Zero K* (2016: 243). To escape the catastrophes that beset the outside world, the increasing signs of human self-destruction (brought on huge TV-screens into the secure space of a quasi-utopian enclave), a transnational community of the superrich plans immortality at a temperature of zero-degree Kelvin, their frozen bodies to be resurrected in a post-apocalyptic future when mankind – represented by a small elite – will transcend itself. The urge to escape death and the desire for immortality are grounded in their deep trust in technology as "[a]nother God" (9). It accepts refrigerated death as a path to everlasting life. ("We will emerge in cyberhuman form" [67].) This new religion – "the billionaire's myth of immortality" [117] – has its own set of priests, monks, artists as well as temples of transformation which may become the "heart of a new metropolis" (33).

The novel's twenty chapters are divided into two parts, each of ten chapters, a symmetrical design reminiscent of *Libra*. The two parts are separated by a six-page interlude enacting the post- or non-consciousness of Artis, the protagonist's stepmother: those mere tremors of self-awareness constantly shifting between first and third person while she is preserved in a frozen state of transition (her "journey toward rebirth"), "alive" only through the words in/by which she exists: "I am made of words. [...] *She tries to see words. Not the letters in the words but the words themselves [...] The words float past*" (157–162).

In the book's second part, DeLillo sets this post-human, quasi-utopian space of ritualized, yet highly artificial perfection – death as a form of 'immortal' art – against the chaotic realm of everyday experience, mostly the disruptive space of Manhattan where life is experienced disjointedly, yet also in a concretely sensuous particularity. It is a space transfigured at the very end when, on a crosstown bus ride, the protagonist watches "the sun's rays align with the local street grit" and the cries of a disabled child enchanted by it, his "howls of awe": "... and I told myself that the boy was not seeing the sky collapse upon us [a fear of apoc-

---

[12] One of the figures speaks of "the promise of a lyric intensity outside the measure of normal experience" (*Zero K:* 48). Lyric intensity and slow-motion film are metaphorically allied in DeLillo's attempt to create a language that transcends habitual ways of seeing and everyday speech. Artis links "lyric intensity" with the expectation of "being reborn into a deeper and truer reality" when her body shall be re-awakened – by the religious-technological endeavor called "The Convergence" – from its deep-frozen state to "a new perception of the world" (47).

alypse that drives 'The Convergence' and its wish for immortality] but was finding the purest astonishment in the intricate touch of earth and sun... I didn't need heaven's light. I had the boy's cries of wonder" (274).

DeLillo's embrace of the boy's "wonder" goes hand in hand with the special function he ascribes to language: On the one hand, by giving or inventing names for persons and objects for which he has – as yet – no names, and by finding definitions and precise meanings for what is in front of his very eyes, he is "getting a grip on things," he is making a sensuously perceived and yet strangely distant reality his own. On the other hand, finding names is his strategy for undermining the new reality as much as the new language that "The Convergence" attempts to develop: a "language system far more expressive and precise than any of the world's existing forms of discourse" (233). It is an endeavor the protagonist rejects, yet that nevertheless runs parallel to his own. In times of "The Convergence" and its push for the Abstract and Artificial (as personified in Artis), it is the function of the protagonist "to subvert the dance of transcendence with my tricks and games" (242) – language being thus at once a means of representation and a living, wonder-preserving entity in itself.[13]

III

With all three writers it is difficult to mark the beginning of what might be called their late phase. Perhaps *John's Wife* (1996) could, in Coover's case, be considered a turning point. On one hand, it seems to be linked to one of his earlier works (*Gerald's Party* of 1985) and a restatement of his aesthetic convictions (of beauty arising out of chaos). On the other, it also defines a break in the history of his publications since it was the last of his novels published by Simon & Schuster and the last one brought out in German translation by the prestigious Rowohlt publishing house. (It dropped his non-profit making books overnight.)

---

[13] Although his later work breaks with the epic scope of *Underworld*, DeLillo continues his attempt to bridge the unbridgeable gap between the harmonies of abstract design (the artificial world of "The Convergence") and the ambiguous rawness of our material existence, absorbing in his own language the abstractness he argues against. The end of *Zero K* echoes the ending of *Underworld* where he contrasts the digital world of the screen and "the things in the room, off-screen, unwebbed, the tissued strain of the deckwood alive in light, the thick-lived tenor of things... the apple core going sepia in the lunch tray;" and tries to overcome their opposition in the word appearing "in the lunar milk of the data stream... a word that spreads longing through the raw sprawl of the city and out a cross the dreaming bourns and orchards to the solitary hills. Peace" (*Underworld*: 827).

In contrast to Thomas Pynchon, who always had a core following of dedicated readers, Coover was thus abruptly made aware that he was losing his audience on both sides of the Atlantic. From then on he had to find, for each new book, a new publisher: *Ghost Town* (1998), a parodistic staging of the Western genre (in film and novel), was brought out by Henry Holt; his bawdy, pornographically enacted reflection on aesthetics, *Lucky Pierre*, by Grove Press (in 2002); *The Stepmother* (2004) and *A Child Again* (2005), both fairy tales for grown-ups, by McSweeney's Books; *Noir* first appeared in French (Seuil, 2008) before it found an English publisher (Overlook Duckworth, Peter Mayer Publishers, 2010); *The Brunist Day of Wrath* came out in 2014 with Dzank Books; and, his most recent novel, *Huck out West* (2017), with Norton & Company. I mention this only because of all postmodernist masters, Coover seems thus to be the most insecure and "alienated," stubbornly clinging to the retelling of stories he believes are deeply engrained in Western culture – such as his hauntingly beautiful recreation of *Briar Rose* (1996); or his re-enactment of one of his literary forebears, Mark Twain; or his return to the life-destroying patterns of collective rituals that he began with his very first novel, *The Origin of the Brunists* (1966), continued in his great political satire of the Nineteen-Fifties, *The Public Burning* (1976), and returned to with *The Brunist Day of Wrath*.

With Coover it is difficult to outline a stylistic or thematic development. From the very beginning he has been (re)telling stories on a large as well as on a small scale, staging their ritualistic function (as in "Charlie in the House of Rue," or "Spanking the Maid"), or unravelling the deeper sexual, social, or political meanings of tales we thought we knew from childhood.[14] Coover created an arsenal of narrative material early in his career and then chose the themes and formats of his story-telling as he went along. Thus, his "development" is not linear but synchronous, even circular. *The Brunist Day of Wrath* is a 1000-page "creative repetition" of *The Origin of the Brunists* published almost fifty years earlier. Both are social novels in their relentless dedication to detail, their meticulous, almost anthropological staging of social life, and their focus on the impact fictions may have on the community. Both show how despair creates its own mythology out of a devastating experience (the explosion of a coal mine somewhere in the Midwest); how poverty and pain turn into religious longing, even into an urgent expectation of a Second Coming.

Chronologically, the events of the two novels are five years apart. The second Brunist novel, even if told almost half a century later, is thus a continuation of

---

14 See Heinz Ickstadt, "History, Fiction, and the Designs of Robert Coover" (2001: 353–374) as well as Elizabeth Bell's dissertation *A Voice of Disturbance – Robert Coover und Mythos* (2009).

the first. It not only frequently refers to characters and events of the earlier book, it also follows the same trajectory of chiliastic hope for a final battle between the forces of the Righteous and of the Antichrist – a plotline modeled on the Book of Revelations that is bound to end in frustration and despair.

Although the second of these novels is twice as long as the first, it does not go much beyond it thematically. Why, then, did he write it? During the ten years Coover worked on it, he brought out a number of smaller publications of tales and fairy tales which confirmed his reputation as a playful, stylistically versatile, if now somewhat marginalized, postmodernist. His re-telling of fairy-tales – such as *Briar Rose, A Child Again* – seemed to continue the stylistic *tour-de-force* of his virtuoso *Pinocchio in Venice* (1991) or his earlier verbal pantomime of "Casablanca" in *Night in the Movies* (1987). With "post-modernism" declared dead by Ihab Hassan (one of its earliest and foremost theorists) at around 1990, Coover may have wanted to insist on the inherent consistency of his work and on the undiminished social relevance of his story-telling, no matter how playfully non-mimetic it might appear, since his return to the story of the Brunists reveals (or, rather, re-confirms) the destructive power of publicly imposed, or collectively invented, fictions.

The Brunist Day of Wrath compounds a collective history of what happened in the mining town of West Condon between March 29 and July 8 (no year given). It presents an immense spectrum of characters from different social classes, ethnic groups, and religious denominations, many of them survivors of the traumatic mine explosion five years earlier who, after the closing of the mine, have lost their jobs and are now stuck in poverty. Their individual stories are embedded in a context of rage, hope, resentment, creating a decentered narrative network of life histories with a kaleidoscopic multiplicity of points of view – a dense web of shifting subjective perspectives and ideological positions. Coover gets into the mindset of the Brunist sect and its fervent believers – their motivations and delusions, their open or repressed sexual desires, their ambitions, their greed, or craving for power. Yet he also explores the intensity of their faith and their longing for redemption: to get rid of this world, this self, this soiled and demeaning life.

"The Brunists [are] an amazing movement!," says Sally Elliot, an off-center observer figure. "Almost like a magic act." The Brunists that Coover magically "conjures almost out of nothing," are the founders of a Church with a hierarchy of bishops and ministers, a growing mythology of martyrs and saints, of rituals and hallowed places, with legends of persecution and redemption, with powerful preachers and folk singers praising "their Myth of the Rapture".[15]

The book begins with a prologue dated July 7, the Day of Wrath, which only happens some 900 pages later, however. It turns out to be a day of collective catastrophe when antagonistic forces clash in apocalyptic blockbuster-film violence, and hopes for salvation die with yet another Second Coming that does not happen. The plot peters out the day after (on July 8) with the fantasies of a poor Brunist nurse hoping to make money from the sect's rich sponsor who has suffered a stroke. But the novel does not end here. It continues with a forty-page epilogue that – much like the Prologue – appears to be an incongruous part of the book. If the latter is focused on a Presbyterian minister called by the town's leading citizen to replace a pastor believing himself to be a reincarnation of Jesus, the Epilogue is centered on Sally Elliot, a minor character in the main plot who records the catastrophic events that partially destroy the town, and is a subversive voice of satire denouncing the collective blind faith in what to her are only mad people enacting crazy fictions.

Prologue and Epilogue can both be seen as part of a strategy of narrative decentering: Jenkins, the *ersatz*-minister for the delusional Mr. Edwards, enters the town in the opening "Prologue" which happens on the day of Rapture close to the book's end. Sally, the main figure of the "Epilogue," writes a novel very much like the one we have just been reading. (As the account we get of Sally's writing career echoes that of Robert Coover.) Yet the "Epilogue" is also part of a strategy of fake-facticity: the biography of the later Sally (her 'marriage,' her literary career, her fight for the lives of some of the Brunists sentenced to death) is rendered in a reportage style meant to underline the factual ("realistic") truth of Coover's fiction. The motto of *The Brunist Day of Wrath* is taken from Sally's first novel: "Against the Cretins," which is, of course, also of Coover's invention and a statement of his life-long creative purpose.

Although he appears to be most of all an advocate of Reason against the collective madness of a new Evangelism, Coover also probes into the emotional (re)source of its antirationalism: a deep resentment tied to their failed hopes for greater social justice. If the historical context of the first Brunist novel may have been the turmoil of the assassinations of the sixties, the Vietnam War, the discovery of poverty and the deep social antagonisms beneath so many American

---

15 In this respect, the novel may also be considered a variant of one of Coover's earliest fictions, *The Universal Baseball Association, Inc., J. Henry Waugh, Prop.* (1968). Coover's invention of an imaginary baseball league complete with players, matches, statistics, rankings, legends and mythologies – of which J. Henry Waugh is the God-like master and most fervent (if arbitrary) player.

dreams, the second echoes the financial crisis of 2008 and the awareness of the growing gap between Rich and Poor. The emotional need and eschatological yearning which, in part, gave rise to Donald Trump may thus have been anticipated metaphorically in the rise of Coover's Brunists.

Thus Coover's "belatedness" seems to be a re-turning to an earlier realistic, less experimental, enactment of his story-telling and not, as with DeLillo,[16] the development of a stylistically distinct and innovative phase. Coover goes back to what he has always been doing – with a difference. His late style is, in Said's phrase, clearly a form of "invention as creative repetition" (128), which is also evident in his recent *Huck Out West* where he reenacts Twain's Huck Finn in (written) voice and gesture.[17] Huck's subversive naïveté unveils the cold inhumanity of the gold-crazy American West (past and present). Turned off by what he sees, he finally sets out South with his Native American friend Eteh who shares with him stories of Coyote – that bawdy spirit of subversion, creativity, and survival. Coyote's "two talking members" puzzle not only Huck but also the reader who may take them as a metaphoric allusion to the instruments that have always been doing Coover's "writing/talking" – the penis and the pen. (In that respect *Lucky Pierre*, which explores the act of creation in its different aspects, is a center piece in Coover's work.) They mark his story-telling as a form of living as surviving. Said speaks of "age masquerading as juvenility" (135) – not with reference to Coover, to be sure, yet not without relevance for him either. Always "a child again," Coover, like Huck, remains an aging figure beyond age, again and again setting out for territories new and yet well-known – telling and retelling stories to the very end.

Works Cited

Berressem, Hanjo. 1993. *Pynchon's Poetics*. Urbana: University of Illinois Press.
Bell, Elizabeth. 2009. *A Voice of Disturbance – Robert Coover und Mythos*. Dissertation, FU Berlin.
Bieger, Laura. 2018. "Say the Words: Reading for Cohesion in Don DeLillo's *Point Omega*." *Narrative*, 26.1: 1–16.
Coover, Robert. 1967. *The Origin of the Brunists*. New York: Ballantine Books.
Coover, Robert. 1996. *John's Wife*. New York: Simon & Schuster.

---

[16] In an interview he gave to *The Guardian* in November 2018, DeLillo speaks of his project for a new novel. Other than Philip Roth, who retired into silence long before his death, DeLillo is determined to go on writing: "It's what's keeping me alive."
[17] This is in line with a long series of Coover-reenactments; see his essay "Reenactments: *Ghost Town* and the American Search for a Sustaining Mythology" (1998).

Coover, Robert. 2014. *The Brunist Day of Wrath*. Ann Arbor, MI: Dzank Books.
Coover, Robert. 2017. *Huck Out West*. New York: W.W. Norton.
Coover, Robert. 2000. "Reenactments: *Ghost Town* and the American Search for a Sustaining Mythology." *Ceremonies and Spectacles: Performing American Culture*. EAAS Biannual Conference in Lisbon, 1998. Amsterdam: VU University Press. 38–47.
Crowley, John. 1999. *The Dean of American Letters*. Amherst: University of Massachusetts Press.
DeLillo, Don. 1997. *Underworld*. New York: Scribner.
DeLillo, Don. 2001a. *The Body Artist*. New York: Scribner.
DeLillo, Don. 2001b. "In the Ruins of the Future." *Harper's Magazine*, December.
DeLillo, Don. 2010. *Omega Point*. New York: Scribner.
DeLillo, Don. 2016. *Zero K*. New York: Scribner.
Ickstadt, Heinz. 1999. "Haunted by Ghosts of a Dream: Thomas Pynchon's *Mason & Dixon* (for Peter Freese, who knows all about Pynchon and entropy")". *Amerikastudien/American Studies*. 44. 4: 555–568.
Ickstadt, Heinz. 2001. *Faces of Fiction: Essays on American Literature and Culture from the Jacksonian Period to Postmodernity*. Heidelberg: Winter.
Ickstadt, Heinz. 2016. *Aesthetic Innovation and the Democratic Principle*. Heidelberg: Winter.
James, Henry. 1984. "American Letters: The Question of the Opportunities." *Henry James: Essays, American & English Writers*. New York: The Library of America. 651–665.
Menand, Louis. 1997. "Entropology." *New York Review of Books*, 12 June 1997: 22–25.
Norris, Frank. 1896, 1986. "Zola as a Romantic Writer." *Novels and Essays*. New York: The Library of America. 1106–1108.
Pynchon, Thomas. 1990. *Vineland*. Boston: Little, Brown.
Pynchon, Thomas. 2003. "Foreword." *Nineteen Eighty-Four, by George Orwell*. New York: Plume. vii–xxvi.
Pynchon, Thomas. 2006. *Mason & Dixon*. New York: Penguin.
Pynchon, Thomas. 2010. *Inherent Vice*. New York: Vintage.
Pynchon, Thomas. 2013. *Bleeding Edge*. New York: Penguin.
Remnick, David. 2018. "Philip Roth." *The New Yorker*. June 4 & 11.
Said, Edward. 2006. *On Late Style: Music and Literature Against the Grain*. New York: Pantheon.
Tanner, Tony. 2000. "Don DeLillo and the American Mystery." *The American Mystery: American Literature from Emerson to DeLillo*. Cambridge: Cambridge University Press. 201–221.

Hubert Zapf
Siri Hustvedt and the Transdisciplinary Knowledge of Literature

Abstract: This essay discusses Siri Hustvedt's writings as an instructive example of the potential of literature as a transdisciplinary form of knowledge at the interface of science and imagination. Siri Hustvedt has more than other writers directly engaged with contemporary scientific theories, while always insisting on the specific contribution of literature to human knowledge and self-knowledge that complements and integrates but can never be completely replaced by scientific knowledge.

The essay has two parts. The first part takes as its reference point the collaborative volume of essays, *Zones of Focused Ambiguity in Siri Hustvedt's Works: Interdisciplinary Perspectives* (2016) to illustrate the broad spectrum of disciplines which Hustvedt's works absorb into their texture and which shape their narrative epistemology – philosophy, art history, psychoanalysis, trauma studies, neuroscience, and medicine. The second part demonstrates how this explorative form of transdisciplinary knowledge is inseparable from processes of aesthetic communication and creativity, taking as an example her experimental novel *The Blazing World* (2014).

The relation between literature and knowledge is at the heart of Siri Hustvedt's writings. In her fictional works, she integrates insights from various disciplines such as philosophy, psychoanalysis, art history, medicine, and neuroscience into her narratives, while in her nonfictional writings, she tests the truth-claims of the contemporary life sciences in the light of the knowledge provided by the literary imagination. In the present paper, I am examining this mutually defining relationship between literature and knowledge as a hallmark of Hustvedt's writings. The paper is structured in two main parts, the first outlining how Hustvedt's writings illustrate some of the ways in which literature can be considered a form of transdisciplinary knowledge, the second indicating how this specific form of explorative knowledge is linked to the processes and structures of literary creativity, taking as my example Hustvedt's art novel *The Blazing World* (2014).

1 The Transdisciplinary Texture of Siri Hustvedt's Writings

Of course, literary texts, and Siri Hustvedt's writings as well, respond to many different needs and fulfil many different functions for readers and the larger culture beyond that of knowledge. Due to their capacity of discursive ecstasy, of *ek-stasis* in its original sense of 'stepping outside of oneself,' as Wolfgang Iser points out, imaginative texts are able to transgress familiar frameworks of consciousness and reality towards unfamiliar territories of the imagination, of dreams, fantasies, and the unconscious, of memory, trauma, and death.[1] Thus they allow author and reader to share intense, intimate, dangerous, and often highly ambiguous psychological or intellectual adventures and explorations, immersing us into the rich but often unacknowledged resonances of our inner lives with our cultural and natural ecosystems, and engaging us, as Siri Hustvedt herself has it, in 'blazing worlds' of the imagination that challenge the sole authority of reality and reason in the definition of what constitutes human life. Because of this transgressive communicational energy, literature, from the very beginning of cultural history, has been regarded as a merely pre-rational and therefore intellectually inferior cultural form, which at best rhetorically embellished and at worst distorted the superior truths of religion, philosophy and, in more recent history, of science. This is also and again true of contemporary debates, in which the hard sciences have gained the status of a master discourse for what counts as truth and knowledge in our techno-scientifically defined world. Siri Hustvedt has actively participated in these debates and has also, more than other writers, directly engaged with contemporary scientific theories and approaches, while always insisting on the specific contribution of literature to human knowledge and self-knowledge that complements and integrates but can never be completely replaced by scientific knowledge.[2]

There is meanwhile a growing number of voices from both the natural and cultural sciences that support this view. Current forms of complexity theory;[3] biosemiotic and biocultural theories of literature;[4] neuroscientific theories of litera-

---

[1] See Iser, *The Fictive and the Imaginary: Charting Literary Anthropology* (1993).
[2] See *The Shaking Woman, or, a History of My Nerves* (2010) and *The Delusions of Certainty* (2017).
[3] See e.g. Wheeler, *The Whole Creature: Complexity, Biosemiotics and the Evolution of Culture* (2006).
[4] See e.g. Easterlin, *A Biocultural Approach to Literary Theory and Interpretation* (2012).

ture as creative engagement of the various faculties of the brain;[5] theories of texts as an alternative form of *Lebenswissen*, of knowledge of living, as Ottmar Ette calls it (2010: 977–993); or cultural-ecological views of literature as a 'reintegrative interdiscourse' that brings together in metaphor and narrative what is separated in institutionalized concepts, categories, and discourses[6] – all of these approaches corroborate the claim that literature has indeed something relevant and indispensable to contribute to contemporary knowledge. Hustvedt's writing explores what she calls "zones of focused ambiguity,"[7] which expresses the transitional, constantly moving but also highly focused dynamics of her texts, in which contradictory images, values, ideas, and interpretations of life are brought together on varying scales and in mutually interacting but never completely definable or conceptually available ways.

The collection of interdisciplinary essays *Zones of Focused Ambiguity* demonstrates especially well this broad range of disciplines and forms of knowledge that shape Hustvedt's works (Hartmann et al. 2016). It contains contributions on life science and life writing, trauma and psychoanalysis, narrative medicine, art history, neuroscience, philosophy, and, of course, on literary and cultural studies – which are all examined as part of the transdisciplinary texture of her works.

2 Historical Excursus: Literature and Knowledge

The relationship between literature and knowledge has been a theme and testing-ground of literary and cultural theory from the very beginnings of critical thought. Ever since Plato discarded any claims of ascribing reliable truth or knowledge to fictional texts, literature has had to struggle for recognition as a field of intellectually serious and respectable cultural practice.[8] All the same, the implicit or explicit truth-claims of imaginative texts could never be completely eliminated from the discourse of literary criticism and theory. The exploration of possible worlds in fictional literature within the principles of verisimilitude and plausibility had already been described by Aristotle as an alternative form

---

[5] See e.g. Armstrong, *How Literature Plays with the Brain: The Neuroscience of Reading and Art* (2013).
[6] See my *Literature as Cultural Ecology: Sustainable Texts* (2016: 114–121).
[7] Hustvedt coined the term in her essay "Borderlands: First, Second, and Third Person Adventures in Crossing Disciplines" (2013) where she emphasizes the inevitable and productive role of perspectivism and personal presence in all forms of disciplinary and cross-disciplinary epistemologies.
[8] See Hazard Adams, *Critical Theory Since Plato* (1971).

of generative, anticipatory knowledge extrapolated from the individual particularity of actual historical fact. In Sir Philip Sidney's Renaissance manifesto *An Apology for Poetry*, the Platonic dictum that poets lie was countered by the proposition of an "as if" logic of the imagination, a logic of "pseudostatements," as I.A. Richards would later call it (1926), that operates beyond the verifiable binaries of true or false, since the poet "nothing affirms, and therefore never lieth" (Sydney, "An Apology for Poetry"; qtd. in Adams 1971: 168). In this virtual space of suspended referentiality, imaginative literature is able to combine the general truth-claims of philosophical knowledge with the particular concreteness of historical narrative, without falling into the complementary traps of worldless abstraction or uninspired factuality. In romanticism, this emancipation of literary knowledge from the prevailing authorities of theology, philosophy, and science became still more pronounced, even as the romantics tried to find ways in their poetic production to fuse different forms of knowledge into one, as put forward in Friedrich Schlegel's influential concept of *progressive Universalpoesie*, or "progressive, universal poetry".[9] In Percy Bysshe Shelley's *Defense of Poetry*, poetry is an intensely communicational form of revisionary world-making, whose truth-claims require no external authorization since it produces a special, performative form of self-recursive truth that unfolds its imaginary worlds as its own authentic evidence. Poetry explores infinite interrelations between mind and matter and is thus a holistic form of knowledge which merges and encompasses all other forms of cultural knowledge, including the sciences. "It is at once the centre and circumference of knowledge; it is that which comprehends all science, and that to which all science must be referred. It is at the same time the root and blossom of all other systems of thought" (qtd. in Adams: 511). From a defensive position towards science and rational philosophy, imaginative literature comes to represent the highest form of cultural knowledge in the period of romanticism, even though science remains an implicit or explicit reference point for all definitions of literary function and significance.

Obviously, this reversal of epistemological priorities has changed significantly in its turn since the era of the romantics. But the evolution of the relationship between literature and science has by no means followed a unilinear path. Rather, it was characterized by shifting polarities and oscillating preferences in which the two poles were alternately seen as opposites, as competing alternatives, or as parts of an interrelated field of cultural knowledge. Thus, while to Keats and other late romantics the natural sciences were a source of reductionism, prosaic disenchantment and positivist impoverishment of the mind, they

---

9 See Friedrich Schlegel, *Athenäum*, Fragment 116 (1798).

represented an important source of inspiration to American Renaissance writers such as Poe, Melville, Dickinson, and the Transcendentalists. The pendulum swung even more in this direction in the era of realism and naturalism, in which the reliance on science became a central criterion for the truthfulness of literary narratives, while in modernism, art tried to incorporate the advances of science into its own experimental processes, without letting itself be subsumed by prevailing scientific epistemologies. In postmodernism, opposition to any authoritative truth-claims of science was radicalized within the framework of a constructivist epistemology, in which the difference between fact and fiction was abolished and the conventional hierarchies of truth were subverted: "The truth of fiction is that fact is fantasy," is John Barth's version of this postmodern constructivism (1972: 246). At the same time, again in an intrinsic countermovement, postmodern writers assimilated knowledge from the postclassical natural sciences such as chaos theory, quantum physics, evolutionary biology, mathematics, and complexity theory into their texts. Representatives of this development include Thomas Pynchon, Raymond Federman, Don DeLillo, and Neal Stephenson, not to speak of the various genres of postmodern science fiction literature anticipating future techno-scientific developments that have gained increasing relevance in the context of recent climate fiction and of environmental utopian or dystopian narratives.

In the twenty-first century, the epistemic framing of the relationship between literature and science has again noticeably shifted as a result of the turn to new forms of realism as well as to ecological and ethical paradigms, whose agendas presuppose some degree of referentiality and shared intersubjectivity of texts. The deep distrust and fundamental critique of science as an expression of Western Enlightenment ideology, which had characterized the radical phase of postmodernism, has been superseded by a new recognition of the inevitability and tentative validity – however relative and socially constructed – of scientific insights and observations as part of contemporary knowledge landscapes with which literature and literary studies are dealing today. Meanwhile, the much-debated "two cultures," whose lack of communication C.P. Snow already deplored in the 1950s, have diversified into ever more different disciplines and subcultures of knowledge, and the urge for their interdisciplinary or transdisciplinary reintegration is as strong as the ever-increasing centrifugal tendency of progressive (over-)specialization. Calls for an all-encompassing "unity" of knowledge as a form of cross-disciplinary 'consilience' (Wilson 1998) are countered by opposite claims of a vital diversity of functionally different and epistemologically complementary cultures of knowledge. In this situation, the problem of literature's relation to science, which has always been an ambivalent one between competition and attraction, has become ever more relevant, but also more contested.

On the one hand, cultural and literary theory have moved from the fundamentalist critique of science towards including the sciences in a more comprehensive, transdisciplinary epistemology of the humanities, as manifest in the growing influence of theorists such as Gregory Bateson, Gilles Deleuze, Bruno Latour, Donna Haraway, Katherine Hayles, or Karen Barad. On the other hand, contemporary literary texts themselves are shaped, more than ever before, by the incorporation of scientific frameworks into their thematic and formal composition, as in the works of Don DeLillo, Richard Powers, T.C. Boyle, and indeed, Siri Hustvedt.

3 Siri Hustvedt and Contemporary Knowledge Landscapes

This situation is the general historical, epistemological, and literary context for the writings of Siri Hustvedt. An underlying assumption of my argument is that literature is, more than ever, significantly influenced, informed, and shaped by issues and developments of modern science, but that at the same time literature represents not just a derivative but a distinct, specifically complex and multilayered form of cultural knowledge in its own right. It is precisely by bringing together apparently opposed, heterogeneous, and seemingly unrelated dimensions of human experience that literature becomes a unique form of cultural self-knowledge, whose potential and productivity consists in the reflexive staging of concretely imagined processes of perception, consciousness, and experience that is not possible in the same way in other forms of discourse. Literature is capable of representing in interrelated polarities what is otherwise separated in thought and cultural practice such as mind and body, intellect and emotion, order and chaos, system and process, self and other, knowledge and life. And it seems that Siri Hustvedt's works are exploring these polarities in specifically multifaceted ways and that, beyond their deeply emotional power of compelling narration, they are also, quite deliberately, forms of such complex exploration and knowledge of contemporary life and culture.

According to Nancy Easterlin's biocultural theory of literature, it is the creation of 'cognitive ambiguities', which result from the fusion of heterogeneous semiotic material and provoke the interpretative engagement of the reader with the world created in the text, which is a major contribution of literature to the evolution of culture (2012). Such cognitive ambiguities open up the space for the interdisciplinary perspectives that are required in the study of Hustvedt's work, but that are also always incomplete and insufficient as explanatory models. This also implies that the various disciplines that are brought into play in this polyphonic dialogue of cognitive frames cannot simply remain unchanged but have to adjust and constantly transcend their own premises in the encounter with the text. In this sense, the knowledge of literature that emerges from this interplay of multiple perspectives is perhaps better described as *trans*disciplinary rather than *inter*disciplinary knowledge, because interdisciplinarity could as well be applied to the relation between given scholarly disciplines to each other without the mediating power of literature and the aesthetic. But it is precisely the latter which accounts for the surplus value of literature as a form of knowledge that both includes and transforms the various frames of disciplinary knowledge that it assimilates into its explorative semiotic processes.

Literature in this sense does not follow a traditional binary logic but a transdisciplinary thinking in complexity, which according to Basarad Nicolescu is based on the 'nonseparability' and fundamental 'indeterminism' that characterize complex living processes from the natural to the cultural levels (2002: 17–19). This thinking in complexity extends the binary logic of mutually exclusive contradictions towards a logic of the 'included middle,' which associates opposite terms in nonlinear correlations interacting on always new emergent levels. "The tension between contradictories builds a unity that includes and goes beyond the sum of the two terms" (ibid: 29–30). Transdisciplinarity in this sense "concerns that which is at once between the disciplines, across different disciplines, and beyond all disciplines," exploring in-between spaces of knowledge that are however not empty but on the contrary, are "full of all potentialities" (44).

Hustvedt's writings work in these boundary-zones between, across, and beyond disciplines, gaining their unmistakable signature by constantly oscillating between biography and fiction, society and psychology, consciousness and the unconscious, intellectual and emotional energies, memory and agency, dialogue and dreams, trauma and therapy. In this interplay, her writings enact some of the main epistemic functions that literature can have in the larger culture – the multiperspectival rendering of experience, empathy as a form of knowledge, the mutual illumination of part and whole through what Paul Armstrong calls the 'hermeneutic circle' at work in literary narrative (2013), and above all, the cognitive ambiguities which generate complex forms of knowledge and self-knowledge that are obliterated in the logocentric constraints of deductive reasoning and monosystemic thought.

4 Literary Knowledge and Literary Creativity: The Example of *The Blazing World* (2014)

The preceding considerations have already indicated the inseparability of questions of knowledge from questions of creativity in Hustvedt's writings that I am going to address in the final part of my essay.

As has been seen, Hustvedt specifically focuses on liminal states and boundary zones, on productive contact spheres and creative spaces, from which always new and shifting views of the psychological and interpersonal issues are produced that she is dealing with – views of multiple, relational selves, of embodied minds and 'transcorporeal' bodies (as Stacy Alaimo would call them; 2010), of deviant psychic states as sources of insight, of identities as products of alterities, of life as both radical singularity and inescapably shared existence, and, by implication, of the difference and yet interconnectedness between the various forms and disciplines of human knowledge that are brought together in her texts.

Let me examine this interconnection of epistemological, ethical, and creative aspects in an analysis of Hustvedt's novel *The Blazing World* (2014). Just like her earlier novel *What I Loved* (2003), *The Blazing World* focuses on the contemporary art scene, on manifold aspects and issues of (post-)modern life and society, as well as on liminal situations with which people are confronted in an undefined space between a humanist and a posthumanist world. As a meta-narrative about a female artist's revenge plot against the male art industry, *The Blazing World* relates, in the form of a posthumously edited collection of voices and documents, the project of Harriet Burden, widow of a celebrated arts dealer, who engages three male artists to pose as creators of her own work in public exhibitions, in order to deconstruct the male-dominated prejudices surrounding the myth of artistic productivity. In comparison with *What I Loved*, however, *The Blazing World* is much more explicitly experimental and multileveled. Instead of the single unifying narrative perspective of Leo Hertzberg in *What I Loved*, the later novel is interspersed with manifold micro-narrations that reveal the multiplicity of lives and voices which shape the macro-narrative of Harriet Burden's stratagem. While *What I Loved* retraces the relationship of an art historian to an individual artist and his works, *The Blazing World* presents various stages and aspects of an emergent art project which unfolds in multiform and unpredictable ways in the course of the narrative. Deliberately taking up a marginalized tradition of women's imaginative writing as represented by Margaret Cavendish's seventeenth-century science fiction novel of the same title, Hustvedt's *The Blazing World* builds on an intertextual dialogue with another female artist, whose unrecognized potential it actualizes in Harriet Burden's art and thought. Whereas in *What I Loved* the creative process retrospectively illuminates traumatic memories of a neglected past, *The Blazing World* projects a neglected past into an ongoing experimental presence.

What is remarkable about this process is that the original intention of positing the 'true' creative authority of Harriet as a female artist against the mythmaking machinations of the commercial art scene becomes ever more difficult to maintain in the face of the complex interactivity that develops between the different players in this trickster game of performative collaboration. The result is that the emphasis shifts from the idea of authentic individualist creativity to a more collaborative, if also competitive, co-creativity of various participants in a transformative interplay between persons, ideas, techniques, objects, and materials. On the one hand, *The Blazing World* clearly rehabilitates the creative potential of female artists against oblivion and patriarchal oppression. On the other hand, it opens up the concept of art itself by expanding the narrative process beyond the boundaries of individuals, genders, genres, and aesthetic programs.

In this respect, *The Blazing World* illuminates a process of literary creativity which corresponds in interesting ways to the findings of creativity research in other disciplines such as philosophy, psychology, or cognitive science[10] – which are all integrated in one way or another into the narrative. Human creativity in this light is not an ahistorical autonomous property and product of isolated individual minds but originates from a complex field of factors involving cultural conditions, intersubjective networks of collaboration and communication, as well as media- and genre-specific codes and repertoires. An ecology of human creativity, as David M. Harrington has outlined, foregrounds the cooperative networks and "creative ecosystems" (1990: 147) through which the acts, products, and circulation of cultural creativity are enabled. These transpersonal ecosystem resources are a necessary precondition of creative processes. At the same time, creativity research also shows throughout its various branches that human creativity cannot be understood unless the "personal resources" (ibid: 155) and productive agency of individual subjects are likewise taken into account.

This co-agency of individual persons, interpersonal relations, and indeed, of the material-environmental conditions within which they are situated, is precisely what characterizes the creative processes that are evolving in *The Blazing World*. Like Harriet Burden's monstrous hybrid creations, the novel is a textual

---

[10] See e.g. Holm-Hadulla, ed., *Kreativität* (2000).

labyrinth, a semiotic puzzle, a polymorphic imaginary wordscape, an intertextual and intermedial hybrid. This is the most polyphonic of all of Hustvedt's books, and one of its fascinating points is that it creates an excessive sense of multiplicity while also bringing the different characters and plot lines into an inevitable, even though not always immediately obvious, connection. One of the ways in which this connection works is reminiscent of the idea of 'mixing,' already familiar to Hustvedt readers from *What I Loved*, in which the individual ego as sole epistemic authority is replaced by the mutually conditioning relation between self and other expressed in the formula "I am because you are".[11] This idea is combined in *The Blazing World* more explicitly with the motif of metamorphosis and the transformative energies of alter ego relations in Harriet's work and in the novel's process. This creativity appears as a continuous form of 'giving birth' to ever new manifestations of the intensely emotional and concretely embodied ideas which inform Harriet's artworks, and which circulate through her and the other characters' lives.

In a rewriting of inherited myths of artistic creativity, Harriet appears as a mixture of Prometheus and a grotesque earth mother figure, being associated with elemental potencies of earth, water, air and fire but also with biomorphic vs. technomorphic forms of generativity. In the context of such icons of creative power, Harriet also resembles a female Faust figure, gaining her productivity through a pact with the 'devil,' specifically with Rune, the Mephistophelian counterpart of Harriet, who represents the sinister, manipulative side of artistic success. "Harry knew that she had struck a Faustian bargain, had made a soul-killing exchange, which had been fraught with risk from the beginning" (307). As a parable about the post-mortem afterlife of art in culture, Harriet's self-enhancing art project nevertheless represents – much like Bill Wechsler's artworks in *What I Loved* – a life-affirming, interpersonal, potentially liberating alternative to the technocentric, ultimately self-destructive cyborg art as embodied by Rune in *The Blazing World* (and, in a different way, by Teddy Giles in *What I Loved*). But perhaps, as in the Faust story, Harriet cannot become herself without her intense, bitter, and conflicted interaction with her more diabolic counterpart (who in the account of his sister, which is also included in the multi-voiced narrative, does not appear so one-dimensionally satanic either).

This adaptation of the Faust model can especially illustrate the connection between knowledge and creativity that is inscribed into Hustvedt's novel. At the beginning of Goethe's eponymic play, Faust is at a point where he recognizes

---

11 See Marks, who takes this phrase from *What I Loved* as a starting-point for her philosophical-phenomenological study of the relational ethics and epistemology of Hustvedt's works (2014).

the insufficiency of institutionalized knowledge provided by the various available disciplines and therefore, in his pact with Mephistopheles, turns to magical forms of alternative knowledge, which open up otherwise inaccessible dimensions of insight and experience, and which make possible the imaginative transformation of mind and life that the Faust story sets free. This transgressive form of creativity, which brings about new ways of knowing and experiencing the living cosmos, is however counterbalanced in its egocentric self-referentiality by the relational dimension of creativity embodied in intersubjectivity and the interdependence between human and nonhuman forces as the larger framework of Faust's experiment. Heather Sullivan elucidates this affinity between aesthetic and ecological processes in Goethe's play when she interprets Faust's final ascent to heaven not just as a humanly but a materially contextualized event, which includes geomorphic and meteorological phenomena of landscape, water, and clouds in an intricately interwoven, open-ended movement that correlates rather than separates soul and body, mind and matter, self and cosmos in complex forms of entanglement (2017).

In Thomas Mann's *Doktor Faustus* as well, a transgressive form of creativity, which goes along with the radical pursuit of human (self-)knowledge, is represented by the composer Adrian Leverkühn, who in his pact with the devil strives for and indeed manages to achieve a musical breakthrough in an avant-garde composition which resembles the twelve-tone-style of Arnold Schönberg. But again, this individualistic concept is counterbalanced in Mann's novel by a relational notion of creativity, by the 'connecting patterns', which, according to Gregory Bateson, link humans to each other and to nonhuman life across different domains (1972). This connective principle is personified by an only apparently marginal character, the prostitute Esmeralda, who in fact leads Adrian Leverkühn to break his contract with the devil – which demanded his denial of any form of love – when he irredeemably falls in love with Esmeralda and is punished for this with a complete breakdown of his personality and premature death due to the syphilis he willfully contracts from this relationship. Esmeralda or *Hetaera Esmeralda*, as he calls her, is clearly a crucial creative influence, who inspires and is literally inscribed into Adrian's experimental compositions in the letters of her name, which metamorphize into musical notations ("Es bedeutet aber diese Klang-Chiffre h e a e es: Hetaera Esmeralda") (*Doktor Faustus* 1947, 2007: 226–227). It is no accident that Esmeralda is symbolically connoted as a half-human, half-animal hybrid being and is described in the features of a green transparent butterfly, thus linking her not only with the literary signifier of metamorphosis but with the biomorphic image of the butterfly named Esmeralda that is introduced early in the novel in the context of the natural science studies of Adrian's father – and that forms a connecting motif in the novel across cultural separations and boundary-lines between self and other, human and nonhuman, culture and nature.

It seems to me that this double structure of artistic creativity is also at work in a comparable, even though completely new way in Hustvedt's adaptation of the Faust myth in *The Blazing World*. Harriet is a female Faust figure who tries to take control of the creative process, only to realize that in the metamorphic projects she is initiating, she is becoming part of an interpersonal, both medially and materially contextualized process which transcends her original intentions but nevertheless manifests a creative power in which she centrally and actively participates.

On the textual level, references such as those to the Faust myth form an intertextual field of metaphors of artistic creativity in the novel, which are translated into personal and interactive presences in the network of narratives and semiotic signifiers that make up the text. This inevitable and inescapable interconnection between the human characters also extends to the world of objects and the nonhuman world in which the urban milieu of the novel is embedded. The frequent references to weather, climate, and atmosphere, as personified in the marginal but sympathetic figure of the Barometer, point to the interdependence between the human and the nonhuman world, between external and internal cultural ecosystems as living spaces of the human characters. They relate to the polarities between 'civilized' and 'wild' forces, social conventions and eruptive energies that pervade the intellectual and artistic *Lebenswelt* that the novel portrays. In this sense, the text is a formally controlled and carefully edited rendering of excessive and unbounded imaginative and intellectual energies, exploring the possibilities of a new form of aesthetically transgressive yet ethically sustainable art, which at the same time offers a transdisciplinary medium of textual exploration of the contemporary world between science and art, everyday life and borderline states of crisis, gender and genre, narrative and drama. *The Blazing World* is a highly complex assemblage of multiple interacting manuscripts, yet it is also an intellectual firework, a blazing world of ideas and images that are reflected and transmitted in language, but also in the life-like metamorphs of Harriet's art objects, which are the products of her intensely empathetic imagination. Early in the novel, she cites Husserl's intersubjective phenomenology as a key inspiration for her art: "Nonexistent, impossible, imaginary objects are in our thoughts all the time, but in art they move from the inside to the outside, words and images cross the border … and they run by and past and through one another. He [Husserl] knew that empathy was a deep form of knowledge" (27–28). Harriet passionately pursues this empathetic imagination in her manifold artworks, which are the source and medium of the transdisciplinary knowledge of life unfolding in the creative process of the novel.

Works Cited

Adams, Hazard. 1971. *Critical Theory Since Plato*. New York: Harcourt Brace Jovanovich.
Alaimo. Stacy. 2010. *Bodily Natures: Science, Environment, and the Material Self.* Bloomington: Indiana University Press.
Armstrong, Paul. 2013. *How Literature Plays with the Brain: The Neuroscience of Reading and Art.* Baltimore: Johns Hopkins University Press.
Barth, John. 1972. *Chimera*. New York: Random House.
Bateson, Gregory. 1972. *Steps to an Ecology of Mind: Collected Essays in Anthropology, Psychology, Evolution, and Epistemology.* Chandler: San Francisco: Chandler.
Easterlin, Nancy. 2012. *A Biocultural Approach to Literary Theory and Interpretation.* Baltimore: Johns Hopkins University Press.
Ette Ottmar. 2004. *ÜberLebenswissen. Die Aufgabe der Philologie*. Berlin: Kadmos.
Ette Ottmar. 2010. "Literature as Knowledge for Living, Literary Studies as Science for Living." *PMLA* 125.4 (October): 977–993.
Harrington, David M. 1990. "The Ecology of Human Creativity: A Psychological Perspective." In: Mark A. Runco and Robert S. Albert (eds.). *Theories of Creativity*. Newbury Park et al.: SAGE. 143–196.
Hartmann, Johanna, Christine Marks, and Hubert Zapf (eds.). 2016. *Zones of Focused Ambiguity in Siri Hustvedt's Works: Interdisciplinary Essays*. Berlin: De Gruyter.
Holm-Hadulla, Rainer M. (ed.) 2000. *Kreativität*. Berlin: Springer.
Hustvedt, Siri. 2003. *What I Loved*. London: Hodder and Stoughton.
Hustvedt, Siri. 2010. *The Shaking Woman, or, a History of My Nerves*. London: Sceptre.
Hustvedt, Siri. 2013. "Borderlands: First, Second, and Third Person Adventures in Crossing Disciplines." In: Alfred Hornung (ed.). *American Lives*. Heidelberg: Winter Verlag. 111–134.
Hustvedt, Siri. 2014. *The Blazing World*. London: Hodder and Stoughton.
Hustvedt, Siri. 2017. *The Delusions of Certainty*. New York: Simon & Schuster.
Iovino, Serenella and Serpil Oppermann (eds.). 2014. *Material Ecocriticism*. Bloomington and Indianapolis: Indiana University Press.
Iser, Wolfgang. 2003. *The Fictive and the Imaginary: Charting Literary Anthropology.* Baltimore: Johns Hopkins University Press.
Mann, Thomas. 1947, 2007. *Doktor Faustus: Das Leben des deutschen Tonsetzers Adrian Leverkühn, erzählt von einem Freunde.* Herausgegeben und textkritisch durchgesehen von Ruprecht Wimmer unter Mitarbeit von Stephan Stachorski. *Thomas Mann: Große kommentierte Frankfurter Ausgabe, Werke – Briefe – Tagebücher.* S. Fischer Verlag: Frankfurt a. M.
Marks, Christine. 2014. *'I am because you are': Relationality in the Works of Siri Hustvedt*. Heidelberg, Winter Verlag.
Nicolescu, Basarab. 2002. *Manifesto of Transdisciplinarity*. Albany: SUNY Press.
Nicolescu, Basarab (ed.). 2008. *Transdisciplinarity: Theory and Practice*. Cresskill: Hampton Press.
Ricoeur, Paul. 1990, 1992. *Oneself as Another*. Trans. Kathleen Blamey. Chicago: University of Chicago Press.
Richards, I.A. 1926. *Science and Poetry*. London: Kegan Paul, Trench, Thrubner.

Schlegel, Friedrich. 1798. *Athenäum*. <http://www.zeno.org/Literatur/M/Schlegel,+Friedrich/Fragmentensammlungen/Fragmente> [accessed 23 November 2021]

Shelley, Percy Bysshe. 1821. *A Defense of Poetry*. In: Hazard Adams (ed.). *Critical Theory since Plato*. New York: Harcourt Brace Jovanovich, 1971. 499–513.

Sidney, Sir Philip. 1595. "An Apology for Poetry." In: Hazard Adams (ed.). *Critical Theory Since Plato*. New York: Harcourt Brace Jovanovich, 1971. 154–177.

Sullivan, Heather L. 2017. "Goethe's Concept of Nature: Proto-Ecological Model." In: Gabriele Dürbeck, Urte Stobbe, Hubert Zapf, and Evi Zemanek (eds.). *Ecological Thought in German Literature and Culture*. Lanham, MD: Rowman & Littlefield. 17–29.

Wheeler, Wendy. 2016. *Expecting the Earth. Life/Culture/Biosemiotics*. London: Lawrence and Wishart.

Wilson, Edward O. 1998. *Consilience: The Unity of Knowledge*. New York: Random House.

Zapf, Hubert. 2014. "Creative Matter and Creative Mind: Cultural Ecology and Literary Creativity." In: Serenella Iovino and Serpil Oppermann (eds.). *Material Ecocriticism*. 52–66.

Zapf, Hubert. 2016. *Literature as Cultural Ecology: Sustainable Texts*. London: Bloomsbury.

Ulfried Reichardt
Shostakovich, Totalitarianism, and Anglo-American Fiction: Powers, Barnes, and Vollmann

Abstract: It is no accident that several important novels about Dmitri Shostakovich's life and music have appeared during the last years. While he is one of the most important and popular composers of classical music of the twentieth-century, he was attacked as elitist formalist by the regime's cultural commissioners in the Stalinist and post-Stalinist Soviet Union. In contrast, in the West, and in particular in the United States, he has been seen by many critics as deeply entangled in Soviet ideology. In three recent novels, U.S.-American authors William T. Vollmann and Richard Powers as well as British writer Julian Barnes explore his life and sound the depths of its complexity in order to understand the political and personal pressure under which his music was written. Yet these novels may also be read as implicit critical interventions into the contemporary debate about the social and political construction of meaning, particularly in the arts. While neither the United States nor Britain have ever experienced totalitarian rule, these texts represent Shostakovich's life as example of the vicissitudes of irony and double-coded expression under political surveillance and as potential warning even for democratic societies. All three novels focus on the inextricable contradictions and paradoxes of art under a regime that assumes the authority to define the meaning of every form of artistic expression. Moreover, they investigate how music signifies, and in which way the affects music causes may be politically used and controlled.

> I wanted to believe that music was the way out of all politics. But it's only another way in. (Powers 2014: 42)

> Probably, no other composer in the history of music had been placed in so political a role. (Volkov 1999: xxxii)

Soviet composer Dmitri Shostakovich plays an astonishingly significant role in several recent Anglo-American novels. While his compositions have been well known for a long time – he died in 1975 – the renewed interest in his life ought to be explained by reference to our contemporary historical and political context. Of course, his music has not changed in the meantime, but the Soviet Union did collapse and break apart, and the euphoria in the West following the fall of the Iron Curtain quickly vanished in the new millennium. The belief in the final victory of Western conceptions of democracy, liberalism, and pluralism has since given way to the realization that liberal democracy not only failed to ultimately triumph, but has since increasingly been undermined from inside. Populist and authoritarian politicians have begun to question and even attack liberties that had been regarded as unquestionable and "sacred." Therefore, even while the reign and raging of totalitarian regimes in the first half of the twentieth-century continue to recede more and more into the past, a resurgence of this danger no longer seems impossible.

Yet there is also a second motivation for the renewed interest in Shostakovich. Parallel to these geopolitical developments, the rise and decline of the dominance of poststructuralism and social constructionism in the humanities and of postmodernism in literature and the arts took place. Very generally, these approaches had questioned the ability of language to represent reality or to render facts truthfully, emphasizing instead that language should be understood as an endless sequence of signs referring to further signs rather than to an empirical reality. Moreover, reality was regarded as being constructed within changing social, cultural, and political contexts which are defined by power relations and that predetermine who decides what is a fact and what is not. In postmodernism, irony developed from a literary trope to an existential attitude that invited detachment and non-involvement. It further raised indifference to an aesthetic ideal, and engendered an atmosphere in which taking a stance or a position felt like a problematic narrowing of possibilities and even potentially dogmatic.

The two seemingly contradictory movements of postmodern skepticism and regressive populism have created a cultural arena in which truth claims and the belief in the (of course, falsifiable) objectivity and reliability of facts are under scrutiny and seen as precarious – ironically from opposing sides and with opposing agendas. While arguments claiming that reality is always to a certain degree constructed, that frameworks of evidence and knowledge are historically contingent, and that irony can be useful for countering dogmatic truth claims are certainly convincing and should not easily be discarded, it has also become evident that such arguments only make sense in systems in which at least a relative degree of security before the law and freedom of speech exist. In a totalitarian state, however, arguments that reality, and versions thereof, are constructed by those in power are rendered moot since such criticism is not only self-evident but also made politically dangerous by the totalitarian state itself. And yet, while irony is a competent survival strategy up to a certain point, it will eventually reach its limits as a mode of genuine social and political resistance.

This is the context, I want to suggest, in which the recent interest in Shostakovich can be understood, and in which his life and his music as traces of an existence under a totalitarian regime are currently being reexamined in American, and to a lesser extent, British fiction. As his compositions remain highly popular with Western audiences, and because he survived Stalinist terror and continued composing in spite of it, his life and music are a test case for questioning not only the possibilities and limits of art, but also for examining implicitly some of the basic predicaments of our current political situation.

I will begin by looking at Richard Powers' *Orfeo* (2014), a novel which dramatizes a convergence of the post-9/11 politics of surveillance in the United States and the difficult relationship between experimental music and audiences throughout the twentieth century. *Orfeo* primarily highlights Shostakovich as a composer whose music had been regarded as dangerous by political authorities in the Soviet Union. Julian Barnes' *The Noise of Time* (2016) focuses on three dilemmatic moments in the composer's life and investigates how Shostakovich reacted to situations in which no morally sound option remained, and how he must have felt trying to survive in a totalitarian world. Finally, within a panoramic view of central Europe under Hitler's and Stalin's rule, William T. Vollmann's *Europe Central* (2005) stages several instances of aporetic conditions under which historical characters had to act, with Shostakovich as one protagonist among others and his music as a "leitmotif." As such, the novels represent a wide spectrum for approaching Shostakovich's life and investigating his music.[1]

All three novels were written by authors who learned their trade in the times of postmodernism, and therefore implicitly negotiate this recent theoretical, literary, and cultural past. One reason why Shostakovich's life and music are interrogated in these novels but also made exemplary for the entanglement of politics, difficult existential decisions, and music and its meaning, is that all three writers are moving beyond the entrapments of mere ironic detachment and searching for what Adam Kelly, in reference to David Foster Wallace, famously called "new sincerity" (cf. Kelly 2010: 131). Kelly's plea is a powerful symptom of a cultural atmosphere still looking to establish a (moral, ethical, metaphysical) grounding for the creation of literature and art after postmodernism that does not resort back to dogmatically fixed positions.

---

[1] Julian Barnes' novel is included in the context of the politics of postmillennial U.S.-American writing as he explores the same constellation as the two U-S.-American texts and his is one of the three major fictional treatments of the composer's life. Both the American and British authors are interrogating Shostakovich's artistic and existential predicament from an outside position, from the vantage point of societies in which music is understood as an artist's free expression and where there is no interference by the state. Yet while exploring the problematic entanglement of music and politics, they implicitly gesture beyond the concrete circumstances of his life. The danger of art being controlled by the state or other institutions is never far away.

There is a further reason for interrogating Shostakovich's music. Since music is generally characterized as being effective mostly on the affective level, it is also a privileged medium for examining how "signs" signify, how art "means," and in what ways meaning is bound to its context. Moreover, novels about Shostakovich must always find a way to render music narratively and linguistically. Communicating about music is necessarily speaking about music. It has to be narrated and semanticized if one does not merely intend to formally analyze musical patterns. As Shostakovich's life had been a point of contestation for some time, narrating his experience and fictionalizing his music constitutes an intervention in an ongoing debate. Because fiction may experiment with voice and juxtapose different perspectives, it can create polyphony on a discursive level. The framework within which I will position the novels, then, includes totalitarianism, the vicissitudes of irony, the potential of music to signify, and the construction of meaning through a political context.

The Debate about Shostakovich

The novels I discuss were not published in an ideological vacuum. Shostakovich had posthumously been at the center of an acrimonious debate for a number of years already. In the last decades of the twentieth century a heated dispute about the Russian composer raged in the United States when several controversial biographies, collections of essays and, finally the volume *The Shostakovich Wars* were published. The Shostakovich Wars were sparked by the publication of Vladimir Volkov's *Testimony* (1979), a book that contains Shostakovich's memoirs as told to and edited by the author. The controversy focuses not only on the authenticity of these memoirs but on the questions whether his compositions contain codes of meaning that were subversive of Soviet ideology and if his later official public image as a representative of Soviet propaganda was accurate. Volkov's version, however, is in many ways just another approximation, itself involved in the question of what was allowed to be said, what could have been said, and which parts of what was said were true. While the widely agreed assessment of Volkov's book today is that it is close to what Shostakovich may have said and thought, the more interesting question is to which extent his music corresponds with the political pressures of his life and whether music can be understood abstractly.

As Ian MacDonald (n. pag.) has pointed out, the debate has almost exclusively taken place in the United States. Defending Shostakovich as a victim who had actually been critical and subversive of Stalinism was regarded by those music scholars, such as Laurel E. Fay, Richard Taruskin, and Malcolm

Hamrick Brown who saw Shostakovich as a straight follower of the party line, as an act of blindness to his involvement in Soviet propaganda, and as a means to sanitize his life (Ho and Feofanov 2011: vii). This fierce controversy and ideological background must be taken into consideration when interpreting recent fictional treatments of Shostakovich's life. The novels discussed in this essay are consciously wrestling with the complexity of a life and of art under a regime that subjected the totality of artistic, cultural, and private expression to the censoring control of the state. Yet the attacks on the composer also targeted his music proper. The compositions were seen as not radical enough, and worst of all, as too popular.[2]

Richard Powers, *Orfeo* (2014)

At the moment when he finally realizes that he is in great danger of being captured by the police for a crime he did not commit, the protagonist of *Orfeo*, the composer Peter Els, thinks of Dmitri Shostakovitch's *Fifth Symphony*, "a condemned man writing the accompaniment to his own execution" (269). The symphony is symptomatic of the dangers, problems, and ambivalences of music that punctured Shostakovich's life and compositions until his death, and which inform Els' predicament in the novel: "Despite himself, in that first bleak figure in the strings [...] Els made out the maker's miserable life; driven into the public arena, forced to choose between penance and revolt, heresy and faith, while his life hung on whatever story the state imagined that it heard" (280). Via Els' thoughts, Powers outlines the very relationship between music and politics which had been dramatically experienced by Shostakovich: "To call any music subversive, to say that a set of pitches and rhythms could pose a threat to real power ... ludicrous. And yet, from Plato to Pyongyang, that endless need to legislate sounds" (282). When he listens to the romantic third movement, Els thinks: "It spoke of whatever was left, after the worst that humans did to each other. At the premiere, they cried openly, not caring that they wept. The whole audience – victims of the present catastrophe – knew what the Largo said. Millions dead,

---

[2] The ideology Shostakovich was confronted with is succinctly captured in a speech given by Zhdanov, the main cultural ideologue of the Soviet Union in 1947: "One trend represents the healthy, progressive principle in Soviet Music [...]. The other trend is that of formalism alien to Soviet art; it is marked by rejection of the classical heritage under the cover of apparent novelty, by rejection of popular music, by rejection of service to the people, all for the sake of catering to the highly individualistic emotions of a small group of aesthetes" (qtd. in Atttali 1977: 7–8).

tens of millions sent to the gulag. And no one had dared speak the fact in public, until this music" (284). While the Soviet composer survived the premiere of his *Fifth Symphony*, he lived the remainder of his life as a "perpetual target in the war against dissonance, dissidents, and discontent" (286).[3]

These passages from *Orfeo* encapsulate some of the main points characterizing Shostakovich's music and stress the degree to which his music cannot be understood apart from the political context in which it was written and first heard. In its discussion of the *Fifth Symphony*, the novel therefore raises the question why totalitarian regimes are interested in controlling music and art in general. Are "dissonance, dissidence and discontent" (286) indeed linked with each other in more complex and intricate ways than the assonance of the prefix "dis" suggests? Why can music be threatening to those in power?[4] Moreover, does the fact that Shostakovich was forced to collaborate with the Soviet state disqualify his music as well as his resistance to the state? There will be no simple answer to this complexly entangled life and musical oeuvre. While Jacques Attali claims that "music is not innocent" (1977: 5), Duke Ellington remarked: "When art ceases to be dangerous, you don't want it" (*Orfeo:* 97).

Powers' reflections, however, are not only far-reaching in that they delineate the contours of the relationship between music and domination. The novel also offers the framing for another reason for the interest in Shostakovich. *Orfeo* can be read as a fictional *tour de force* through twentieth century musical composition, mediated through the lived experience of the composer Peter Els. As described in the novel, the main dilemma of experimental music in the West was that it explored unknown realms of sounds, yet was only able to reach a rather small audience of specialists and was thus never popular. The contrast between music by avant-garde composers such as John Cage and Karlheinz Stockhausen on the one hand and more accessible composers like Shostakovich on the other constitutes one of the novel's main arguments. Why is his music,

---

[3] Shostakovich had been a celebrated composer in the Soviet Union until 1936. In January of that year, Stalin attended a performance of his successful but also formally highly complex and experimental opera, *Lady Macbeth of Mtsensk*, in Moscow, left after the first act, and anonymously published a devastating review two days later in the Prawda entitled "Muddle Instead of Music," which also declared that this might become very dangerous for the composer. At this time, show trials and political purges were taking place, and tens of thousands were shot or disappeared in the Siberian camps. Since then, Shostakovich would be constantly observed by state agencies and could be confronted with devastating consequences at any time.

[4] Jacques Attali writes that "Music [...] explores [...] the entire range of possibilities in a given code [...]. For this reason musicians, even when officially recognized, are dangerous, disturbing, and subversive; for this reason it is impossible to separate their history from that of repression and surveillance" (1977: 11).

which was written under the highest pressure in the totalitarian world, much more successful even in the West than the music based on individualism and unencumbered experiment, music that allows free individuals to search for new ways of expressing themselves? [5] Is this artistic freedom only possible for a rather privileged elite who are able to gain pleasure by opposing listening expectations and enjoying the unexpected? Or should the search for new forms itself be understood not exclusively as a sign of liberty but rather of what has been called "compulsory *individualization*" (McGuigan 2014: 233)? The tension between popularity and formal exploration may be one of the defining contradictions of twentieth century classical music, and I may add, of Powers' own career.

While Els in Powers' novel led an entire life of avant-garde composing, extending the limits of music far beyond what had been known before, his works "were performed twice, seven years apart, for a dozen puzzled listeners each time" (53). Avant-garde music is presented as an already historical phenomenon: "Much of twentieth century music had been lost to the idea that the diatonic scale was arbitrary and exhausted, part of the bankrupt narrative that had led to two world wars" (76). Yet Els' wife Maddy tells him just before she prepares to leave him: "The Game's over. Nobody's listening" (201). And his friend and fellow experimentalist Bonner finally realizes: "Turn the crank, and out comes the little predictable spurts of stylized outrage" (259). Thus, after being attuned to sounds in nature, Els begins inscribing a simple melody into a bacteria's DNA. Having given up the hope to win an audience in the present, he opts for handing over his song to an evolving organic yet unknowable future, thus merging his musical creativity with nature's contingent emergence. One could speak of a "posthuman" approach to music and composition.

The concrete political context for this act of aesthetic defiance *qua* genetic engineering is the Patriot Act instituted after 9/11. *Orfeo* thus explicitly connects Shostakovich's music with the present. Els is tracked by the police as he is suspected of having conducted dangerous biohacking experiments and possibly preparing acts of bioterrorism.[6] While this is not the case, Els has to flee his

---

5 "'No composer wholly of the twentieth century currently enjoys a higher standing amongst audiences of classical music, at least in the West'. In North America, Shostakovich ranked [...] among the most frequently performed composers of orchestral music [...]" (Michael Mishra, *A Shostakovich Companion*, Westport, CT: Praeger, 2008, ix)." (Ho and Feofanov 2011: vi) For the relationship between individualism and the political dimension of art in the United States focusing on Abstract Expressionism in the 1940s, see Serge Guilbaut (1985).
6 The novel's plot is based on the actual story of Steve Kurtz, an American artist who was arrested in 2004 for an act of bioterrorism. He had been working on an exhibit about genetically modified agriculture when his wife suddenly died of a heart attack. Police detained him and

home to escape the unfounded allegations. On the way, the novel presents excursions into pieces of music from Mozart to Mahler and throughout the twentieth century.

Yet the two most decisive works that are examined at length and literally "sounded" in *Orfeo* are Shostakovich's *Fifth Symphony* and Olivier Messiaen's *Quartet for the End of Time*. The latter was composed by Messiaen while he was a prisoner of war in Germany and premiered in a German concentration camp on January 15, 1941 by musicians who were forced laborers and who nearly starved to death. Despite its context of creation, the *Quartet* is not a simple tune intended to give hope to the inmates but rather a complex piece of modernist music: "The music is Messiaen's escape from the grip of meter, from the plodding thump of heartbeats and the ticking of clocks. His jagged lines struggle to defeat the present and put an end to time" (112). As Messiaen himself is quoted: "*Never was I listened to with such attention*" (119; emphasis in the original). Both the *Quartet* and the *Fifth Symphony* were written and performed under the threat of death, and thus symbolize that classical music can be difficult to listen to and nevertheless find an audience. One could argue that the meaning of the two pieces is located in the situation in which they were composed and the function the music had for the listeners at this moment. Furthermore, these pieces take on a much more urgent significance now that Els himself is threatened with capture and persecuted. Thus, the context of the musical pieces' composition and first performance correspond with his present predicament. The music's "meaning" cannot be separated from the context of its composition yet cannot be reduced to it either.

However, does Powers argue that only music composed in dangerous situations is meaningful? Do meaning and significance depend more on the context than on form?[7] While the two compositions are in fact masterpieces, not every masterpiece is widely recognized. Nor is every tune played under duress good music. Nevertheless, as it is argued in the theory of popular culture, what people

---

searched his apartment and equipment, yet he was released, as no dangerous material was found.

[7] For Theodor W. Adorno music has a semantic dimension, even while it can only be heard in the structure of the form itself: "While art opposes society, it cannot position itself outside; art's opposition only succeeds through identification with what it revolts against" (*Ästhetische Theorie* 1973: 201; my translation). It is oppositional only in its immanent movement against society, not in its manifest position taking. However, we also have to think about music as a communicative act. Symptomatically, Shostakovich's music did not do much for Adorno. As one critic writes, he could not see that composers in the Soviet Union as well had to find an idiom which they could use to express themselves, and through which they could communicate with audiences and still survive (Feuchtner 2017: 23–25).

'do' with the music is at least as important as the work of art itself (cf. Fiske 2010). It is in its actual reception that music becomes politically effective. And it is also here that we encounter a thorny paradox. If everything is allowed and possible, very little counts or has an effect. In contrast, if art is controlled and the spectrum of expression is policed, even slight forms of subversion do make a difference. Powers seems to be critical of the cultural leveling in contemporary Western societies, of a condition in which anything goes but nothing matters as well as of avant-garde music's loss of contact with listeners. At the same time, he does not discard the need for music, and art in general, to investigate new formal territories of sound and expression. As music is a profoundly social phenomenon, the novel emphasizes that its meaning is largely dependent on the context, which may change, and that form and function are intricately intertwined. Music's form is always interacting with the context yet the meaning ensuing from this interaction is rarely unambiguous. Even while it is not explicitly expressed in *Orfeo*, we can interpret the critique of experimentalism ("Formula transgression" [259]) also as an implicit critique of the idea of language as "free play," signifiers only referring to other signifiers, without any direct contact with the world.[8] Powers' novel may thus be understood as an attempt to go beyond the formal openness of "anything goes," in order to search for an ethical, existential, or political grounding without falling back on dogmatically asserted truths.

Julian Barnes, *The Noise of Time* (2016)

Julian Barnes, a writer whose postmodernist novels have previously dealt with biographical material (*Flaubert's Parrot* 1984), focuses exclusively on Shostakovich's life in *The Noise of Time*. The question he was confronted with when writing the novel was how to represent the life of a man whose existence was fragmented and distorted by the controlling voice of the Soviet state apparatus, who was forced to sign statements he did not endorse, and about whose biography several historically shifting versions are available. Barnes comments that "Shostakovich was a multiple narrator of his own life. [...] truth was a hard thing to find, let alone maintain, in Stalin's Russia" (2016: 184). While the novel is not explicitly metafictional and uses material from the main biographical sources (Vol-

---

[8] This critique can also be found in Powers' novel *Galatea 2.2* (1995), where he stages signs and literary texts without reference in the context of artificial intelligence as being ultimately pointless.

kov 1999, Wilson 2006), the manner in which it constellates the puzzle pieces is opposed to any attempt at creating a coherent picture of the composer. Authenticity is a concept invented in the context of the rise of bourgeois individualism. Yet the interest in the inner life and motivation of significant persons has evidently persisted beyond postmodernism's claim that identity is always retrospectively and performatively constructed.

The fragmentation and aphoristic quality of Barnes' novel – it consists of a sequence of vignettes – pays tribute to the contradictions, the striking masking, and the layers of lying as well as enforced proclamations that complicate any direct access to the composer's life. The structure of the text mimics the form in which Shostakovich's biography is available: Its distortions are symptomatic of an era and a specific political formation, thus reaching far beyond the composer's life. While Ilya Ehrenburg declared that "Music has a great advantage: without mentioning anything, it can say everything" (qtd. in Volkov 1999: xxxiv), the book's title *The Noise of Time* questions this view and stresses the context, the non-musically structured "sounds" of history that nevertheless affect music. Can the music be separated from the acts of the man, and moreover, can we hear "the noise of time" in his music? The novel persistently interrogates how a person was able to survive under extreme totalitarian pressure. Although Shostakovich never agreed with the Party line, he neither revolted nor was he an open opponent of the system. This semblance of conformity allowed him to compose his music within rigid limitations, albeit not without cooperating personally and compromising himself. If total rule makes the oppressed into collaborators of terror, what does this complicity do to a person?

Barnes selects three decisive biographical moments in which Shostakovich was forced to decide in hopelessly dilemmatic situations – Stalin's verdict in 1936 that Shostakovich's opera was not only "muddle" but that such music might become very dangerous for the composer, his visit to New York as a representative of the Soviet Union when he had to denounce Stravinsky and humiliate himself publicly in 1948, and the time when he was forced to join the Communist Party and sign letters attacking the main dissidents Andrei Sakharov and Aleksandr Solzhenitsyn in 1960.

The political system in which Shostakovich lived may best be described by reference to Hannah Arendt's *The Origins of Totalitarianism* (1951), where she analyzes the practices of Hitlerism and Stalinism. Under these totalitarian regimes, the search for truth or empirical proof and the verification of facts were no longer possible; while lying, even in the face of blatantly contradicting facts, became the rule. People were condemned to die even as victims as well as prosecutors knew that the accused were innocent. Every form of human relationship, whether friendships or family relations, became suspect (cf. Arendt 1951: 323). According to Arendt, people in Stalin's Soviet Union "had realized that their lives and the lives of their families depended [...] exclusively on the whims of the government which they faced in complete loneliness [...]" (Arendt 1951: 320). Terror is the true character of total domination, and the victims themselves are made accomplices of the crimes of total regimes. No last resort is left.[9] Truth and reality are dependent on the lies of the leaders and thus, indeed, "constructed."[10] Totalitarianism implies complete existential insecurity.[11]

The Noise of Time begins by emphasizing the constant threat that had characterized Shostakovich's existence since 1936: "*He had become a technique for survival*" (1). "*Enquiring about the movement of trains – even if you were passenger on one – could mark you as a saboteur*" (2; emphasis in the original). The novel's narrative devices, short sentences, and empty spaces between statements and descriptions, prevent coherence and underline the impossibility of the emergence of any meaning concerning Shostakovich's situation. Parataxis, the juxtaposition of seemingly unrelated pieces of thought, stresses the lack of any causal connection, of logic or reason for what Shostakovich is experiencing: "All he knew was that this was the worst time. [...] His situation had come out of the blue, and yet it was perfectly logical" (7). The predominant feeling is fear, to be completely at the mercy of unpredictable forces that cannot be argued with. The novel does not develop a psychologically rounded picture of the composer. While the narrative instance focalizes from within, it speaks in the third person. Occasionally, the text offers up bits and pieces of a stream of consciousness, the impression of immediacy, of an ongoing process, of trying to make sense of what happens to the protagonist, and of the emotions as well as sensa-

---

9 "When a man is faced with the alternative of betraying and thus murdering his friends or of sending his wife and children, for whom he is in every sense responsible, to their death; when even suicide would mean the immediate murder of his own family – how is he to decide? The alternative is no longer between good and evil, but between murder and murder. [...] Through the creation of conditions under which conscience ceases to be adequate and to do good becomes utterly impossible, the consciously organized complicity of all men in the crimes of totalitarian regimes is extended to the victims and thus made really total" (Arendt 1951: 52).
10 Stunning is the fact, fictionalized by Arthur Koestler, that many of the operative elite confessed to being guilty when they were tried. In *Darkness at Noon* Koestler writes about how it must have felt to be loyal and accused. The interrogator claims: "The greatest temptation for the like of us is: to renounce violence, to repent, to make peace with oneself" (2005: 124). And the accused Rubashov declares: "There is nothing for which one could die, if one died without having repented and unreconciled with the Party and the Movement" (2005: 199).
11 Other books that could be cited would be Vasily Grossman's epic war novel *Life and Fate* (1980), also forbidden in the USSR, Danilo Kiš's *A Tomb for Boris Davidovich* (1978), Nadezhda Mandelstam's memoirs *Hope Against Hope* (1970) and recently Timothy Snyder's *Bloodlands* (2012). All of these also refer to the shared antisemitism of Hitler and Stalin.

tions circulating through him: "They always came for you in the middle of the night" (15). Short pragmatic explanations are given: "He had therefore proposed that he spend those inevitably sleepless hours out on the landing by the lift" (15). The narrative is factual, the tone unpoetic, straight forward. The description of the performance of Shostakovich's opera, for instance, when Stalin left abruptly and then indicted the composer as a formalist and thus enemy of the people, is presented from the composer's point of view. He is trying to make sense of the irrational; because the government box is located directly above the very loud percussion and brass section, the noise might have irritated Stalin: "Indeed, that might be the best way of looking at it: a composer first denounced and humiliated, later arrested and shot, all because of the layout of an orchestra" (18). In totalitarian regimes, aesthetics is regarded as being highly political; form matters, but must be controlled by the state. Shostakovich's compositions had an immense value for the party, and therefore were intensely monitored. Soviet music could not be left to the will of an individual alone.

A central motif as well as a subject of the novel is irony. The text interrogates the effectiveness and function of irony with regard to life under totalitarian regimes. While irony is a central category of postmodernist literature, where it is used as a trope for staying aloof and not engaging with conflicts,[12] in times of persecution, saying something and meaning something else is a political and artistic strategy of survival: "All his life he had relied on irony. [...] Irony allows you to parrot the jargon of Power [...] You write a final movement to your Fifth Symphony which is the equivalent of painting a clown's grin on a corpse, then listen with a straight face to Power's response [...] And part of you believed that as long as you could rely on irony, you would be able to survive" (173–174). Yet towards the end of his life Shostakovich finally comes to realize that "irony had its limits. For instance, you could not be an ironic torturer; or an ironic victim of torture" (175). He comprehends that "This was the final, unanswerable irony to his life: that by allowing him to live, they had killed him" (177). Irony has turned against itself.

The novel presents irony on several levels and balances incompatible aspects. Because his compositions were censured and controlled, Shostakovich resorted to using indirection and double-speak in his music. Complex tonal forms and structures were officially declared as politically incorrect and dangerous. In order to have his compositions performed at all, Shostakovich had to "voice" his criticism, had to package his idea of music in sounds that could be heard as conforming to the Soviet dogma. He had to walk the utterly thin line between wholly

---

[12] See for example David Foster Wallace's unfinished novel *The Pale King* (2011).

accommodating the Party line (which was neither predictable nor based on any aesthetic expertise) and conveying what he wanted in his music.

The law of aesthetic form cannot withstand the attacks of those in power if it is precisely the form of music that is targeted. As totalitarian power does not allow any outside position, the situation Shostakovich was forced into no longer allowed him to abstain from political involvement. The only, if dangerous, alternative was to respond indirectly to the forces that dominated every aspect of his life, to comment on oppression and violence allegorically, in a way that is "readable" yet not explicitly critical. The last movement of the *Fifth Symphony* is a symptomatic instance – a march in celebration of the State, or a march to the camps, a funeral march lamenting the millions dead and never mourned – depending on the tempo, half time sounding the death march. To some audiences, however, this double-speak may sound like pompous music that has accepted the Party's verdicts. These are the vicissitudes of allegory.

The novel's three-part structure carries location-specific titles, underlining the central importance that time, context, and historical events play here. The composer's political involvement increases against his will over time, while simultaneously distancing himself from his public persona. Towards the end of his life, and the novel, he observes himself as if he were another person. Looking back, "he was even beginning to see his own life as a farce" (164). Although still performing public lip service to the Soviet State Shostakovich "hoped [...] that death would liberate his music" (179). But can his music be liberated from his life? Barnes does not answer this question. Meaning has and had been projected onto Shostakovich's compositions, has and had been politically constructed. His music remains entangled with his life's pressures, veiled by strategies of musical irony and indirection. Never completely owned by himself, a thick layer of interpretations, narratives and projections obscures the sounds' immediacy. We cannot know how his music might have developed without Stalinist censorship.

Shostakovich's life, Barnes' novel argues, is not only exemplary for the atrocities the composer had to live through, but also for the humiliations he was forced to live with in order to continue composing music. Stalin once called him personally on the telephone and ordered him to endorse Soviet cultural ideology and denounce emigrated composers at a congress in New York City in 1948: "He had betrayed Stravinsky, and in doing so, he had betrayed music" (110). Ultimately the composer is crushed between opposing forces, none of which leave him space to breathe freely. He was no hero, but isn't his survival itself an act of heroism? Can we understand such a predicament at all, living in a safe world ourselves? His music has resisted all attempts to strangle it, but it also carries the scars and inscriptions of its time and thus is not innocent. "The noise of time" can be heard in it.

William T. Vollmann, *Europe Central* (2005)

Julian Barnes focuses exclusively on Shostakovich's lived experience. He neglects his music and dramatizes the noise of the time only in so far as it affected the composer. No wider angle on historical, social, and political structures and events brings other factors and persons into the novel's spotlight. In contrast, William T. Vollmann's novel presents the composer within a kaleidoscopic panorama of Central Europe in the first half of the twentieth century, depicted as a network of forces and counterforces. A broad spectrum of historical characters dramatizes how persons confronted with radical evil in the forms of totalitarian politics, war, and violence attempted to act as morally as was possible in the situation. In the novel music is used as a leitmotif, as a medium for accessing experiences, as a trace of events, and as a foil onto which the defining aspects of the times can be projected. Vollmann explores extreme existential conditions, war and totalitarianism, "the ambiguity of good" (Friedlander 1969),[13] with violence and sex at the center and "Shostakovich's doublespeak" (Vollmann 2005: 800) as a main characteristic. The prime motivation is a moral one.

Vollmann paints an epic panorama of several lives under totalitarianism.[14] His concern is a collective portrait of an epoch in Central Europe, mostly of the 1930s and 1940s, and the ways in which Soviet as well as German women and men behaved within the web of systems that confronted them with impossible moral choices. By way of what has been called a contrapuntal method, *Europe Central* (almost) consistently pairs a story featuring a German and a Soviet person as respective protagonist. The novel's systemic view is structured by presenting fragments consisting of stories of acting people. Almost all of the protagonists are historical figures, such that the novel is based on extensive research which is documented in a long apparatus of footnotes. Nevertheless, *Europe Central* is the stylistically most experimental one among the novels under consideration.

An explicitly metafictional aspect is the use of dynamic focalization and the shifting narrative point of view. The most prominent narrator is Comrade Alexandrov, a fictional Soviet secret police officer spying on Shostakovich, co-telling

---

[13] Cf. Saul Friedlander, *The Ambiguity of Good* (1969).
[14] In scope and aim it may be compared with Leo Tolstoi's *War and Peace* (1869), and more directly with Vasily Grossman's *Life and Fate* (1980), which was confiscated in the USSR by the agencies, and only smuggled into the West later. In terms of the analysis of the comparability of Hitlerism and Stalinism, *Europe Central* may be linked to Grossman's novel, to Hannah Arendt's analysis of totalitarianism (1951), and to Timothy Snyder's *Bloodlands* (2012).

his story and thus signifying the never ending observation under which the composer spent his life. Being an omniscient observer, Alexandrov's cynical remarks function to contrast the dogmatic view of the ideologues in power with the creative artist or any free individual. Alexandrov is constantly present and commenting on everything, like an internalized external gaze. Yet there are other fictive non-diegetic narrators, and also a voice that has to be attributed to Vollmann himself when he projects his own "imaginary content analogies" (Wolf 1999: 50–51) onto Shostakovich's compositions. This flexibly shifting spectrum of narrative voices creates a heterogeneity of perspectives as well as an intricately composed polyphony that is confusing at times, yet helps to create the complexity and moral ambiguity which is itself the subject of the novel. Comrade Alexandrov's comments are complicated by statements taken out of Volkov's version of the composer's memoirs as well as the letters to his friend Isaak Glikman.

Other important characters include Käthe Kollwitz, the two generals Friedrich Paulus and Andrey Vlasov, as well as Kurt Gerstein, among others. Paulus, who was the commander of the German army in Stalingrad and became a prisoner of war after surrender, returned to East Germany and became a Communist. Vlasov commanded the army that defended Moscow against the Nazi attack in 1941 and was captured by the Germans when he attempted to lift the siege of Leningrad. He organized the Russian Liberation Army with the help of the Germans to fight Bolshevist terror, was captured after the defeat of the Nazis, and executed in August 1946 in Moscow. Finally, Kurt Gerstein who became an SS officer, was involved in organizing gas for extermination camps but actually attempted to subvert the system by informing Western politicians as well as the Catholic Church about the mass murder of Jews – although he was ultimately not heard. His testimony, nonetheless, became an important document in the Nuremburg trials. As such, the novel presents a whole array of persons who were involved in the atrocities of the war and the two bloody regimes, yet also acted in morally difficult constellations. Shostakovich in Vollmann's novel, therefore, is one actor within a spectrum of women and men who became guilty but at the same time attempted to act in favor of other humans. Moreover, the novel presents a network structure with nodes and intricate entanglements that cannot be dissolved. As these are the "agencies," we have a posthumanist view of agency, with systemic, discursive, contingent, and object-related configurations: It is totalitarianism itself that acts.

The second important aspect of *Europe Central* is Vollmann's attempt to fictionalize several of Shostakovich's works. The novel presents some of his major compositions as media for accessing the era and its emotional and experiential "atmosphere." In contrast to the other two novels, Vollmann explicitly translates music into words by narrativizing it, by imagining hearing compositions telling real stories. Problematically, he hereby functionalizes Shostakovich's music as a symptom of the age. He projects a meaning onto the compositions and imaginatively creates concrete semantic references. He interrogates them as "material traces" of the epoch, a representation we can still listen to today, and use it as a way of access.

The novel's major themes are violence and death, and their relationship to music, art, and memory. The first chapter is staged as a retrospective look at WWII in 1945. The main metaphor is the telephone as an all-connecting device of control and impersonal agency, another one is moving steel, that is, weapons, tanks, and other means of destruction. Central Europe is connected by telephone wires and communications. From the beginning the text foregrounds that Hitler and Stalin, that Nazi and Soviet Power are closely interlinked: "A squat black telephone, I mean an octopus, the god of our Signal Corps, owns a recess in Berlin (more probably Moscow [...] The ever-wakeful sleepwalker in Berlin and the soon-to-be-duped realist in the Kremlin get married" (3). The project is to dramatize the territory as well as the civilians, politicians, and soldiers as one system of interacting forces, an internally corresponding entity. Hitler and Stalin are named, but they merge into an impersonal force of destructive power, no longer distinguishable by ideology, but "married" by violence. Vollmann uses metaphors, comparisons, and poetic images to introduce the system of totalitarianism and war: "According to the telephone (...), Europe Central's not a nest of countries at all, but a blank zone of black icons and gold-rimmed clocks whose accidental, endlessly contested territorial divisions (...) can be overwritten as we like [...]" (4). Shostakovich is the novel's main protagonist, and his music could be called the text's 'leitmotif'.[15] His life is presented as symptomatic, and the novel punctures the narrated sequence of events by focusing on important compositions.

Fictionalizing Music

Vollmann describes his approach to music as follows: "Shostakovich would not be happy with my portrayal of his music, because he claimed to hate program

---

[15] Vollmann writes in a note: "When I think of Shostakovich, and when I listen to his music, I imagine a person consumed by fear and regret, a person who (like Kurt Gerstein) did what little he could to uphold the good – in this case, freedom of artistic creation, and the mitigation of other people's emergencies. He became progressively more beaten down, and certainly experienced difficulty saying no – a character trait which may well have kept him alive in the Stalinist years" (2005: 808).

music, and, in fact, what I did was to attach all the specific horrors from his life, and from the war, to his music. Because, when I listened to his music, I felt that it expressed the spirit of his time so much" (Vollmann "Gespräch," qtd. in Delazari 2018: 68). Werner Wolf has introduced the term "imaginary content analogies" (1999: 50–51) for the narration of musical compositions and explains that "the narrator [...] attributes an imaginary literary content to individual movements. This content is subjective and actually not 'there' in the music, of course, but still sufficiently related to [the] 'pretext' to justify a classification of what happens here as a (peripheral) form of literary imitation of music" (51). While the score is materially real, the music's meaning and the experience that may have motivated the composition are not present – they have to be re-presented.

Ivan Delazari regards Vollmann as representative of a mimetic approach that uses diegetic music as transporting an explicit message and stresses Vollmann's "'dedication to emotive musical description' [he quotes Peter Christensen] [...] In *Europe Central*, music is intermingled with and isomorphous to *reality*, so its 'depictions' and reinventions are similar to a fictional treatment of any other familiar experience" (2018: 83). The first musical reference is the *Cello Sonata Opus 40*, a romantic piece written in 1934, before the composer came under the crossfire of Stalin's purges. The *Sonata* is exemplary of an earlier "unburdened" phase of his life. Vollmann analogizes it with memories of a love affair at the time of composition and thus gives the composition a straightforward meaning: a positive counterpoint to the composer's later difficult and sad pieces. The translation of the musical sequence into erotic scenes, however, is awkward: "his tongue seeking as tenderly as a true pianist's fingers, obeying the timbre of her sighs, to give pleasure as exactly as he could: in short, her sighs were the score; his kisses were the performance" (87). At the same time, the novel quotes Shostakovich saying that when in a "*symphony Soviet civil servants are represented by the oboe and the clarinet, and Red Army men by the brass section, you want to scream!*" (91). Interpreting the sonata as being mimetic of a love affair seems somewhat reductionist. As a romantic piece it contains sounds that may be associated with ecstasy and the emotion of being in love, but it is neither program music nor is it expressionist in the sense that a singular emotion can be heard.

In a chapter called "The Palm Tree of Deborah" the *Seventh*, also known as the *Leningrad Symphony*, is contextualized and "sounded": "Barbed wire like music – lines taut in bunches of five, claimed either by the bass cause or the treble – for there was nor can be a neutral instrumental zone – now embraced Leningrad [...] From within the city (treble, tremolo) arose the countervailing piccolo music of screams" (140). Autobiographical scenes and information about Shostakovich's life are mixed with images of Russian history. When the symphony was first performed in Leningrad it was still under the nine hundred days siege by the German Wehrmacht – more than a million people died of hunger and cold. The conductor Karl Eliasberg searched for musicians who were left in the city, pulled some out of the trenches at the front, yet most were too starved and sick to play at all. Nevertheless, the concert took place with half-dead musicians and constituted an exceptional moment of the will to live. It is probably the only symphony the performance of which was supported by a military counterattack against the invaders. In terms of meaning in music, the *Leningrad Symphony* is probably the most interesting case, as it does in fact contain a message, if not an unambiguous one. It contains several codes at once, pointing in different directions. M. T. Anderson refers to "secret messages and double-speak, and [...] how music is itself a code [...]" (7). Shostakovich's own statements are ambivalent and directed at the fascist siege as well as at Stalinist terror. *Europe Central* fictionalizes the sounds of the invasion by merging it with the description of the war: "Now in came the orchestra's processional drums, the Rat Theme going national-patriotic, and in the seventh go-round it was positively stern with the snare drum sounding like a rattlesnake" (197).

The last work the novel fictionalizes is the *Eight Quartet* which, for Vollmann, expresses Shostakovich's statement that "The majority of my symphonies are tombstones" (qtd. in Volkov 1999: 156). Its central motivation is characterized by Anna Akhmatova, who insists "that whoever doesn't make continual reference to the torture chambers all around us is a criminal" (695). The narrator again translates the music into words: "Some notes of Opus 110 get confined up in chords, while others, solo, coffinless, become Leningraders falling one by one into the snow to die. As for the rhythm, if you've ever been present when our Blackshirts in Berlin or their NKVD cadres in Leningrad are beating enemies of the people, you'll know how it is, the screams alternating with gasps. What's that sound? That's the *allegro molto*" (699). According to Vollmann's ear, "Shostakovich becomes every victim [...] striving not to scream and scream" (702). There is sadness and melancholy because of the dead, but also the indissolubility of his entanglement in the system of the Soviet Union; guilt, responsibility, and ambivalence with regard to his own moral record are presented as context and existential horizon. It is a piece sounding as if it came from beyond the grave, by a dead man walking. It commemorates the murdered friends and people sent to the camps, people who vanished without tombs, names, or graves.

While Powers argues that music may be given a meaning by the context, enforced by political power, which, however, is not intrinsically tethered to the music, Vollmann attaches a concrete semantic element to the musical pieces.[16]

---

[16] Ivan Delazari summarizes that for "Vollmann, historical events and biographical circum-

While I agree with much of the argument of the novel, it seems problematic that *Europe Central* does not take the music on its own terms. Vollmann consciously subordinates the art of music, his topic and subject, to the art of fiction, his medium of representation. Thus, he does not primarily write about the predicament of music in totalitarian times but about totalitarianism as a historical tragedy. He is less interested in how these forces affected the music than in how the music may express the historical forces, interpreting them as traces of these.

Conclusion

Sounds are materially given yet music is always culturally and historically coded. Because he lived in times of totalitarianism, Shostakovich's compositions are politically charged and burdened like few other instances of serious music in the twentieth century. We cannot understand his compositions fully without relating them to the context of his life although the music cannot be reduced to their circumstances either. Music does possess meaning, but the meaning is not explicit, is rarely one-dimensional, and, moreover, may be defined by powerful agencies. Shostakovich's compositions are scarred by his dangerous and troubled life, yet they are, because of or in spite of this, very popular. They may be interpreted as double-coded, using irony and allegorical double-speak. Yet Shostakovich's biography as well as his music remain as complex as complicated. This may be the main reason why the composer, his life, and his music continue to be so attractive to writers of fiction.

The controversies surrounding Shostakovich are relevant to debates about our contemporary condition. While *Orfeo* explicitly refers to the present and the danger of surveillance in the contemporary United States, the ways in which the other two novels interrogate how music is or is not politically effective, has ramifications for our current situation as well. As music is one of the most often present and pervasive media which, however, is often pushed into the background as non-signifying "noise," it is important to consider criteria for its affective and political dimensions. Moreover, the critique of dogmatism and totalitarian tendencies as well as of the double-edgedness of a detached ironic attitude seems of particular urgency in today's highly charged and unstable political condition.

---

stances explain Shostakovich's music, and the other way around: his music contains essential clues for understanding history and psychology, both social and personal – hence the pivotal role of music in the novel" (2018: 36).

Works Cited

Adorno, Theodor W. 1973. *Ästhetische Theorie*. Frankfurt am Main: Suhrkamp.
Anderson, M. T. 2017. *Symphony for the City of the Dead: Dmitri Shostakovich and the Siege of Leningrad*. Somerville, MA: Candlewick Press.
Arendt, Hannah. 1951. *The Origins of Totalitarianism*. New York: Harcourt, Brace, Jovanovich.
Attali, Jacques. 1977. *Noise*. Trans. Brian Massumi. Minneapolis: University of Minnesota Press.
Barnes, Julian. 1984. *Flaubert's Parrot*. London: Jonathan Cape.
Barnes, Julian. 2016. *The Noise of Time*. London: Jonathan Cape.
Delazari, Ivan. 2018. "Musical Experience in Fictional Narrative: William T. Vollmann, William H. Gass, and Richard Powers." *Open Access Theses and Dissertations*. 487. <https://repository.hkbu.edu.hk/etd_oa/487>. [accessed 23 November 2021]
Feuchtner, Bernd. 2017. "Flaschenpost mit Sklavensprache – Schostakowitsch und Adorno." Conference Paper. 1–26. <https://www.researchgate.net/publication/321481829_Flaschenpost_mit_Sklavensprache__Schostakowitsch_und_Adorno/link/5a23baae4585155dd41cda0f/download>. [accessed 23 November 2021]
Fiske, John. 2010. *Understanding Popular Culture*. Milton Park, UK: Taylor and Francis.
Friedlander, Saul. 1969. *Kurt Gerstein: The Ambiguity of Good*. Trans. Charles Fullman. New York: Alfred A. Knopf.
Grossman, Vasily. 2006 [1980]. *Life and Fate*. Trans. Robert Chandler. London: Vintage.
Guilbaut, Serge. 1985. *How New York Stole the Idea of Modern Art*. Chicago: University of Chicago Press.
Ho, Allan B., and Dmitry Feofanov. 2011. *The Shostakovich Wars*. <https://www.siue.edu/~aho/ShostakovichWars/SW.pdf>. [accessed 23 November 2021]
Kelly, Adam. 2010. "David Foster Wallace and the New Sincerity in American Fiction." In: David Hering (ed.). *Consider David Foster Wallace: Critical Essays*. 131–146. Austin, TX: SSMG Press.
Kiš, Danilo. 2017 [1978]. *A Tomb for Boris Davidovich*. Trans. Duška Mikić-Mitchell. Dalkey Archive Press.
Koestler, Arthur. 2005 [1940]. *Darkness at Noon*. Trans. Daphne Hardy. London: Vintage.
MacDonald, Ian. "The Shostakovich Debate: A Manual for Beginners." *Music Under Soviet Rule*. Website. Southern Illinois University at Edwardsville. <https://www.siue.edu/~aho/musov/deb/begin.html.> [accessed 23 November 2021]
Mandelstam, Nadezhda. 1999 [1970]. *Hope Against Hope: A Memoir*. Trans. Max Hayward. New York: Modern Library.
McGuigan, Jim. 2014. "The Neoliberal Self." *Culture Unbound* 6: 223–240.
Powers, Richard. 2014. *Orfeo*. London: Atlantic Books.
Powers, Richard. 1995. *Galatea 2.2*. New York: Picador/Farrar, Straus and Giroux.
Snyder, Timothy. 2012. *Bloodlands: Europe Between Hitler and Stalin*. New York: Vintage.
Volkov, Solomon. 1999 [1979]. *Testimony: The Memoirs of Dmitri Shostakovich*. As related to and edited by Solomon Volkov. Trans. Antonia W. Bouis. New York: Limelight.
Vollmann, William T. 2005. *Europe Central*. New York: Penguin.
Vollmann, William T. 2013. "William T. Vollmann: 'Europe Central': Im Gespräch mit Clemens J. Setz, Lesung von Ingo Hülsmann." <https://www.youtube.com/watch?v=EYL9B-pH4W4>. [accessed 23 November 2021]

Wilson, Elizabeth. 2006. *Shostakovich: A Life Remembered*. London: Faber and Faber. New Edition.
Wolf, Werner. 1999 [1997]. "Musicalized Fiction and Intermediality: Theoretical Aspects of Word and Music Studies." In: Walter Bernhart, Stephen Paul Scher and Werner Wolf (eds.). *Word and Music Studies: Defining the Field. Proceedings of the First International Conference on Word and Music Studies at Graz*. Word and Music Studies 1. Amsterdam: Rodopi. 37–58.

Joseph C. Schöpp
History is Suffering: Reading Teju Cole's *Open City* in Light of Walter Benjamin and W. G. Sebald

Abstract: I argue in my article that Teju Cole can be read as an heir of Walter Benjamin and W. G. Sebald, two writers with whom *Open City* shares the view that history is suffering and historiography "a document of barbarism." Like Benjamin he aims to "brush history against the grain," to write a history of the non-victorious and disregarded. Julius, the protagonist, is a *flâneur*, as described by Benjamin in his *Arcades Project,* who like a detective with "eyes open, his ear ready," is in search of things disregarded by the crowds. He leads his readers to vanished times and forgotten places of history. He questions the historical monuments, looks behind their, at times monstrous and glorifying, facades, and with a cold eye records the acts of a worldwide colonial barbarism which defies national borders.

We undeniably live in a globalized age. Gigantic international cash flows circulate unimpeded around the globe and numerous people migrate through a more or less borderless world. The nation-state has had its day and has to make room for more cosmopolitan concepts. Fiction as a worldly art (*welthaltige Kunst*) will need to take these changed conditions into account and "undergo significant cosmopoetic transformation" (Schoene 2017: 88). As early as 1989 Maxine Hong Kingston had already foreseen the end of the nation-based American novel and predicted a new "global novel" that would ensure her and her fellow-writers that they "would all have a sequel" (Kingston 1989: 39–40). The sequel, it seems, has come to a full fruition in the twenty-first century. Critics now increasingly observe transnational drifts, cosmopolitan visions, and see fiction on its way to a "geopolitical novel" (Irr 2013: 11). The fictional space of such "world novels" would be defined by permeable and fluid, if not entirely absent borders, within which highly mobile figures move more or less freely from country to country, from continent to continent. Apart from this transnational tendency, Caren Irr observes a "renewed commitment" to the real in fiction which self-reflexive postmodern novels had largely lost sight of. Novels of the 21st century increasingly "gesture toward reality," as a collection of essays on David Foster Wallace insinuates (Bolger 2014). In a time of fake news, we have to restore the faith of our readers in what is real and true, Salman Rushdie recently demanded in *Süddeutsche Zeitung* (2018). Thus, the real and the transnational, it seems, are two predominant tendencies in contemporary fiction.

Teju Cole's *Open City* (2011) is a piece of writing whose success somehow chimes in with the transnational mood and the faith in what is real. The beginning of the book already sets the tone of a borderless world. Julius, the protagonist, watches birds that ignore borders and migrate freely in the sky, stirring up hope of a "natural immigration;" he tunes in to online classical music stations from countries thousands of miles away whose announcers he could not even understand (*Open City:* 3f.) Julius is a typical product of transnationalism. Born in Nigeria of a German mother and a Nigerian father he lives in the United States and travels effortlessly from country to country, from America to Nigeria to Belgium and back. In part the author's alter ego, a hybrid who is in part "similar to me in certain ways and different in some other ways," as Cole characterized the narrator of his first novel *Every Day is for the Thief* (2007), he appears as a figure wavering between autobiography and fiction. His writing blurs the boundaries not only on a geographical and figural level but also in a generic sense. *Open City* is strictly speaking not a novel; as a plotless, free-flowing form of narration it disregards generic boundaries and oscillates between literary genres like the writings of W. G. Sebald, who freely mixes forms and whose work, like Cole's writings, comprise "history, memoir, biography, autobiography, art criticism, scholarly arcana, and invention" (Cole 2016: 38). Cole repeatedly argued against strict genre conventions; in his eyes "the novel is overrated" and the writers he finds most interesting "find ways to escape it" (Cole 2014).

Open City is a book which relies heavily on facts of history and, as one character in the book puts it, "that is history: suffering" (123), a view that Cole shares with Walter Benjamin and W. G. Sebald, two writers he feels especially close to. If Sebald is the heir of Benjamin, as Jessica Dubow argues, Cole can be seen as the heir of both Benjamin and Sebald (Dubow 2007: 822). Benjamin, in "On the Concept of History" (1942), expresses the view of history as "a document of barbarism" (and Sebald in his writings "draws us into history's shadow" (Cole 2016: 41)). In *Open City*, Cole explicitly pays tribute to Benjamin as one who might help better understand the structure of history (114). What Benjamin aims at in his essay is "to brush history against the grain" (1942: n. pag.), to write a history from the bottom up, as it were, of the non-victorious and the disregarded. Sebald, in Cole's eyes, is a poet of the disregarded whose books are "reflections on the history of violence" (Cole 2016: 38). A closer analysis will show how the voices of these two German posthumous friends resonate in *Open City*.

Julius, the protagonist of *Open City*, works as a psychiatrist in a New York hospital conducting "a clinical study of affective disorders" (*Open City:* 7). As a counterpoint to his busy days in the hospital he, on free weekends, walks the streets of Manhattan as the narrator of Sebald's *The Rings of Saturn* walks the country in East Anglia when emptiness takes hold of him. Julius goes to *Tower Records* and *Blockbuster* stores, attends concerts in Carnegie Hall, visits Ground Zero, goes to shows in museums and photo galleries, loves Mahler, reads Roland Barthes, Tahar Ben Jelloun, and Peter Altenberg's *Telegrams of the Soul*, a book in praise of "little things" which supplant the great events (*Open City:* 5). Images of little objects – "schoolbooks, pens, dresses, shoes" – are sometimes more powerful than human faces, Cole once remarked in his essay "Object Lesson" (2016: 137). Like Sebald, Julius has a "feeling for the inanimate [...] places that have been reduced to their smallest units by the forces of nature and history" (ibid: 42). As a reader of Barthes' *Camera Lucida*, he roams the streets of the city, nailing decisive moments not unlike Cole, a passionate street photographer and photo critic of *The New York Times*. Julius and his author, the psychiatrist and the photographer, have also in common that their work is largely done in dark rooms where things must be developed before they come to the fore.

Julius is a typical *flâneur* as described in Benjamin's *The Arcades Project*, a child of the Parisian boulevards, an aimless, idle walker, forever curious, his "eyes open, his ear ready searching for something entirely different from what the crowd gathers to see." (*Arcades:* M20a, 1) His maxim is that "in our standardized and uniform world, it is right here, deep below the surface, that we must go" (M14a, 4). "The street conducts the *flâneur* into a vanished time. For him every street is precipitous. It leads downward – if not to the mythical Mothers, then into a past that can be all the more spellbinding because it is not his own, not private" (M 1, 2). The *flâneur* resembles the detective who on his way downward uncovers hidden layers of the past. Or as Benjamin puts it: "Preformed in the figure of the *flâneur* is that of the detective" (M 13a, 2).

Two museums, which Julius visits, conduct the idle walker into a vanished time. Avoiding the rain and noise of the street, he enjoys the quiet atmosphere of the American Folk Art Museum, a place of non-spectacular, little art objects showing "weather vanes, ornaments, quilts, paintings" which lead him, the only visitor, into a half-forgotten past. "The sense of having wandered into the past [is] complete" once Julius reaches the third floor and sees a special exhibition of John Brewster's work, a painter of the Early Republic, whose portrait paintings show the "sealed-away world" of the artist's deafness. Julius loses "all track of time before these images, [falls] deep into their world, as if all the time between them and me had somehow vanished." From the quiet place he is hurled back into the standardized and uniform world of the noisy New York streets; he leaves the museum "with the feeling of someone who had returned to the earth from a great distance" *(Open City:* 37–40). The *flâneur* according to Benjamin legitimizes his idleness by his haphazard discoveries of things lost. The *flâneur* Julius is a kind of memorial artist, a photographer, as it were, who with his lens wide open "wards off total oblivion" and helps "frame our losses" (Cole 2016: 197). *Tower Records* and *Blockbuster,* once trade names of the music and movie industries, have disappeared in the book within weeks. Thanks to the memorial art of the *flâneur,* we can still remember the losses.

In the International Center of Photography Julius, the alter ego of Cole, the passionate photographer one day visits a show of the Hungarian photographer Martin Munkásci. Julius is mainly interested in the photographs as works of art, the carefully composed snaps of Munkásci's early period that had inspired Henri Cartier-Bresson to develop his idea of the "decisive moment" in photography, an "uncanny art" which captures one single moment in history while the moments before and after disappear "into the onrush of time." Two visitors of the show, a man in his sixties and a young Hasidic couple seem to "spoil" Julius' artistic experience. The one visitor, an ex-Berliner who had emigrated in 1937 and has lived in New York ever since, seems to be less interested in the artful patterns of the photographs, he elaborates on the incorrect spelling of the *Berliner Illustrirte Zeitung* in which Munkásci's photos of the 1920s and 1930s had appeared. "The man spoke with the slowness of someone who was entering a memory, but it was not a foggy memory, and he spoke about it clearly, as though it had only just happened" (*Open City:* 151). He literally draws Julius into history; the single decisive moment of the picture expands into the before and after. Viewing Munkásci's photo of the infamous Day of Potsdam with Hitler and Goebbels, Julius feels an "undiluted hatred." What the young Jewish couple standing next to him would feel Julius will never know. They stood close to each other, not speaking. Each of the visitors viewing the photos, Julius realizes, would have his or her stories. The one moment of standstill – without a before or an after – develops into stories that have a before and an after. Benjamin, who in his *Arcades Project* devotes a whole section to photography, speaks of "a dialectics at a standstill":

> It's not that what is past casts its light on what is present, or what is present its light on what is past; rather, image is that wherein what has been comes together in a flash with the now to form a new constellation, in other words, image is a dialectics at a standstill [...] Only dialectical images are genuine images [...] and the place where one encounters them is language. (N2a, 3)

For Julius, who had come here for purely photographic reasons, the stills turn into dialectical images and the place where one encounters these dialectical images is language. "The afternoon," he remarks, "was poisoned, and I wanted only to get home and sleep" (*Open City:* 151–155). In a flash of a moment, he finds himself in an uncomfortable new constellation.

In what follows, I hope to show that Julius' walks are first and foremost walks into vanished times, shedding some light on disregarded events in American history. On one of his first walks, he visits his grandfatherly friend, the Japanese-American Professor Saito, 89 years old and suffering from terminal prostate cancer; who had taken Julius under his wings in college and to whom he feels closer than to his own family or any other person in the book. After his medieval studies in England, Saito had returned to the Pacific Northwest from where he and his family were deported and incarcerated in an internment camp, as were over 100,000 Japanese-Americans after Pearl Harbor: a shameful racist chapter in American history. Saito, an American citizen, was "all confused about what was happening; we were American, had always thought ourselves so, and not Japanese" (*Open City*: 13). To fill his time of waiting meaningfully as an internee, Saito begins to memorize great English poetry, not knowing if he would ever see his books again. It taught him the "value of memory," which is especially needed in a country marked by a "crisis of historical memory," as Nancy Peterson argues in her book *Against Amnesia* (2001). His reveries, Julius notes, not only took Saito "out of the everyday" in Saito's memories, Julius is also taken back in time to the days of the Japanese detention. The past for him becomes present and what mainstream American history tends to omit is remembered in Saito's memorization of his time in the camp, where he learned the lesson about the value of memory that he tries to pass on to the next generation.

"I adore imaginary monsters, but I am terrified of real ones," (11) Saito had remarked in their conversation and shortly after their meeting, Julius encounters such a real historical monster. In a bookshop he spots *The Monster of New Amsterdam*, a historical biography of the largely forgotten Cornelis Van Tienhoven, who is mentioned in one breath with other infamous historical monsters like Pol Pot, Hitler, and Stalin. Julius had wanted to look at the book since it was authored by V., one of his patients. Van Tienhoven had arrived in New Amsterdam in 1633, had climbed up the social ladder and became known for his cruel attacks of the Canarsie on Long Island and the Hackensack tribe, raids in which thousands of natives were brutally murdered. In the historical records, V. discovers that these mass murders were treated as little more than the regrettable side effects of colonization. For V., a member of the Delaware tribe, this is a historically untenable position; in her eyes, it is pure racism and needs to be redressed. V.'s depression, for which Julius treats her, developed while working on her book, a typical academic study with an extensive critical apparatus and written from a non-partisan, objective point of view. Her partisanship for her fellow-natives, which she had to suppress professionally, came to the fore on a private level. The horrors her people had to suffer affected her deeply. For her it was "a difficult thing to live in a country that has erased your past," but what had happened, she argues, is "not in the past, it is still with us today, at least, it's still with me" (*Open City:* 27). Julius as a professional therapist behaves the same way as V. the professional historian; he casts a cold eye on his patient's illness as she hides her personal sympathy for the suffering tribes. In her book, he merely looked for "those moments when it left the strict historical record and betrayed some subjective analysis," hoping to gain "further insight into her psychological state" (*Open City:* 27). In his therapeutic efforts, however, Julius appears not to have been successful. At a dancing event in Central Park, he, by pure chance, spots V.'s obituary in the *New York Times*. While he "could hardly imagine the kind of raw pain her family – her husband, her parents – would be experiencing," he reacts to her death as a pure professional; it does not seem to affect him personally. "I returned to the knoll in the park, where I had come in. The dancers had just started again," he comments briefly (*Open City:* 165). His research project on "affective disorders" seems to have been aptly chosen. A relentless affective deficit is, as I hope to show later, his problem.

As an African American, Julius is drawn on his walks to historic sites of African American importance largely disregarded by the public. In this sense, he is a true Sebaldian "poet of the disregarded" (Cole 2016: 42). One of the sites is in Battery Park, within sight of the Statue of Liberty, now a children's playground and once a mercantile center for the building, outfitting, insuring and launching of slavers' ships. Though slavery had been officially abolished in 1820, the slave trade continued to flourish and from the New York ports, "human cargo" was shipped to Cuba, where the deportees worked as slaves on the sugar plantations. Moses Taylor, board member and later president of the New York City Bank, which happens to be Julius' bank, "made massive profits from brokering the sale of Cuban sugar" (*Open City:* 161). The other site on his walk is in Bowling Green, not far from the financial district, which once had been used "for the executions of paupers and slaves," now a place where erhu players perform and Chinese women dance doing their calisthenics (*Open City:* 162). Hidden under the smooth, glittering surface of financial wealth, echoes of a darker, more violent past reverberate.

On a patch of grass on a small security island near the A&T Long Lines Building in Church Street, Julius spots a "curious shape," barely visible amidst the high-rise buildings and difficult to make out. On closer inspection it turns out to be a monument designed by a Haitian artist commemorating the site of an African burial ground: In the eighteenth century a large, quiet piece of land where 20,000 Blacks were buried "outside civilization," then at the outskirts of the city, now reduced to an inconspicuous spot amidst "the endless hum of quotidian commerce and government" (*Open City:* 220). Corpses who frequently bore traces of suffering were often stolen and passed on to surgeons and anatomists who were in need of human material. Slavery, it seems, does not end with one's death. In the course of time the place was forgotten but to this day the dead still return when construction workers "routinely" uncover little objects and human remains. What Julius is steeped in is "the echo across centuries, of slavery in New York" (*Open City:* 220). The city, he realizes, is a palimpsest: written – erased – rewritten – overwritten. Before the Twin Towers were erected, now erased to make room for a new construction, there had been pre-Columbian communities, later pushed away, relocated or exterminated by Dutch and English settlers (58). In Sebald's *Austerlitz*, the new massive building of the Bibliothèque National in Paris rests on ruins of a huge warehouse where German soldiers had collected the loot taken from Parisian Jewish homes. We must go deep down into a vanished time below the surface, Benjamin would argue, to understand the city (M 14a, 4). Or as Cole put it in an interview in *Die Zeit:* "Die Stadt auch aus der Tiefe der Zeit begreifen" (Cole 2013: n. pag.).

On his flight to Brussels, where Julius will continue his lonely city walks, Annette Maillotte, his neighbor on the plane, happens to touch on the history of Heliopolis, a luxurious suburb of Cairo; literally a 'sun city,' "a fantastical place" with fantastic buildings in the style of Ankor Wat or Hindu temples and the currrent home of the Egyptian president. It was designed and built with the money of the Belgian industrialist Baron Édouard Empain (91). When she gives Julius her phone number, a whole series of associations is set in motion in his mind, ranging from the Paris Métro that Empain had built to Heliopolis architecture that he designed, and "the numberless dead, in forgotten cities, necropoli, catacombs" (*Open City:* 94). Baron Empain not only modernized Cairo – as a true believer in *travail et progress*, the motto of the Belgian Congo, he was also a colonizer; a modernizer of cities like Léopoldville where he built an extensive tram system, and to this day he is remembered as the father of the Paris Métro, another symbol of "optimism and progress" (*Open City:* 93). What these modernizing efforts suppress, however, is 'the depth of time,' what Don DeLillo in *Underworld* calls the city's "underhistory, the way archaeologists dig out the history of early cultures" (1997: 791). The history of Heliopolis is one with multiple layers: Pharaonic, Hellenistic, Roman and still later Islamic, with "numberless dead." Ancient Heliopolis has been overwritten by discourses of those who were in power at a time.

"The one who has the power controls the portrayal" (*Open City:* 119), Farouq, a Moroccan Neo-Marxist remarks, whom Julius meets in Brussels and on whose desk he espies a study on Walter Benjamin's "On the Concept of History." In his own essay Benjamin had expressed a similar view:

> Whoever until this day emerges victorious, marches in the triumphal procession in which today's rulers tread over those who are sprawled underfoot. The spoils are, as was ever the case, carried along in the triumphal procession. They are known as the cultural heritage. In the historical materialist they have to reckon with a distanced observer. For what he surveys as the cultural heritage is part and parcel of a lineage which he cannot contemplate without horror. (VII)

Whereas "the historical writer of historicism" irrefutably empathizes with the victor, the historical materialist who "regards it as his task to brush history against the grain," dissociates himself as far as possible from power-controlled portrayals of triumphal victories and empathizes with the victim. In his eyes there "is no document of civilization which is not at the same time a document of barbarism" (Benjamin 1980: 254). As a counter-historian Julius wants to foreground the "footnotes" of history – mass death, plague, famine – rather than the triumphal processions of the Nazis in Nuremberg, the Soviets in Moscow's Red Square or the Chinese rulers in Bejing's Tiananmen. Stalin's Gulags and Hitler's death camps in Europe, the massacres of the Pol Pot regime in Asia, the victims of slavery, and Van Tienhoven's brutalities against the native Americans, the murderous regimes in Uganda and Rwanda in Africa – all mentioned in *Open City* – document the worldwide atrocities. History is not only a triumphal march of the victors but first and foremost a record of suffering.

Belgium, where five chapters in the center of the book are set, is remembered for its brutal colonizers in Africa and for the "corpse-filled cities, camps, beaches, and fields," the slaughter and destruction on the Somme, in Ypres and much earlier at Waterloo (*Open City:* 96). Brussels, where Julius spends four weeks unsuccessfully searching for his German grandmother, is described as a city whose age manifests itself mainly in stone. In these chapters the Sebaldian echoes are most prominent. Julius is as obsessed by monumental buildings as Jacques Austerlitz. Sebald's eponymous novel *Austerlitz* is partly set in Belgium that manifests its history in megalomaniac railroad stations like the one in Antwerp, in historic monuments, and massive fortifications. In *Open City* Brussels presents itself as a city with monuments of an inhuman scale. During his aimless flâneries, Julius discovers countless nineteenth-century "architectural monstrosities" (*Open City:* 97) erected all over town under king Leopold II, also known as the Congo Monster responsible for millions of victims. Their monstrous magnitude is oppressive; it dwarfs the viewers who look like toys, "tiny and drab, like midgets" (*Open City:* 100, 116). The parks abound with statues made of bronze and stone. A bronze bust of the poet Paul Claudel, praised by W. H. Auden as one "writing well," leads the *flâneur* below the surface to discover a more "problematic figure" who had collaborated with Marshal Pétain and the Nazis. A bronze plaque honors the Belgian kings – among them the Monster of the Congo – with an inscription that reads: *Hommage à la dynastie la Belgique et le Congo reconnaissants MDCCCXXXI*. A typical portraiture of those in power or as Julius remarks: "Not triumph, then, but gratitude, or gratitude for triumphs achieved" while those sprawled underfoot, as Benjamin would argue, remain unmentioned (*Open City:* 100). Brussels owed the preservation of its historic monuments to a decision of the city fathers in 1944, which declared it an open city exempt from bombardment and its reduction to rubble. In sharp contrast to the grandeur of the preserved city stand the numberless dead in two World Wars, "ferocious to a degree rarely experienced in history" (*Open City:* 97).

In Farouq's Internet café in Brussels, where customers from all over the world come and go to make their worldwide phone calls, Julius, a cosmopolitan of sorts who travels freely from country to country, experiences genuine cosmopolitanism. The café is, as it were, a small-scale version of a cosmopolitan world with Farouq as its spokesperson. A polyglot in command of several languages, "he flipped seamlessly into French, and back again into English" (*Open City:* 103). Having applied for an M.A. in critical theory, Farouq casually bandies big words and theories by Benjamin, Said, Deleuze and de Man, and now at work on his new master's degree in translation, he practices cosmopolitanism as a translator in his international café. Rejecting such high-flown ideas as the melting pot, the salad bowl or multiculturalism, he firmly believes in cultural and personal difference not as a folkloristic entertainment, "but difference with its own intrinsic value" (*Open City:* 104). A moderate Marxist à la Benjamin, Farouq not only propagates but also lives his beliefs. His Moroccan friend, Khalil, despite his extremist Marxist view remains Farouq's best friend. Julius senses "something powerful about him, a seething intelligence, something that wanted to believe itself indomitable" (*Open City:* 129). He secretly admires Farouq, yet he remains "isolated from all loyalties" (*Open City:* 107). He is the non-committed observer, who, during the heated debates of the two Moroccan friends, keeps more or less silent, gives no indication of what he thinks, only nods, "signaling that [he] was listening" (*Open City:* 115). Farouq is the active cosmopolitan figure, as Katherine Hallermeier argues: "Whereas Julius is relentlessly detached, Farouq is passionately engaged" (2013: 244). Julius, the erudite, disengaged flâneur, never at a loss with words, suddenly falls silent when he should take a personal stand. After his return to New York, he sends Kwame Anthony Appiah's *Cosmopolitanism* to Farouq in memory of the conversations but alos to hide behind Appiah's position, as it were. He asks the postal clerk for a stamp with no American flags, who misinterprets Julius' wish and claims him as his soul brother, a "visionary," one "we call a journeyer" who has traveled far, an ascription from which Julius promptly distances himself. The postal worker, a politically engaged Black rapper, invites him to a poets café, an invitation that he does not explicitly turn down but makes "a mental note to avoid that particular post office in the future" (*Open City:* 186–188). Pieter Vermeulen sees Julius' posture as one of "a cosmopolitan flâneur [...] shadowed by the contours of a more sinister, and mostly forgotten nineteenth-century figure of restless mobility, the fugueur [as] the pathological flip-side of the flâneur" (2013: 42).

On numerous occasions Julius behaves like a typical *fugueur* who flees from taking on responsibility and shows his affective disorders. Hearing of the death of his neighbor's wife, he avoids an embrace because it would in his eyes look like a "false intimacy" (*Open City:* 21). After his separation from Nadège, his female companion, both agree that they "would make an effort to work things out at a distance but we had said the words without meaning them" (24). After a one-night stand with a Czech women in a Brussels hotel, he uses a pseudonym although she tells him her name, which he immediately forgets. Upon completion of "the needful", he gets dressed, kisses her on the neck, and leaves the room wordlessly (*Open City:* 110). In a detention facility, which he reluctantly visits with Nadège and a group of female do-gooders "with that beatific, slightly unfocused expression" on their faces, he meets Saidu, a Liberian migrant, who tells him the story of his adventurous escape, a story that to Julius' ears sounds too good to be true and to which he gives "as best as [he] could, a sympathetic ear" (*Open City:* 62–64). When Saidu invites him to visit again if he is not deported, Julius flatly responds that he would but never does (*Open City:* 70). Only the news of Saito's death affects him deeply, his only real friend who "was so kind to me" (*Open City:* 184). Saito's legacy that he "must be careful about closing too many doors," goes unheeded (172). The doors of sympathy and affection remain closed. His affective disorders are reflected in the flat, "affectless tone" of the book (Vermeulen 2013: 53). Julius' friend, to whom he refers only briefly, does not even have a name. What the reader learns about the basis of their friendship is that his interests went beyond the professional specialty, that he had a taste for fashionable French philosophers, that he had strong opinions about books, films and jazz: an intellectual friendship entirely to Julius' taste, but no word about affections (*Open City:* 23). And there is "that other girl" who appears time and again in the book. When she makes her first appearance, she is "tied to Nadège" and obviously a one-time lover, hidden in his memory for more than twenty-five years, whose name he does not remember (*Open City:* 60). The same girl, it seems, makes her physical appearance many years later in a grocery store in Manhattan; she expects him to remember her but he doesn't. When she introduces herself as Moji Kasali, "the memory was restored" (*Open City:* 156). Pages later the reader learns that she is an engaged environmentalist who "actively" worries about the ecology while Julius' response that we all worry sounds like unengaged prattle "filling in the silence" (*Open City:* 198, 204). The reader senses that there is something unacknowledged in their tense relationship, which is only disclosed near the end of the book when Moji reveals that years ago in Nigeria Julius had sexually abused her – it left her with a life-long "stain or a scar" while he acts as if he knows nothing about the abuse and that he had even forgotten her. "The luxury of denial had not been possible for her" (*Open City:* 244). Julius leaves Moji's demand to say at least a word of apology unanswered. As a typical fugueur, he flees and hides behind a Nietzsche anecdote that refers to a scar the philosopher had carried for the rest of his life (*Open City:* 246).

In an interview discussing the novel, Cole explicitly states that he didn't want his narrator to be innocent but to be directly implicated in his own narration (Knörer 2012: n. pag.) This makes Julius an ambivalent figure, both reliable and unreliable. As a *flâneur* he can be trusted, observes acutely with a cold, almost photographic eye minutest details, dives deeply into vanished times, and unearths forgotten layers of history. When confronted with his own biography, he acts as a *fugueur* who tends to forget, suppress, and avoid self-confrontation, which "disqualifies him as a reliable focalizer" (Schoene 2017: 95). The title of the book is as ambivalent as its narrator. As a form of surrender to the enemy, Brussels declared itself an 'open city' in World War II to save people's lives. A such, it is a fixed political term. More questionable is its sociological meaning, and Brussel's openness to ethnically 'others'. Despite the free European borders, Julius feels a "palpable psychological pressure in the city" (*Open City:* 98). The color-blindness that Dr. Maillotte claims for her native city would be strongly refuted by Farouq, who has "lost all [his] illusions about Europe" (*Open City:* 128). New York's cultural and ethnic diversity, the openness on a textual level with diverse narratives that coexist next to each other and prevent a coherent legibility and textual closure cannot be denied. Yet to "this strangest of islands" there is still another side. It is a city self-absorbed, turned in on itself, its shore "a carapace, permeable only at certain points" (*Open City:* 54). *Open City* reflects both its openness and closedness in two symbolic scenes at the very beginning and end of the book. Before Julius begins his aimless flâneries, he had "fallen into the habit of watching bird migrations [...] hoping to see the miracle of natural immigration," a futile hope, as it turns out in the final scene of the book (*Open City:* 3). During an excursion to the Statue of Liberty, "massive and towering over us," Julius remembers a moment in the history of Bartholdi's statue, once the biggest working lighthouse in the country, guiding ships safely into Manhattan's harbor but at the same time fatally misguiding the birds. One morning "more than fourteen hundred dead birds were recovered from the crown, the balcony of the torch, and the pedestal of the statue" (*Open City:* 259). Whereas the mighty ships, representatives of commercial power, were guided safely into Manhattan's harbor, the powerless birds, hoping to see the miracle of natural immigration, fell prey to the massive and towering monument. Their carcasses were at first commercially used by milliners and fancy stores and later sent off to the Smithsonian Institution where they would be retained in the service of science (258). Reading this final scene, Walter Benjamin and W.G. Sebald come to mind again: It is a Sebaldian scene that "draws us into history's shadow" (Cole 2016: 41) and an echo of Benjamin that "there is no document of civilization which is not at the same time a document of barbarism" (1942: n. pag.).

Works Cited

Benjamin, Walter. 1942. "On the Concept of History." Trans. Lloyd Spencer. <https://www.sfu.ca/~andrewf/CONCEPT2.html>. [accessed 23 November 2021]
Benjamin, Walter. 1980. "Über den Begriff der Geschichte." *Illuminationen: Ausgewählte Schriften*. Frankfurt: Suhrkamp. 251–263.
Benjamin, Walter. 1999. *The Arcades Project*. Trans. Howard Eiland and Kevin McLaughlin. Cambridge, MA: The Belknap Press of Harvard University.
Bolger, Robert K. (ed.). 2014. *Gesturing Toward Reality: David Foster Wallace and Philosophy*. New York: Bloomsbury.
Cole, Teju. 2011. *Open City: A Novel*. New York: Random House.
Cole, Teju. 2013. "Die Situation in den USA ist abscheulich." *Die Zeit*. June 12, 2013. <https://www.zeit.de/kultur/literatur/2013-06/interview-teju-cole-open-city>. [accessed 23 November 2021]
Cole, Teju. 2014. "By the Book." *The New York Times*. March 9, 2014. <https://www.nytimes.com/2014/03/09/books/review/teju-cole-by-the-book.html>. [accessed 23 November 2021]
Cole, Teju. 2016. *Known and Strange Things*. London: Faber and Faber.
DeLillo, Don. 1997. *Underworld*. New York: Scribner.
Dubow, Jessica. 2007. "Case Interrupted: Benjamin, Sebald, and the Dialectical Image." *Critical Inquiry* 33.4: 820–836.
Hallemeier, Katherine. 2013. "Literary Cosmopolitanisms in Teju Cole's *Every Day is for the Thief* and *Open City*." *Ariel: A Review of International English Literature*, 44.2–3: 239–250.
Irr, Caren. 2013. *Toward the Geopolitical Novel: American Fiction in the Twenty-First Century*. New York: Columbia University Press.
Kingston, Maxine Hong. 1989. "The Novel's Next Step." *Mother Jones*, 14.10: 39–40.
Knörer, Ekkehard. 2012. "Interview mit Teju Cole." *Merkur*, Oct 8, 2012. <http://.www.merkur-blog.de/2012/10/interview-mit-teju-cole/>. [accessed 23 November 2021]
Peterson, Nancy J. 2001. *Against Amnesia: Contemporary American Women Writers and the Crisis of Historical Memory*. Philadelphia: University of Pennsylvania Press.
Rushdie, Salman. 2018. "Wahrheit, stets eine umstrittene Größe." *Süddeutsche Zeitung*, May 18, 2018. <https://www.sueddeutsche.de>kultur>salman-rushdie-fake-1.3985387>. [accessed 23 November 2021]

Schoene, Berthold. 2017. "Contemporary American Literature as World Literature: Cruel Cosmopolitanism, Cosmopoetics, and the Search for a Worldlier American Novel." *Anglia* 135.1: 86–104.

Vermeulen, Pieter. 2013. "Flights of Memory: Teju Cole's *Open City* and the Limits of Aesthetic Cosmopolitanism." *Journal of Modern Literature* 37.1: 40–57.

Christa Buschendorf
Greek Passion Revisited: Appropriations of Medea in African American Fiction

Abstract: Writers involved in the revision of classical myths necessarily engage in what Hans Blumenberg terms "work on myth." Whether they retain the ancient setting or transpose the stories about gods and heroes of antiquity into their own time and place, they transform earlier versions of the myths according to the questions relevant in their societies. In the twentieth and twenty-first centuries, feminists and African Americans have shown a particular interest in rewriting and revising the Medea myth. Whereas many Black intellectuals of the early twentieth century argued that African Americans should be entitled to and thus should thrive for the cultural and symbolic capital of a literary taste defined as legitimate by whites, the attitude towards the Western canon changed with the civil rights movement and the development of a genuinely Black aesthetics. In the ensuing canon debates, the adoption of consecrated authors of the Western tradition was often interpreted as an act of submission. More recently, however, there is a revived interest among African American writers in classics and in classical myths, often referred to as "Black classicism." In the following, I will discuss three appropriations of the Medea myth in Black fiction – W. E. B. Du Bois' *The Quest of the Silver Fleece* (1911), Percival Everett's *For Her Dark Skin* (1990), and Jesmyn Ward's *Salvage the Bones* (2011).

The multiple murderess Medea is one of the most terrifying female figures of Greek myth. The desperate act of infanticide she is said to have committed after her husband Jason had left her for Creusa, the young daughter and only child of king Creon, ruler of the city state of Corinth, has for centuries fascinated writers and visual artists alike. While her current notoriety is based almost exclusively on the horrifying act of murdering her two sons, the mythic figure of Medea that evolved in numerous sources of antiquity, shows a high degree of complexity. According to an early mythic strand, she was of divine ancestry, granddaughter of the powerful Greek sun god Helios and also direct descendant of Hecate, a non-Olympian goddess from Asia Minor whose realm is the night and who is well-versed in magic and witchcraft; in other words, Medea simultaneously represented the opposing forces of light and darkness, good and evil. It was only later, when she became associated with Greek cults and served as priestess of Hecate, that she turned human. Even so, she remained a renowned expert in magic and potions, who true to her bipartite heritage was capable of both rejuvenating and destroying lives. In fact, she was often portrayed as a wise counselor, thus fulfilling the promise of her Greek name, which, after all, means 'knowing good counsel.'[1]

When Jason and the Argonauts, in quest of the Golden Fleece, arrive in the kingdom of Colchis situated on the eastern shore of the Black Sea, the king's daughter Medea acts in the classic role of helping-maid to the Greek hero: without her superior knowledge and unfailing support Jason could not have survived the dangerous tasks assigned to him by Medea's father Aeëtes, nor could he have stolen the Golden Fleece guarded by an unsleeping vicious dragon. Medea's loyalty towards the Greek hero, with whom – due to the interference of Aphrodite – she fell in love at first sight, leads to the betrayal of her family. Not only is she instrumental in robbing her father of the most valuable treasure of his kingdom,[2] but she is even responsible of the death of her brother Apsyrtos sent by the king to pursue the Argo. Upon entering Greece, Medea, a princess in her homeland, intelligent and beautiful, is allotted the social status of an outsider by a society that regards itself as superior vis-à-vis a 'barbarian.'

The story of Medea and Jason combines two themes. On a psychological level, it tells about the raging jealousy of an individual woman deeply hurt by the betrayal of a man whom she loves passionately. On a socio-psychological level, it displays the fate of a foreigner who experiences exclusion for being considered inferior. The two aspects become intertwined when we read the story as addressing what in terms of a controversial theory of cultural history is the transition from a matriarchal to a patriarchal order.[3] From this perspective, Medea's

---

[1] For a helpful survey of the major episodes in Medea's 'biography' and their ancient sources, see Fritz Graf, "Medea, the Enchantress From Afar: Remarks on a Well-Known Myth," *Medea: Essays on Medea in Myth, Literature, Philosophy, and Art*, eds. James J. Clauss, and Sarah Iles Johnston (Princeton: Princeton University Press, 1997), 21–43.

[2] The material basis of the legend of the ram's golden fell is the ancient technique of prospecting for gold: it is believed that fells were used to collect particles of gold in water. Colchis is located in today's Georgia, a region famous for its long history of gold winning and goldsmith's art going back to the second half of the third thousand BC; for the connection between the practice of gold winning and the saga of the Argonauts, see, for example, the article by Nino Lordkipanidze, "Gold aus Georgien," in *Medeas Liebe und die Jagd nach dem Goldenen Vlies*, ed. Vinzenz Brinkmann (catalogue of the exhibition *Medea's Love and the Quest for the Golden Fleece*, Liebighaus, Frankfurt a.M., 2018–2019).

[3] The concept of matriarchy, established by J. J. Bachofen's *Das Mutterrecht* (1861), while being refuted by scholars of ancient history, had been taken up by feminists of the 1970s and 1980s and is often used in connection with the myth of Medea; see, for example, Inge Stephan, *Medea: Multimediale Karriere einer mythologischen Figur* (Köln, Weimar, Wien: Böhlau, 2006), 36, 155, 163–165.

resistance and revenge stand for a collective uprising of women which ultimately is doomed to fail. Medea's murder of Creusa and her own children appear then as calculated strikes against patriarchy: Medea successfully extinguishes two pedigrees. But while she can claim victory with regard to destroying individual genealogies, she cannot possibly reverse the kind of male domination under which she suffers. In the male-dominated world of Jason, women are treated as means to an end in the competitive conflicts men impose upon each other for power and riches as well as for securing their genealogical line. Yet, in Euripides' tragedy *Medea* (431 BC), undoubtedly the most influential literary appropriation of the myth, the story of Jason and Medea famously ends with the latter's escape from Corinth in the sun chariot of Helios drawn by two dragons. If this innovation is "touching upon apotheosis,"[4] Euripides is also said to have invented Medea's infanticide. According to earlier versions of the myth, the Corinthians killed the children in order to prevent Jason's off-spring of mixed heritage ever to ascend the throne.[5] Thus in their attempt to exonerate Medea, feminist writers often build their revisions upon pre-Euripedean sources or decide to omit the infanticide.[6]

In the twentieth century, the story of Medea and Jason was frequently taken up by African Americans authors. Most adaptations, based on Euripides' tragedy, were written for the stage.[7] In the following, I will discuss three appropriations of the Medea myth in Black fiction. W. E. B. Du Bois' *The Quest of the Silver Fleece* (1911) and Jesmyn Ward's *Salvage the Bones* (2011) employ Medea and Jason as mythic foils, against which the novels' characters are set off. Both authors create modern heroines who, in stark contrast to the ancient Medea, serve as benevolent models to the Black community of their day. In contrast, Percival Everett's *For Her Dark Skin* (1990), is a satirical take on the myth. While Everett retells the story in the ancient setting, he reverses the power relations between Jason and Medea even more radically than Du Bois and Ward.

---

4 Christina Dokou, "The Mother of All Horrors: Medea's Infanticide in African American Literature," *The Palgrave Handbook to Horror Literature*, edited by Kevin Costorphine and Laura R. Kremmel (New York: Springer International Publishing, 2018), 409.
5 For recent discussions of the infanticide motif, see Sarah Iles Johnston, "Corinthian Medea and the Cult of Hera Akraia," Clauss and Johnston, eds., *Medea*, 44–65.
6 See for example, Christa Wolf, *Medea. Stimmen* (1996); cf. Stephan, *Medea*, 9–12; on Wolf's doubt as to Euripides' version and her reliance on other ancient sources, see 155.
7 See Helene P. Foley's seminal chapter on "Reimagining Medea as American Other," *Reimagining Greek Tragedy on the American Stage* (Berkeley: University of California Press, 2012), 190–228.

For centuries, Greek myths have functioned as a fathomless treasure trove of the artistic imagination. The postmillennial novel in the United States is no exception; in fact, the popularity of myth adoptions in European and American literature has been increasing in the last two decades. In light of the ongoing struggle for women's rights, it does not come as a surprise that there is a growing emphasis on myths that present strong women in their battle against male authority and abuse, among whom Antigone and Medea stand out. While each epoch inscribes its own social and political issues into the mythic tales, in the case of Black literature we find – in addition to such expected changes – a reoccurrence of specific themes that relate to the long and enduring tradition of the Black freedom struggle. For example, African American appropriations of the classics are usually interconnected to the demand of higher learning. One of the most rigorous and eloquent advocates for unlimited Black education in the twentieth century was Du Bois, but as the example of Ward's postmillennial novel demonstrates, one hundred years after his application of the Medea myth, the fight still continues; Ward, too, feels the need to justify the use of Greek myth. In view of this challenge, both authors employ myth in their fiction as an educational tool that helps their protagonists to mature. In addition, both novels – in an effort to create appealing identity figures – highlight Medea's charitable aspects. Yet, as the following interpretations will demonstrate, Ward's postmillennial coming-of-age story differs significantly from Du Bois' vision of Black socialism. In contrast, choosing the genre of parody by definition saves Everett the obligation to justify his adoption of classic myth, and it even gives him the liberty to portray Medea as murderess of her children and simultaneously as a captivating figure.

I

In *Souls of Black Folk*, W. E. B. Du Bois famously declares: "I summon Aristotle and Aurelius and what soul I will, and they come all graciously with no scorn nor condescension."[8] To claim writers of antiquity as intellectual property of Blacks was an important demand in Du Bois' battle for full recognition of African Americans in U.S.-American society. While he already briefly refers to the myth of the Argonauts in *The Souls of Black Folk* (1903),[9] he uses it extensively in his first

---

8 *The Souls of Black Folk* (Oxford, New York: Oxford UP, 2007), 52.
9 On the eighth essay in *The Souls of Black Folk*, "On the Quest of the Golden Fleece," as "the most important intertext for the novel," see Jackie Murray, "W.E.B. Du Bois' *The Quest of the Sil-*

novel *The Quest of the Silver Fleece*. In what he later maintains is "really an economic study" about the mechanisms of cotton production and trade in the post-Reconstruction period,[10] the myth of Jason and Medea functions as a matrix for the socio-historical plot of exploitation and robbery. In the heroine Zora, Du Bois creates a profound revision of Medea. Although Zora, like Medea, is raised in an uncivilized realm, in her case, the dark territory of a swamp in Alabama, and although as a young girl she is sexually exploited by Harry Creswell, offspring of the local planter elite, Du Bois' Black Medea overcomes her early socialization and grows into a morally mature, well-educated young woman who finally becomes a genuine force for good to the Black community. In contrast to the spirited and beautiful young woman, her mother Elspeth, "an old woman – short, broad, black and wrinkled, with fangs and pendulous lips and red, wicked eyes,"[11] is, according to Zora, "a witch and can conjure" (19). She is an ominous presence in the swamp, hosting nightly gatherings of white men in her cabin. Just as Du Bois emphasizes that the swamp is both a dismal, inhospitable as well as a beautiful, fertile natural habitat, he juxtaposes the ugly depravity of Elspeth with Zora's admirable striving for decency. Elspeth, who stands in the tradition of Medea as demonic witch,[12] is a creature shaped by the institution of slavery, while her daughter, embodying Medea's beneficial side, represents the emancipated Black woman's potential and future. Yet, as Du Bois shows, both women suffer from the effects of white and male supremacy, the backbone of slavery that has survived the institution.

Apart from the allusion to the Golden Fleece in the title,[13] the myth of the Argonauts is explicitly introduced in the text by Miss Mary Taylor, a young teacher from the North who mentions it to Blessed Alwyn, the most promising pupil in

---

ver Fleece: The Education of Black Medea," *Transactions of the American Philological Association* (TAPA) 149, no. 2 (Supplement, 2019), 154–157; 145–146.
10 Du Bois, *Dusk of Dawn: An Essay Toward an Autobiography of a Race Concept* [1940] (Oxford, New York: Oxford UP, 2007), 134.
11 Du Bois, *The Quest of the Silver Fleece* (Oxford, New York: Oxford UP, 2007), 5; further references to this edition in the text.
12 For a portrait of Medea as a powerful witch and sorceress, closely associated with the snake, see e.g. Seneca's tragedy *Medea*. On the serpentine nature of Elspeth, see David H. Sick, "Alabamian Argonautica: Myth and Classical Education in *The Quest of the Silver Fleece*," *Classical World* 110, no. 2 (Spring 2017), 389–390.
13 "The Quest for the Golden Fleece" was Du Bois' first choice of title that he had to modify because there already existed a popular romance with that title: *Golden Fleece: The American Adventures of a Fortune Hunting Earl* (1903) by David Graham Phillips; see William C. Cook and James Tatum, *African American Writers and Classical Tradition* (Chicago and London: University of Chicago Press, 2010), 129.

the Smith School for Negroes, who falls in love with Zora and then refutes her after having learned that she is not "pure." Bles' reaction takes Mary Taylor by surprise:

> "All yon is Jason's."
> "What?" she asked, puzzled.
> He pointed with one sweep of his long arm to the quivering mass of green-gold foliage that swept from swamp to horizon.
> "All yon golden fleece is Jason's now," he repeated.
> "I thought it was—Creswell's," she said.
> "That's what I mean."
> She suddenly understood that the story had sunk deeply.
> "I am glad to hear you say that," she said methodically, "for Jason was a brave adventurer—"
> "I thought he was a thief."
> "Oh, well—those were other times."
> "The Creswells are thieves now." (14)[14]

In this passage, Du Bois establishes an interpretation of the myth of Jason and the Argonauts as a story of a raid by colonizers, thereby turning Jason into an anti-hero. In contrast to Mary Taylor's idealization, Bles' down-to-earth application of the myth to the present characterizes the economic structure in the South as exploitative and its planter class as criminal. When Bles passes the saga of the Argonauts on to Zora, they again discuss its meaning for their own situation. Zora poses the question: "Do you s'pose mammy's the witch?" (23) Bles, who at that point does not know that Elspeth operates as a kind of madam of a brothel where white men meet and sexually abuse black girls, among them her own daughter, denies the possibility: "No; she wouldn't give her own flesh and blood to help the thieving Jason." But Zora contradicts him: "Yes, she would, too." "Then we must escape her," Bles responds. Bles' plan to flee the influence of Elspeth-Medea involves utilizing the very resources the sorceress has to offer. In a particularly fertile patch, the "heart of the swamp" (23), they plant the "wonder seed" (37) supplied and, in an uncanny ritual, sowed by Elspeth.[15] After great toiling, the benevolent forces of nature turn the cotton seed into two bales of the most beautiful Silver Fleece.

Rather than inventing fictional characters who fully correspond to figures of Greek myth, Du Bois limits mythological references to isolated features of gods

---

14 For an extended interpretation of this scene and the complicated relationship between white teacher and Black pupil, see Murray, "Du Bois' *Quest*," 154–157.
15 As Sick argues, "Du Bois is combining separate aspects of the Greek myth, both of which involve snakes. Elspeth is both the dragon that protects the Fleece, and she is the source of the dragon's teeth for planting." "Alabamian Argonautica," 389–390.

and heroes. These fragmentary allusions serve various purposes. Elspeth embodies a mythic type rather than a fully developed fictional character capable of change. In contrast, when Zora compares Bles to Jason, the parallel remains vague, but it leads the reader's imagination to look for further points of reference between the mythic couple Jason and Medea and the relationship of Bles and Zora. The mythic Jason betrays Medea, thereby revealing ingratitude and selfishness. Bles also acts selfishly when he condemns Zora for not having preserved her "purity." Ignoring what Zora tries to convey to him, namely, that she and the other girls were sexually exploited by Creswell whom they considered their "master" (90), he is preoccupied with preserving his male pride. Whereas Bles recognizes that the ancient Jason is a thief, he overlooks that the myth also tells about masculine domination, which, albeit unconsciously, he exerts himself.

Zora resembles Medea in that she is a 'barbarian' whose education is based on the workings of nature and magic practices, and who, in encountering Bles, is for the first time confronted with scientific knowledge that she initially rejects. Yet, in contrast to the myth of Medea, Zora's story is a *Bildungsroman*;[16] the successful process of Zora's acquisition of higher learning underscores Du Bois' demand that all Blacks should have access to whatever knowledge they aspire. Zora also resembles Medea in her passionate love for Bles, her loyalty, and her subsequent desire to help him; but unlike Medea she will not commit crimes for him. Rather, true to her mythic model's name, Zora provides good counsel to Bles,[17] and she does so even after their separation, when at a crucial point of his career as a politician he is running the risk of sacrificing his integrity for political advantage. At first raped and later robbed of the true value of the bales of Silver Fleece by her "master," young Harry Creswell, and abandoned by her lover Bles, Zora seeks independence from both Jasons. Like Medea, she "asserts herself as independent of husband and patriarchy generally."[18] But unlike Medea, she never seeks revenge for the grave injustices suffered. Moreover, completely

---

[16] Cf. Murray, "Du Bois' *Quest*", 144: "But what *The Quest of the Silver Fleece* is really about is Zora's education." See also David Withun, "Zora's Bookshelf in *The Quest of the Silver Fleece* by W.E.B. Du bois [sic]," *The Explicator* 77, nos. 3–4 (2019), 124–127, on the significance of Zora's small collection of books.
[17] According to Murray, her own name, Zora, "is Slavic, meaning 'Dawn.' In Greek mythology, Dawn is the mother of Memnon, the king of the Ethiopians. Zora's connection (via her name) to the Sun and the Ethiopians is strengthened by Du Bois' great emphasis on the brightness of Zora's eyes." Murray, "Du Bois' *Quest*," 154.
[18] Marianne McDonald, "Medea as Politician and Diva: Riding the Dragon into the Future," Clauss and Johnston, eds., *Medea*, 303.

reversing literary tradition, Du Bois rewrites the tragedy of Jason and Medea as a romance. As a consequence, there is a clandestine bond of love that keeps Zora and Bles connected, which in the end, in a thorough negation of the myth, even leads to the reunion of the lovers. But what can be achieved by transforming a myth to the point of revising even some of its core elements?[19]

The sociologist and historian Du Bois uses fiction writing as a kind of shorthand that allows him to present in a condensed manner the economic and political forces that shape an historical period. He invents a fictional plot evolving around agents who are types of the social classes engaged in the respective conflicts of interest. Set off against them are the characters of the subplot developed into full-fledged personalities. Inscribed into the structure of the historical novel, mythical allusions function as an additional technique of condensation. Mythic labelling produces an identification that serves to depict the characters, no matter whether they affirm the myth or deviate from it. As mentioned before, once we apply the matrix of the story of Jason and Medea to Bles and Zora, the patriarchal attitude of Bles is immediately exposed. But in contrast to his self-interpretation as a leader and protector, Bles will eventually have to realize that Zora is the stronger of the two. Starting out as an "heathen hoyden," "steeped body and soul in wood-lore" (19), she does not remain a 'barbarian,' but leaves the limited world of the swamp behind, constantly maturing in mind and soul. Morally repelled by rampant corruption in Washington, she finally decides to assume responsibility for the struggling Black farmers back in Alabama. Returning to the swamp she tries to build a Black community completely independent of whites, and what is more, she does so by way of creating a Black cooperative, one of Du Bois' favorite economic concepts.[20] While the heroine is shaped both in reference to and in deviation from the mythic figure, she participates in Medea's heroic grandeur. In her courageous and victorious struggle against patriarchy and racism, Zora achieves a stature larger than life. More importantly, though, in foregoing rage and revenge she surpasses Medea in moral grandeur.

---

19 See Hans Blumenberg, *Work on Myth* (Cambridge, Mass., London: MIT Press, 1990), for two essential principles of the reception of myth, namely first, that "everything we are acquainted with is myth that has already entered into the process of reception," and secondly, that "the limit concept of work on myth would be to bring myth to an end, to venture the most extreme deformation, which only just allows or almost no longer allows the original figure to be recognized." (266)

20 Mythologically, one might argue, Du Bois follows Pindar's *Pythian* 4, where Medea appears as a prophetic voice who predicts a founding of a colony in North Africa; see Dolores M. O'Higgins, "Medea as Muse: Pindar's *Pythian* 4," *Medea*, eds. Clauss and Johnston, 1997, 114–115. For Du Bois' propagation of the concept of "the Negro co-operative movement," see *Dusk of Dawn*, 107, and passim.

Besides using the literary genres of historical novel and romance in combination with mythology as a means of reinterpreting post-Reconstruction history, Du Bois employs his pronounced rewriting of the mythic figure of Medea for promoting Black feminist agenda, for which he most notably advocates in his essay "The Damnation of Women" (1920). Du Bois' call for "the uplift of women," is also a very special homage to Black women as well as a severe critique of "the white South" for "its wanton and continued and persistent insulting of the black womanhood which it sought and seeks to prostitute to its lust."[21]

II

In the course of the civil rights movement, when intellectuals and artists focused on the development of a genuinely Black aesthetics, appropriations of classical myths were often suspected to be an act of submission to the cultural hegemony of whites.[22] More recently, though, there has been a renaissance of the classical tradition among African American writers.[23] One of the most famous examples of twentieth-century fiction is Toni Morrison's novel *Beloved* (1987). It has been interpreted as a revision of the Medea myth, although it does not attempt to retell the ancient story. The novel's reception of the figure of Medea merely consists in the refutation of Medea's motif for committing infanticide: "Medea is recast not as the malicious wife who mercilessly kills her children, but as a victimized slave who desperately tries to protect her brood."[24] Tracey L. Walters sees a potential source of inspiration for Morrison in Edith Hamilton's *Mythology* (1942), the famous American classicist's popular retelling of Greek myths.[25] In fact, according

---

21 *Darkwater: Voices from Within the Veil* (Oxford, New York: Oxford University Press, 2007), 87; 82. In the *Silver Fleece* Du Bois had already made the same point by establishing the prostitution of Black women as the 'dark' secret of the Creswell family.
22 See, for example, Trey Ellis, who claims a change of aesthetic in the 1980s, when Black artists "no longer need to deny or suppress any part of our complicated and sometimes contradictory cultural baggage to please either White people or Black," "The New Black Aesthetic," *Callalloo* 12 (1989), 235; cf. Tracey L. Walters, *African American Literature and the Classicist Tradition: Black Women Writers from Wheatley to Morrison* (New York: Palgrave MacMillan, 2007), 139.
23 Apart from numerous studies on single Black writers' adaptations of myths since the 1980s, see the following surveys: Walters, *African American Literature* (2007); Cook and Tatum, *African American Writers* (2010); Foley, *Reimagining Greek Tragedy* (2012).
24 Walters, *African American Literature*, 109. For an extended discussion of Medea as "the terrible and primal authority of a mother as a dealer of life *and* death," her relation to the situation of mothers in slavery, and an interpretation of *Beloved*, see Dokou, "Mother of all Horrors," 409.
25 Walters, *African American Literature*, 36.

to Hamilton, Medea comes to the following conclusion: "There was no protection for her children, no help for them anywhere. A slave's life might be theirs, nothing more. 'I will not let them live for strangers to ill-use,' she thought."[26]

The story of Medea as retold by Hamilton plays a central role in Jesmyn Ward's novel *Salvage the Bones*.[27] The female protagonist Esch encounters the myth of the Argonauts through her summer reading assignment of Hamilton's *Mythology*. To the fifteen year-old pregnant teenager, who feels betrayed by the father of her unborn child, Medea becomes a character who helps her to come to terms with her own situation. As Ward states in an interview: "It infuriates me that the work of white American writers can be universal and lay claim to classic texts, while black and female authors are ghetto-ized as 'other.' I wanted to align Esch with that classic text, with the universal figure of Medea, the antihero, to claim that tradition as part of my Western literary heritage."[28] By asserting the classic tradition as part of her own intellectual heritage, Ward turns it into an act of empowerment both for her protagonist and herself.

The setting of the novel is Bois Sauvage, a small town on the Mississippi Gulf Coast, in August 2005. Esch's family, her father Claude Batiste, her elder brothers Randall and Skeetah, and her younger brother Junior, are preparing for the arrival of the storm that will turn into hurricane Katrina. Esch's mother died in childbed, and since then the family has been wrestling psychologically and economically. The Batistes still live on the land the parents of Esch's mother owned and that grandfather Papa Joseph had nicknamed the "Pit." (14) But the property is neglected; the fields "are overgrown with shrubs" (14); the yard is filled with scrap metal: "refrigerators rusted […], pieces of engines, a washing machine." (89) Moreover, if Bois Sauvage is a place where nature tends to undo all efforts of the community "to impose some order, some civility" (117), then the Pit, in aggravation, is the "black heart of Bois Sauvage" (97), or, as Skeetah claims: "We savages up here on the Pit" (95; emphasis in original). Esch's home, like Medea's Colchis, is the realm of wilderness opposed to civilization.

Each of the twelve chapters of the novel corresponds to a day in the family's life: after ten days of anticipation, the hurricane makes landfall on the eleventh

---

26 Edith Hamilton, *Mythology* (Boston: Little, Brown & Co., 1949), 178; Hamilton quotes Euripides, v. 1059–1064, yet Euripides does not refer to slavery, but to the danger that the Corinthians might kill the children: "To die by other hands more merciless than mine." (ibid.)
27 For an interpretation that stresses different aspects of Ward's appropriation of Medea, see Benjamin Eldon Stevens, "Medea in Jesmyn Ward's *Salvage the Bones*," *International Journal of the Classical Tradition* 25, no. 2 (2018), 158–177.
28 "Q&A with Jesmyn Ward," Jesmyn Ward, *Salvage the Bones* (London, New York: Bloomsbury, 2011), 264–265; further references to this edition in the text.

day leading to severe flooding, in which the family struggles for survival, until, on the twelfth day, they find refuge at their friend Big Henry's house. Apart from the actions connected to the approaching storm, there are two subplots evolving around Skeetah's dog China and Esch's pregnancy. Parallel to the development of the novel's plot, the story of Medea and Jason unfolds in the form of reflections by Esch who keeps reading Hamilton's *Mythology*.

The theme of motherhood is introduced in the first scene of the novel, in which Skeetah's white pit bull China gives birth, as simultaneously Esch remembers the day her mother died from complications giving birth to Junior. The two scenes of birth anticipate the result of the pregnancy test that on the second day confronts Esch with the "terrible truth of what I am" (36), a mother. From age eight, when her mother died, Esch was growing up among males. She first had sex, when she was twelve years old. From then on, several friends of her brothers would take advantage of the girl who finds it "easier to keep quiet and take it" (23). Whereas she seems to accept having sex regularly and even compares it to "swimming through water" as the "only thing that's ever been easy" (22) to her,[29] to the reader it is obvious that the teenage boys exploit her as an easily available sexual object, which they reveal by paying her with fake money, "chocolates covered in golden foil to look like coins, that the boys leave behind once they get up, once we pull apart." (30) Not only does she succumb to sexual exploitation, but naturalizing the abuse, she also suffers from what Pierre Bourdieu calls "symbolic violence" exerted upon her in the form of masculine domination.[30] For Esch, the situation changes, when she falls in love with Manny. Her mythological reading helps her understand her emotions. When she first encounters "the story of Jason and the Argonauts," in Hamilton's *Mythology*, she muses "if Medea felt this way before she walked out to meet Jason for the first time, like a hard wind

---

[29] Hence the protagonist's first name Esch, another word for the fish that more commonly is called "grayling" (in German: "Äsche"). Ward underlines Esch's affinity to fish and the element of water by the protagonist's repeated use of fish imagery: she compares the moving of the puppies to "swimming in the dirt" (39) or "swimming blindly, as if through very deep water" (114); some of the dogs Skeetah used to bring home were "so skinny their bones looked like a school of fish darting around under their skin" (33); watching Manny and Randall "wrestle, giggling," they are "looking like fish yanking against a line" (53); when Esch is running "the air coming into my nose feels like water. I am swimming through the air." (66); once her hand "slides through his [Skeeta's] grip like a wet fish" (72); and when Esch cannot concentrate, it is because "thoughts of Manny kept surfacing like swimmers in my brain" (109).
[30] Pierre Bourdieu, *Masculine Domination*. Trans. Richard Nice (Cambridge, UK : Polity, 2001), 33–42.

come through her and set her to shaking." (7)[31] Esch identifies with Medea as she feels the same helplessness vis-à-vis love at first sight that grips her with the force of a storm. Esch realizes that even such a powerful woman like Medea becomes weak face to face with the man with whom she is madly in love:

> In *Mythology*, I am still reading about Medea and the quest for the Golden Fleece. Here is someone that I recognize. When Medea falls in love with Jason, it grabs me by the throat. I can see her. Medea sneaks Jason things to help him: ointments to make him invincible, secrets in rocks. She has magic, could bend the natural to the unnatural. But even with all her power, Jason bends her like a young pine in a hard wind; he makes her double in two. I know her. (38)

While Esch is yearning for a bond of love and tenderness, Manny, who by then has entered a steady relationship with Shaliyah, is out for mere sex. He will neither kiss her nor even look at her, and when she dares to express her desire for affection, he reproachfully draws back: "You crazy? [...] Naw, Esch. [...] You know it ain't like that." (56) Clearly, Manny-Jason has the power to define their relation. Esch compares the pain set off by Manny's rejection to " a sudden deluge" (56) that she fights with the counterforce of the burning fire of her own love projected again upon Medea: "I imagine that this is the way Medea felt about Jason, when she fell in love, when she knew him; that she looked at him and felt a fire eating up through her rib cage, turning her blood to boil, evaporating hotly out of every inch of her skin." (56–57)

Apart from seeking orientation in Greek mythology, Esch's perception is deeply rooted in nature; she constantly relates her sensations to natural phenomena. Her comparisons show that she is an acute observer, for example, as-

---

[31] See Stevens, "Medea in Ward's *Salvage*," for an in-depth discussion of the motif of the wind and its origins in Apollonius' *Argonautica* and Euripides. Stevens maintains that the "simile 'like a hard wind come through her' derives from Hamilton, who describes Medea's and Jason's first meeting as follows: 'The two stood face to face without a word, as lofty pine trees when the wind is still. Then again when the wind stirs they murmur; so these two also, stirred by the breath of love, were fated to tell out all their tale to each other' (Hamilton, 172)" (166). Stevens then presents the evidence that "Hamilton's language is closely modeled on Apollonius' *Argonautica*. There the relevant moment is the first time Medea and Jason find themselves together in what passes for private, with Medea's attendants at a discreet distance (3.967–971; translation is Peter Green's): 'Silent and speechless the two were left face to face like oaks or tall pine trees, side by side in the mountains standing deep-rooted and quiet, while a calm stillness prevails, but then a breeze comes blowing and stirs them to endless murmuring converse'" (166). As Stevens mentions, the comparison between humans and trees, employed by Hamilton after Apollonius, goes back to Homer (167 n.31); in *Salvage* it reappears inconspicuously as the natural imagination of the protagonist.

sociating various shades of dark skin with the color of trees. She remembers her mother's skin as "dark as the reaching oak trees." (22) In contrast, Manny's lighter "skin was the color of fresh-cut wood at the heart of a pine-tree." (6) Esch also refers to "Manny's golden skin." (102) In fact, she transfers the golden hue of his skin to his whole appearance: "I saw [...] gold, Manny." (15) In Esch's story, in contrast to the myth of the Argonauts, the preciousness of the golden fleece is projected upon the hero, Manny-Jason. Esch links the color golden to heat; in her eyes, he blazes like the sun, "golden, burning" (45): "Manny catches all the light from the fire, eats it up, and blazes." (50) In contrast to Esch, but in accordance with his mythic model Jason, Manny appreciates the material value of gold, in this case, jewelry worn by Esch's rival: Esch sees "the bit of metal that Shaliyah wears on her arm catch the sun through the tree and throw it back gold." (118)

Apart from gold, the color red plays an important role in the novel. It is connected to the clay typical of the ground in Mississippi: "the color of the red earth after someone has dug in it to plant a field or pull up stones or put in a body. It is Mississippi red." (8) More importantly, as it signifies the color of blood, it references the body. *Salvage* abounds in injured and scarred bodies, bodies losing blood in giving birth, bodies wounded from accidents, animal bodies spilling blood being killed or fighting each other. The color red is then indicative of the violence that is ubiquitous both in Medea's story and Esch's narrative. Whereas Esch seems to accept frequent bloodshed as integral to her natural and social environment, the reader is made aware of the excess of aggression in Esch's life by the text's emphasis on the redness of blood.

Whiteness functions as a counter-force signaling beauty, embodied, above all, in China: "She is white, so white. She is the pure white heart of a flame." (171) It is in vain that Manny tries to "convince us she wasn't white and beautiful and gorgeous as a magnolia on the trash-strewn, hardscrabble Pit, where everything else is starving, fighting, struggling." (94) The admiration of perfection in the white dog serves as a precious vision of a better world for the inhabitants of the Pit. At the same time, whiteness is a sign of symbolic violence, for Blacks, by adoring it, succumb to the cultural hegemony of white supremacy. But in addition, China, admired for her strength and fighting spirit, simultaneously becomes a symbol of resistance to white supremacy. When China aggressively attacks and almost kills Twist, the dog of a white neighbor, she acts, as it were, vicariously for the Black community, who has no efficient means of fighting back. Skeetah, accompanied by Esch, had broken into the white man's barn to steal some cow wormer he needed – and could not afford to buy – in order to cure China and the litter from parvo. The old white man who surprises them, has his dog chase after the fleeing siblings. "Then rifle shots." (79) This encounter between the armed white citizen and unarmed Black youth evokes the traditional power disparities that have shaped the relation of the two groups for centuries. In this particular case, however, China provides victory: "Twist jumps and runs, limping like his master [...]. Behind him he leaves red rain." (82)

China gains further complexity as a Medea figure. To the horror of Skeetah, she kills first one and later another one of her puppies. On the mythological level, China's first choice suggests that the puppy stands in for the father, egoistic Jason: "He is the one that is a model of the father [...], the most well-fed, the bully." (129) To Esch, the incident again raises the question of motherhood: "China is bloody-mouthed and bright-eyed as Medea. If she could speak, this is what I would ask her: *Is this what motherhood is?*" (130)

Corresponding to the traditional preconception of a ferocious and cruel Medea, China functions as a counter-image to Esch as Medea. The protagonist undergoes a significant development from a girl weakened by infatuation, to a pregnant teenager who, taking responsibility for her child, turns into a self-confident woman. Her growth towards maturity is reflected in a sequence of Medea metamorphoses. Esch shows the first sign of strength, when watched by Manny she imagines herself "tall as Medea, wearing purple and green robes, bones and gold for jewelry" (170). Later, when Esch confronts Manny telling him that the child she bears is his, she turns into a fighter: "I am on him like China." (203) And while she is attacking him she identifies with her mythic model: "This is Medea wielding the knife. This is Medea cutting. I rake my fingernails across his face, leave pink scratches that turn red, fill with blood." (204) However, by "wielding the knife" directly at Jason, i.e. hurting the father rather than her child, Esch-Medea transforms into an anti-Medea, a role she maintains, when she struggles to keep herself, her child, and the three puppies she carries in a bucket alive in the rising water: "*The babies*, I think." (235)

Earlier, there is a moment, when Esch watching Manny and Shaliyah in playful banter, feels the impulse of killing both herself and her child: "If I could, I would reach inside of me and pull out my heart and that tiny wet seed that will become the baby." (122) But after Katrina made landfall, the Pit flooded, and the family barely survived, Esch no longer considers the baby as a somewhat alien fruit within her body, for example, a "melon" she would like "to knead [...] to pulp" (102), but thinks of it as an individual, a person who will need a name. "If it is a girl, I will name her after my mother: Rose." (247) "If it is a boy, I will name it after Skeetah. *Jason.*" (248) Acknowledging the need for a loving, caring mother as well as a caring, tender father, of the type Skeetah had proven himself towards China and her puppies, Esch completely revises the myth. The life-threatening storm makes her accept motherhood and the name "Mama" that goes with it (219), and she now builds on her own experience and, as a consequence, emphasizes love as caritas. Moreover, she expresses her belief in the capacity of human beings to act on behalf of social units, family or community, rather than focusing on their individual well-being. In the moment of danger, Skeetah, who in the past days by constantly taking care of his beloved dog and her puppies had prioritized the animals over his family, finally reverses course and sacrifices China, in order to save his pregnant sister from drowning. Furthermore, acknowledging motherhood, Esch is able to disown Manny-Jason. When Big Henry, a character who throughout the novel has shown responsibility and compassion while at the same time refuting the macho image most of the other Black males display, asks Esch, who the father of her child is, she answers: "It don't have a daddy." (254) He moves her to tears, when he reassures her through words and body language: "'This baby got a daddy, Esch.' He reaches out his big soft hand [...] and helps me stand." (255). Big Henry's hand, indicative of his caring, gentle nature, is juxtaposed to Medea's "merciless hands": Katrina is "the mother that swept into the Gulf and slaughtered. Her chariot was a storm so great and black the Greeks would say it was harnessed to dragons. She was the murderous mother who cut us to the bone but left us alive [...]. Katrina is the mother we will remember until the next mother with large, merciless hands, committed to blood, comes." (255)

Before the rising water forces the family out of the house, Esch ends her reading of the story of Medea and Jason: "Jason has remarried, and Medea is wailing. *An exile, oh God, oh God, alone.* And then: *By death, oh, by death, shall the conflict be decided. Life's little day ended.* I shut the book, don't even mark my place, and sit on it." (225) Esch will no longer look for orientation in Hamilton's *Mythology*; instead, she thinks of her own mother who, according to Skeetah, "told us to be good. To look after each other." (222) The myth of Medea as the mother who murders her children serves as a negative foil to be completely inverted. Rose and Esch take care of their children as best as they can. Instead of Medea killing her brother Apsyrtos, brother Skeetah saves his sister's life. In contrast to the enmity that shapes the relation between Medea and her father Aeëtes, Esch's father sincerely regrets his aggressive reaction to learning that she was pregnant. Fueled by patriarchal wrath he pushes her and she falls into the water, an impulse he regrets immediately. Later, in safety, he apologizes to her and expresses genuine concern for his daughter and her child.

By the end of the novel, the destructive potential inherent in the mythic figure of Medea has been completely relegated to the harmful forces of nature embodied in water and wind. As has been pointed out above, in the beginning, water seemed to be Esch's natural element. Yet her reading about Greek myth taught her that water is potentially dangerous: "Medea's journey took her to the water, which was the highway of the ancient world, where death was as close as the waves, the sun, the wind. Where death was as many as the fish waiting in the water, fanning fins, watching the surface, shadowing the bottom dark." (159) On the eve before the storm hits, Esch formulates the insight she has gained from reading: "In ancient Greece, for all her heroes, for Medea [...], water meant death." (216) It will almost mean death to herself and her unborn child, when soon after she falls into the raging water flooding the Pit. Watching the water rise, Esch expresses the threat it poses by comparing it to a devouring animal: "There is a lake growing in the yard. It moves under the broken trees like a creeping animal, a wide-nosed snake. [...] The snake has swallowed the whole yard and is opening its jaw under the house." (226–227)[32] As the wind gets stronger, its hissing noise also reminds Esch of a snake (219). Since the snake is one of the attributes of Medea, Esch's associations anticipate the identification of Katrina with Medea.[33]

Besides nature's dangerous forces of wind and water, there are also harmful forces of human nature that rage both in the figures of the Medea myth and in the novel's protagonists. They appear in the form of unleashed emotions, emotions, moreover, that tend to reinforce selfishness, such as love as infatuation, jealousy, revenge, aggression, or desire of domination. These passionate feelings – promoted by the intense heat in the days before the storm and by the hurricane itself – yield now to soberness and thus form a parallel to nature's calmness after the storm. What is more, in view of the vast destruction wreaked by Katrina,[34] the characters' former self-regard gives way to gestures of charity and solidarity. Sensing the fundamental change, Esch reflects: "Suddenly there is a great split between now and then." (251)

In *Salvage the Bones*, the shift from ubiquitous violence to incidents of gentleness, from love as passion to love as charity, from bouts of the irrational to a

---

[32] Cf. Apollonius' description of the dragon guarding the golden vlies: "the serpent [...] was relaxing the long ridge of his giant spine, and lengthening out his myriad coils, like a dark wave, dumb and noiseless, rolling over a sluggish sea; but still he raised aloft his grisly head, eager to enclose them both in his murderous jaws." *The Argonautica*. Trans. R. C. Seaton (London: Heinemann, 1912), Book IV, 150–155.

[33] Cf. Stevens, "Medea in Ward's *Salvage*": "The snake is an important image in stories about Medea: there is the serpent she helps Jason defeat, and there are the dragons that draw the chariot in which she makes her final escape. In *Salvage*, the snake is both the wind and, slightly later again, the water taking over the land [...]. Threatened thus is Esch's family's way of life, as the household risks collapse." (170)

[34] It is interesting to note that in *Salvage* Katrina also destroys white supremacy in the form of an architectural style that functioned as symbolic violence: "All the old white-columned homes that faced the beach, that made us feel small and dirty and poorer than ever [...] are gone. Not ravaged, not rubble, but complete gone." (252–253)

moderation of feelings, is a promise of a new, less violent world. What is temporarily destroyed, will be rebuilt; there is no need for Esch-Medea to kill her child: it will have a future in the community. Like Du Bois, Ward creates a vision of a better Black world by juxtaposing it to the Medea myth. As Stevens puts it, "by depicting a Medea-figure who does not, and will not, kill, *Salvage* suggests that Esch – like Ward – has found in Greek myth a way of responding to such violence without perpetuating it."[35] Moreover, Stevens sees in the verb "to salvage" a term that can be applied to Ward's method of appropriating classical myth, "offering a model for classical reception as a kind of 'salvage'"[36]: "[B]y, as it were, saving Medea's children, Ward's novel embodies the sort of response to 'ancient tales' that is simultaneously a powerful expression of hope for transformation of the present world."[37]

III

Parody has often proved a particularly creative way to claim a tradition. Percival Everett's novel *For Her Dark Skin* (1990) is a case in point. In contrast to Du Bois and Ward, who transpose the mythical plot to the United States and choose as time-frame the recent past, Everett in place and time retains the setting of the ancient world. Nevertheless, his retelling of major episodes of the myth of the Argonauts differs substantially from classic versions. In fact, by using anachronisms, present-day language, and modern psychology, Everett inscribes late twentieth-century culture into the ancient world. The resulting discrepancies create comic effects; yet, the humor that evokes our laughter is a highly subversive force undermining what we may take for granted in connection with the Medea myth.

In stark contrast to the elaborate rhetoric of Greek tragedy, Everett uses colloquial expressions, slang, and obscenities throughout the novel, for example, in the scene when Jason informs King Aeetes that he "must take" Medea "to Hellas and show her off. [...] Her beautiful dark skin will make her a queen in my land. [...] Aeetes shook his head and laughed when they were gone. 'A queen for her dark skin. That shit will last for a day.'"[38] Notwithstanding their casual use of language, Everett's characters repeatedly reflect on it. For example, Medea com-

---

[35] Stevens, "Medea in Ward's *Salvage*," 159.
[36] Ibid.
[37] Ibid., 162.
[38] Percival Everett, *For Her Dark Skin* (Seattle: Owl Creek Press, 1990), 11–12; further references to this edition in the text.

ments sarcastically on the rhetoric of the sermon during her wedding ceremony: "Greek gibberish. Empty words. Like all their words. *Democracy.*" (59; emphasis in original) Medea's mocking remark goes beyond language criticism; it expresses skepticism of the political system. Everett reverses here the traditional understanding of the allegedly superior civilization Greece and Medea's barbaric home country, as it is the 'barbarian' Medea who reveals the incongruity between noble words and reality. Moreover, due to the technique of merging the Greek world and the modern western world, Everett indicates that this critique should also be applied to contemporary democracy.

Another example of juxtaposing the two worlds is the following anachronistic description of an antique chariot by Jason: "we sat, ate, and watched the chariots rattle by. I would have to purchase one. The fashion was to personalize one's vehicle with wood-cutting of a distinctive design. Many were very sporty." Jason then discovers the princess Creusa in "a red chariot with sloping sides which curved up into fins in the rear. Carved wings adorned its front." (85) Antiquity and contemporary consumer culture become visually intertwined as we recall presentations of chariots on Greek vases and simultaneously, owing to the color red and the words "sporty" and "fins," American sports cars.

Furthermore, the mythic characters display the mental dispositions of the twentieth century. A rich source of humor derives from the discrepancy between the activities of Greek gods, who on the level of plot regularly interfere with human beings, and the lack of reverence the characters exhibit towards them. For example, Medea is angry at Eros who she knows to be responsible for her falling in love with Jason, a man she loathes for his weakness, vanity, and cowardice. As Medea's first statement illustrates, her disrespect vis-à-vis the Greek pantheon extends to despising the Greek hero:

> They came in their *mighty* ship and we weren't that impressed. [...] But there it was. And there he was. He was not much to look at and really not much for anything else. Seeing him strut around as he did, I expected the son of a god, but all I got was a pale man just off a boat. [...] I would not have let him touch me, but the gods ... not even my gods, but some chalk-skinned bitch voyeur caused me to fall in love with this Jason. (10)

One of the great heroes of Greek myth is deconstructed, not only by Medea, but also by his own men who know that their leader is a coward. At one point, Jason takes flight, when he is confronted with the giants who "sprouted from the furrows" of the field he had sowed with the seed of "the serpent's teeth." (17) As Polydeuces comments: "Jason ran. We caught him and tossed him back into the fray." (17) The most valiant warrior among the Argonauts, Polydeuces, is clearly superior to Jason; he sees through him and even declares him a "fool" and a "simp." (38) Medea's downsizing of Jason often occurs through sexual innuendo and is also directed towards his lack of intelligence: "That he was not overly bright was apparent, though he was a talker." (10) Obviously, Everett plays with common racial stereotypes by exposing or reversing them. While Jason praises Medea's dark skin, Medea considers Jason's outward appearance, his slight stature and blond hair, to be revoltingly ugly. Eros may have the power to make Medea 'love' Jason; however, since she is fully aware of being forced, she is paradoxically able to keep an emotional distance: "Loving a man I despise" (46), she explains, is her problem.

Although the novel covers major events of the myth of Medea and Jason, from the arrival of the Argonauts at Colchis to the moment Jason discovers that Medea just killed the twin boys, Everett turns the story of heroic adventure, ominous witchcraft, and tragic murder into a series of brief melodramatic scenes highlighting the psychological conflicts among the characters. The commonplace nature of these emotional struggles is underlined by an emphasis on everyday life situations and colloquial language. The eight chapters of the narrative are subdivided into short sections of differing length, headed by the name of the respective narrator. Besides Jason, Medea, Polydeuces, there is an invented figure, the Corinthian woman Tamar, friend of Medea and wife of Polydeuces, who also happens to be a cousin of Euripides (to whom she writes a letter assuming he would "appreciate this story" (81), addressing him as "dear Rip" (110)), as well as a male nurse, and Eros. There are two sections, named after Medea's father Aeetes and her brother Apsyrtos, but told by an anonymous narrator, thus denying narrative agency to the two men from Colchis. Thus the story is retold in a fragmented manner by multiple, highly subjective voices, whose emotional bias is enhanced when the episodes are told twice, offering different, if not opposing interpretations. From Jason's point of view a confrontation between himself and Medea ends as follows, when Medea "walked away toward her chamber": "'Medea,' I shouted. She stopped. 'I have not dismissed you.' She turned to face me. 'Would you repeat that?' she asked. 'I have not dismissed you.' Her eyes teared." (102) Medea's perception of the same situation differs significantly: "I could find no words that this creature would understand [...] So, I stood and started for my bed. He stopped me with a shout and I turned to hear him say – I have not dismissed you. Twice he said it. 'And you do well not to,' I said." (103) While Jason's rendering the scene suggests Medea's humiliation, Medea herself expresses both silent contempt and out-spoken defiance.

For Her Dark Skin transforms tragic myth into a hilarious travesty. Everett's retelling of the Medea myth allows for a particular radical transgression of traditional gender roles. The novel's literary devices of humor and satire are used to deconstruct the white hero, to critique colonialism, patriarchy and racism, in fact, more generally, to reveal and to denounce the "wellsprings of power."[39] By contrast, it is Everett's Black Medea who is finally empowered. Everett invents an attempt by Medea to prevent the birth of her twins hoping they would dissolve in her body, because, as she cries in childbed: "Life is vicious and unjust." (107) But her magic fails: not only does she give birth, but immediately afterwards an intoxicated Jason tries to rape her. Later, her infanticide becomes a calculated act of resistance that is not condemned. Medea has then the last – mocking – word testifying to her pugnacious spirit: "Why do *you* cry? I asked. You are alive. You have not been burned. You have not been cut. Oh, I see—your *smile* is gone. Grieve for your *smile*. 'You are wicked,' he muttered through his tears. 'No, Jason, motivated.'" (152)

To sum up, apart from standing in the well-established western tradition of appropriating classical myth, the three novels are firmly grounded in the Black literary tradition in that they highlight the systemic racism that has shaped the lives of Black people from the time the first enslaved Africans set foot on American soil to the present. Moreover, while the three novels differ widely with regard to subgenre and style, their authors share a specific revisionary approach to the Medea myth. Rejecting the image of Medea as a malefactor, bound by overwhelming passion, all three writers develop female characters, whose first struggle consists in achieving a balance between passion and rationality. Thus equipped, Zora, Esch, and Medea take up the feminist battle against patriarchal domination. Conveniently, the Jasons they wrestle with are morally weak figures, and yet the fights the three Medeas have to fight are extremely arduous, because grappling with the Jasons of their world they have to stand up against deeply ingrained power structures, often comprising class, race, and gender privileges. Not surprisingly, while all of them are granted some success, their victory is far from complete.

Notwithstanding Du Bois' conventional choice of the genre of romance and the genteel language he employs, he creates with his inverted Medea a benefactress who leads her people towards a utopian vision of Black socialism projecting the hope of overcoming one day the power structures of capitalism – respectively colonialism – racism and male domination that have shaped western

---

[39] See Pierre Bourdieu's comparison of sociology and comedy with regard to exposing the machinations of power in "Revealing the Wellsprings of Power." *Political Interventions: Social Science and Political Action*, eds. Frank Poupeau and Thierry Discepolo. Trans. David Fernbach (London, New York: Verso), 133–136; cf. Christa Buschendorf and Astrid Franke, "The Implied Sociology and Politics of Literary Texts: Using the Tools of Relational Sociology in American Studies." *American Studies Today: New Research Agendas*, eds. Winfried Fluck et al. (Heidelberg: Universitätsverlag Winter, 2014), 80.

societies for centuries. Du Bois, pointing out the analogies between myth and fictional reality, employs the classical myth of the Argonauts to illuminate the ongoing suppression and economic exploitation of Black people. In contrast, the postmillennial novel *Salvage the Bones* no longer carries Du Bois' hopeful expectation of revolutionary political change. While Esch, like Zora, is also an inverted Medea and while her shift of focus from erotic love to mother love and charity also signifies the hope of a ground-breaking transformation of Black life, it seems typical of the postmillennial novel that it refrains from the revolutionary zest of its predecessor and instead applies the myth of Medea and Jason anthropologically. Ward stresses the resemblance of female experience in ancient myth and in contemporary (fictional) reality, highlights the similarities between animals and human creatures, and even posits an identity between the forces of myth and nature as well as between natural phenomena and emotional states. Countervailing these ahistorical, if not essentialist, assumptions that pervade the text, the novel's present-day setting evokes in lively detail a world of violence deriving from systemic racism, white supremacy and male supremacy. But notwithstanding such clear-cut references to sociological factors such as inequality of wealth, education and housing that in the end define how hard members of the Black community are hit by the destructive vehemence of Medea-Katrina, the novel focuses on a teenager's initiation into motherhood. Accordingly, the emphasis is on the authenticity of the protagonist's voice and experiences, and any societal changes hoped for are expected to derive from individual processes of maturation rather than from systemic transformation. While undoubtedly socially conscious, the postmillennial novel assuages its social criticism by foregrounding the protagonist's desire for bonding and love.

Juxtaposing the postmillennial novel with its early twentieth-century predecessor reveals the former's indebtedness to the Black literary tradition in general and to the Black tradition of the reception of the classics in particular. At the same time, it uncovers Ward's emphasis on an anthropological usage of myth as opposed to Du Bois' more critical socio-political viewpoint. By means of genre, Everett's satire also helps to expose the postmillennial novel's less radical stance. *For Her Dark Skin*, set in antiquity, does not provide any visions of a better future. Although the novel stands in the postmodern tradition of rewriting myth, reminiscent, for example, of John Barth's three novellas *Chimera* (1972), it does not share the insincere playfulness that often typifies postmodern irony. Instead, indebted to the social criticism of Black satirical writing, it concentrates on critique, and its critique of racism and patriarchy is as witty as it is scathing. In Everett's parody, Medea's transformative strength lies in the utter irreverence against the powers-that-be, including the Olympian gods. In contrast to Du Bois and Ward, who both created beneficial Medea figures, Everett's heroine is not an inverted, but rather an enhanced Medea, an unflinching truth-teller.

However, notwithstanding the aesthetic and political differences pointed out above, all three novels are manifestly devoted to the firmly established agenda of Black writing. Consequently, all three Medeas – even Ward's postmillennial version – are distinguished by a strong spirit of resistance that eventually turns them into powerful forces of change. "Medea, as the exploited barbarian, can be the symbol of the freedom fighter."[40] Therein lies Medea's attraction for Black writers.

Works Cited

Apollonius Rhodius. 1912. *The Argonauts*. Trans. R. C. Seaton. London: Heinemann.
Blumenberg, Hans. 1990. *Work on Myth*. Cambridge, Mass., London: MIT Press.
Bourdieu, Pierre. 2001. *Masculine Domination*. Trans. Richard Nice. Cambridge, UK: Polity.
Bourdieu, Pierre. 2008. "Revealing the Wellsprings of Power." In: Frank Poupeau and Thierry Discepolo (eds.). *Political Interventions: Social Science and Political Action*. Eds. Trans. David Fernbach. London, New York: Verso, 133–136.
Buschendorf, Christa, and Astrid Franke. 2014. "The Implied Sociology and Politics of Literary Texts: Using the Tools of Relational Sociology in American Studies.". In: Winfried Fluck, Erik Redling, Sabine Sielke, and Hubert Zapf (eds.). *American Studies Today: New Research Agendas*. Heidelberg: Universitätsverlag Winter, 75–104.
Cook, William C., and James Tatum. 2010. *African American Writers and Classical Tradition*. Chicago and London: University of Chicago Press.
Dokou, Christina. 2018. "The Mother of all Horrors: Medea's Infanticide in African American Literature." In: Kevin Costorphine and Laura R. Kremmel (eds.). *The Palgrave Handbook to Horror Literature*. Springer International Publishing, 407–421.
Du Bois, W. E. B. 2007. *Darkwater: Voices from Within the Veil*. Oxford, New York: Oxford University Press.
Du Bois, W. E. B. 2007. *Dusk of Dawn: An Essay Toward an Autobiography of a Race Concept*. Oxford, New York: Oxford University Press.
Du Bois, W. E. B. 2007. *The Quest of the Silver Fleece*. New York: Oxford University Press.
Du Bois, W. E. B. 2007. *The Souls of Black Folk*. New York: Oxford University Press.
Ellis, Trey. 1989. "The New Black Aesthetic." *Callaloo* 12: 233–243.
Everett, Percival. 1990. *For Her Dark Skin*. Seattle: Owl Creek Press.
Foley, Helene. 2012. *Reimagining Greek Tragedy on the American Stage*. Berkeley: University of California Press.
Graf, Fritz. 1997. "Medea, the Enchantress From Afar: Remarks on a Well-Known Myth." In: James J. Clauss and Sarah Iles Johnston (eds.). *Medea: Essays on Medea in Myth, Literature, Philosophy, and Art*. Princeton: Princeton University Press, 21–43.

---

40 McDonald, "Medea as Politician," 301–302.

Hamilton, Edith. 1949. *Mythology*. Boston: Little, Brown & Co.
Johnston, Sarah Iles Johnston. 1997. "Corinthian Medea and the Cult of Hera Akraia." In: James J. Clauss and Sarah Iles Johnston (eds.). *Medea: Essays on Medea in Myth, Literature, Philosophy, and Art*. Princeton: Princeton University Press, 44–70.
Lordkipanidze, Nino. 2018. "Gold aus Georgien." In: Vinzenz Brinkmann (ed.). *Medeas Liebe und die Jagd nach dem Goldenen Vlies*. München: Hirmer, 40–69.
McDonald, Marianne. 1997. "Medea as Politician and Diva: Riding the Dragon into the Future." In: James J. Clauss and Sarah Iles Johnston (eds.). *Medea: Essays on Medea in Myth, Literature, Philosophy, and Art*. Princeton: Princeton University Press, 297–323.
Murray, Jackie. 2019. "W.E.B. Du Bois' *The Quest of the Silver Fleece*: The Education of Black Medea." *Transactions of the American Philological Association* (TAPA) Vol. 149, No. 2, Supplement, 143–162.
O'Higgins, Dolores M. 1997. "Medea as Muse: Pindar's *Pythian 4*." In: James J. Clauss and Sarah Iles Johnston (eds.). *Medea: Essays on Medea in Myth, Literature, Philosophy, and Art*. Princeton: Princeton University Press, 103–126.
Sick, David H. 2017. "Alabamian Argonautica: Myth and Classical Education in *The Quest of the Silver Fleece*." *Classical World* Vol. 110, Number 2 (Spring): 373–397.
Stephan, Inge. 2006. *Medea: Multimediale Karriere einer mythologischen Figur*. Köln et al.: Böhlau.
Stevens, Benjamin. 2018. "Medea in Jesmyn Ward's *Salvage the Bones*." *International Journal of the Classical Tradition* 25.2: 158–177.
Ward, Jesmyn. 2011. *Salvage the Bones*. London, New York: Bloomsbury.

Section Two: **Realisms and Representing the Anthropocene**

Sabine Sielke
The Newly Conventional U.S.-American Novel and the (Neo-)Liberal Imagination: on Franzen, Eggers, and the Like

Abstract: This paper interrogates the aesthetics, tonality, and cultural function of what I call the "newly conventional" U.S.-American novel that has dominated the literary marketplace during the last decades. Capitalizing on the fiction of Jonathan Franzen and Dave Eggers, my argument proceeds in two parts. In part one, I briefly reengage Lionel Trilling's 1950 intervention into the political domain of literature which highlighted the proximity of politics and ideas with emotions and sentiments – a move recently promoted as novel. In my second part, I adopt Trilling's register to explore how Franzen's and Eggers's distinct realist, ironic, and sentimental modes take part in forming, profit from, yet also challenge and exploit the current "neoliberal imagination," its globalized ideology as well as its sense of (political) agency. My final 'footnote' confronts the (predominantly male) 'canon' of the newly conventional to reassess our faith in the (gendered) politics of contemporary literature.

The success of what I call the "newly conventional" – and here I mean: aesthetically conventional – U.S.-American novel is both noteworthy and somewhat disturbing. I find it disturbing in part because this 'genre' realigns certain literary styles, first and foremost versions of realism – Jeffrey J. Williams speaks of a "resigned realism" (2013), Mark Fisher of "capitalist realism" (2009) – with processes of cultural and political conformity or, more precisely, with the interrogation of such processes. So, what do we make of the fact that after the prominence or privileging of an experimentalist postmodernist aesthetics, retained in the writing of Mark Z. Danielewski and David Foster Wallace as well as in certain moves in the fiction of Siri Hustvedt, Jennifer Egan, and Michael Chabon, for instance, a more "readerly" prose has been applauded again in the last two or three decades?

The newly conventional texts, I like to suggest, quite consciously partake in a far-reaching general trend to accommodate, if not adapt to (both imaginary and real) neoliberal economic environments and mindscapes – time-spaces which, to different degrees, they help to create and reaffirm, yet also challenge. With its reflections and interpretations this essay aims at accounting for the (dis-)comfort we may feel reading the twenty-first-century work of Jonathan

https://doi.org/10.1515/9783110771350-008

Franzen and Dave Eggers or rediscoveries, such as the fiction of Richard Yates and John Williams which, unfortunately, I cannot go into at length here. Suffice it to say that, too conventional for the common 1960s reader, Yates' *Revolutionary Road* (of 1961) and Williams' *Stoner* (of 1965) speak to a contemporary audience in part, because they foreground the complicity between literary etiquettes and the proprieties of our newly encoded lives; and so does the work of Franzen and Eggers. As a consequence, the new conventionality, characteristic for much of what we consider contemporary U.S.-American fiction – the bulk of which seems produced by a predominantly male cast –, may not pave revolutionary roads. Much the opposite, as Christian Kloeckner poignantly argues, recent novels such as Eggers' *A Hologram for the King* are informed by a pervasive "androcentric nostalgia" for economically 'good times' (unpublished: 36; see also Kloeckner 2017). As a consequence, the newly conventional modes invite us to reconsider how literature engages politics and the ongoing transformation of what Lionel Trilling called "the liberal imagination."

My argument proceeds in two steps and is supplemented by a concluding, though by no means conclusive or even closural, footnote. In step one I briefly return to Trilling's 1950 intervention into the politics of literature and literary criticism which is of interest now, I like to suggest, less for its faith in literature than for closely aligning politics and ideas with emotions and sentiments – an insight which, e.g. in debates on the new rise of populism, has misleadingly been hailed as original and novel. In step two, I map a part of the discursive terrain covered by the newly conventional novel. Engaging the appropriation of Trilling's terminology in current critical debates on the "neoliberal imagination," I try to assess in what way the aesthetics of Franzen's and Eggers' fiction shines a novel light on what Trilling once called "Reality in America" (1951: 3). Delineating the particular twists Franzen and Eggers take on what is commonly known as realism, I engage two representatives of this mode of writing who intervene into and challenge, with distinct effects, yet also (re-)produce our current neoliberal imaginary. My final footnote proposes to extend and complicate this reading which ultimately, though, cannot escape the neoliberal framework of all of our work as readers and critics. This work includes the very 'canon' of the newly conventional which raises yet another question: that of gender. Is the new conventionality, I wonder, first and foremost a male affair (as was Trilling's literary canon, of course)? Figuring in how recent U.S.-American realist novels partake in their neoliberal economic conditions, this essay shows how this dominant mode of contemporary fiction may also both limit and enlarge our faith in the (gendered) politics of literature.

Engaging these questions, my contribution to this volume also pays tribute to the work of Susanne Rohr, picking up on her suggestive reading of Franzen's

The Corrections (2001) whose focus on a Midwestern family, as she writes, raises "the question of lost order in a perplexing world" and engages "the challenge to try out and re-establish various systems of order. These epistemological concerns," Rohr argues,

> are closely related to those of modernism and post-modernism, yet this novel chooses a unique narrative strategy for staging them. It follows the narrative conventions of literary realism but metaphorically uses the symptoms of the father's Parkinson's disease – that is the patient's eroding capacity to meaningfully interpret reality – to develop a fictional world of collapsing order, general disorientation, insecurity and imbalance within the bounds of a seemingly known and familiar world. (2004: 91)

Rohr's essay "explores how this narrative strategy serves a double goal": how it both drives "what literary criticism has identified as the 'new conventionalism' in literature" and "adds a new form to the genre of the novel: the novel of globalization" (ibid). My argument revisits Rohr's concerns by readdressing the new conventionalism in its (neo-)liberal framework. What, I wonder, does it mean to narrate the disorder of our globalized existence in an 'orderly' manner?

Step One. The "Liberal Imagination" and the Politics of Literature

In his 2008 essay "Regrets Only: Lionel Trilling and His Discontents," published in *The New Yorker*, Louis Menand called *The Liberal Imagination* – Trilling's 1950 collection of essays on "Reality in America," on "Manners, Morals, and the Novel," and on writers including Mark Twain, Sherwood Anderson, John Dos Passos, and F. Scott Fitzgerald – "a phenomenon. It did something," Menand holds, "that very few books have ever done: it made literary criticism matter to people who were not literary critics" (n. pag.). Since this is quite an accomplishment indeed, how was it done then?

Trilling, we may want to recall, invited his readers to engage literature and its primary concern with "the politics of culture" in order "to look at liberalism" – for him "not only the dominant, but even the sole intellectual tradition" "[i]n the United States at this time" – "in a critical spirit" (1951: ix–xv). For liberalism in "its present particular manifestations" had lost, Trilling deemed, what he called its "primal imagination" (xv). "It is one of the tendencies of liberalism to simplify," Trilling wrote in his preface, "and this tendency is natural in view of the effort which liberalism makes to organize the elements of life in a rational way" (xiv). One of the tasks of literature, so he suggests, is to retain "the lively sense of contingency and possibility and of those exceptions to the rule which may be the beginning of the end of the rule – this sense [that] does not suit well with the impulse to organization" (xv). In order to make literature work as a force of democracy against tendencies of totalitarianism, "[t]he job of criticism would seem to be, then," he concluded,

> to recall liberalism to its first essential imagination of variousness and possibility, which implies the awareness of complexity and difficulty. To the carrying out of the job of criticizing the liberal imagination, literature has a unique relevance, not merely because so much of modern literature has explicitly directed itself upon politics, but more importantly because literature is the human activity that takes the fullest and most precise account of variousness, possibility, complexity, and difficulty. (ibid)

Menand bemoans that "the term 'liberal' is never defined in 'The Liberal Imagination'" (2008: n. pag.). Political theory, he in turn explains, distinguishes various types of liberals: "There is, in Isaiah Berlin's famous distinction, the liberal who believes in negative liberty, 'freedom from,' and the liberal who believes in positive liberty, 'freedom for.' There is the classical liberalism of free markets and individual rights, and the left liberalism of state planning and class solidarity" (ibid). Trilling, by contrast, conceives of liberalism as "a large tendency rather than a concise body of doctrine," and emphasizes what he believes to be the proximity of ideas and sentiments – an interdependence, in fact, that creates the connection between politics and literature he considered, in 1950, characteristic of U.S.-American fiction of the last 150 years (1951: xii). At the same time, he acknowledges that

> liberalism [stands] in a paradoxical relation to the emotions. The paradox of liberalism is concerned with the emotions above all else, as proof of which the word happiness stands at the very center of its thought, but in its effort to establish the emotions or certain among them, in some sort of freedom, liberalism somehow tends to deny them in their full possibility. (xii–xiii)

Liberalism, Trilling holds, "unconsciously limits its view of the world [...] and tends to develop theories and principles, particularly in relation of the human mind, that justify its limitation" (xiii). To Trilling, it is the inherent paradox of liberalism that "in the interest [...] of its vision of a general enlargement and freedom and rational direction of human life [...] it drifts toward a denial of the emotions and the imagination" (xiii–xiv).

I quote Trilling at length here because more than 70 years after their publication his perspectives of 1950 remain suggestive, explaining, at least in part, the close alliance between our current neoliberalist "Zeitgeist" and socially progressive ideas. "Gay marriage, new laws of citizenship, help for self-help, freedom and personal autonomy as central terms of self-determination made neoliberalism attractive even beyond the circles of economic players," comments political scientist Thomas Biebricher in a recent interview (2020: 27). What remains, however, of Trilling's sense of literature's "unique relevance" "[t]o the carrying out of the job of criticizing the liberal imagination"? More particularly, what is the "politics" of the currently bestselling newly conventional literature, what its "precise account of variousness, possibility, complexity, and difficulty" (1951: xv)?

Step Two. The "Neoliberal Imagination" and the Tonalities of the Newly Conventional Novel: the Cases of Franzen and Eggers

Now what has been called "the neoliberal imagination" by some, including Walter Benn Michaels in an article of that very title (2005: n. pag.), and "the plutocratic imagination" by others, like Jeffrey J. Williams (2013), works in similarly paradoxical ways as does the liberal imagination: it celebrates freedom and individualism, yet regulates lives and channels the cultural imagination on a large scale. Promising choice and liberties from governmental regulations and central planning, neoliberalism has at the same time created new mechanisms of control and surveillance. Accordingly, if we trust the assessment Williams makes in his discussion of Franzen, Eggers, Jennifer Egan, and Joseph O'Neill, among others, in a 2013 issue of *Dissent*, Trilling's faith in the power of literature is a thing of the past:

> If we still take the novel as a register of politics and culture, it is not a good time for social democracy. Since around 1990, a new wave of American fiction has emerged that focuses on the dominance of finance, the political power of the super-rich, and the decline of the middle class. This new wave marks a turn in the political novel: the fiction of the 1970s and 1980s tended to expose conspiracies under the surface of formal government, whereas this new wave tends to see government as subsidiary, with the main societal choices occurring within the economic sphere. The novels animate the turn to neoliberalism, and thus we might aptly categorize them as "the neoliberal novel." (n. pag.)

Identifying Bret Easton Ellis' *American Psycho* (1991) as the "first major" representative of this genre, Williams's essay features Franzen's *Freedom* of 2010 as "perhaps the most prominent novel of the past decade," a text that "portrays contemporary America as a plutocracy rather than a democracy," a place where "social problems can be more effectively handled through private means than public ones" and "the super-rich are not only entitled to political power but also make the best political choices" (ibid).

> It is not that Franzen advocates neoliberalism, and in fact he exposes some of its dubious values, but, adhering to the conventions of literary realism, he cannot imagine any other possibility. It is a disturbing sign of the times that the most bruited novel of the past decade, declared on the cover of *Time* magazine to "show us the way we live now," [...] assume[s] that there is little chance for fundamental change through normative democratic channels. Liberal procedures have been tossed in the nostalgia bin of history, supplanted by a direct appeal to the super-rich. (ibid)

One may even add that central U.S.-American democratic institutions are, to a large part, being operated by the "super-rich." Still, I'd like to level some of the sweeping claims Williams makes when putting the blame on realism. For just as Mark Twain, Henry James, William Dean Howells, and Theodore Dreiser practiced rather different versions of this once indeed new literary mode which Trilling engages in his essay "Reality in America," so do Franzen and Eggers (while Ellis' *American Psycho* was, as I argued elsewhere, mistakenly read as a version of realism; see Sielke and Hofmann 2002). Unlike their literary predecessors, though, Franzen and Eggers interrogate the "neoliberal imagination" with different degrees of ironic distance and therefore specific emotional effects.

Let us thus turn to *Freedom* and recall how on its second page the novel anticipates the 'evolution' of its liberal protagonists Walter and Patty Berglund from "young pioneers of Ramsey Hill" to well-settled citizens:

> In the earliest years, when you could still drive a Volvo 240 without feeling self-conscious, the collective task in Ramsey Hill was to relearn certain life skills that your own parents had fled to the suburbs specifically to unlearn, like how to interest the local cops in actually doing their job, and how to protect a bike from a highly motivated thief, and when to bother rousting a drunk from your lawn furniture [...]. There were also more contemporary questions, like, what about those cloth diapers? Worth the bother? [...] Were the Boys Scouts OK politically? Was bulgur really necessary? Where to recycle batteries? How to respond when a poor person of color accused you of destroying her neighborhood? [...] Could coffee beans be ground at night before you used them, or did this have to be done in the morning? (2010: 2)

In the course of this paragraph, as past concerns morph into contemporary anxieties and the suburbs sprawl back into the gentrified cityscape, the narrator's bitterly ironic, if not cynical tone ushers us into an environment whose inhabitants are both affluent and leisurely enough to ponder questions about "kitchen water filters" and "good Volvo mechanics" (ibid). Entitled "Good Neighbors," referencing the Berglunds, their local social environment, and the passage's narrative perspective, the opening pages of Franzen's *Freedom* leave no doubt, though, that its protagonists are all but free – in the eyes of those nearby residents that is. As prototypical liberals, they organize all elements of their lives in a (seemingly) "rational way" (Trilling 1951: xiv), that is, with clear limits – their estranged son Joey comes to see liberalism "as a weakness on par with self-abuse" (*Freedom*: 27) – and with the efficiency of good (neoliberal) citizens whose ultimate task is to engage in a new kind of conspicuous consumption, an activity practiced often, it seems, as a mode of evasion or skip action.

As James Ley recalls in his review of *Freedom*, Franzen, in an (uncollected) essay published in 1996, went so far as to claim "that American writers face 'a totalitarianism of commercial culture analogous to the political totalitarianism with which two generations of Eastern Bloc writers had to contend'" (2011: n. pag.). Or as he succinctly put it in "Perchance to Dream" (also in 1996): "The dollar is now the yardstick of cultural authority" (qtd. in ibid). Meanwhile somewhat less polemically outspoken, Franzen has come to voice his concern over the "infernal," "overwhelming," and "oppressive" "machine of technological consumerism," so Ley holds, in his ambition "to write big social novels" (ibid). Evidently, in this endeavor *Freedom* followed the tracks successfully laid out by his first bestseller *The Corrections*, published on 1 September 2001, on the brink of what was mistakenly hailed as a new (post 9/11) era and "the end of irony" (see Sielke 2002).

I find it less ironic than Ley that novels which critically engage the economic framework they emerge from come to thrive and sell perfectly well in this very environment; this has always been the case, necessarily, and to mind comes fiction ranging from Susanna Rowson to Harriett Beecher Stowe to Edith Wharton and Upton Sinclair to Toni Morrison, Tom Wolfe, and beyond. More remarkable is how more recently this success manifests itself in newly conventional modes of realist narration, thus reaffirming the faith in a nineteenth-century mode of literature and literariness. This confidence Franzen shares with Richard Powers, for instance; the unbroken allegiance to the art of the novel positions both authors closer to nineteenth-century predecessors than to their contemporaries. "*Freedom* is an almost classically middlebrow novel," Ley contends. "It is a big, readable work of character-driven social realism, solidly grounded in domestic drama, but with an overlay of concerned political conscience" (2011: n. pag.).

Aimed at assessing the impact of this kind of retroaesthetics, we may want to recall, as does Kloeckner, that "literary realism has come to be considered the 'aesthetic mode most intimate to capitalism' that despite its insights into and critiques of bourgeois class culture was itself already capitalist and actually committed to the status quo, 'producing the very subjects and objects that the mode claim[ed] to document'" (Schonkwiler and La Berge 2014: 1); and this "is most evident," writes Kloeckner, "in the social novels and other literary writings that deal directly with economic matters in the second half of the nineteenth century" (2017: 16–17). Those texts by Herman Melville, William Dean Howells, Edith Wharton, and Frank Norris, among others, which "may have let financial markets appear in a questionable light," were also "highly instrumental," however, in making market mechanisms "'legible for their readers,'" and thereby "'helped [...] call [them] into being'" (Peter Knight, *Reading the Market*; qtd. in ibid: 17). Hence Fisher's aforementioned term "capitalist realism" (see also Schonkwiler and La Berge 2014).

As we acknowledge realism's cultural work of (re-)production and reaffirmation – as opposed to its supposed function of 'reflection' and critical interrogation –, it becomes all the more interesting to note that the newly conventional "drive" by way of characters marks considerable common ground between Franzen and Powers, even if Powers, unlike Franzen, in his attempt "to reconnect representations of character to broader explorations of those selves' rich and immense environments," takes refuge in the generic frame of the systems novel (Powers 2008: 306). Like systems theory itself, the systems novel aims at understanding the whole not in terms of its parts but in terms of the whole, Powers explains, framing its "new family genealogy" – the very term calls on Darwin, Foucault, and the kinship between the two that Philipp Sarasin has traced so insightfully (2009) – as "a kind of bastard hybrid" splicing realism and metafiction (Powers 2008: 305, 308; see also Sielke 2012).

As Rohr notes in her illuminating reading of *The Corrections*, characters also take a leading role in Franzen's (family) novel which employs its "five main characters" – "no longer sure how to interpret and cope with their disturbing reality of globalization, gender crossings, nationalism as redefined according to the laws of the international market, changing role behavior, deteriorating patriarchy, conventions of political correctness, materialism gone haywire, addiction, eroding family structures, and the like" (2004: 99) – quite strategically: The main characters enact the dominant cultural discourse of the 1990s (ibid). Rohr finds "this new conventionalism hardly surprising" (102). The renewed significance of characters as 'focalizers' and impersonators of current cultural debates, is noteworthy, however, and, as Rohr suggests, closely related to a return of the subject in literature: "After so many decades of laborious efforts in both literature and literary criticism to undermine subjects and subject positions in every imaginable way," she argues,

> attempts to resurrect the subject, especially since the 1990s, seemed a plausible move. Given this trend, the attraction of the narrative conventions of literary realism is evident.

> The realist construction of a novel, particularly a family novel, allows for extended studies of character and social relations, and these form the center of *The Corrections*. (ibid)

The very use of the term subject is, of course, an effect of the crisis the nineteenth century individual or self – and, as a consequence, these concepts themselves – have undergone, concepts that have been contested for some time now; for manifold good reasons, we have come to preferably speak of a subject or, as Julia Kristeva suggested, a subject in process. In this "state of post/individualism" (Reichardt 2018: 114) though, questions of agency also regained relevance, in critical theory as much as in neoliberal economic practice. Neoliberal governmentality made "[c]onsumer choice" the kind of agency allowed for a "sort of subject," as Guthman and DuPuis note (2006: 442). Along with it, the neoliberal agenda revitalized the individual by relegating "a wholesale shift of responsibility" and risk, especially for "life's failures onto the shoulders of life's actors" (Baumann 2017: 126), while, on the other hand, eroding the spaces that may allow for both (truly non-standardized or "non-customized") individual choices and acts as well as concerted action on politically produced problems (ibid: 12).

"So pervasive has neoliberalism become," writes George Monbiot in an article on neoliberalism and its theorists from Hayek and Mises to Friedman and Fukuyama, "that we seldom even recognise it as an ideology." Instead, we take it as "a kind of biological law, like Darwin's theory of evolution. But the philosophy arose as a conscious attempt to reshape human life and shift the locus of power" (2016: n. pag.). Monbiot's register foregrounds one of the central questions that systemic (principally Foucauldian) perspectives on the effect of power, understood as decentralized and discursive, have raised: If neoliberalism has turned into our natural environment, more or less globally, how much freedom – of choice and agency – remains for the neoliberal subject? What impact do our choices in turn have on that environment? What has become of the "job" of – and our faith in – both literature and criticism? And is it indeed on us, in our hands, as Franzen's clichéd – shall we say: conventional? – suggestion holds: "When you hold a book in your hand, nothing will happen unless you work to make it happen. When you hold a book, the power and the responsibility are entirely yours" (Franzen 1996: 40).

Notions of agency shift as do choices, and there are several ways to reassess subjectivity that allow for agency while acknowledging its limits. Judith Butler's well-known take on gender performativity seems highly suggestive even in this context. For just as we do not embody gender, we do not literally embrace and embody neoliberalism. Instead, just as we perform gender, we also perform and enact the identities that neoliberalism feeds us only partially, with variation and, possibly, even with ironic distance. "The body is not passively scripted with cultural codes," Butler wrote in "Performative Acts and Gender Constitution" in 1988, "as if it were a lifeless recipient of wholly pre-given cultural conventions. But neither do embodied selves pre-exist the cultural conventions which essentially signify the body. Actors are always already on the stage, within the terms of the performance" (526). Likewise, none of our acts and choices are merely "individual," but neither are they "imposed or inscribed upon the individual, as some [...] would contend" (ibid). It is this limited range of "freedom" that still allows for degrees of individual variousness and possibility; and just as gender performativity also challenges gender norms, the newly conventional characters do not preexist literary conventions. At times, they may even venture off the beaten tracks. As does Enid Lambert on the final page of Franzen's *The Corrections*. The novel ends with Alfred Lambert taking his time to die, still refusing his wife's "corrections": "He was as stubborn as the day she'd met him. And yet when he was dead, when she'd pressed her lips to his forehead and walked out [...] into the warm spring night, she felt that nothing could kill her hope now. She was seventy-five and she was going to make some changes in her life" (*Corrections* 2001: 568). Hinting that hope never dies, this surprisingly happy ending is both yet another beginning, a sign even of the sustainability of "social hope" and "visions of a better future" (Rorty 1998: 126–127) and a highly ironic and self-referential form of critique, containment, and closure. After all, Enid's transformation materializes solely in the reader's mind – or rather: his or her (neo-)liberal imagination. Accordingly, Richard Rorty's distinction, undertaken in his Massey Lecture with the provokingly conventional title "The Inspirational Value of Great Works of Literature" (1998), the binarism "between a literature of 'knowingness' (or protective cynicism) and a literature of 'inspiration' (or utopian romance)" does not hold (Mahon 2014: 91).

Likewise, even as Franzen's *Freedom* undoubtedly interrogates the reshaping of our lives and the relocation of power that Monbiot speaks of, the political effect of this revisionary take on realist modes remains hard to measure. Somewhere along the lines we have lost our faith in irony which was once deemed either to challenge the system or, as Rorty would have it to be accountable for "a palpable condescension toward national pride" (Mahon 2014: 91); nowadays, some even consider irony the "artistic norm" and a "constraint" (Assheuer 2020: 50). Whether it functions as critique or reaffirmation of what it critically engages – or, most likely, as both –, irony depends both on the eye of the beholder, on cultural literacy, and on previous experiences of reading (novels). Contesting Rorty's "straightforward division between a book's 'aesthetic' and 'moral' value," Áine Mahon argues that, "at once sharply satirical," with its parody of "a very particular type of American liberal," "and deeply compassionate," Franzen's *Freedom* "still opens to the possibility of personal and social redemption in the context of a yet-to-be-achieved America" (Mahon 2014: 91–92). At worst, the novel's ironic distance and range of tonality, stretching from cynicism to humor, may have backfired and contributed to populist backlashes against political correctness and the politics of symbolism. At best, Franzen's *Freedom* may suggest, as Lauren Berlant recommends in her study *Cruel Optimism* (2011) that, "we need to think about agency and personhood not only in inflated terms but also as an activity exercised within spaces of ordinariness that does not always or even usually follow the literalizing logic of visible effectuality, bourgeois dramatics, and lifelong accumulation or self-fashioning" (99). Maybe, however, all of these assumptions simply overrate the "inspirational value" of contemporary fiction.

Now, whereas in *Freedom* irony manages to foreground the uneasy proximity of liberal politics and the neoliberal agenda, the newly conventional aesthetics of Eggers' writing uncannily resonates with a sediment of cultural anxieties and manifests the cracks in the façade of the globalized neoliberal regime and mindset. Most notably in this context, Eggers' writing, at times, challenges the neoliberal imagination by an attempt to refrain from irony. "At the end of history," writes Lee Konstantinou in his 2016 study *Cool Characters: Irony and American Fiction*, "irony transformed from an instrument of revolution to a symptom of the impossibility of revolution" (n. pag.). Konstantinou reads Eggers' novels as a successful popularization of a post-ironic impulse; with Eggers, he argues, post-irony turns into a literary brand that promises consumer reenchantment, a kind of (nonprofit) retail avant-gardism, "a theoretical project," and "a literary intervention" (ibid).

The opening of his 2012 novel *A Hologram for the King* – a paradigmatic example of the novel of globalization – may seem to exemplify this "new sincerity" perfectly, setting its tone and anticipating its protagonist's fate with a line from Samuel Beckett's play *Waiting for Godot* (1952) that serves as epigraph and renders the paratextual frame to the fictional universe we are about to enter: "It is not every day," Beckett's Vladimir remarks, "that we are needed." From there Eggers' text proceeds with a matter-of-fact kind of precision and economy while mapping the movements of protagonist Alan Clay's body and mind – a mind under pressure and eager to remain clear-headed and rational. This is how we meet him in the novel's first short paragraph: "Alan Clay woke up in Jeddah, Saudi Arabia. It was May 30, 2010. He had spent two days on planes to get there." Bound to connect with "his team" at the "King Abdullah Economic City" and "set up a holographic conference system" to be presented to King Abdullah who, "if [...] impressed, [...] would award the IT contract for the entire city to Reliant, and Alan's commission, in the mid-six figures, would fix everything that ailed him" (*Hologram* 2013: 3). The conditional form anticipates what's ahead – "the characters," as Williams put it, "await the king in the desert for several weeks before he finally breezes in and awards the contract to the Chinese" (2013: n. pag.) – and we soon learn more about Alan's ailments. In accordance with the dominant neoliberal agenda, the sleepless protagonist puts the blame on himself, "because he had made a series of foolish decisions in his life," "decision that would leave [...] Alan, as he now was – virtually broke, nearly unemployed, the proprietor of a one-man consulting firm run out of his office" (*Hologram*: 4). Four pages into the novel, we know that Alan is deeply into debt, his life in ruins; at its very end he is still waiting, secretly hoping for a potential return of the king.

Eggers' novel certainly files neatly under the rubric of "capitalist realism," as Kloeckner suggests (unpublished: 36); *A Hologram for the King* exhibits, he holds, what Ursula Heise termed the "aesthetics of uncertainty" (2009), a term that, like "capitalist realism," coins a category of content, though, rather than form. According to Richard Sennett, Kloeckner explains, uncertainty is "the defining temporal challenge for modern subjectivity [...], demanding a new type of habitus, which Sennett skeptically describes as "a self oriented to the short term, focused on potential ability, willing to abandon past experience'" (qtd. in Kloeckner: 36). Reconsidering the past as "a series of foolish decisions," Alan certainly shows such willingness; remembering an era before the decline of U.S. manufacturing and "his time as a successful salesman [and] consultant at the Chicago headquarters of the Schwinn bike factory" (ibid: 74), he also nostalgically reinvents the good times of a "happier past" (ibid). Accordingly, Eggers' *Hologram* varies considerably in tone, enacting literature's "variousness" and "complexity" in newly conventional ways. Yet the very fact that its protagonist's unreliable employer goes by the name Reliant leaves no doubt that "post-irony" may be a trendy critical term, but an undoable literary practice in the twenty-first century. Irony seems to remain the privileged "post-postmodernist" strategy for indicating distance, awareness, maybe even a new variety of omniscience, and a critique self-referentially aware of its own limits.

Likewise, Eggers' 2013 novel *The Circle* (2013) marks post-irony as an impossibility. Preceded by lines from John Steinbeck's *East of Eden* of 1952 – "There wasn't any limit, no boundary at all, to the future. And it would be so a man wouldn't have room to store his happiness" – the novel opens as follows:

> My God, Mae thought. It's heaven.
> The campus was vast and rambling, wild with Pacific color, and yet the smallest detail had been carefully considered, shaped by the most eloquent hands. On land that had once been a shipyard, then a drive-in movie theater, then a flea market, then blight, there were now soft green hills and a Calatrava fountain. And a picnic area, with tables arranged in concentric circles. And tennis courts, clay and grass. And a volleyball court, were tiny children from the company's daycare center were running, squealing, weaving like water. Amid all

> this was a workplace, too, four hundred acres of brushed steel and glass on the headquarters of the most influential company in the world. The sky above it was spotless and blue. (*Circle:* 1)

"Paradise regained" – this is where we enter *The Circle*, Eggers' dystopian utopia of how "the world's most powerful internet company" (ibid: book cover) – its obvious reference being Google – may shape our existence and how its totalitarian ideal of total transparency may regulate and limit our lives. Eight pages later, assigned to a dilapidated desk with an "ancient" computer, our happy-go-lucky protagonist is "baffled, and found her mood sinking into the same sort of abyss in which she spent the last five years" (ibid: 8).

In this circular world, happiness is closely linked with and contained by order, control, and what sounds like a secular kind of intelligent design, all of which resonate in the controlled mimicking, seemingly "transparent" tone of Eggers' text. *The Circle*'s ode to transparency and truisms such as "SHARING IS CARING," "PRIVACY IS THEFT," "all knowledge must be democratically accessible," and "[i]t's the natural state of information to be free" (ibid: 302–303) shared with an enthused audience of thousands of "Circlers" in Mae's onstage appearance with Eamon Bailey, one of the "Wise Men" who run the Circle, all of this sounds like distant echoes of the famous "greed is good" monologue, delivered by financial guru Gordon Gekko (Michael Douglas) in Oliver Stone's 1987 feature film *Wall Street:* "Greed is right. Greed works. Greed clarifies, cuts through and captures the essence of the evolutionary spirit. Greed in all of its forms: greed for life, for money, for love, [for] knowledge has marked the upward surge of mankind" (qtd. in Kloeckner: 44). With its multiple discursive indebtedness, Eggers makes the neoliberal mindset and environment his novel projects appear natural, indeed. Moreover, as the text exposes the simplicity and lack of variousness, and possibility of the ideas traded by the "neoliberal imagination," it produces a significant side-effect: a surplus of sentimentality, yet another of the various modes of the nineteenth century American novel. With its taint of – at times rather "embarrassing" (*Circle*: 301) – sentimentality, *The Circle* foregrounds that, just like the cultural politics of liberalism, neoliberalism "is concerned," as Trilling insisted, "with the emotions above all else." Even more so, it seems to aim at reducing the political to the emotional, and in turning the lack of complexity into a new kind of freedom.

Footnote. The Newly Conventional Novel on the Literary Market, and: Does Gender Matter?

What does all this suggest for the "job of criticism"? It sometimes seems to me that we have followed Trilling both too little – when it comes to tracing literature's "account of variousness, possibility, complexity, and difficulty" – and too faithfully – when projecting its cultural politics. Yes, literature provides the writer with "a ground and vantage point," as Trilling wrote, "from which to judge and condemn, and perhaps revise the culture that produced him" or her, for that matter, "the habits of thoughts and feeling that the larger culture imposes" (1951: xii). At the same time, literature is very much part of the (neo-)liberal imagination and economy that it ponders, part of a market that defines citizens as consumers – a fact from which Franzen, Eggers, and the like, whose texts sell quite successfully, of course, do profit. Accordingly, just as our sense of the politics of culture has changed since Trilling mapped the mid-twentieth-century liberal imagination, so has our sense of how literature engages the complexities of our lives.

As forms of entertainment both literature and politics have, to a certain degree, been subsumed under the dominant drift of current event cultures. When the 2016 "Lit Cologne" festival featured Jonathan Franzen in a reading from the German translation of his novel *Purity*, moderator Denis Scheck did not even try to conceal that the evening was dedicated to marketing the book Rowohlt published under the misleading title *Unschuld*. Whereas a few decades ago, author's readings were free-of-charge outings for the truly dedicated, the Lit Cologne assembles huge audiences that, in addition to (still) spending money on printed matter, are willing to purchase tickets from € 20,00 upward for book promotions camouflaging as cultural events. This willingness to invest in the very process of marketing underscores the true ingenuity of the neoliberal imagination – or what we used to call late capitalism; and mind you, that latter term has returned, too, not only in the work of Thomas Piketty who, interestingly enough, was himself an invited guest to the Lit Cologne 2020 (that got canceled due to the Covid-19 pandemic). By contrast, when we tried to invite Eggers for a reading during the annual conference of German Association for American Studies (GAAS) which the North American Studies Program hosted at the University of Bonn in 2015, his German publisher, Kiepenheuer and Witsch, declined. Eggers' appearance during the 2014 Lit Cologne was a financial disaster, I was informed.

Now don't get me wrong: I do not expect publishers to engage in a cultural politics that calls into question the very dynamics they thrive on. Rather, figuring in the market may limit our faith in the cultural politics of literature and reframe our view of the newly conventional. No doubt, such a move also makes us accommodate "the tendencies of [neo-]liberalism to simplify" – and I am echoing and appropriating Trilling here –, to "give up something of the largeness and modulation and complexity" of literature in order to make our "job" of literary and cultural criticism survive (1951: xiv). It survives best, we have come to believe, not primarily because we stimulate the cultural conversation with illuminating expertise and suggestive insights; rather, we think we matter most as long as we manage to successfully position and circulate undercomplex observations on the neoliberal marketplace. Perhaps literary criticism, perhaps *we* need to take more seriously our job of accounting for literature, "the human activity that takes the fullest and most precise account of variousness, possibility, complexity, and difficulty" (ibid: xv); and perhaps in doing that, our readings and cultural literacy need to, once again, dare more "variousness, possibility, complexity, and difficulty," at the risk of selling even worse.

So, what about my initial point about the gender of the newly conventional novel? Could we convincingly argue that Hustvedt's international bestsellers *What I Loved* (2003) and *The Summer Without Men* (2011) and Jennifer Egan's *A Visit from the Goon Squad* (2010) shift generic conventions more playfully than Franzen and Eggers do in their fiction; that they thus sustainably retain the subversive potential of the postmodernist impulse? Isn't such a claim in itself highly nostalgic and, yes, conventional, not least in the way it reaffirms traditional gender binarisms and norms? Or is it even ironic, perhaps? After all, was not postmodernism a literary mode explored and practiced predominantly by male writers? What then would it suggest when women writers keep echoing and advancing this mode? More insightful, I find, is Kloeckner's suggestion to read the novels of Eggers and the like as an interrogation of masculinities "partaking in a 'pervasive' nostalgic turn in recent fiction and popular culture" (2017: 60), a turn that takes part of its self-referential shape in the newly conventional novel.

Works Cited

Assheuer, Thomas. 2020. "Der Vulkan brodelt, das Magma des Unmuts steigt auf." *Die Zeit*, March 19, 2020: 50.
Bauman, Zygmunt. 2017. *Retrotopia*. Cambridge: Polity Press.
Berlant, Lauren. 2011. *Cruel Optimism*. Durham: Duke University Press.
Butler, Judith. 1988. "Performative Acts and Gender Constitution." *Theatre Journal* 40. 4: 519–531.
Eggers, Dave. 2012. *A Hologram for the King*. New York: Vintage Books.
Eggers, Dave. 2013. *The Circle*. New York: Knopf.

Fisher, Mark. 2009. *Capitalist Realism: Is There No Alternative?* Winchester: Zero Books.
Franzen, Jonathan. 1996. "Perchance to Dream." *Harper's Magazine* (April 1996): 35–54.
Franzen, Jonathan. 2001. *The Corrections*. New York: Farrar, Straus and Giroux.
Franzen, Jonathan. 2010. *Freedom: A Novel*. New York: Farrar, Straus and Giroux.
Guthman, Julie, and Melanie DuPuis.2006. "Embodying Neoliberalism: Economy, Culture, and the Politics of Fat." *Environment and Planning D: Society and Space* 24. 3: 427–448.
Heise, Ursula. 2009. "Cultures of Risk and the Aesthetic of Uncertainty." In: Klaus Benesch and Meike Zwingenberger (eds.). *Scientific Cultures – Technological Challenges: A Transatlantic Perspective*. Heidelberg: Winter. 17–44.
Kloeckner, Christian. "Financialization and Nostalgia in US Literature and Culture." Unpublished Manuscript.
Kloeckner, Christian. 2017. "Risks and Nostalgia: Fictions of the Financial Crisis." In: Sabine Sielke (ed.), in collaboration with Björn Bosserhoff. *Nostalgie: Imaginierte Zeit-Räume in globalen Medienkulturen | Nostalgia: Imagined Time-Spaces in Global Media Cultures*. Transcription 9. Frankfurt: Lang, 2017. 225–241.
Konstantinou, Lee. 2016. "'We had to get beyond irony': How David Foster Wallace, Dave Eggers and a New Generation of Believers Changed Fiction." Excerpt from *Cool Characters: Irony and American Fiction*. Salon, March 28, 2016. <https://www.salon.com/test/2016/03/27/we_had_to_get_beyond_irony_how_david_foster_wallace_dave_eggers_and_a_new_generation_of_believers_changed_fiction/.> [accessed 24 November 2021]
Lau, Mariam. 2020. "Neoliberalismus." Interview with Thomas Biebricher. *Die Zeit*, Februar 27, 2020: 27.
Ley, James. 2011. "*Freedom*, by Jonathan Franzen." *Australian Book Review* no. 327. <https://www.australianbookreview.com.au/abr-online/archive/2010/45-december-2010-january-2011/183-jonathan-franzen-freedom.> [accessed 24 November 2021]
Mahon, Áine. 2014."Achieving Their Country: Richard Rorty and Jonathan Franzen." *Philosophy and Literature* 38.1: 90–109.
Menand, Louis. 2008. "Regrets Only: Lionel Trilling and His Discontents." *The New Yorker*, September 22, 2008. <https://www.newyorker.com/magazine/2008/09/29/regrets-only-louis-menand.> [accessed 24 November 2021]
Michaels, Walter Benn. 2005. "The Neoliberal Imagination." *n+1*. No. 3. <https://nplusonemag.com/issue-3/essays/the-neoliberal-imagination/.> [accessed 24 November 2021]
Monbiot, George. 2016. "Neoliberalism – the Ideology at the Root of All Our Problems." *The Guardian*, April 15, 2016. <https://www.theguardian.com/books/2016/apr/15/neoliberalism-ideology-problem-george-monbiot.> [accessed 24 November 2021]
Powers, Richard. 2008. "Making the Rounds." In: Stephen J. Burn and Peter Dempsey (eds.). *Intersections: Essays on Richard Powers*. Champaign: Dalkey Archive Press. 305–310.
Reichardt, Ulfried. 2018. "Self-Observation in the Digital Age: The Quantified Self, Neoliberalism, and the Paradoxes of Contemporary Individualism." *Amerikastudien/American Studies* 63.1: 99–117.
Rohr, Susanne. 2004."'The Tyranny of the Probable' – Crackpot Realism and Jonathan Franzen's *The Corrections*." *Amerikastudien/American Studies* 49.1: 91–105.
Rorty, Richard. 1998. "The Inspirational Value of Great Works of Literature." In: Richard Rorty (ed.). *Achieving Our Country: Leftist Thought in Twentieth-Century America* Cambridge, MA: Harvard University Press. 125–140.

Sarasin, Philipp. 2009. *Darwin und Foucault: Genealogie und Geschichte im Zeitalter der Biologie*. Frankfurt: Suhrkamp.

Shonkwiler, Alison, and Leigh Claire La Berge (eds.). 2014. *Reading Capitalist Realism*. Iowa City: University of Iowa Press.

Sielke, Sabine. 2002. "Das Ende der Ironie? Zum Verhältnis von Realem und Repräsentation zu Beginn des 21. Jahrhunderts." In: Sabine Sielke (ed.). *Der 11. September 2001: Folgen, Fragen, Hintergründe*. Frankfurt: Lang. 255–273.

Sielke, Sabine. 2012. "The Subject of Literature: (Re-)Cognition in Richard Powers's (Science) Fiction." In: Antje Kley and Jan D. Kucharzewski (eds.). *Ideas of Order: Narrative Patterns in the Novels of Richard Powers*. Heidelberg: Winter. 241–262.

Sielke, Sabine, and Anne Hofmann. 2002. "Serienmörder und andere Killer: Die Endzeitfiktionen von Bret Easton Ellis und Michel Houellebecq." In: Andrew Johnston and Ulrike Schneider (eds.). *Anglo-Romanische Kulturkontakte: Von Humanismus bis Postkolonialismus*. Berlin: Dahlem University Press. 283–318.

Trilling, Lionel. 1950, 1951. *The Liberal Imagination: Essays on Literature and Society*. 1950. London: Secker and Warburg

Williams, Jeffrey J. 2013. "The Plutocratic Imagination." *Dissent* (Winter 2013). <https://www.dissentmagazine.org/article/the-plutocratic-imagination.> [accessed 24 November 2021]

Thomas Claviez
Neorealism, Metonymy, and the Question of Contingency

Abstract: Since the publication of Roman Jakobson's famous 1956 essay "Two Aspects of Language and Two Types of Aphasic Disturbances," we have tended to read the relationship between metaphor and metonymy as a dialectical one. The essay argues that this approach stands in need of revision, since metonymy, as a trope – and as a trope, moreover, of contingency – undermines the dialectical relationship between the syntagmatic and the paradigmatic axes. This has far-reaching implications, specifically for the assessment of both literature in general, and its realistic varieties in particular. Since metaphor functions structurally analogous to dialectics itself, metonymy and its role in realism and neorealism might offer us a way to think a "poetics of contingency" that acknowledges the role of contingency, rather that suppressing it and its role in preventing closure through sublation.

In what follows, I would like to connect my first foray into Neorealism – my introductory essay to the special edition of *Amerikastudien/American Studies* with the title *Neorealism Between Innovation and Continuation* – to a more recent one that came out in the volume *Literatur und Politische Philosophie*, edited by Michael Festl and Philipp Schweighauser, with the title "Dramas of Mis(re)cognition: Critical Theory as Literary History" (Claviez 2004: 2017). In the first essay from 2003, I argued that the two realms of epistemology and representation would have to be kept apart in order to assess Neorealism as not simply a 'return' to traditional strategies of representation; that is, neorealist works are not simply an expression of a nostalgic desire to return to 1) a pristine, transparent language prior to the onslaught of the Linguistic Turn, and to 2) classical Realism's agenda to base an understanding of the world upon a (preferably violent-free) process of dialogical deliberation. In my more recent essay, I approached both Realism and Neorealism from another vantage point. Here I argued that Critical Theory's recent neglect of aesthetics and the realm of culture – specifically as it is observable in Habermas' oeuvre, but even more so in what has become known as Phi-

---

Note: A longer version of this article was published in a special issue of *Humanities* with the title "Ethics and Literary Practice," in 2019, guest edited by Adam Zachary Newton. doi:10.3390/h8040176n.

losophy of Recognition, as pursued by Axel Honneth and Nancy Fraser – constitutes a step back behind Modernism, and specifically Modernism's emphasis on self-alienation. In what follows, I would like to draw out some of the ethical ramifications of these critiques, and to connect them with an overarching project devoted to the concept of a "Metonymic Community" and an "Ethics of Contingency" that I have laid out in more detail elsewhere (see Claviez 2014 and 2016). In order to do so, however, I will have to ask my readers to indulge in a kind of longer excursus in order to show where the ethical stakes as regards metonymy and contingency lie, and what both Neorealism and Recognition have to do with it.

Recognition, Modernism, and the Problem of Alienation

As regards the above-mentioned connection between contemporary philosophies of recognition and literary practice – or rather, their disconnect – here is how Winfried Fluck assesses this process:

> In both of these cases, Habermas as well as Honneth, a programmatic rejection of theories of self-alienation is designed to pave the way for an alternative theory of subject-formation: the shift is one from self-alienation to intersubjectivity, from a theoretical framework in which the subject is cut off from self-knowledge, either by forces of modernity or by an anthropological lack, to a theory of subject-formation in which the subject is constituted through intersubjective relations. (2015: 126)

And, in the vein already pointed out above, he also notes that

> [...] in the case of Honneth (but in the final analysis also Habermas) the price for exchanging a narrative of self-alienation by a narrative of intersubjectivity is to analytically disregard the realm of culture (in the sense of cultural practices and cultural representations) as a sphere of subject-formation. In Honneth's intersubjective theory of recognition, culture plays hardly any role at all. (130)

While I wholeheartedly agree with this assessment, I argued that we would have to raise two questions: a) whether, if that diagnosis is correct, we can simply assume that the concept of intersubjectivity can simply leave all modernist claims of alienation behind, and b) if the neglect of recent Critical Theory of the realms of literature and culture is in some way connected to the former assumption. I concluded that theories of recognition simply constitute a step back behind Modernism, as it shares with classical Realism the assumption a) that self-alienation does not constitute a problem, that b) processes of recognition can be assumed to take place through dialogical deliberation, and that c) these processes of recognition can be assumed to work unperturbed by either the insights of deconstruction and phenomena of alienation and self-alienation. It is on the basis of such questionable assumptions that, in the case of Honneth, literature can have only one function: that of the diagnosis of 'pathologies' which disturb the processes of recognition. Consequently, Honneth can only offer a rather poor description – I'd hesitate to call it an interpretation – of Franzen's recent novel *Freedom*. Thus, he discerns in it the (questionable) "tendency […] to use friendship in order to construct advantageous relationships and thus to abuse it for instrumental purposes" (2010: 355, FN 35). Furthermore, he reads it as an indication "that the troubles and conflicts that arise in the heretofore intact family Berglund are triggered by the increased chances to openly articulate ones needs and moods, but are solved through the caring of the children for their parents, who thus turn into something like their parents' parents" (361, FN 116). Besides the fact that such a reading flies in the face of Honneth's own assumptions about recognition, I would venture to say – and I think many of us would agree – that the novel has much more to tell us than that. And in order to do that, please allow me to take a little detour through Aristotle, Jakobson and de Man in order to take up once again the two main issues that I addressed in the first essay: those of epistemology and representation, and the latter specifically after the Linguistic Turn.

Metonymy, Contingency, and Representation

In his philosophy, Aristotle points at two different strategies to overcome what he considers to be the inherent contingency of the world that surrounds us: In his *Poetics*, one is the fabula or *muthos* that he considers poetry to provide us with, in order to impose order upon the sheer contingency of history; the latter of which he delegates to the historiographers to represent (*Poetics*, 23.1459a16–24). Myth, as we all know, is a narrative; its job is thus to impose a narrative order – through selection, omission and compression; a process which necessarily means to distance oneself from the pure contingency of reality. Or, to make the point even stronger: The more we try to create order out of the contingency of historical reality, the more we by default distance ourselves from this very reality. Narrative is, however, a process that takes place on what structuralists would call the syntagmatic axis; and I will come back to this soon. The other strategy to impose order is conceptual thinking, the early form of which he inherits from Plato: that of dialectics.

As far as the *Poetics* are concerned, Aristotle clearly favors metaphor over metonymy – an attitude that he shares with about 95% of his colleagues to come, including Jakobson. Still, in *De Memoria*, he reminds us of the fact that one is reminded of a thing by something "either similar, or contrary, to what we seek, or else from that which is contiguous with it" (451b 24–25). While similarity clearly belongs to metaphor, and contiguity belongs to metonymy (with certain reservations as regards Aristotle's definition of contiguity), opposition occupies a very strange position in this triangle; it will be, however, a central part of Hegel's later dialectics. Interestingly enough, any abstraction, be it philosophical or poetic is – indeed, can only be – based upon the assumption of – a third! A third that, in both instances, takes us away from the true contingency of history, in order to establish – order. Thus, it might not come as a surprise that a similarity is being forced upon us: that between philosophical dialectics and poetic metaphor:

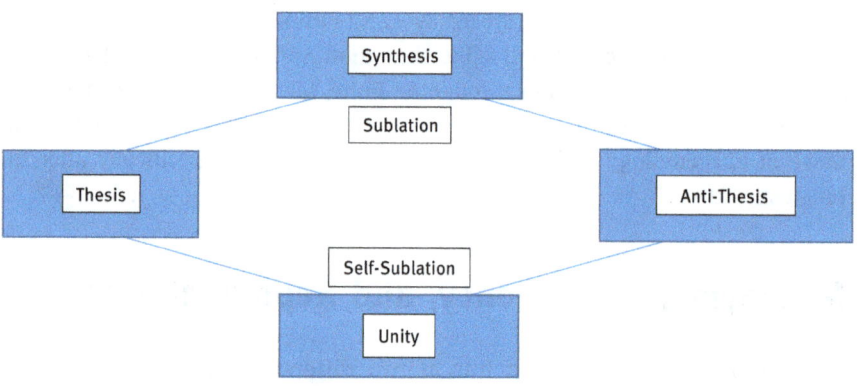

Fig. 1: Dialectics

Interestingly, contingency is what is categorially excluded by, through being juxtaposed to, both dialectics and metaphor (and the dialectics *of* metaphor). Moreover, it also forms a highly problematic sting in Hegel's dialectical philosophy.[1]

In fact, dialectics can only work if it assumes a prior unity – and thus a basis for comparison or a 'third' – that self-sublates itself into thesis and anti-thesis, in order to then be, in a second step, sublated into a synthesis. That is, dialectics is in fact a process that implies not a triangle, but a quadrangle; a unity that is being undone by what Hegel calls the self-sublation of the previous unity into thesis and anti-thesis, which is in turn sublated again by the dialectical process

---

1 On the problematic role of contingency, see Thompson (2014), Siani (2015) and Padui (2010).

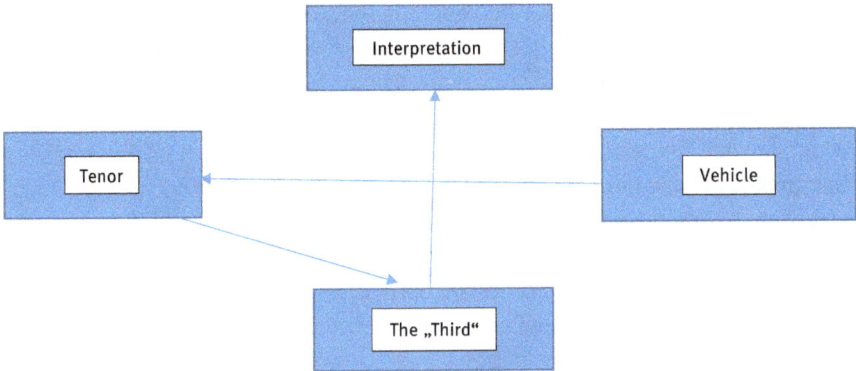

Fig. 2: Metaphor

into the synthesis. The same, interestingly, holds true for a metaphor: Only on the basis of a presumed third, which guarantees the similarity and comparability of tenor and vehicle, can a metaphor be successful. As in dialectics, a presumed unity (1) is split up into tenor (2) and vehicle (3), to be reunited by the reader (4) on the basis of the presumed former similarity (see Hegel, *Encyclopedia*, §§ 79–81).

Fast forward to Roman Jakobson's famous essay "Two Aspects of Language and Two Types of Aphasic Disturbances"; a text that has massively influenced structuralist and post-structuralist thinking. While evoking the distinction between metaphor and metonymy – the former of which Jakobson connects with the paradigmatic axis of selection, substitution and similarity, while the latter he relates to the aspect of contiguity and syntagmatic combination – he defines the two tropes as follows: While metaphor relies on an abstract 'third' to establish the conjunction of tenor (that which should be expressed) with vehicle (that with which it is actually and figuratively expressed), metonymy relies on the concept of 'contiguity in space.'

Furthermore, he attributes metaphor to Romanticism and Modernist Surrealism, and metonymy to the more prosaic forms of Realism. And although he identifies metaphor – very much in the tradition of Aristotle – as a sort of 'queen of tropes,' he surprisingly adds:

> [...] when constructing a metalanguage to interpret tropes the researcher possesses more homogeneous means to handle metaphor, whereas metonymy, based on a different principle, *easily defies interpretation*. Therefore nothing comparable to the rich literature on metaphor [...] can be cited for the theory of metonymy. (1995: 132; emphasis mine)

Now, what is so strange about this quote is that, on the one hand, he connects metonymy with the prosaic genre of Realism – which, in order to achieve its closeness to reality, usually avoids figurative language and is thus deemed 'artless'; however, on the other hand, he tells us that it "easily defies interpretation," which is what one would certainly not usually accuse Realism of. So, what is it that makes prosaic metonymy the 'ugly duck' of tropology – and such a difficult one at that? And does the fact that it is hard to decipher have any repercussions on the role it could possibly play to think of Realism in a new way? In what way might Realism and Neorealism "easily defy interpretation?"

Moreover, another problem arises, as Jakobson, in another essay, establishes the following – and in the meantime almost classical – distinction between metaphor and metonymy:

> The selection is produced on the base of equivalence, similarity and dissimilarity, synonymity and antonymity, while the combination, the build up of sequence, is based upon contiguity. The poetic function projects the principle of equivalence from the axis of selection into the axis of combination. (1960: 358)

And he adds a little later: "Poetry and metalanguage, however, are in diametrical opposition to each other: in metalanguage the sequence is used to build an equation, whereas in poetry the equation is used to build a sequence" (ibid).

Now, the problem that arises is as follows: Metonymy occupies a very strange position in this "equation": Qua trope it belongs to the paradigmatic axis, which is the axis of selection; and I select a metonymic expression to express something it is not. Which becomes even clearer when we take into account that metonymy originally means 'misnomer.' On the other hand, it 'embodies' the syntagmatic principle of contiguity. This would suggest the following conclusion: If the poetic – which would be the metaphoric – function "projects the principle of equivalence from the axis of selection into the axis of combination," does then not metonymy do the exact opposite, namely "project the principle of contiguity from the axis of combination into the axis of selection?" This would be a feasible – and, indeed, the only logical – conclusion to draw. However, there arises another, huge problem: Because that option is already taken, in Jakobson's scheme, by the *metalinguistic* function, the most important aspect of which is to "interpret" the poetic one. If, however, the poetic function of language seems to be reserved to metaphor – which embodies the paradigmatic in a much more straightforward way than metonymy, since it dances on both weddings, and thus undercuts any clear dialectical opposition – this would imply that we interpret metaphor by means of a metonymic operation, which could then explain the difficulties as regards interpretation that Jakobson mentions. That, however, doesn't really help because he explicitly singles out metonymy as the trope 'easily defying interpretation.' Moreover, this would go straight against the assumption of David Lodge, who, in his *Modes of Modern Writing*, concludes that the metalinguistic operation would have to be by default metaphoric, as we can interpret any text only by establishing a third that would allow us to make sense of it:

> The solution would seem to lie in a recognition that, at the highest level of generality at which we can apply the metaphor/metonymy distinction, literature itself is metaphoric and nonliterature is metonymic. The literary text is always metaphoric in the sense that when we interpret it, when we uncover its 'unity' [...], we make it into a total metaphor: the text is the vehicle, the world is the tenor. Jakobson himself [...] observed that metalanguage (which is what criticism is, language applied to an object language) is comparable to metaphor, and uses this fact to explain why criticism has given more attention to metaphorical than to metonymic tropes. (1977: 109)

This would prove the close relatedness of metaphor and dialectics that I have suggested above: The reader has to 'retranslate' the metaphoric operation of the author on the assumption of an existing third, on the basis of which this retranslation can be more or less successful. Fact is, however, that if the Linguistic Turn itself has shown us anything, it is that language does emphatically *not* work 'metaphorically,' in that it is exactly that 'third' that language, according to Saussure actually lacks: Not only is there, due to the arbitrary nature of the sign, no third between the signifier and the signified; language's negatively-differential character on the level of both signifier and signified precludes *any* third between the signifiers and the signifieds, respectively. Saussure's assumption that the signifiers attain their value only through "opposition" to others is a lame – and failed attempt – to retain some form of dialectics:

> The moment we compare one sign with another as positive combinations, the term difference should be dropped. It is no longer appropriate. [...] Two signs, each comprising a signification and a signal, are not different from each other, but only distinct. They are simply in opposition to each other. The entire mechanism of language [...] is based upon oppositions of this kind and upon the phonetic and conceptual differences they involve. (ibid: 119)

While it is rather strange that the quote ends on "differences" – the very term he insists should be dropped – there is no reason why the value of a sign, achieved through being different from others, should be conceived as "opposition": 'cat' is by no reasonable means the opposite of either 'hat' or 'cut.' Thus, the negative-differential relationship is one of pure contingency, also known as – metonymy. Enter: Paul de Man.

In "Semiology and Rhetoric," de Man takes up Jakobson's rather uneven and uneasy opposition between metaphor and metonymy, in order to give metonymy the due that Jakobson claims it hasn't been given. De Man's main objective in the essay is, in good old poststructuralist fashion, to show that metonymy plays an even more important role than Jakobson is willing to concede it, and to put into question the 'tendentious' opposition it is based upon. All this in order to show – another well-known deconstructive move – that a clear-cut distinction cannot be drawn, and that Proust's text, which de Man analyzes, deconstructs itself. To make this move possible, de Man basically erases – reference:

> By an awareness of the arbitrariness of the sign (Saussure) and of literature as an autotelic statement 'focused on the way it is expressed' (Jakobson) the entire question of meaning can be bracketed, thus freeing the critical discourse from the debilitating burden of paraphrase. [...] It (semiology) demonstrated that the perception of the literary dimensions of language is largely obscured if one uncritically submits to the authority of reference. (1979: 5)

Reference – that is, the metalinguistic aspect – is thus reduced to reflect upon the inner closedness of the literary text; an assumption that Proust's text, which de Man reads, underscores through its own self-reflectiveness. The text, with its references to reading and other structures of *mise en abyme*, provides its own metalinguistic interpretation. Without going into further details, what I am interested in are de Man's conclusions:

> A rhetorical reading of the passage reveals *that the figural praxis and the metafigural theory do not converge* and that the assertion of the mastery of metaphor over metonymy owes its persuasive power to the use of metonymic structures. [...] For the metaphysical categories of presence, essence, action, truth, and beauty do not remain unaffected by such a reading. (ibid: 15; my emphasis)

And he describes the difference between the two as follows:

> [...] the difference between metaphor and metonymy, necessity and chance [is] a legitimate way to distinguish between analogy and contiguity. *The inference of identity and totality that is constitutive of metaphor* is lacking in the purely relational metonymic contact: an element of truth is involved in taking Achilles for a lion but none in taking Mr. Ford for a motor car. The passage is about the aesthetic superiority of metaphor over metonymy, but this aesthetic claim is made by means of categories that are the ontological ground of the metaphysical system that allows for the aesthetic to come into being as a category. *The metaphor for summer [...], guarantees a presence which, far from being contingent, is said to be essential, permanently recurrent and unmediated* by linguistic representations or figurations. (14; my emphases)

What is so strange about this distinction that, on the one hand, metonymy as part of the syntagmatic axes is relegated to 'chance and contiguity'; on the other hand, grammar exerts its iron fist to ensure that chance and contiguity are being held in check. But then, the syntagmatic axis cannot stand for contiguity and chance anymore! Metonymy's own contingency either evaporates when being projected upon the paradigmatic axis, or it is reined in by the rules of grammar. What is it that seems to conspire against metonymy to such a degree that it is repeatedly being invoked, just to be ground to naught between the prominence of metaphor and the logic of grammar? Somehow, dialectics doesn't seem to work in this case; metonymy seems to be based on a mythic both/and logic, but is being crushed at the same time. On the other hand, there is metaphor which, rather surprisingly, de Man characterizes as evoking a presence that is 'essential, permanently recurrent and unmediated by linguistic representations or figurations!' Proximity – a.k.a. contingency – as de Man rightly observes, can only "pass the test of truth" if it acquires "the complementary and totalizing power of metaphor" and is thus "not reduced to the 'chance of a mere association of ideas. [...] The relationship between the literal and the figural senses of a metaphor is always, in this sense, metonymic, though motivated by a constitutive tendency to pretend the opposite" (71). The challenge then would be to see through such pretentiousness, and not read literature as metaphoric, but to acknowledge that it might actually just offer the "chance of a mere association of ideas" that defy metaphorico-dialectical totalization.

Narrative and the Problem of Contingency

In order to illustrate this further, let us take the example of a *muthos*; to be more precise, a Native American origin myth. In "The Iroquois Depict the World on the Turtle's Back," we learn the story about twins who mutually vie for predominance; a fight that actually already starts in the mother's womb. The right-handed one is born in the normal way, the left-handed through the mother's armpit. The right-handed one tries to do everything the normal way; the left-handed does everything in a 'crooked' manner. A chart of the respective characteristics of the two twins would look something like that:

Right-handed twin	Left-handed twin (favored by grandmother)
Born the normal way	Born through the armpit, killing the mother
Does everything like he should	Does things in a devious way
Straight mind	Crooked mind
Herbivore	Carnivore
Collects berries and fruits	Collects briar and poison ivy; knows about medicine
Makes man	???
Tells the truth	Lies
Decides to lie	Decides to tell the truth

While thus, as the myth tells us, serves to create 'a balanced and orderly world,' the twins still keep on fighting, but neither twin can decisively beat the other. In order to solve the conundrum, the story then offers a rather surprising turn: Just once, the right-handed twin lies to the left-handed twin, while the left-handed twin decides to tell the truth. In the final duel, the right-handed twin kills the left-handed one, and throws him "off the edge of the world," but "some place below the world, the left-handed twin still lives and reigns" (Albert and Iverson 1994: 22).

Both the oppositional structure, as well as the chiasmic turn that the story takes, lend themselves perfectly to a structuralist, as well as a poststructuralist reading, as the story does not only create oppositional pairs, but also lets them switch places and thus insinuates that none of the binary oppositions is as 'pure' as one might think. However, and this is my main point, narratively speaking all of this hinges on a moment in the story – both twins simultaneously, but unbeknownst to each other – deciding to suddenly change their roles: a highly improbable scenario. But what then is the *muthos* or the fable in this Iroquois myth? Is it the oppositional structure that, in a Lévi-Straussian reading looks like an early form of dialectics, or is it a totally contingent turn in a strange story? Well, it was exactly this 'narrative' strangeness or eventfulness that Lévi-Strauss wanted to overcome with his structuralist analyses, in trying to carve out, in a kind of vertical reading, the columns that he so famously introduced in his seminal essay "The Structural Analysis of Myth." However, what is getting lost in this procedure is exactly that narratively highly contingent and utterly improbable moment that leads to the chiasm, that in turn deconstructs the purity of the binary pairs, but that in itself cannot be dialectically accounted for.[2]

If that holds true, however, what does the difference between mythical and syllogistic reason that he so emphatically insists on really consist of? As I have argued elsewhere, it consists of a logic that is not syllogistic (a logic, that is, that follows an either/or structure), but cosmo-logic (based upon a both/and structure) (see Claviez 1998). In Lévi-Strauss' dialectic-structuralist reading, an important part of this difference gets blurred, in that the narrative moment of contingency that makes the chiasm both possible, but at the same time questionable and 'impure,' simply disappears. Only then is the *muthos* able to introduce the very order that Aristotle ascribes to it.

However, the both/and cosmo-logic itself creates a problem, in that it defies syllogistic reasoning so dear to dialectics from Plato and Aristotle to Hegel and beyond. In fact, we can define a syllogistic contradiction as a special form of contingency: The coexistence in space and time of $A = B$ and $A \neq B$. Or rather, instances where A and B simply are not oppositions, but differences.

Having looked at contingency from both the Aristotelian and the structuralist side, we are now in the position to distinguish two levels of contingency: An epistemological contingency that characterizes reality proper, upon which either a narrative *muthos* or a dialectical/metaphorical order can be imposed, and a representational contingency that affects the means by which this order is being imposed. One could argue that, talking about the axes of combination and selection, or metaphor and metonymy, we are in the face of an 'impure' dialectics, as the combinatory character of metonymic narrative and the conceptual/dialectical character of metaphor are by no means equivalent: Narrative and metonymy constitute something like a 'first line of defense' against contingency, while the conceptual/dialectical character of metaphor is clearly given pride of place. Myth, then, is emphatically not a compressed or 'mini'-metaphor (or is so only when one chooses to read it dialectically): If anything, myth works metonymically.

---

[2] The binary structure, by the way, is by no means strictly upheld. And it is quite telling that the right-handed twin, after having won the fight, even kills the grandmother who favored the left-hand twin. To impose order can entail quite a lot of collateral damage, as the story seems to suggest.

Neorealism, Mimesis, and Contingency

Neorealism – and in our case, Franzen's *Freedom* – thus has to address two challenges: On the one hand, it has to face the representational challenges imposed by the Linguistic Turn; on the other hand, it still tries to represent the contingency of real facts – without, however, giving in to the didactic agenda of classical Realism that tries to achieve a consensus by means of a violence-free dialogical deliberation, since – at least on the side of the reality depicted – such an attempt seems doomed to fail: Both alienation and self-alienation are part and parcel of this reality. Moreover, one of the earliest instances of American Realism – Henry James' short story "Daisy Miller" – already shows, that even if there exists the wish to make both two persons (who are moreover attracted to each other) mutually decipherable to each other, and to decipher the cultural environment they operate in, success is by no means guaranteed: The tragic end of the protagonist Daisy Miller is caused, in the final instance, through her inability to read her suitor, Winterbourne, and to read the writings on the wall as regards the danger of catching Roman Fever.[3] That is, even if Neorealism were simply to 'go back' behind the agendas of Modernism or Postmodernism, it would most likely reach the spot again that James reached at the end of his literary career, when all hopes and pretensions to reach 'consensus by dialogical deliberation' are given up in the hermetic short story "The Turn of the Screw."

However, as my new take on structuralism's attitude to metonymy was supposed to show, this latter contingency does not necessarily entail a complete 'blockage' from reality through language. One could define Neorealism as an inherently ironic as-if attempt: How can we possibly address reality's contingency if language always poses an obstacle that makes it impossible to get there? That is, what if language *were* able to represent reality? What if this new Realism were to 'mime' – even if only metaphorically, as we now know – a reality ripe with contingencies that cannot be sorted out, as the early James hoped, through a form of 'communicative reason'? And I am using the concept of Aristotelian mimesis here in the sense that Jacques Rancière has given it in *The Politics of*

---

[3] Winterbourne's attempts to decipher Daisy, and to finally find out who she really is, weave like a thread through the novella: "Poor Winterbourne was amused, perplexed, and decidedly charmed: [...] Was she simply a pretty girl from New York State – were they all like that, the pretty girls who had a good deal of gentlemen's society? Or was she also a designing, an audacious, an unscrupulous person?" ("Daisy Miller" 1967: 24); "He had assented to the idea that she was 'common'; but was she so after all; or was he getting used to her commonness?" (41); "Daisy, on this occasion, continued to present herself as an inscrutable combination of audacity and innocence" (54).

Aesthetics: Not as "resemblance, as some appear to believe, but the existence of necessary connections between a type of subject matter and a form of expression" (2004: 53). Now, what 'forms of expression' can a Neorealism take whose subject matter is not, as in classic Realism, the dialogic creation of a consensus designed to overcome the contingency of the 'real' world, but the sobered realization that this doesn't work, as well as the realization that the 'forms of expression' themselves are 'infected' or 'poisoned' by the contagious contingencies of language proper?

That is, both layers of contingency are reconnected again in Neorealism: an epistemological one and a representational one. The epistemological one is narrative, or the *muthos*, that forms a first front line to capture metonymically (even if the syntagmatic axis is subjected to the 'laws' of grammar, as we have seen) the contingency of reality. The second one, the representational one, language itself, which is exposed to the same contingencies as is reality. The problem with metonymy, which Jakobson defines as being "more difficult to decipher," could thus be explained by the fact that, qua trope, it belongs to both the syntagmatic and the paradigmatic axis. But if it forms one of the main characteristics of Realism, then one could argue that it is so difficult because *it contains remnants of this very contingency* that dialectics or metaphor try to overcome. Through such remnants, it contaminates – as contingency is prone to do – the metaphorical attempts to overcome it. Or, as de Man puts it: "it fails to acquire the complementary and totalizing power of metaphor and remains reduced to 'the chance of a mere association of ideas'"; or a metonymy "motivated by a constitutive tendency to pretend the opposite" (1979: 71). Since de Man is talking about a modernist text by Proust, we might then simply add that what distinguishes Neorealism from both Modernism and classic Realism that is has given up on just such pretense.

What Susanne Rohr has claimed in connection with Franzen's novel *The Corrections* – that the novel develops "a fictional reality of disorientation, insecurity and imbalance within the bounds of the seemingly known and familiar" (2004: 93); a claim strongly reminiscent of Freud's 'uncanny,' which is also echoed by Shklovsky's modernist definition, in "Art as Technique," as the defamiliarizing aspect of art – holds even truer for *Freedom*: No dialogical/dialectical deliberation is able to overcome the almost total collapse of 'recognition' (and we can 're-cognize' only what is familiar, a.k.a. the metaphorical 'third') that the novel traces. Moreover, giving the reader more insights into the Berglund family than they have of themselves, he can witness the total failure of communication, even in everyday language. That is, we as readers have to be able (more or less successfully) to read the protagonists in order to read their communicative failure; another instance of an 'allegory of misreading.' Alienation and self-alienation, that is, affect not only language after the Linguistic Turn, but are still – or maybe even more – part and parcel of our contemporary, and highly contingent, times. That is why Neorealism (or, for that matter, any other genre) cannot possibly serve any other purpose – at least for philosophers of recognition such as the Hegelian Honneth – than as a pathology-diagnostic one. However, I would argue that, if anything, Neorealism constitutes a rather 'difficult' negotiation of the basic tenets of any theories of recognition – be they epistemological or representational ones. It is characterized, in a manner similar to Late Romanticism, by an ironic 'as-if' quality: If Late Romanticism irony is inspired by matured insight that early Romanticism's attempt to consciously reach an unconscious state is doomed to fail, Neorealism might be defined by the similarly ironic quality to show that, even if one were to achieve referentiality by means of resorting to a metonymic quality in language (representative contingency), a second layer of contingency opens up (epistemological contingency). It thus stands in a matured-ironic relationship to early Realism's optimistic assessment that consensus can be reached dialogically: Even if the linguistic means to establish a consensus *were* available, the transcendental homelessness, to which early Realism offers a first reaction, and to which we are still exposed, effectively prevents to reach a consensus in a world characterized by utter contingency. The *Freedom* that Franzen's novel alludes to is thus mainly the freedom to misread and misrecognize the other and the world around us; this, however, is something that already Hegel was aware of: That freedom depends upon contingency to exist in the first place; otherwise we would simply be the pawns in a dialectical game that might as well go on without us.

What *Freedom* also shows us is that one of the central assumptions of theories of intersubjectivity – the fact that we, as Fluck puts it with reference to George Herbert Mead, to whose theories Honneth resorts in *The Struggle for Recognition*, "cannot possibly not know each other because we only learn who we are in interactions with others" (1995: 75) – is just half of the truth: The claim 'we cannot possibly know ourselves because we only learn who we are in interactions with others' could claim equal validity; as would, for that matter, the statement 'We cannot know ourselves because we cannot know the others through which we allegedly come to learn ourselves.' This hints at the conceptual impasse at the heart of recognition: I need the recognition of others who, qua others, are not qualified to recognize me, and thus prone to misread me, and especially my particularity, which is what distinguishes me from them (see also Claviez 2013).

I'm thus afraid that simply to Houdini-like make the implications of self-alienation go away, as theories of recognition try to do, works neither on a conceptual nor on a historical level. Moreover, if we indeed are who we are only through the input and recognition of others, what does that do to the assumption that we all have a particular potential which we (and others) are ethically urged to help develop? Nor – and again, *Freedom* (and countless other novels) can serve as examples – does the emotional attachment of a parent guarantee that recognition succeeds, as Honneth seems to presuppose; an emotional attachment that not only precedes recognition for Honneth, but that actually constitutes a *precondition* of the latter – even if, as I argued, a questionable one.

One of the most important distinctions between literature and metaphysics – or literary theory, for that matter – might actually be the fact that the former is there to show us that the millennial fantasies of philosophy, be they of an Aristotelian, Kantian, or Hegelian provenance, sometimes offer rather bad storylines. Readers of Kant are still stupefied when he offers, in his dispute with Benjamin Constant, a series of utterly improbable stories that might induce someone to indeed tell the truth to a potential murderer pursuing my friend (Kant 1993: 65). Readers of Hegel are still baffled to witness the master suddenly craving for the recognition of the slave (Hegel 2018: 108–116). And even John Rawls' fiction of us being suddenly blindfolded might qualify for a Nobel Prize – but certainly not that for literature (Rawls 1999). The desperate attempt to suppress, overcome, or explain away contingency might be the philosopher's business; it's not the poet's one. In Kant, there remains the problem of free choice in the (veiled) face of the Moral Law; and even in Hegel's dialectics, freedom is closely connected to choice.

In Franzen's novel, the one thing we are free to be is to be free to self-alienate, and to mis-recognize others; even to do evil. In fact, freedom might manifest itself exclusively *in these categories*. The dream to return to a state of referential stability in order to get back to an Adamic, unspoiled state of linguistic transparency, individual authenticity and a disambiguated reality miserably fails, and thus won't do the trick to reconnect us with a world – realistic, romantic, philosophical – long gone. One that might as well have never existed; should it become reality, I wouldn't want to be part of it.

Works Cited

Aristotle. 1906. *De Sensu and De Memoria*. Trans. G. R. T. Ross. Cambridge: Cambridge University Press, 1906.
Aristotle. 1995. *Poetics*. Trans. Stephen Halliwell. Loeb Classical Library. Cambridge, MA: Harvard University Press.
Claviez, Thomas. 1998. *Grenzfälle: Mythos – Ideologie – American Studies*. Trier: Wissenschaftlicher Verlag Trier.

Claviez, Thomas. 2004. "Introduction: Neorealism and How to Make It New." In: Thomas Claviez and Maria Moss (eds.). *Neorealism: Between Innovation and Continuation*. Amerikastudien/American Studien. Heidelberg: Winter. 5–18.

Claviez, Thomas. 2013. "Done And Over With, Finally? Otherness, Metonymy, and the Ethics of Comparison." *PMLA* 128.3: 608–614.

Claviez, Thomas. 2014. "Traces of a Metonymic Society in American Literary History." In: Winfried Fluck, Erik Redling, Sabine Sielke, and Hubert Zapf (eds.). *American Studies Today*. Winter. 299–322.

Claviez, Thomas. 2016. "A Metonymic Community? Toward a Poetics of Contingency." In: Thomas Claviez (ed.). *The Common Growl*. New York: Fordham University Press. 39–56.

Claviez, Thomas. 2017. "Dramen der An(v)erkennung: Kritische Theorie als Literaturgeschichte." In: Michael Festl and Philipp Schweighauser (eds.). *Literatur und Politische Philosophie*. Paderborn: Fink. 21–49.

De Man, Paul. 1979. *Allegories of Reading*. New Haven: Yale University Press.

Fluck, Winfried. 2015. "Literature, Recognition, Ethics: Struggles for Recognition and the Search for Ethical Principles." In: Ridvan Askin and Philipp Schweighauser (eds.). *Literature, Ethics, Morality: American Studies Perspectives*. SPELL 32. Tübingen: Narr. 9–41.

Franzen, Jonathan. 2010. *Freedom*. New York: Farrar, Straus and Giroux.

Hegel, G. W. F. 1991. *The Encyclopedia Logic: Part 1 of the Encyclopaedia of Philosophical Sciences*. Trans. T.F. Geraets, W.A. Suchting, and H.S. Harris. Indianapolis: Hackett.

Hegel, G. W. F. 2018. *The Phenomenology of Spirit*. Trans. Terry Pinkard. Cambridge: Cambridge University Press.

Honneth, Axel. 1995. *The Struggle for Recognition*. Cambridge: Polity Press.

Honneth, Axel. 2010. *Freedom's Right*. Cambridge: Polity Press.

Hurtado, Albert and Peter Iverson (eds.). 1994. "The Iroquois Depict the World on the Turtle's Back, n.d." *Major Problems in American Indian History*. Lexington, Mass.: D.C. Heath.

Iser, Wolfgang. 1994. *Der Akt des Lesens*. Munich: Wilhelm Fink.

Jakobson, Roman. 1960. "Closing Statement: Linguistics and Poetics." In: Thomas Sebeok (ed.). *Style in Language*. Cambridge, MA: The MIT Press. 350–377.

Jakobson, Roman. "Two Aspects of Language and Two Types of Aphasic Disturbances." In: Linda R. Waugh and Monique Monville-Burston (eds.). *On Language*. Cambridge, MA: Harvard University Press. 115–133.

James, Henry. 1967. "Daisy Miller: A Study." *The Bodley Head Henry James*, Vol. XI. New York: The Bodley Head. 15–78.

Kant, Immanuel. 1993. *Grounding for the Metaphysics of Morals/On a Supposed Right to Lie Because of Philanthropic Concerns*. Trans. James W. Ellington. Cambridge: Hackett Publishing Company.

Lévi-Strauss, Claude. 1955. "The Structural Study of Myth." *The Journal of American Folklore* 68.270: 428–444.

Lodge, David. 1977. *The Modes of Modern Writing*. London: Edward Arnold.

Padui, Raoni. 2010. "The Necessity of Contingency and the Powerlessness of Nature: Hegel's Two Senses of Contingency." *Idealistic Studies* 40.3: 243–255.

Rancière, Jacques. 2004. *The Politics of Aesthetics*. London: Continuum.

Rawls, John. 1999. *A Theory of Justice*. Cambridge: Harvard University Press.

Rohr, Susanne. 2004. "'The Tyranny of the Probable: Crackpot Realism and Jonathan Franzen's *The Corrections.*" *Amerikastudien/American Studies* 49.1: 91–105.

Saussure, Ferdinand de. *Course in General Linguistics*. La Salle, Ill.: Open Court Classics, 1983.

Siani, Alberto. 2015. "Hegel's Logic and Narration of Contingency." *Revista Opinião Filosófica* 6.2: 8–27.

Thompson, Peter. "Hegel and the Metaphysics of Contingency." *Verso*. [blog post] 01 July 2014. <https://www.versobooks.com/blogs/1639-hegel-and-the-metaphysics-of-contingency.>. [access 24 November 2021]

Astrid Böger
For the Birds: Nell Zink's and Jonathan Franzen's Environmentalist Fiction

Abstract: This article discusses two novels by Nell Zink and Jonathan Franzen that serve as compelling examples of an environmentally-engaged branch of U.S.-American literature, which has emerged roughly since the millennial turn. More generally, it emphasizes literary responses to the increasing endangerment of the natural environment due to various human interventions including its overuse or even downright destruction. Notably, both novels highlighted here have in common a deep appreciation of birds, which have played an ambiguous role as harbingers of an uncertain future at least since biblical times, a symbolism underlying both works, as well. And yet, they present rather different storylines focusing on the uneasy relationship between humans and non-human animals, at times shown to be on a collision course (Zink); at others, well-meaning individuals create a sanctuary for an imperiled avian species but further degrade the natural habitat in the process (Franzen). Above and beyond their differences, both novels negotiate the chances of survival in an era now known as the Anthropocene, where finally all species appear endangered somehow.

Around the millennial turn, a branch within North American literature has moved into focus, broadly labeled environmentalist fiction or, to use a somewhat older term, eco-fiction, which encompasses such diverse genres as mysteries, romances, and speculative fiction, among others. For all their differences regarding genre and style, one thing nearly all environmentalist works have in common is their explicit and critical engagement with humanity's impact on nature. What is more, a striking number of these increasingly popular literary interventions continue to explore the *ur*-American apocalyptic imagination familiar since Puritan times, albeit in a strictly contemporary vein. These include, for instance, Margaret Atwood's dystopian *Maddadam* Trilogy (2002–2013) and, more recently, Jeff VanderMeer's post-apocalyptic novel *Borne* (2017), to name but two well-known examples. In this essay, by contrast, I am interested in works that are set in a world that is recognizably ours, and that do not follow any such (post-)apocalyptic narrative scripts. More specifically, my focus here lies on literature per-

---

Note: I would like to thank Nino-Raimondo Torricelli for his insightful feedback and for pointing me toward Haraway for further inspiration.

haps best termed neo-realist for its insistence on the more or less truthful representation of the world we inhabit. With considerable urgency, a growing number of these works expose the shortcomings of Western societies when it comes to protecting our planet from destructive human overuse typical of the present era now known, and as of 2016 officially acknowledged by the International Geological Congress, as the Anthropocene (see Subramanian 2019).

In order to narrow my focus further, I will discuss in what follows two authors in particular, Jonathan Franzen and Nell Zink, whose novels I consider particularly compelling specimens of contemporary, environmentally engaged literature. In fact, their respective works are perhaps all the more engaging for their critical takes on a range of environmental issues that they negotiate. Indeed, both authors address with remarkable complexity some of the most pressing concerns of today. However, rather than postulating any clear-cut environmentalist agendas, they do so by presenting stories and characters many readers find utterly relatable – another distinctive feature of neo-realist fiction –, which allows them to explore a range of perspectives and attitudes toward nature, broadly defined, as well as our increasingly harmful role in it. Regarding the human presence in nature, it is interesting to note that both authors share a passion for birds and birding, which supposedly brought them together in the first place (Sehgal), and which has not only had a notable impact on the respective fictional universe they have created but also, even more strikingly, on their writing itself. This, in turn, gave me the idea to take a closer look at how birds appear in two of their novels, and what their presence might signify to readers and, indeed, all of us, when placed in the broader context of contemporary environmentalist discourses.

Birds, of course, have appeared across cultures as ambiguous harbingers of an uncertain fate at least since biblical times. Thus, while a single dove equipped with an olive branch protruding from its beak has widely come to symbolize peace in the Christian imagery, in the *Book of Revelation* the narrator who refers to himself as John witnesses the calling of "all the birds that fly in the sky" by an angel to feast like vengeful vultures on the Antichrist's armies:

> I saw an angel standing in the sun. He cried with a loud voice, saying to all the birds that fly in the sky, "Come! Be gathered together to the great supper of God, that you may eat the flesh of kings, the flesh of captains, the flesh of mighty men, and the flesh of horses and of those who sit on them, and the flesh of all men, both free and slave, and small and great." (The Rev. to John 19:17:18)

In modern times, cultural renditions of bird appearances have safely moved beyond the realm of Christian symbolism, even though they have retained some of their portentous significance as potentially bad omen for, if not downright devastation of, humanity as we know it. This notion was perhaps most iconically conveyed in Alfred Hitchcock's proto-environmentalist horror film classic *The Birds* from 1963, which has scared audiences around the world into the discomfiting realization that angry nature has a way of getting even. The film, based on a short story by the British author Daphne du Maurier originally published in 1952, is arguably all the more unsettling for the absence of a cause given for the recurring, violent bird attacks on apparently innocent people in an otherwise unremarkable seaside town in California. It is worth noting that it is precisely this absence of an explanation for the unfolding catastrophic events, which gives the narrative an apocalyptic bent while denying viewers and, by implication, humanity as a whole (or, in any case, the Christian part of it) an escape route toward salvation as envisioned in the ancient biblical texts invoked above.

Considered in a more positive vein, it is striking that in recent years birds have quite officially been recognized as important indicators of environmental health and integrity – or, as the case may be, their increasing endangerment. Thus, in the publication *The State of the Birds, United States of America, 2009* issued by the U.S. Department of Interior, we find the following assessment undoubtedly intended to enlist public support for conservationist efforts to protect the United States' "wealth of natural resources, and spectacular wildlife, including more than 800 bird species" praised in the opening paragraph:

> Birds are bellwethers of our natural and cultural health as a nation—they are indicators of the integrity of the environments that provide us with clean air and water, fertile soils, abundant wildlife, and the natural resources on which our economic development depends. (*The State of the Birds:* n. pag.)

Lest readers miss the urgency of the situation for all the natural beauty of the American habitat that the text evokes, it is clarified elsewhere that "since the birth of our nation, four American bird species have gone extinct, including the Passenger Pigeon, once the world's most abundant bird. At least 10 more species are possibly extinct" (ibid: n. pag.). In this passage as well as the document as a whole, birds are thus considered not merely as somehow representative of the state of nature, but indeed of the nation's wellbeing more generally. Moreover, it is remarkable to note that birds are regarded as "bellwethers," giving them a previously implausible position of leadership within the natural world, albeit one inevitably moving in the direction of endangerment and even extinction, largely due to continuously detrimental human interventions. Therefore, as the statement from the government-issued document above suggests, birds do indeed connect the nation's nature with its culture, but with an obvious frictional loss. It is precisely this clash between nature and culture increasingly imperiling (not only) bird populations in the United States and elsewhere that both Franzen and Zink foreground in their respective novels I will now turn to.

Jonathan Franzen's critically acclaimed *Freedom* (2010) employs several elements of his signature prose style already at work in *The Corrections*, which had come out nine years earlier. Thus, the more recent novel also focuses on an average American family, the Berglunds, who are busy leading what at first appear to be rather ordinary lives in St. Paul, Minnesota. Apart from the parents, Walter and Patty, there are their two adolescent children, Joey and Jessica. Over the course of the book, the family slowly falls apart as each of its members turns away from the others in search of happiness or, more precisely, the eponymous freedom more often than not involving new partners, as these things frequently go. The narrative is as plot-driven as most fictional works published by Franzen so far, and builds great momentum as we are gradually drawn into the various relationships between and among parents and children becoming increasingly tainted in the course of the novel. Carefully avoiding any taking of sides, the narrative point of view alternates throughout between the individual protagonists, another familiar element of Franzen's fictional universe.

For our purposes here, however, I will single out Walter, who at first strikes us as not only a dedicated husband and father as well as a liberal-minded, middle-class Midwesterner but also a lawyer with unshakable environmentalist convictions. Thus, while nominally doing advocacy work for an organization named Cerulean Mountain Trust, Walter's real passion is a campaign against human overpopulation, in his eyes the most pressing global predicament of all. Considering that Walter has fathered several children with his wife and impregnates another woman in the course of the narrative, his earnestness as a dedicated environmentalist is thus cast in an ironic light from the start. What is more, all good intentions notwithstanding, he soon becomes entangled in ever-deeper moral dilemmas. To begin with, the Cerulean Mountain Trust, so named after the cerulean warbler, a small, new-world songbird with strikingly blue plumage, whose actual status is currently listed as "species of concern" according to the U.S. Fish and Wildlife Service ("Species of Concern"), is funded by a profit-driven coal-mining mogul. Worse, the mogul's stated plan is to forcefully vacate, subsequently strip-mine, and thereby debase a designated area in West Virginia before finally turning it into a preserve for the vulnerable warbler. When the obviously fraught real estate scheme eventually falls apart, Walter leaves his wife and children in order to team up romantically with his attractive assistant, and after her sudden death in a car accident decides to move back into his family's old lakeside house scenically situated next to a new residential development in rural Minnesota. While staying there, he spends much of his time trying to persuade his mostly uncooperative neighbors to keep their predatory cats inside so that nesting birds would have a chance to survive and, if all goes well, procreate. After this campaign, too, thoroughly fails (rather hilariously, one might add), Walter ends up leaving for New York City, while turning the lakeside property into a bird sanctuary, protected by "a high and cat-resistant fence around the entire property" (*Freedom:* 562) and named after his deceased lover, Lalitha. The novel's memorable closing lines poignantly encapsulate the ironies involved in creating a gated and supposedly safe environment for an otherwise endangered bird population, and thereby invariably encroaching on the freedom of most parties involved:

> To this day, free access to the preserve is granted only to birds and to residents of Canterbridge Estates, through a gate whose lock combination is known to them, beneath a small ceramic sign with a picture of the pretty young dark-skinned girl after whom the preserve is named. (562)

With this final image of the cordoned-off bird sanctuary tantamount to an exclusive, private zoo, the narrative nicely captures the underlying moralistic premises of the likes of Walter Berglund, a concerned environmentalist driven by the will to intervene into and, ideally, change the course of an endangered bird habitat in an effort to protect it from further harm. While some readers might find the outcome laudable and even consider it a happy conclusion of sorts, upon second thought the book's final outlook appears ambiguous at best. For, in the end, the survival of the birds can only be ensured by the creation of a human-made, entirely controlled, and therefore thoroughly unnatural, closed environment. What is more, throughout the novel, different and at times conflicting attitudes toward the impact of humans upon the environment are forcefully negotiated, often in the form of intense arguments in all likelihood familiar to many readers. For instance, when Walter tries to persuade his God-and-cat-loving neighbor Linda Hoffbauer to keep Bobby, her overly predatory feline pet inside because "small cats aren't native to North America, and so our songbirds never evolved any defenses against them. It's not really a fair fight," she simply retorts, "[c]ats kill birds […]. It's what they do, it's just part of nature" (542). Predictably, Walter's follow-up point that "[t]hey are not part of our nature. They wouldn't be here if we hadn't introduced them" (ibid) does not change her mind; nothing does. After finishing *Freedom*, readers are left pondering precisely such imponderables foregrounded throughout the novel: What, indeed, is the true state of nature? Furthermore, what exactly do we even mean when we invoke nature? Above all else, who has the right to intervene in its course, and to what end? Finally, whose freedom is really at stake? Without offering definitive solutions to such quandaries, the book goes a long way in unsettling any preconceived, simple answers to these important questions.

Nell Zink takes us on a very different road in *The Wallcreeper*, her debut novel published in 2014. In fact, the road is anything but a tired metaphor in this case, as the novel opens with a car accident of serious consequence that occurs while the protagonists, a recently married couple, are on a birding trip in Switzerland, and when the husband, Stephen, tries but fails to avoid hitting first a rock and then the eponymous bird. The opening sentence, considered "unimprovable" by some critics including Kathryn Schulz, who reviewed the novel for *The New Yorker* (Schulz), is both hilarious and deeply disturbing: "I was looking at the map when Stephen swerved, hit the rock, and occasioned the miscarriage" (2015: 1). To call Zink's prose surprising is a serious understatement, as the many plot turns and leaps will indeed "give you vertigo," as Parul Sehgal warned readers rather admiringly in his review for *The New York Times* (2014: n. pag.). In fact, one would be hard pressed to call the narrative structure of *The Wallcreeper* a plot in any conventional sense at all. Instead, we move seemingly without a clear sense of direction from episode to episode, frequently switching gears and settings along with the personnel. One critic even went so far as to coin a new genre label by calling the book an "ornithological novel" in an attempt to describe not only the presence of numerous avian species in it but also, more poignantly, the fluttering, quasi bird-like style of writing itself (Sethi 2016: n. pag.). What holds this novel together, then, is the unique perspective of the protagonist Tiffany, through whose voice rendered in the first person the narrative unfolds.

Going beyond questions of style, however, there is also a concrete ornithological interest displayed throughout the book. Stephen, in particular, strikes us as a true lover as well as a connoisseur of birds. For example, after he inadvertently hit the wallcreeper, retrieved the bird and took it into their car, Stephen offers the following explanation to his wounded wife, who seems incapacitated and therefore remains rather quiet throughout the scene, likely from having suffered a head injury in the accident:

> I thought it was dead. I just wanted to get it off the road. I was going to have it prepared or something, I don't know. You should see its wings. For me it's a lifer. It's like the most wonderful bird. But it's a species of least concern and actually they're all over the place except anyplace you would normally go. I identified it even before I hit it. *Tichodroma muraria!* It was unmistakable, just like they said it would be. So this is great. Dead is not a tick as far as I'm concerned. I identified it before I hit it anyway. It really is unmistakable. You should see it, Tiff. I'm rambling on like this because you might have a concussion and you're not supposed to sleep. (*The Wallcreeper* 2014: 2)

In the passage above, Stephen insists that he *knows* birds, as proven by his impressive ability to identify them in a mere instant if need be. Moreover, he also turns out to be thoroughly familiar with their natural incidence and, consequently, the value of individual species as indicated by their position on the official scale of concern, the wallcreeper obviously ranking low on the list, being "all over the place." Remarkably, however, Stephen appears to be able to see beyond the assumed commonplaceness of the wallcreeper, which comes to the fore when he admiringly describes the bird's "essential duality" to his friends:

> "Okay, what I mean is, it has this essential duality. It's tiny and gray and you'd never notice it, and then these wings. Woo. You have to see them." He spread his hands like outfielders' mitts and shook them to express his incapacity to understand the wallcreeper. The gesture was like a prayer of desperation, but he never raised his eyes, as if to say, there is no one to appeal to for help, not even me. It was an effective gesture. Omar's wife leaned back, nodding, believing in the wallcreeper. (9)

While rendered somewhat humorously, this passage nicely encapsulates the friends' appreciation of birds going well beyond merely knowing them. Rather, looking at Stephen's attempt at embodying the bird in flight, they seem to experience a sentiment akin to religious awe. More specifically, they admire the special capacity of "the most wonderful bird" (2) to spread and move its wings in a fashion that somehow magically transforms its otherwise unassuming appearance into a quasi-sacred presence that does not seem to require anything or anyone for its perfect if, to humans, unfathomable self-realization. Unsurprisingly, it is the wallcreeper's special ability to combine flying and climbing with great agility, which captures the imagination of Stephen and his friends. In this context, it is worth noting that Stephen's "incapacity to understand the wallcreeper" is shared by professional ornithologists, as well, as there appears to be an actual "lack of knowledge on the behavioural patterns of this bird species" (Saniga 2001: 225). Of course, birds' capacity for flight as well as their general elusiveness has ensured humans' admiration bordering on envy throughout the ages, as testified by countless depictions of flying humanoid figures such as angels in the long history of art. In reality, this special ability gives birds an obvious advantage over earth-bound animals including humans in most situations, while also making them more vulnerable in certain others. As Tiffany explains elsewhere,

> Birds are braver than the other animals, because they have an ace up their sleeve: flight. Maybe Europe had flightless birds once, but nobody ever saw them because they hid instead of fleeing. And then they were gone, like the lavender in the book that was never opened. The marbled teal is almost gone. It doesn't hide. It flies away, low and slow and in a straight line. (*Wallcreeper*: 156)

Tiffany does not feel a need to add the obvious, namely that flying "low and slow and in a straight line" naturally spells danger in an environment dominated by human animals equipped with rifles and deeming themselves masters over the life and death of other species. Consequently, many of the latter have been decimated to near or even complete extinction, in Europe as elsewhere, over the course of just a few centuries.

Compared to Franzen's earlier book, encounters between birds and humans in *The Wallcreeper* are unpredictable, occasionally transformative, and at times even traumatic, as seen in the opening scene discussed earlier. However, unlike Tiffany's unborn child, the injured bird survives, and is nourished back to health and in the process gradually domesticated under the couple's diligent care. They even give it a name, Rudolf Hess, "because its colors were those of a Nazi flag, with black on its chin for the SS in spring" (*Wallcreeper*: 12). When Rudi, as they affectionately call the bird, is well again but slowly going crazy from being trapped inside during the breeding season, the couple decides to set him free. Sometime later, when he unexpectedly returns to their place, they connect him to a GPS transponder in order to be able to "visit him in the summer, assuming he wasn't hanging around in some inaccessible chasm. Maybe meet his family!" (43). However, domestication turns out to be a fatal misstep. For, in a twist of fate typical of this novel, they do in fact "visit" Rudolf in the following summer, only to witness how the small bird, quite possibly because the GPS device weighed him down too much, is brutally killed by a hawk. This violent incident leaves Stephen furious and wishing for a gun so that he could "shoot every motherfucking sparrowhawk in the whole goddamn Alps" (45). Clearly, nature in Zink's book is anything but kind or inherently good; nor are humans. Not even habitual bird-lovers such as Tiffany and Stephen romanticize nature or feel that it has to be protected at all cost. Referring to the birds' lifestyle as "breeding and feeding" (13), which becomes the couple's running gag equally summing up basic human behavior patterns including their own, Stephen rather considers birds as

> ludicrously tragic animals, always fleeing the slightest hint of bad weather in a panic, yelling for months on end to defend territories the size of a handball court, having brief, nerdy sex and laying clutch after clutch of eggs for predators, taking helpless wrong turns that led them to freeze to death, drown, starve, or be cornered by hunters on frozen lakes, too tired to move. (13)

Thus devoid of human idealization or the projection of an enthusiast's vision of nature transformed into a somehow perfected state, as can be observed in Franzen's novel discussed earlier, birds in *The Wallcreeper* are for the most part simply present, frequently unfathomable, and mainly *doing their thing*. Human intervention in their ways and habitats seems like a bad idea, to say the least, as evidenced by Rudolf's sad fate. Yet, there is more to the human-bird connection in this book than first meets the eye. In fact, throughout, the lives of birds and humans often run curiously parallel courses. In one scene, for instance, as Stephen kisses Tiffany with the convalescing wallcreeper nearby, he notices that "[Rudi's] tiny heart is throbbing with love for someone he's never seen," which moves him to confessing to his wife, "I love you, too, you know" (13). When the couple soon thereafter lets Rudolf free to find a mate, Stephen tells Tiffany that they "should try again to have a baby, right now" (17). In short, the avian lifestyle of 'breeding and feeding' extends well into the human habitat, where people fall in and out of love seemingly at random, have occasional and at times not only nerdy but fairly violent sex, and generally flutter from one place to another without any apparent long-term plans or goals. While this parallelism makes for great comical effects throughout the novel, I believe there is also a larger point, with which I would like to conclude my discussion, via a brief detour engaging some related ideas shared by speculative philosopher Donna Haraway in her recent book *Staying with the Trouble: Making Kin in the Chthulucene* from 2016.

Building on her earlier work, Haraway envisions a multispecies world where interactions that she describes as 'making kin' can principally take place among different species thought of as equals. As she explains, the utopian concept of the "Chthulucene" appearing in the book's subtitle imagines a world where linear, man-made history disappears in favor of a continuity of past, present, and future (Haraway 2016: 101). The term itself is "a compound of two Greek roots (*khthôn* and *kainos*) that together name a kind of timeplace for learning to stay with the trouble of living and dying in response-ability on a damaged earth" (2). Moreover, her concept of the Chthulucene implies a strong critique of the Anthropocene as that age, which by definition casts humans as potent agents and all others as somehow less empowered, thereby invariably promoting an ideology of human exceptionalism in turn perpetuating the damaging dynamics of overuse and exploitation if not downright destruction of natural resources. Unsurprisingly, in Haraway's verdict, the Anthropocene and its concomitant ideology of human exceptionalism have been thoroughly discredited or, in her own words, they have become "[s]eriously unthinkable: not available to think with."

> Biological sciences have been especially potent in fermenting notions about all the mortal inhabitants of the earth since the imperializing eighteenth century. *Homo sapiens* – the human as species, the Anthropos as the human species, Modern Man – was a chief product of these knowledge practices. [...] What happens when organisms plus environments can hardly be remembered for the same reasons that even Western-indebted people can no lon-

ger figure themselves as individuals and societies of individuals in human-only histories? Surely such a transformative time on earth must not be named the Anthropocene! (30–31)

In an attempt to overcome such pernicious positing of the human species at the center of everything, Haraway's work goes a long way in envisioning a utopian world in which human exceptionalism gradually disappears, making room for multispecism instead.

Taking my cue from Donna Haraway, I would like to return to the realm of environmentalist fiction of the realist variety once more by suggesting that Nell Zink's work is perhaps so compelling precisely because it likewise challenges the ontological basis on which we habitually differentiate between *us* and *the rest* – be it nature, wildlife, or the environment. All these different entities are, in fact, referring to the same principal idea of human self-empowerment entirely typical of this age now called the Anthropocene, which invariably casts the human species in the role of the agentic subject vis-à-vis the less empowered, and therefore far more vulnerable, others. In Zink's work, by contrast, there is no safe terrain or sanctuary, for anyone; instead, human and non-human animals – who in her book clearly share the same basic urges – struggle while moving through the world as it presents itself, and which is full of surprises, some good, some not so good, and some not good at all. I delight in the thought that we have books like Zink's that deal head-on with this messy world of ours; that give us complex characters who navigate it, more often than not without map or compass, and which do so not earnestly or idealistically, as one might expect from more conventional environmentalist works of fiction, but seriously.

Works Cited

Du Maurier, Daphne. 2004 [1952]. "The Birds." *The Birds & Other Stories*. London: Virago Press. 1–39.

Franzen, Jonathan. 2001. *The Corrections. A Novel.* New York: Farrar, Straus and Giroux.

Franzen, Jonathan. 2010. *Freedom. A Novel.* New York: Farrar, Straus and Giroux.

Haraway, Donna J. 2016. *Staying with the Trouble. Making Kin in the Chthulucene*. Durham and London: Duke University Press.

Saniga, Miroslav. 2001. "Characteristic types of flight and climbing and variability in coloration of the throat and breast of the Wallcreeper *Tichodroma muraria*." *Monticola. Zeitschrift für die Vogelwelt der Berge* 8: 225–232.

Schulz, Kathryn. "Outside In. Nell Zink turned her back on the publishing world. It found her anyway." *The New Yorker*, 18 May 2015. <https://www.newyorker.com/magazine/2015/05/18/outside-in>. [accessed 24 November 2021]

Sehgal, Parul. "A Blithe Spirit, Created by a Birder, Initially as a Lark." *The New York Times*, 2 December 2014. <https://www.nytimes.com/2014/12/03/books/the-wallcreeper-is-nell-zinks-debut-novel.html>. [accessed 24 November 2021]

Sethi, Anita. "The Wallcreeper by Nell Zink review – powerful call of the wild." *The Guardian*, 13 March 2016. <https://www.theguardian.com/books/2016/mar/13/wallcreeper-nell-zink-birds-review>. [accessed 24 November 2021]

"Species of Concern: Cerulean Warbler (Dendroica cerulea). U.S. Fish & Wildlife Service – Midwest Region." 2007. Washington, D.C.: U.S. Department of Interior. <https://www.fws.gov/midwest/es/soc/birds/cerw/>. [accessed 24 November 2021]

Subramanian, Meera. "Anthropocene now: influential panel votes to recognize Earth's new epoch." *Nature*, 21 May 2019. <https://www.nature.com/articles/d41586-019-01641-5>. [accessed 24 November 2021]

The Birds. 2001 [1963]. Dir. Alfred J. Hitchcock. Universal. DVD [The Hitchcock Collection].

"The Revelation to John." *Early Christian Writings*. <http://www.earlychristianwritings.com/text/revelation-web.html>. [accessed 24 November 2021]

The State of the Birds, United States of America, 2009. US Fish & Wildlife Publications. 2009. Washington, D.C.: U.S. Department of Interior. <https://digitalcommons.unl.edu/usfwspubs/398/>. [accessed 24 November 2021]

Zink, Nell. 2014. *The Wallcreeper*. London: Fourth Estate.

Jan D. Kucharzewski
"...the Wood for the Trees": Scale, Sentience, and Sentiment in Richard Powers' *The Overstory*

Abstract: Ostensibly an ecocritical text revolving around the so-called "Timber Wars" of the 1990s, Richard Powers' most recent novel, *The Overstory* (2018), is not only an exploration of the non-human sentience of trees, but also a meditation on the question if a novel, by its very nature (or lack thereof), is maybe too much of a humanist enterprise to ever move beyond an anthropocentric perspective. Even though the novelistic form itself can be regarded as a product of humanist philosophies and practices, *The Overstory* sets out to harness the inherent humanism of its form as a means of bending the anthropocentrism of fiction towards entities whose potential sentience and agency cannot be conceptualized in human parameters. The essay argues that by integrating the anthropocentric biases of fiction and the affective qualities of sentimentalism into a complex narrative structure which often relegates the novel's protagonists to mere focalizers for a plot unfolding on vastly larger scales, *The Overstory* eventually reveals how "likeness is the sole problem of men," whereas trees "are, in fact, like nothing but themselves."

Can there be a novel about non-human entities that does not personify its subjects and that still functions as a novel? Is the anthropomorphization of nature the principal misconception of environmentalist fiction or a fitting strategy for articulating ecocritical concerns in the age of the Anthropocene? What form does fiction have to take in order to trace the impact of human existence on the earth's ecosystems without letting go of human narratives and focalizers? How to tell the story of nature in the cadences of human language? Richard Powers' twelfth novel, *The Overstory* (2018), directly addresses these questions about fiction and form in the Anthropocene while wrestling with the realization that "the world is failing precisely because no novel can make the contest for the *world* seem as compelling as the struggles between a few lost people" (382; original emphasis). The novel is a five-hundred-plus-page epic about the solipsism of humanism and the sentience of trees which won the Pulitzer Prize for Fiction in 2019, but which was also criticized for heavily relying on anthropomorphic elements and for engaging in an unfashionable eco-sentimentalism that humanizes nature rather than accepting that nature is an ontological Other beyond the reach of human categories and concepts. This chapter argues that anthropomorphism and sentimentalism are features, not bugs, of a text that repeatedly acknowledges the inherent humanism of narrative fiction, the inability of language to speak beyond itself, and the generic conventions of the novelistic form that make it not particularly suitable for engaging with the non-human. I will argue that the novel is not about trees that are like people, but about the human fallacy to require anthropomorphization in order to accept an ontological linkage to the natural world. It will therefore be shown that *The Overstory* deploys anthropomorphic language, sentimentalist tropes, and a narrative structure of constant rescaling to evoke empathy for non-human entities while simultaneously scrutinizing and criticizing the need for such artifices.

Into the Wood

The first recorded English language usage of the phrase to "not be able to see the wood for the trees" is attributed to the Renaissance dramatist John Heywood (1497–1580), who writes in a 1546 collection of proverbs: "*Plentie is no dainte; ye see not your owne ease. / I see, you can not see the wood for trees*" (107; original emphasis). As it is often the case with firsts, the original saying is more complex than most subsequent iterations: "I see, you can not see the wood for the trees." Here, the act of seeing someone *not* seeing both accentuates and complicates the notions of perspective and scale which inform the proverb. The speaker in Haywood's version not only sees both the wood and the trees, the speaker also sees the person in the wood not seeing the wood and only seeing the trees. In being able to see this 'not-seeing,' the speaker almost obtains the paradoxical God's eye view of the Emersonian "transparent eyeball" of being nothing yet seeing all (1836, 2014: 20).

Like Heywood's proverb, the most famous passage from Ralph Waldo Emerson's "Nature" (1836) frames the forest as a site of shifting scales and epistemic entanglements. According to Emerson's sylvan soliloquy, "[i]n the woods we return to reason and faith" (n. pag.). Within his transcendentalist vision, knowledge and belief are not mutually exclusive capacities; to think of them in terms of a dichotomy is to not see the wood for the trees. Surrounded by the forest's verticality, one can be "standing on the bare ground" and yet be "uplifted into infinite space" (n. pag.). To be rooted in an actual place or to be uprooted in imaginary space is, in Emerson's view, merely a question of scale. Scale also determines the difference between "mean egotism" and the "Universal Being," or parcels God into parts (n. pag.).

In the semantic field of the forest planted by Emerson, the gap between the individual and the divine, between seeing and being, becomes the gap between the trees and the wood: a question of scale, not of category. While Haywood and Emerson argue that woods are a matter and a mystery of perspective, Powers suggests in *The Overstory* that the problem of not seeing the wood already begins with the problem of not seeing the trees:

> No one sees trees. We see fruit, we see nuts, we see wood, we see shade. We see ornaments or pretty fall foliage. Obstacles blocking the road or wrecking the ski slope. Dark, threatening places that must be cleared. We see branches about to crush our roof. We see a cash crop. But trees – trees are invisible. (422)

Since *The Overstory* contains almost one thousand instances of 'seeing,' 'looking,' and 'watching' (i.e. approximately two per page), it is programmatically invested in making trees visible – or rather: legible – to a species that is innately "[p]lant-blind" (114). Inspired by the agricultural nonfiction of Peter Wohlleben, Colin Tudge, Robin Wall Kimmerer, and David George Haskell,[1] the novel reframes trees as "alien agents doing things beyond the narrow consciousness of humans" (463), while simultaneously wrestling with the extent to which human consciousness remains "blind to intelligence around it" (281).

The human inability to recognize that this "is not our world with trees in it," but a "world of trees, where humans have just arrived" (424), fuels both the ecocritical agenda and the aesthetic grammar of a text which positions itself as a counterargument to the "grand, luxurious act of self-deceit" and "outright lie" of Kant's claim that "*[a]s far as nonhumans are concerned, we have no direct duties. All exists merely as means to an end. That end is man*" (*Overstory*: 250; original emphasis). Since "trees and humans are at war over the land and water and atmosphere" and it is evident "which side will lose by winning" (133), this Kantian anthropocentrism and all of its subsequent iterations will ultimately be the undoing of the species that deems itself privileged:

> Life will cook; the seas will rise. The planet's lungs will be ripped out. And the law will let this happen, because harm was never imminent enough. *Imminent*, at the speed of people, is too late. The law must judge *imminent* at the speed of trees (498; original emphasis).

But although environmental immanence must be judged at the speed of trees, "the only place where people really live" is "the few-second-wide window of

---

[1] See Wohlleben, *The Hidden Life of Trees* (2016), Tudge, *The Secret Life of Trees* (2006), Kimmerer, *Braiding Sweetgrass* (2015) and Haskell, *The Forest Unseen* (2013).

Now" (278). *The Overstory* therefore sets out "to capture the tree and see what the thing looks like, sped up to the rate of human desire" (11). In its attempt to synch arboreal time and sapiens time, the novel deploys narrative strategies of temporal flexing and chronological conflating already celebrated by the self-aware narrator of Powers' *Generosity* (2009) as one of the greatest feats of fiction:

> Time passes, as the novelist says. The single most useful trick of fiction for our repair and refreshment: the defeat of time. A century of family saga and a ride up an escalator can take the same number of pages. Fiction sets any conversion rate, then changes it in a syllable. The narrator's mother carries her child up the stairs and the reader follows, for days. But World War I passes in a paragraph. I needed 125 pages to get from Labor Day to Christmas vacation. In six more words, here's spring. (168)

On the one hand, Powers' novels have frequently demonstrated how narrative can level the epistemological playing fields between different forms of knowledge, modes of existence, and constructions of time. But on the other hand, *The Overstory* serves as a meditation on the question of whether narrative is perhaps too much of a humanist enterprise to ever capture non-human sentience. If novels are indeed a reprieve from or response to what Georg Lukács calls our "transcendental homelessness" (1971: 41), the novel is by default prone to presenting the tangled wood of existence through the twisted metonymies of individual trees. For even in its most fragmented or misanthropic manifestations, narrative fiction is still inherently anthropocentric: Story interprets life as human life and perspective as human perspective. And whereas non-human sentience is indeed a matter of perspective, perspective itself is a human privilege (at least when viewed from a human perspective). Hence, *The Overstory* attempts to narrativize the paradox that humans are "chosen by creation to *know*" (281; original emphasis), even though everything "alive is just outside their field of view" (293). Rather than simply shifting notions of sentience from the species that climbed down from the tree to the tree itself, Powers actually examines the epistemological feedback loop of the human capacity to see its own blindness and to know its own ignorance. The central premise of *The Overstory* is therefore not that trees are like people, but that due to the very nature of stories, the story of nature will always be a human story.

The title of the novel already indicates a conceit of fiction and foliage which Powers expands into the conceptual template for the entire text: An 'overstory' is the agricultural term for the highest layer of tree crowns in a forest canopy. Indeed, the official definition of the relation between overstory and understory pulled from the *United States Department of Agriculture's Glossary of Forest Engineering Terms* reads as if Todorov and Genette donned flannels, exchanged the diegetic axis for actual axes, and yelled 'Timber!': "Two-Storied Stand: Forest stand in which two height classes of considerable difference occur: the overstory and understory. Does not apply to a forest in the process of reproduction, in which the appearance of two stories is due to a seed tree or shelterwood cut before the final cut."[2]

Powers is too much of a conceptualist to let such polysemes stand untapped and the structure of the novel mimics the relationship between an overstory and an understory by deploying character-driven narratives as mere understories for the larger, but also elusive, story of trees. Since the overstory has to be told cumulatively via a human understory, the first part of *The Overstory*, titled "Roots," consists of eight initially unrelated short-stories about protagonists who experience aboral epiphanies and become dedicated eco-activists. Their stories converge during the so-called 'Redwood Summer' (also known as the 'Timber Wars') in 1990 when protesters tried to stop a massive deforestation of the Pacific Northwest. The protests culminate in a moment of violence that leaves one character dead and the others reeling from the aftermath of their failed attempt to protect the redwoods. While the protagonists become emotionally attached to trees and frequently regard them as entities with agency and social behaviors, the novel also cautions that any attempt to make plants seem like people, to grant them semblances of personhood, is fraught with category errors, confirmation biases, and an idealist tendency to gauge the world according to human parameters. Yet, Powers and his protagonists are still invested in "the belief that affection might solve the problems of freedom yet" (255). After all, the "best arguments in the world won't change a person's mind. The only thing that can do this is a good story" (488). To tell this story, the novel engages in a program of anthropomorphic anti-humanism: *The Overstory*, so my central thesis, relies on the anthropomorphic in order to reach beyond the anthropocentric.

Because we suffer from "Adam's curse" and "only see things that look like us" (114), *The Overstory* posits that before we can really see the tree or the wood and understand their agency and sentience, we first need to see ourselves in them. The human proclivity towards pareidolia – a cognitive disorder described in the novel as "the adaptation that makes people see people in all things" and "turn two knotholes and a gash into a face" (393) – only allows us to relate to non-human entities if we can conceptually remake them into something that they are not.

The utopian hope of *The Overstory* is that such metaphorical remaking would eventually affect the maker of metaphors, because "all good stories" also "kill you a little. They turn you into something you weren't" (412). Concord-

---

[2] cf. https://www.srs.fs.usda.gov/forestops/glossary/.

antly, a line from Ovid's *Metamorphoses* serves as the novel's leitmotif: "Let me sing to you now, about how people turn into other things" (466). Thus, the text's transformative impetus is not to turn trees into people but to make people recognize their kinship with trees. There is literalism at the roots of the tree of life: "You and the tree in your backyard come from a common ancestor. A billion and a half years ago, the two of you parted ways. But even now, after an immense journey in separate directions, that tree and you still share a quarter of your genes" (132).

In order to illustrate the roles of anthropomorphic language, scale, sentience, and sentiment in the novel, this discussion will primarily focus on the narrative arcs of three protagonists: The biologist Patricia Westerford, who hypothesizes that trees have agency and forests are social structures; Neelay Mehta, a quadriplegic Silicon Valley tycoon who made his fortune with the most comprehensive simulation video game ever developed; and Nicholas Hoel, a struggling artist from the Midwest who becomes the heir to an elaborate art project started by one of his ancestors. Whereas the stories of Neelay and Nicholas address the extent to which notions of sentience are contingent upon scale and perspective, Patricia's narrative is a self-referential discussion of the novel's use of language and metaphor.

Arboreal Ventriloquism

Like some of its non-fictional intertexts – especially Wohlleben's *The Hidden Life of Trees*[3] – *The Overstory* has been criticized for anthropomorphizing the natural world and for imposing human categories of intelligence and agency onto flora in order to evoke empathy via slanted analogies. Eoin McNamme detects "sins of anthropomorphism and personification" (2018: n. pag.) in the novel and *The New York Times* book critic Barbara Kingsolver points out that while dendrologists "carefully avoid the word 'behavior' and other anthropomorphic language, lest they be accused of having emotional attachments to their subjects," the "novelist suffers from no such injunction" (2018: n. pag.). Setting aside that assertions of a privileged scientific epistemology which successfully circumvents 'emotional attachments' have been repeatedly challenged by the various contributions to the field of Science Studies, passages like the following nevertheless seem to validate a criticism which cringes at the novel's unabashed anthropomorphism:

---

3 See Kingsland, "Facts or Fairy Tales? Peter Wohlleben and the Hidden Life of Trees" (2018).

> These slow, deliberate creatures with their elaborate vocabularies, each distinctive, shaping each other, breeding birds, sinking carbon, purifying water, filtering poisons from the ground, stabilizing the microclimate. Join enough living things together, through the air and underground, and you wind up with something that has *intention*. Forest. A threatened creature. (283; original emphasis)

However, critics dismissing the 'plants-are-like-people' trope of *The Overstory* conveniently ignore the novel's equally present meta-discourse about the legitimacy and functionality of this trope. Whereas the generic conventions of a dendrological research paper indeed demand the avoidance of anthropomorphic and affective language to evoke a sense of scientific detachment, the novel can directly address and contextualize such practices of representation and mediation. For Powers, novels are "second-order representations" that "are free to speculate not only about circulating and context-free truths but also about how those truths appear to and function for various focal positions inside reciprocal and interdependent webs" (Kucharzewski 2011: 457).

Accordingly, the anthropomorphic language in *The Overstory* does not exist independently of a corresponding discourse of scrutiny, skepticism, and self-referentiality. To simply transfer the criticism of decidedly non-fictional writings like *The Hidden Life of Trees* to *The Overstory* is akin to pointing out all the zoological inconsistencies in the 'Cetology' chapter of *Moby-Dick*: Such an approach takes a critical position already immanent in the text and turns it into external critique. Like Melville's reluctant taxonomist Ishmael who attempts the "classification of the constituents of a chaos" (1851, 2018: 109) only to leave his "cetological system standing thus unfinished" (118), *The Overstory* never claims to truthfully represent the ecosphere. Instead, the novel serves as a second-order observation of the various processes by which we either relate to this sphere or try to separate ourselves from it.

It is the narrative of the biologist Patricia Westerford that explicitly explores the (im)possibility of being non-human in human language while additionally making a case for the necessity of anthropomorphic representations. Patricia's groundbreaking graduate work in dendrology proposes that "trees are social creatures" (122) and that "the biochemical behavior of individual trees may make sense only when we see them as members of a community" (126). Even though "her data are sound and no one can find any problems except commons sense," the scientific "journal that ran the piece prints a letter signed by three leading dendrologists" (126) who discredit her claims without bothering "to replicate Patricia Westerford's findings" (127). After all, "[n]o other animal closes ranks faster than *Homo sapiens*" (127).

Patricia subsequently gets ousted from her academic community, takes up work as a forest ranger, and starts reading "Thoreau over wood fires at night" (129). In a direct echo of Emerson's 'transparent eyeball' passage cited above, Henry David Thoreau also regards the individual as "part and parcel of nature" rather than as "a member of society" (1851, 2001: 225). Patricia, too, discovers how the forest allows the "particle of her private *self*" to rejoin "everything it has been split off from" (225; original emphasis).

The Overstory is infused with this transcendentalist vision of integration and interconnectedness. Not only does the novel open with an epigraph by Emerson contemplating "an occult relation between man and the vegetable" (1), Thoreau also has a cameo appearance on the very first pages of the opening chapter, which describes a chestnut harvest in nineteenth-century America:

> People are hurling stones at giant trunks. The nuts fall all around them in a divine hail. [...] Up in Concord, Thoreau takes part. He feels he is casting rocks at a sentient being, with a duller sense than his own, yet still a blood relation. *Old trees are our parents' parents, perchance. If you would learn the secrets of Nature, you must practice more humanity...* (5; original emphasis).

The original quote from Thoreau's journals reads as follows:

> The thought that I was robbing myself by injuring the tree did not occur to me, but I was affected as if I had cast a rock at a sentient being, – with a duller sense than my own, it is true, but yet a distant relation. Behold a man cutting down a tree to come at the fruit! What is the moral of such an act? (qtd. in Higgins 2017: 47)

Thoreau's acknowledgment of this 'distant relation' resonates with Patricia's conviction that extending notions of kinship and sentience to the non-human is in itself a form of humanism; not because nature is human(-like), but because humans have conceptually extracted themselves from nature, thereby granting themselves a false and ultimately destructive independence from the ecosphere that sustains them. She wonders: "What is it within us that gives us this need not just to satisfy basic biological wants, but to extend our wills over things, to objectify them, to make them ours, to manipulate them, to keep them at a psychic distance?" (250).

Patricia wants to close this 'psychic distance' by embracing the anthropomorphic rather than rejecting it: To recognize kinship is not only to see nature as human but to also see humans as nature. For Patricia, the fables in Ovid's *Metamorphoses* "seem to be less about people turning into other living things than about other living things somehow reabsorbing, at the moment of greatest danger, the wildness inside people that never really went away" (116–117). In

Patricia's view, anthropomorphization is a two-way street that could revive "the dead metaphor at the heart of the word *bewilderment*" (390; original emphasis) and force us to ask: "What use are we, to trees?" (221). Since "words [are] a ruse" (8) to begin with, any description of nature – be it scientific or poetic, ostensibly objective or obviously sentimental – is artifice. The ontological othering of nature is just as anthropocentric as the personification of trees, yet one kind of anthropocentrism potentially legitimizes exploitation, whereas the other demands responsibility.

Instead of insisting on scientific detachment and objectivity – values that might keep her discipline pure but will not change the way of the world – Patricia starts writing a non-fiction book about her research that deliberately dabbles in poetic language and anthropomorphic images and that very much resembles *The Hidden Life of Trees* by Peter Wohlleben (with whom she shares her initials). When describing how dying Douglas firs send chemicals into the soil that benefit the surrounding flora, Patricia, for example, refers to them as "giving trees" (220) – not because this is a scientifically accurate way of capturing ecological processes, but because the "reading public needs such a phrase to make the miracle a little more vivid, visible. It's something she learned long ago, from her father: people see better what looks like them. *Giving trees* is something any generous person can understand and love" (220; original emphasis).

Even as Patricia is consciously manipulating her readers in a way that "seals her own fate" as a scientist and changes "the future of trees" (220) – at least in the public imagination –, she never loses awareness of the fallacy she is committing: "All day and all night long, her only people are the trees, and her only means of speaking for them are words, those organs of saprophytic latecomers that live off the energy green things make" (218). *The Overstory* is neither Patricia's non-fiction book and eventual bestseller nor Wohleben's *The Hidden Life of Trees*, but a text examining the agendas and aesthetics of such writings. Powers clearly shares the sentiments of both Wohleben and his fictional proxy, yet he does not take them at face value. Instead, he provides second-order observations about a larger network of connections, mediations, and transformations in which nature cannot escape the semantic colonialization by humans.

I have argued elsewhere that Powers' poetics of what he calls "systems novels" (Powers 1999b: n. pag.) and "dialogical fiction" (Kucharzewski 2011: 455) share an understanding of representation and mimesis with Bruno Latour's Actor-Network-Theory (ANT).[4] Like Powers, Latour concludes that the "more

---

4 For an extended analysis of the connection between Bruno Latour's 'Actor-Network-Theory" and notions of agency in Powers' texts see my "The Irreducible Complexity of the Analog

human-made images are generated, the more objectivity will be collected. In science there is no such a thing as "mere representation" (2002: 21–22). The presence of additional representational levels is also what distinguishes a non-fiction book about trees which merely uses anthropomorphic language from a novel about an author writing such a book. *The Overstory* clearly cannot shed the anthropocentric in its representational framework, but it can reproduce anthropomorphic discourses, criticize the role of anthropocentrism in our understanding of nature, *and* investigate the limitations of the novelistic form itself when it comes to dealing with the non-human.

After all, the novel *per se* has often dreamed of being consciousness' closest cousin, of capturing what it means to be one of those 'saprophytic latecomers' from within. But because of this, the novel is also humanism's most verbose vanguard. Or as one protagonist in *The Overstory* observes: Books "share a core so obvious it passes for given. Every one imagines that fear and anger, violence and desire, rage laced with the surprise capacity to forgive – *character* – is all that matters in the end" (382; original emphasis). 'Character' is both the generative catalyst and the limiting perimeter of the novelistic form and any novel attempting to move beyond character, to speak about and for the non-human, faces the danger of leaving behind the very genre itself. Through the character of Patricia, Powers emphasizes that his own puppet printed on pulped wood can only speak the language of trees in a human lexicon. However, this arboreal ventriloquism is a feature, not a bug, of a text that understands how fictional "heroes, villains, and walk-ons are better than truth. *Though I am fake*, they say, *and nothing I do makes the least difference, still, I cross all distances to sit next to you* [...], *keep you company, and change your mind*" (382; original emphasis). The fakery of fiction can be the facilitator of an affective truth with truly transformative potential and hence palpable extra-textual consequences.

Powers' focus on anthropomorphic affect as the principal vehicle for the novel's (environmental) politics has led some critics to compare *The Overstory* to Harriet Beecher Stowe's *Uncle Tom's Cabin* (1852). In his review of the novel, Nathanial Rich wonders if "all that stands in the way of enlightenment the lack of a robust public-information campaign or a climate-themed *Uncle Tom's Cabin?*" (2018: n. pag.). Along similar lines Steven Donoghue writes:

> If you write a long book in which trees talk, you run the risk looking silly, which is the green kryptonite of serious fiction. Likewise, if you preach, you run the risk that your preaching will outstrip your storytelling – if it doesn't, you have a work of mind-changing art like

---

World" (2015). The connection is also relevant for the present discussion of *The Overstory*, but will not be examined in more detail.

Uncle Tom's Cabin, but if it does, you're stuck with a leaden piece of polemic like *The Jungle*. (n. pag.)

Since even the novel's characters wonder if they are "just being sentimental about pretty green things" (238), *The Overstory* might indeed be the "*Uncle Tom's Cabin* of the Tree." After all, how can a novel that presents trees as sentient creatures and mourns their cutting not be sappy? Yet, *The Overstory* is probably not an example of sentimentalism in the same way that Anna Sewell's *Black Beauty* (1877) was initially advertised as "The *Uncle Tom's Cabin* of the Horse."[5] Instead, *The Overstory* is a self-aware "*Uncle Tom's Cabin* of the Tree," fully cognizant of its own biases, prescriptions, inscriptions, manipulations, and limitations; a novel which deploys the power of sentiment in order to facilitate connections, shift perspectives, and inspire action. Because to move us into recognition, the sentimental novel always had to latch on to the most common aspects connecting people and entities, the emotional base line of shared experience. Concordantly, *The Overstory* openly concedes that to "be human is to confuse a satisfying story with a meaningful one, and to mistake life for something huge with two legs" (382). But since life is actually "mobilized on a vastly larger scale" (382), the novel has to scale the arboreal "to the rate of human desire" (11) in order to make the story of trees narratively satisfying, 'meaningful,' and affecting – an act of distortion that, like the text's anthropomorphic language, is refracted in a second-order discourse about the possibilities and problems of such narrative scaling.

Scaling Sentience

Especially the storylines of the artist Nicholas Hoel and the programmer Neelay Mehta examine how the recognition of sentience is often a question of scale and how fiction can move seamlessly between radically different gauges, thus enabling a scaling of sentience. Like the other six protagonists of the novel, Nicholas and Neelay experience epiphanic moments in connection with trees and forests that turn them into eco-activists. Whereas Nick actively participates in the 'Timber Wars' by living in the crown of a Redwood tree in order to prevent its cutting, Neelay, who is paralyzed due to a childhood accident, attempts to use coding to

---

5 To this day, some royalty-free editions of *Black Beauty* still use the novel's original full title: *Black Beauty: His Groom and Companions; The "Uncle Tom's Cabin" of the Horse*. Later editions usually changed it to *Black Beauty: His Groom and Companions; The Autobiography of a Horse*.

do what he believes is the bidding of trees, those products "of the Earth thinking aloud" (390).

As a teenager, Neelay stumbles upon a science fiction story about aliens whose perception of time and intelligence is radically different from humans:

> Aliens land on Earth. They're little runts, as alien races go. But they metabolize like there's no tomorrow. They zip around like swarms of gnats, too fast to see—so fast that Earth seconds seem to them like years. To them, humans are nothing but sculptures of immobile meat. The foreigners try to communicate, but there's no reply. Finding no signs of intelligent life, they tuck into the frozen statues and start curing them like so much jerky, for the long ride home. (97)

At the end of *The Overstory*, Neelay has become utterly disillusioned by the fact that the massive multiplayer online simulation game with which he made his fortune has "no endgame, just a stagnant pyramiding scheme. Endless, pointless prosperity" (410). When his project managers refuse to follow his plan of tweaking the game to include environmental damage and resource depletion as didactic tools, Neelay accepts that the "massively parallel online experience will go on, faithful to the tyranny of the place it pretends to escape" (413). Instead of reprogramming the virtual world, he releases a complex self-learning algorithm into the global data sphere with the intention of compiling and advancing all available knowledge about the world in order to save humanity. The bots "watch and match, encode and see, gather and shape all the world's data so quickly that the knowledge of humans stands still" (487). This "next new species" (496) of self-replicating code will "read every sentence in every article that every field scientist ever published" and "binge-watch every landscape that anyone has pointed a camera at" in order to "speculate on what it takes to live and put those speculations to the test. Then they'll say what life wants from people, and how it might use them" (493). At this point in the novel, Neelay has forgotten the apocalyptic ending of the science fiction tale that impressed him so much as a teenager and *The Overstory* closes with the implication that humanity might meet the same fate as in the story: Replaced and consumed by a species existing on an accelerated temporality.

Against this looming extinction – whether at the hand of sentient machines or self-inflicted – the novel articulates the hope that art and artifice can harmonize divergent frames of reference as a means of providing perspective – if not answers: On the very last page of *The Overstory*, satellites controlled by Neelay's emergent agents of the singularity take pictures of an art installation created by the artist-turned-activist Nicholas Hoel – the word 'Still' spelled out in fallen tree trunks across an entire forest, the letters so large that they are "legible from space" (501). 'Still' as in 'still here' but also 'not moving'.

This concluding attempt at communication between vastly different scales mirrors the opening set piece of the novel in which Hoel's ancestor, a Norwegian immigrant to the United States, plants a chestnut tree somewhere in the middle of a midwestern prairie sometime in the middle of the nineteenth century. At the turn of the century, the chestnut blight, an aggressive fungus, is introduced to North American from Asia. Within three decades the blight destroys almost the entire chestnut population of the United States, reducing it from approximately three billion trees to less than a hundred. Because the chestnut planted by Hoel stands as a sole sentinel in a midwestern nowhere, it escapes the blight. Over several generations the planter and his descendants take monthly pictures of their tree from the same angle in order "to document what time hides forever in plain sight" (11), eventually producing a flip book which covers almost 150 years:

> More than a hundred frames along, the oldest, shortest, slowest, most ambitious silent movie ever shot in Iowa begins to reveal the tree's goal. A flip through the shots shows the subject stretching and patting about for something in the sky. A mate, perhaps. More light. Chestnut Vindication. (11)

The novel contrasts the time-lapse photography of the chestnut with a time-lapse narrative of the blight spreading across North America as well as with vignettes outlining the history of the Hoel family:

> The handiwork of heroin and Agent Orange that comes home with nephews from 'Nam. The hushed-up incest, the lingering alcoholism, a daughter's elopement with the high school English teacher. The cancers (breast, colon, lung), the heart disease, the degloving of a worker's fist in a grain auger, the car death of a cousin's child on prom night. (16)

The family tree and the family's chestnut tree are thus spliced together by literal photosynthesis and the alchemy of narrative. Whereas Nicholas Hoel's final installation makes the human visible to the cameras of Neelay's rapidly evolving digital overlords, the flip book makes the tree visible to the humans living in its shadows. But it is only the novel itself that actually includes *all* frames of reference: The flip book does not tell the surrounding tales of the family because "everything a human being might call the story happens outside his photo's frame" (16); the word 'Still' spelled in wood is not legible to any person standing right in front of it; and the satellites that can see the word cannot see the artist who dragged the trunks into meaning. The only instance that actually integrates all perspectives, positions, and scales – be they non-human, human, and posthuman – is the eponymous *Overstory*.

Like many of Powers' previous works, *The Overstory* makes an implicit case for the novel as a "supreme connection machine" (1999b: n. pag.), a form of expression that can serve as what Powers describes to be an "intermediary between seeming incompatibles, an interlocutor that managed to coax mutually hostile materials onto speaking terms" (*Gain* 1999a: 46). In Powers' oeuvre this type of mediation (in the dual sense of the word) between incongruent epistemes, scales, chronologies, and perspectives manifests as neatly constructed conceits and "stereoscopic" (Harris 1998: 98) narrative designs which suggest patterns and symmetries, where contemporary fictions more evidently situated within modern and postmodern traditions tend to see chaos and entropy. As the narrator of Powers' debut *Three Farmers on Their Way to a Dance* (1985), who refers to himself only as "P-", admits: "[S]ymmetry is my only vice" (12).

This vice of symmetry has resulted in a distinct narrative mode that evokes the conventions of literary realism without ever fully creating conventionally realistic characters or narratives. Powers' realism is often too self-aware to satisfy most readers of realistic fiction and not metafictional enough to situate him within the postmodern canon of self-congratulatory self-implosion. According to Powers, his writings are driven by the thesis that the "individual human cannot be adequately understood solely as an autonomous, self-expressing, self-reflecting entity, but must be seen as a node on an immensely complex network of economic, cultural, historical forces" (2008: 305). Therefore, "fiction needs to reconnect representations of character to broader explorations of those selves' rich and immense environments" (305).

Whereas Latour praises this approach as a "systematic inquiry into what it means to realistically represent the question of what it means to exist" (2008: 266–267), literary scholarship shaped by post-structuralism often points out how Powers' novels deal with postmodern themes of structural dissemination and ambiguous agency without deploying matching postmodern styles and devices. In a somewhat exemplary academic reception of the novels, Ursula Heise argues that Powers' writing "consistently restores context, control, and orientation" (2008: 175). Even though his texts portray with "astonishing conceptual sophistication individuals' inability to resist or even comprehend the worldwide networks that entangle them," his "readers can rely on the comprehensive map the self-assured omniscient narrator unfolds before them" (175). According to Heise, Powers fails to engage in the disruptive aesthetics of postmodernism since the "narrative structure" of his novels "does not in the end offer a persuasive formal correlative" (175) to the overwhelming complex worlds his characters inhabit. Although Heise's analysis is concerned with Powers' sixth novel *Gain* (1998), such criticism is echoed in the more unfavorable responses to *The Overstory* which similarly claim that the reader is put into "the middle of a storm of thought which has been wrestled into the shape of a novel by a writer's act of will," while the novel's cast of characters does not feature any of those "side-of-mouth protagonists" and "dead-eyed ironists squinting at the end of the world through cigarette smoke" (McNamee 2018: n. pag.) who have become a staple of American fiction.

Here, the underlying assumption seems to be that novels *should* dramatize disconnection rather than connection, that the fake openness of the writerly text is preferable to the fake symmetries of the readerly text, and that fragmentation is a marker of literary authenticity. Postmodern fiction and the literary criticism it spawned is never anti-realist or utterly dismissive of mimesis, it simply interprets mimesis as accurately representing the non-representability of the world. Powers' novels are equally invested in the problem of representationalism. However, they negotiate the fundamental inability of literature to capture life by deliberately imposing patterns, conceits, and symmetries so blatantly artificial that they always point to their own inaccuracy. As the narrator of Powers' pseudo-autobiographical novel *Galatea 2.2* (1995) concludes: "Meaning was not a pitch but an interval. It sprang from the depth of disjunction, the distance between one circuit's center and the edge of another. Representation caught the sign napping, with its semantic pants down" (144–145).

In this sense, Powers' "encyclopedic" (Strecker 1998: 68) novels do not strive for more authority, congruence, or comprehensiveness than the more obviously entropic and non-linear expressions of postmodernism. His narrative mode which restores "context, control, and orientation," actually serves as map meant to lead us to a place where the hyperbolic, reductive, and ridiculous aspects of cartography become blatantly obvious, where the abstract placeholder for a forest runs into the actual thing. The very limitations of fictions *ex negativo* always validate, as Powers puts it, the "irreducible complexity of the analog world" by reminding us of how "finely narrated is the life outside this constructed frame, a story needing only some other minds pale analogies to resensitize us to everything in it that we've grown habituated to" (2000: n. pag.).

The assumption that narrative symmetries, elaborate conceits, and extended puns are means of engaging with rather than escaping from the "world's living concepts" (*Galatea 2.2* 1995: 249) is at the core of Powers' unique meta-realism that neither fully matches the deconstructionist fictions of his postmodern predecessors Barth, Barthelme, Gaddis, and Pynchon nor the neo-realism of his literary contemporaries like David Foster Wallace, Jonathan Franzen, Nicole Krauss, or Jennifer Egan. Powers is neither a reluctant postmodernist nor a failed realist. Instead, he is essentially an American pragmatist in the tradition of James,

Pierce, Dewey, Rorty and their literary counterparts Gertrude Stein, Wallace Stevens, and Robert Frost.[6]

Many of Powers' novels tackle a conundrum exemplary expressed in the last lines of Wallace Stevens' "The Snow Man" (1921): "For the listener, who listens in the snow, / And, nothing himself, beholds / Nothing that is not there and the nothing that is" (1997: 8). Once the human factor is removed from the equation, once the experiencing subject attains the absurd position of the Emersonian 'transparent eyeball' by being "nothing himself," this purely ontological entity will indeed no longer hear "any misery in the sound of the wind" (8) blowing across the winter landscape, not regarding the "bare place" (8) as the extension of some inner topography. But although this 'snow man' will hear "[n]othing that is not there" – will not project, assess, interpret, or anthropomorphize – it will also be confronted with "the nothing that is" (8).

Or, as Patricia contemplates in *The Overstory:* Even though "life will not answer to reason and *meaning* is too young a thing to have much power over it" (132; original emphasis), life is also "speculation, and speculation is life" (454). Significantly, 'speculation' "means to guess. It also means to mirror" (454). The paradoxical duality of mirroring and guessing informs the pragmatist poetics of both Stevens and Powers who maintain that nature indeed has no meaning, but that without meaning the question of nature's lack thereof is also meaningless. There are no *noumena* without phenomena and the thing itself is an invention of its idea. Meaning has no say in the grand scheme of things, but for us it also means everything.

In *The Overstory*, the human desire and capacity for meaning are identified as the facilitators of a "cognitive blindness" that "will forever prevent people from acting in their own best interests" (235). If our understanding of the entanglement with, connection to, and dependence on the natural world is so utterly contingent upon finding human meaning in the non-human, eco-critical literature has to pragmatically embrace the anthropocentrism of the novel to generate anti-humanist wonder. The primary strategy implemented by Powers for this purpose is to follow an Emersonian principle which also resonates with Ovid: "All thinking is analogizing, and it is the use of life to learn metonymy. The endless passing of one element into new forms, the incessant metamorphosis, explains the rank which the imagination holds in our catalogue of mental powers" (*Poetry and Imagination* 2015: n. pag.). In *Galatea 2.2*, Powers expands on this notion by

---

[6] For a detailed discussion of pragmatism's influence on American literature, see Jonathan Levin, *The Poetics of Transition* (1999); for a further examination of Powers' meta-realism and its pragmatist elements, see my *Propositions About Life* (2011) and Kley and Kucharzewski, "Introduction" (2012).

adding that "[l]ife *was* metonymy, or at least stood for it" (154–155; original emphasis). Since, as was discussed above, *The Overstory* posits that good stories "kill you a little" by turning "you into something you weren't" (412), it is important to stress the metonymic dimension of the novel's anthropomorphism. Whereas metaphor substitutes, metonymy associates. Metonymy therefore cuts both ways: It relies on concrete connections rather than conceptual resonances and the metonymies of *The Overstory* are not meant to recast trees as people but to trace the contiguities of people and trees: "Men and trees are closer cousins than you think. We're two things hatched from the same seed, heading off in opposite directions, using each other in a shared place. That place needs all its parts" (454).

Concordantly, characters who throughout the novel assume that "the most wondrous products of four billion years of life need help" (170), eventually realize that their various efforts were never about the trees: "Not them; us. Of course, it's not the world that needs saving. Only the thing that people call by the same name" (494). *The Overstory* therefore not only rejects a Kantian anthropocentrism that derives epistemic privilege from the inability of human consciousness to step out of itself; it also does not fully embrace the anti-correlationalism associated with Speculative Realism or Object Oriented Ontology. Human meaning and human perspective, however slanted, crooked or bent, actually *do* matter because they can and do affect the world we inhabit, especially in the age of the Anthropocene. In fact, the "problem begins with the word *world*. It means two opposite things. The real one we cannot see. The invented one we can't escape" (465–466; original emphasis). Because we cannot reach through our invented world to the one we cannot see, because the "nothing that is" will always provoke a misguided, yet inevitable *horror vacui*, *The Overstory* emphasizes entanglements where most new materialist positions would rather focus on autonomy. While objects exist independent of human perceptions and categorizations, humans do not exist independent of objects: "Our brains evolved to solve the forest. We've shaped and been shaped by forests for longer than we've been *Homo sapiens*" (454). Even the language that cannot adequately speak of and for the tree is rooted in a forest beyond its telling, a realm in which "the word *tree* and the word *truth* come from the same root" (501; original emphasis) and in which "the word *beech* becomes the word *book*, in language after language," so that "*book* branched up out of beech roots, way back in the parent tongue" (116; original emphasis).

The Overstory fully embraces the etymological logic by which trees branch into books and books can unmake the human truth of trees as a remedy to rather than extension of anthropocentrism. While fiction cannot capture the scale of the tree without the scope of the human, it can still make us see how and why we cannot see the wood for the trees. The novel points out that the problem of not seeing the wood for the trees or the world for the human is, after all, not the result of an epistemological bias. Instead, the bias is ontological: There is no difference between the wood, the tree, and the spectator – they are the same entity viewed form different scales: Trees and wood are part and parcel of a "great, joined, single clonal creature that looks like a forest" (131). Since there are "no individuals in a forest, no separable events," it is "useful to think of forests as enormous spreading, branching, underground super-tree" (218), for "[e]verything in the forest is the forest" (142).

The Overstory does not personify trees in order to make them relatable, but attempts to metonymically unearth the roots which connect the creature that looks like a forest to the creature who cannot see the tree beyond itself. In one of the novel's branching stories, researchers stumble upon a tree trunk in a Brazilian jungle that looks exactly like a human. They "laugh at the stupefying odds against anything accidental growing exactly like this, like us, out of mindless wood" (394). However, after seeing that a tree can grow into human form, the researchers are suddenly able to marvel at non-human forms of life as well: "Every trunk now appears like an infinitely lifelike sculpture too complex for any sculptor but life to have made" (394). The fact that there is a tree which looks like a human does not make the other trees less special, less alive, less significant, or dependent on human perspective, recognition, and interpretation. Instead, the unlikely likeness of the human trunk reminds the researchers of the unlikeliness of the human form: In the anthropomorphic shape of the tree, the researchers can see the elusive contours of life itself. Through the self-evident falsities of semblance, imitation, and mimesis, the tree, like the novel itself, allows the researchers to realize that they, too, are but the accidental growth of mindless matter – not fundamentally different from the tree, just differently scaled. And they begin to see that while, "*likeness* is the sole problem of men," trees "are, in fact, like nothing but themselves" (355; original emphasis).

Works Cited

Donoghue, Steven. 2018. "Review of *The Overstory*, by Richard Powers." *Open Letters Review*. 07 April 2018. <https://openlettersreview.com/posts/the-overstory-by-richard-powers>. [accessed 24 November 2021]

Emerson, Ralph Waldo. 1836, 2015. *Essays of Ralph Waldo Emerson: Poetry and Imagination*. Editora Dracaena. Ebook.

Emerson, Ralph Waldo. 1851, 2014. "Nature." In: Jeffrey S. Cramer (ed.). *The Portable Emerson*. New York, NY: Penguin. 15–54.

Harris, Charles B. 1998. "'The Stereo View': Politics and the Role of the Reader in *Gain*." *The Review of Contemporary Fiction* 18.2: 97–108.
Haskell, David George. 2013. *The Forest Unseen: A Year's Watch in Nature*. New York, NY: Penguin.
Heise, Ursula K. 2008. *Sense of Place and Sense of Planet: The Environmental Imagination of the Global*. Oxford: Oxford University Press.
Heywood, John. 2018. *The Proverbs of John Heywood*. Philadelphia, PA: Franklin Classics.
Higgins, Richard. 2017. *Thoreau and the Language of Trees*. Oakland, CA: California University Press.
Kimmerer, Robin Wall. 2015. *Braiding Sweetgrass: Indigenous Wisdom, Scientific Knowledge and the Teachings of Plants*. Minneapolis, MN: Milkweed Editions.
Kingsland, Sharon Elizabeth. 2018. "Facts or Fairy Tales? Peter Wohlleben and the Hidden Life of Trees." *Bulletin of the Ecological Society of America*. 27 August 2018. <https://doi.org/10.1002/bes2.1443>. [accessed 24 November 2021].
Kingsolver, Barbara. 2018. "The Heroes of This Novel Are Centuries Old and 300 Feet Tall." Review of *The Overstory*, by Richard Powers. *The New York Times*. 15 April 2018. <https://www.nytimes.com/2018/04/09/books/review/overstory-richard-powers.html>. [accessed 24 November 2021].
Kley, Antje and Jan D. Kucharzewski. 2012. "Introduction." In: Antje Kley and Jan D. Kucharzewski (eds.). *Ideas of Order: Narrative Patterns in the Novels of Richard Powers*. Heidelberg: Winter. 1–20.
Kucharzewski, Jan D. 2011. *Propositions about Life: Reengaging Literature and Science*. Heidelberg: Winter.
Kucharzewski, Jan D. 2011. "In the Lakehouse of Language." Richard Powers in Interview with Jan D. Kucharzewski. *Propositions about Life: Reengaging Literature and Science*. Heidelberg: Winter. 454–461.
Kucharzewski, Jan D. 2015. "The Irreducible Complexity of the Analog World: Nodes, Networks, and Actants in Contemporary American Fiction." *Amerikastudien/American Studies* 60.1: 121–138.
Latour, Bruno. 2002. "What is Iconoclash? Or is there a world beyond the image wars?" In: Peter Weibel and Bruno Latour (eds.). *Iconoclash: Beyond the Image-War in Science, Religion, and Art*. Cambridge, MA: MIT Press. 14–37.
Latour, Bruno. 2008. "Powers of the Facsimile: A Turing Test on Science and Literature." In: Stephen J. Burn and Peter Dempsey (eds.). *Intersections: Essays on Richard Powers*. Champaign, IL: Dalkey Archive Press. 263–291.
Levin, Jonathan. 1999. *The Poetics of Transition: Emerson, Pragmatism, and American Literary Modernism*. Durham, NC: Duke University Press.
Lukács, Georg. 1971. *The Theory of the Novel*. Trans. Anna Bostock. Cambridge, MA: MIT Press.
McNamee, Eoin. 2018. "*The Overstory* Review: A Ranter's Sermon." *The Irish Times*. 14 April 2018. <https://www.irishtimes.com/culture/books/the-overstory-review-a-ranter-s-sermon-1.3455978>. [accessed 24 November 2021].
Melville, Herman. 1851, 2018. *Moby-Dick*. New York, NY: W.W. Norton & Company.
Powers, Richard. 1985. *Three Farmers on Their Way to a Dance*. New York, NY: William Morrow and Co.
Powers, Richard. 1991. *The Gold Bug Variations*. New York, NY: Harper Perennial.

Powers, Richard. 1995. *Galatea 2.2*. New York, NY: Harper Perennial.
Powers, Richard. 1999a. *Gain*. New York, NY: Farrar, Straus and Giroux.
Powers, Richard. 1999b. "The Last Generalist." Interview with Jeffrey Williams. *Cultural Logic* 2.2. <http://www.eserver.org/clogic/2-2/williams.html>. [accessed 24 November 2021].
Powers, Richard. 2000. "Being and Seeming: The Technology of Representation." *Context 3*. 12 April 2004 <http://www.dalkeyarchive.com/article/show/120>. [accessed 24 November 2021].
Powers, Richard. 2008. "Making the Rounds." In: Stephen J Burn and Peter Dempsey (eds.). *Intersections: Essays on Richard Powers*. Champaign, IL: Dalkey Archive Press. 305–312.
Powers, Richard. 2009. *Generosity: An Enhancement*. New York, NY: Farrar, Straus and Giroux.
Powers, Richard. 2018. *The Overstory*. New York, NY: W.W. Norton & Company.
Rich, Nathaniel. 2018. "The Novel That Asks, 'What Went Wrong With Mankind?'" Review of *The Overstory*, by Richard Powers. *The Atlantic*. June 2018. <https://www.theatlantic.com/magazine/archive/2018/06/richard-powers-the-overstory/559106/>. [accessed 24 November 2021].
Stevens, Wallace. 1997. *Collected Poetry and Prose*. New York, NY: Library of America.
Strecker, Trey. 1998. "Ecologies of Knowledge: The Encyclopedic Narratives of Richard Powers and His Contemporaries." *The Review of Contemporary Fiction* 18.3. 67–72.
Thoreau, Henry David. 1851, 2001. "Walking." *Collected Essays and Poems*. New York, NY: Library of America. 225–255.
Tudge, Colin. 2006. *The Secret Life of Trees*. New York, NY: Penguin.
Wohlleben, Peter. 2016. *The Hidden Life of Trees: What they Feel, How they Communicate – Discoveries from a Secret World*. Trans. Jane Billinghurst. Berkeley, CA: Greystone.

Catrin Gersdorf
Forests, Sustainability, and the Ecological Cynicism of the Anthropocene: Reading Annie Proulx's *Barkskins*

Abstract: This essay reads Annie Proulx's *Barkskins* (2016) as a novel that represents forests as a crucial part of the human condition. Covering 320 years of human interactions with the arboreal world in North America, Proulx's narrative reimagines modern history as one that is marked by but rarely recognized for its ecological cynicism. As such, *Barkskins* engages in a form of literary ecocriticism that is diagnostic rather than celebratory or elegiac, and that reveals the story of modernity as one that hazards the very conditions of its existence – "earthly nature" (H. Arendt).

This is not an academic article. It is an essay that veers towards more non-academic forms of writing. And yet it is still intended as a critical contribution to a larger conversation about the human condition, a conversation that is necessary to have in light of enormous ecological and environmental changes, often summarized under the rubric of the Anthropocene. I hope to provide a 'critical' contribution to that conversation, not in the sense of 'critique' as a form of suspicion, of mistrusting a literary text for its tendency to omit and occlude, and for its failure to know and comprehend the reality that it purports to represent.[1] Rather, the following essay hopes to be critical in the sense that a comprehensive diagnosis is critical for finding the appropriate cure for an illness; that breathable air, drinkable water, and edible food are critical for the continuation of

---

[1] In *The Limits of Critique* (2015), Rita Felski reproaches the practice of literary studies in the idiom of critique for its tendency to always mistrust the ethical and political attitudes, as well as the epistemological value of literary texts. "A toolkit of methods ... ready to hand," the critic engaging in the critique of literature "draw[s] out what a text does not know and cannot comprehend. The scalpel of political or historical diagnosis slices into a literary work to expose its omissions and occlusions, its denials and disavowals. Reading becomes ... an act of resistance rather than assent, a way of unbinding oneself from the power of the text" (16). Or literature itself was seen as a form of critique, as a mode that would forge an "alliance of mutual distrust" between the critic and the work "vis-à-vis everyday forms of language and thought" (16).

https://doi.org/10.1515/9783110771350-012

plant and animal life; that music, art, poetry, and perhaps even religion, are critical forms of human self-expression.

This essay is also the product of two aspirations: one, to write something meaningful that would approach literature and art as a modes of memorizing, memorializing, and historicizing worlds made by humans and that confront us with otherwise unspeakable cruelties and incomprehensible atrocities, or more generally, with the absurdities and paradoxes of human existence; two, to write something meaningful about Annie Proulx's *Barkskins* (2016) as a novel that provides us with a historical perspective on forests as a critical component of the human condition.

Beginning and End: Two Images

Annie Proulx's *Barkskins* begins in 1693 and it ends in 2013. It begins with the arrival of two French immigrants, both indentured servants, in the ecological luxuriousness of North America. They are not the first Europeans to enter the seemingly impenetrable forests of the New World; that is, the novel does not introduce them as the drivers of European colonialism. But ultimately, Charles Duquet (who later reinvents himself as Charles Duke) and René Sel, as well as their descendants, will participate in its project of cultural and ecological subjugation. In the 320 years of history that is covered by the novel, Proulx tells the stories of the Sels and the Dukes whose family histories do not only intertwine, they are also closely linked to the boreal forests of North America. While the Sels become a scattered dynasty of woodsmen and lumberjacks who form friendships and enter connubial relationships with members of the Mi'kmaq, a First Nation people indigenous to the Gaspé Peninsula in present-day Quebec, Nova Scotia, and parts of northern Maine, the name of the Dukes becomes synonymous with a lumber empire which, at its peak, is a global business with ties to Europe, China, India, Japan, Brazil, and New Zealand. At first glance, *Barkskins* appears to be a multi-generational family saga that stretches across more than three centuries and tells the stories of up to nine generations. But ultimately, and in spite of the family trees printed at the back of the novel, the Dukes and the Sels merely provide the hinges for the various historical articulations of the novel's prime subject – deforestation. Or perhaps not "merely." But unlike novels in which forests, prairies, swamps, deserts, rivers, and oceans provide the backdrop of human history (a backdrop that can be picturesque, sublime, or apocalyptic, or something else entirely), in Proulx's *Barkskins* the forest is more than that: it is narratively positioned as the ecological antagonist to the human protagonists; and it appears to be defeated at the narrative's end.

The novel closes with an ekphrastic image that draws on the aesthetic sensibilities, as well as the technology, of 35 mm black-and-white photography. Reducing the human presence in that image to a hand holding on to the most precious, and most paradoxical machine ever invented – the car, Proulx writes:

> In the eastern quadrant of the sky the moon was small and very white and its impersonal brilliance showed the rocky coast, ravaged forests, silent feller bunchers, a black glowering mass of peat bog and spiky forest like old negatives. It showed Onehube's white-knuckled grip on the steering wheel. The sea lifted toward the light. And kept on lifting. (713)

The nocturnal scene captured in these lines shows a landscape punctuated by the tools of destruction and the ghost-like remnants of what one can only imagine as its former arboreal grandeur. Proulx ends her novel in her readers' present, with a post-Romantic image in which the moon casts its light, not on an imaginary Hawthornean fairy-land but on a scene in which the actuality of modernity's destructiveness merges with the narrative's recognition of a cosmological continuity that remains undisturbed by *homo faber*. But the comfort of the novel's transcendental dénouement is oddly cold – not just because of the nightly atmosphere. Its power to provide intellectual, emotional, and spiritual solace seems weak, and ultimately ineffective, given that the reader has just finished an epic story of "slow violence" (Nixon 2011): the "slow and long lasting" (6) calamity of deforestation.

Set in approximately the same geographical region as the novel's closing scene, the tableau that opens *Barkskins* is lit by the "twilight" (3) of a new day and, metaphorically, a new era. It contrasts starkly with the moon-lit apocalyptic landscape at its end. Zooming in from a "remote riverbank settlement" somewhere in the "Tadoussac, Kébec and Trois-Rivières" region in New France on René Sel and Charles Duquet, the narrative very soon veers towards the description of an overpowering environment:

> Mosquitoes covered their hands and necks like fur. A man with yellow eyebrows pointed them at a rain-dark house. Mud, rain, biting insects and the odor of willows made the first impression of New France. The second impression was of dark vast forest, inimical wilderness. (3)

Later, after they are claimed by their master, Monsieur Trépagny, "[t]hey plunged into the gloomy country, a dense hardwood forest broken by stands of pine" (3). After walking through this imposing forest for several hours,

> the sodden leaf mold gave way to pine duff. The air was intensely aromatic. Fallen needles muted their passage, the interlaced branches absorbed their panting breaths. Here grew hu-

geous trees of a size not seen in the old country for hundreds of years, evergreens taller than cathedrals, cloud-piercing spruce and hemlock. The monstrous deciduous trees stood distant from each other, but overhead their leaf-choked branches merged into a false, dark sky. (4)

The contrast of this scene with the landscape at the end of the novel could not be greater. Read back to back, the black-and-white sterility of the twenty-first-century photo negative at the end of the novel underscores the visual and sensual intensity of the story's late seventeenth-century origin point. And not only that. While Charles and René may enter the new space of Nouvelle-France, they simultaneously enter an earlier stage of the Northern hemisphere's ecological history. Or does this forest, rather than being indicative of the absence of human progress, suggest a different, more sustainable interaction between humans and arboreal forms of life? Proulx seems to plant that interpretive seed when she has Monsieur Trépagny point to the white trunks of birch trees and explain to René and Charles that "the *sauvages* made houses and boats from the bark" (4). René's refusal to believe Trépagny's explication, combined with Trépagny's racism (which becomes apparent later in the novel), represents the cultural and ethical myopia of the colonizer's gaze – even when the colonizer's social status equals that of the Indigenous population ousted from their own land. It is one of the ironies of modern existence that René Sel will become the male progenitor of a biracial family of "Barkskins," people who earn their living by cutting down trees, while at the same time many of them will try to hold on to cultural and medicinal practices dependent on a functioning forest ecology, practices that are part of the heritage of the Mi'kmaw side of the family.

In-between: The Stories of Deforestation and Ecological Cynicism

Barkskins' narrative arc is anchored in the diurnal symbolism of twilight before dawn and moonlight after dusk. The twilight that illuminates the opening scenes of the novel is associated with the human protagonists' entry into the primeval "forest of the world" (5); the moonlight at the end of the novel heightens a sense of demise and destruction. The two images bracket the story of deforestation.[2]

---

[2] In a review article written by Lucy Rock for *The Guardian* shortly after the novel's publication in 2016, Proulx is cited as having said: "The deforestation is what *Barkskins* is all about" (Rock). When it was first published, the novel received an ambivalent reception. In her dissertation on *Postcolonial Cli-Fi: Advocacy and the Novel Form in the Anthropocene* (2018), Rachel Hodges Ro-

Proulx suggests such a reading by prefixing her narrative with two epigraphs, one by philosopher George Santayana, the other by medievalist Lynn White, Jr.

The first epigraph is an excerpt from a letter Santayana wrote to Logan Pearsall Smith, a writer well-known in the transatlantic intellectual circles of the early twentieth century but mostly forgotten today. In that letter of May 24, 1918, Santanyana responded to Smith's *Trivia*, a collection of aphoristic texts that was originally published in 1902 and republished in 1917. The anthology contains short pieces on such 'trivial' matter as "Seats" to be held in politics, the legal system, and the Church. "Front seats, Episcopal, Judicial, Parliamentary Benches—were all the ends then, I asked myself, of serious, middle-aged ambition only things to sit on?" (Smith: 29). Santayana commends Smith's "love of pleasure, and your humour and malice," writing: "it is so delightful to live in a world that is full of pictures, and incidental divertissements, and amiable absurdities" (*The Letters of George Santayana* 2:319; emphasis in the original). He then adds the two sentences that would end up as an epigraph in *Barkskins:* "Why shouldn't things be largely absurd, futile, and transitory? They are so, and we are so, and they and we go very well together" (319). While the rhetoric of this passage may not be fully cynical (there are no hints of vulgarity or animality, attitudes commonly associated with Diogenes of Sinope, arguably the first cynic[3]), its tone is somewhat reminiscent of the tone of a philosopher-cynic. We hear the voice of someone who finds the absurdities of life amusing, "amiable" rather than disconcerting. Something similar can be observed in *Barkskins:* while the dominant narrative tone is realistic, we find particles of philosophical cynicism scattered throughout the novel. I will return to and expand on that issue below. Those particles are, as I will argue, indicative of the cynicism underlying mod-

---

chester assesses the critical reception of *Barkskins*. For Rochester, Anthony Cummins' review for *The Guardian* is representative of some critics' reservations against the novel. Cummis holds against Proulx that in her novel "the environment is at least as important as anyone in it, a view held by the book's indigenous people but rubbished by almost all of its foreigners" (qtd. in Rochester 167). According to Rochester, "Cummis echoes other critics who viewed the novel as more of an elegy than a call to environmental action, which flouts one of the central goals of effective locus-colonial fiction" (167).

3 Diogenes of Sinope was said to have lived like a dog, masturbate in public, and ridicule Plato's philosophical abstractions. The anecdote most often cited as an example of that critique of Platonic concepts pertains to Plato's description of humans as featherless bipeds. In this anecdote, Diogenes plucked the feathers from a rooster, brought it into Plato's school, and said: "Here is Plato's man." Cf. https://www.laphamsquarterly.org/animals/miscellany/plato-and-diogenes-debate-featherless-bipeds. Accessed March 16, 2021.

ernity's paradoxical relationship with what Hannah Arendt called "the fundamental conditions of human existence on Earth."[4]

That Proulx conceived her novel as a critical comment on Christianity's and, by extension, Western modernity's problematic relation to "earthly nature" (Arendt 1998: 2) becomes obvious in the second epigraph. It is an excerpt from Lynn White, Jr.'s "The Historical Roots of Our Ecological Crisis," an essay originally published in *Science* in 1967, and anthologized in Cheryll Glotfelty and Harold Fromm's *Ecocriticism Reader* (1996). With this epigraph Proulx reveals herself as a writer interested in both the current condition of our material environment, and the intellectual history of human attitudes towards nature. In the paragraph Proulx selected, White speaks of the ecological damage caused by Christianity when it abandoned pagan animism and began treating non-human nature as merely an exploitable resource. "In Antiquity," White writes,

> every tree, every spring, every stream, every hill had its own *genius loci*, its guardian spirit. These spirits were accessible to men, but were very unlike men; centaurs, fauns, and mermaids show their ambivalence. Before one cut a tree, mined a mountain, or damned a brook, it was important to placate the spirit in charge of that particular situation, and to keep it placated. By destroying pagan animism, Christianity made it possible to exploit nature in a mood of indifference to the feelings of natural objects. (1967, 1996: 10)[5]

One does not have to agree with White about the sentience of all "natural objects." But his diagnosis of "indifference" touches the ecologically sore spot of modern attitudes towards nature as merely a resource for satisfying human

---

4 This is my own translation of Arendt's formulation in the "Einleitende Bemerkungen" of *Vita Activa oder Vom tätigen Leben*, first published in 1971. Distinguishing between "Neuzeit" (Arendt 1992: 12), the modern era that began at the end of the seventeenth century, and "moderne Welt" (12), the modern world that began with the nuclear age in the mid-twentieth century, Arendt writes: "... diese moderne Welt bleibt im Hintergrund meiner Erwägungen, die noch voraussetzen, daß das Grundvermögen des Menschen, die den Grundbedingtheiten menschlicher Existenz auf der Erde entsprechen, sich nicht ändern" (13). Clearly, Arendt's text precedes what we could call an Anthropocene consciousness – the realization that fundamental conditions of human existence on Earth, such as a relatively stable global climate, are currently in flux. In the original English version of her text, first published in 1958 as *The Human Condition*, the passage from which I quote elides the reference to Earth. Writes Arendt: "I confine myself, on the one hand, to an analysis of those general human capacities which grow out of the human condition and are permanent, that is, which cannot be irretrievably lost so long as the human condition itself is not changed" (Arendt 1998: 6). However, in an earlier passage of the "Prologue," Arendt had defined "earth" as "the very quintessence of the human condition," and "earthly nature" as "unique in the universe in providing human beings with a habitat in which they can move and breathe without effort and without artifice" (2).

5 This entire passage serves as one of the novel's two epigraphs.

needs. White was one of the earliest voices who called for a critique of modernity that looks at "the *presuppositions* that underlie modern technology and science" (5; emphasis added). By the time his essay was included in the *Ecocriticism Reader* as one of the ecocritical *ur*-texts, the investigation of "presuppositions," i.e. of ways of thinking and speaking about nature and the environment, had started to become the methodological center piece of the new, but rapidly growing movement of ecocriticism. In the "Introduction" to the *Ecocriticism Reader*, Glotfelty defined ecocriticism with a list of questions such as the following: "How do metaphors of the land influence the way we treat it?" (xix). A year earlier, Lawrence Buell, one of the stalwarts of American ecocriticism, observed that "environmental crisis involves a crisis of the imagination the amelioration of which depends on finding better ways of imaging nature and humanity's relation to it" (1995: 2). For Buell, the ecocritical responsibility lay in the scholar-critic's ability to (re-)discover texts whose symbolic structure and narrative preoccupations support an alternative, ecologically benign vision of the nature-culture relationship, one that would "practice restorationism by calling places into being" (267). In other words, Buell understands ecocritical work as archival and programmatic – to identify and create a canon of "environmental texts" (267) that would support the political project of ecological restoration. In contrast, White's project can be conceived as primarily diagnostic[6] – to read texts for a display of symptoms that point at the ecological flaws and errors in systems of thought, cultural practices, and philosophical presuppositions that have contributed to the current ecological crisis. This is the key to *Barkskins*, a novel that, in the end, may be cynical about literature's capacity to remedy ecological ills, but is self-confident about the diagnostic capacities of storytelling, even if the story that is being told relentlessly addresses the truth of deforestation.

The excessive, destructive use of forests as a resource is not an exclusively modern phenomenon. Nor is it solely a problem caused by the pursuit of European economic interests, at home and abroad. Long before humans became a major geological force, heralding the age of the Anthropocene,[7] forests under-

---

[6] I say "primarily" because at the end of his essay White shifts rhetorical gears towards the proscriptive when he offers Saint Francis of Assisi as a proponent of "An Alternative Christian View" (12), one that does not operate on the divine decree to "replenish the earth, and subdue it" (Genesis 1:28).

[7] With Pieter Vermeulen, I understand the Anthropocene less as a name for the current geological epoch and more as "a rubric that has, since the beginning of [the twenty-first] century, increasingly come to cluster concerns over the human impact on the planet" (2020: 8). And I agree that the "term has been undeniably productive as a catalyst for ecological concerns, and for discourses and practices through which human anxieties and aspirations are articulated" (8).

went major existential fluctuations. Far from being stable or sedentary ecological systems, they are, as historical geographer Michael Williams observes,

> a living, ever-changing, dynamic entity that is affected directly by both short- and long-term environmental changes, particularly climate, but it is also severely affected by quite minor human disturbances. Agriculture, domestication, and the control of fire have all been roughly coincident with the formation of modern forests during the last 10,000 years, and their interaction is inseparable. (2003: pos. 233)

Historically, wood is one of the oldest resources used by humans for making tools, cooking food, building shelters, vehicles, and fires, and for creating objects for symbolic purposes and ritualistic uses. In some cases, "minor human disturbances" had major societal consequences. For example, historians suggest that "the Aztec empire was on the verge of collapse from declining agriculture before European intervention, because of intense population pressure and deforestation culminating in land degradation" (Williams 2003: pos. 965). This is not to minimize the violence deployed to enforce European colonial interests but to highlight the societal vulnerability of states or empires when they neglect to take into political account the ecological and environmental conditions of their existence. At roughly the same historical moment that saw the demise of the Aztec empire and the beginning of the establishment of European settler-colonialist communities in the Americas, Chinese states seem to have developed a way of meeting the continued demand for wood by using a system of forestry that was economically viable, albeit not necessarily ecologically sustainable. About the development of what could be perceived as the early-modern prototype of a modern timber industry in China, environmental historian Ian M. Miller writes:

> By maximizing the production of quantifiable commodities like timber, tree farmers caused a clear decline in unquantified ecological goods. They destroyed or degraded habitats for commercially marginal flora and fauna, especially large mammals like tigers and elephants. (2020: 8)

China had found a way to overcome its eleventh-century wood crises by countering deforestation with "a massive *transformation*" (11) of its primary forests into tree farms, but at the expense of other environmental sectors.

More recent historical research tells a similar story about Europe and its forests. The theory that deforestation (and concomitant soil depletion) was the major cause for the decline of the ancient Greek and Roman empires – a hypothesis that was first introduced by Edward Gibbon's *History of the Decline and Fall of the Roman Empire* (1776–1789) and, in spite of its critics, was still de rigeur during much of the twentieth century (cf. Williams 2003: pos. 1588) – has become less tenable today. One of the scholars who questions the theory that deforestation led to the political predicaments of ancient Greece, and who is cited by Williams, is Classical archeologist John Bintliff. Drawing on paleo-botanical as well as archeological and climatic evidence, Bintliff raised serious doubts about the conventional wisdom that connects long-term environmental degradation of the Mediterranean with the political projects of the Greek and Roman empires. According to Williams, Bintliff argued that "pollen analysis" in the northeastern part of Aegean Macedonia,

> together with the corroborative evidence of travelers in the region during the last five hundred years, suggests that the forest could, and did, regenerate successfully; and that it was the massive clearances of the last couple of centuries with greater accessibility by road and rail that have created the present bare landscape, not the activities of the classical past. (2003: pos. 1618–1634)

In other words, while Bintliff does not deny the historical reality of deforestation during Europe's classical age, he also suggests that the damage inflicted during that era was not irreversible, and the stark, treeless landscapes of today's Mediterranean rim are the result of modern, not ancient human actions.

For the purposes of this essay, the history of deforestation must remain brief and eclectic. But it shows that independent of their cultural identity, geopolitical ambitions, and economic interests, humans, like most organisms, modify their environments. Where they differ – from each other and from other, non-human organisms – is the extent to which they go beyond the basic existential interest of securing the life of their individual and communal bodies. As soon as wood is used commercially, and trees as well as forests become "abstractions" (Miller 2020: 6) measured in board feet and marketed as timber, environmental modification runs the risk of becoming ecological devastation. While Miller's focus is on the state of forests and forestry in early modern China, the perception of forests as supplier of raw material, rather than complex ecological systems, is also characteristic of attitudes towards forests in the transatlantic West, the geopolitical and cultural region that is of interest to Proulx.

Barkskins links the history of deforestation with the transatlantic histories of feudalism, settler-colonialism, and capitalism – social, economic, and cultural systems that all are bolstered by the ideological tenets of Christianity and the scriptural decree for humanity to subdue the earth. The novel not only unfurls the environmental effects of those systems, it also confronts European and Euro-American ecological attitudes with those of North America's and New Zealand's Indigenous cultures. More specifically, Proulx offers four narrative frameworks in which she explores the consequences of cultural attitudes and socio-economic systems on the state of North America's (and the world's) forests. These frameworks are connected with individual characters, such as Monsieur Trépagny, with family groups, the Dukes and the Sels, and with the individuals and social groups indigenous to the territories Europeans and US-Americans colonize, as represented by Mari, a Mi'kmaw woman who serves as Trépagny's housekeeper and concubine and later becomes René Sel's wife, or the Maori of New Zealand, who revere the ancient kauri trees but cannot prevent their destruction by nineteenth-century English and American lumber companies. What exactly do these characters and groups of characters exemplify?

After landing in North America, René Sel and Charles Duquet have to work off their debt to Claude Trépagny, a *seigneur* in colonial New France's semi-feudal system of land tenure. For Trépagny, woodland clearing is his life's mission, one that is authorized by the joined economic interests of the King and the fur company operating on his behalf, and legitimized by ethical values of Christianity, the anthropological self-image of European civilization as the avant-garde of progress, and conventional images of white masculinity. In Trépagny's thinking, historical progress and the emergence of great civilizations presupposes deforestation. For René Sel, the logic of rigorous deforestation on which Trépagny operates is not self-evident. On their way from the landing place to their *seigneur*'s abode in the wilderness they pass several clearings. "Why do we cut the forest when there are so many fine clearings?" René asks. "Why wouldn't a man build his house in a clearing ...? Wouldn't that be easier?" (*Barkskins*: 17). To which Trépagny replies: "Easier? Yes, easier, but we are here to clear the forest, to subdue this evil wilderness" (17). Not only does he equate deforestation with being a man, he perceives it as a "necessity" and a "duty" (17). "I don't see the trees," he ends his "droning sermon" (17); "I see cabbages. I see vineyards" (17). The transformative character of Trépagny's vision is apparent, while the ecological cynicism that feeds it may go largely unnoticed. Yet it is subtly planted into the narrative bed of the novel. In this dialogical encounter between master and servant, cabbages and vineyards first and foremost represent French (culinary) culture, with Potée Lorraine (which uses cabbage as its main ingredient) and wine the two most recognizable items. But cabbages and vineyards also carry symbolic meaning, with the latter signifying imperial power and divine omnipotence (think of the expansion of the Roman empire into the northern parts of Europe that facilitated the introduction of grapevines into a new ecosystem, as well as the metaphorization of God's domain on earth as vineyards), and the former standing in for moderation and humility. Cabbage enjoys a particular historical link with cynicism, given that it was the vegetable of choice for Diogenes of Sinope, the philosopher widely considered to be the original cynic. His choice to live in the street like a dog, with only a barrel as shelter, and on a frugal diet of cabbage meant freedom from the tyranny of consumption and wastefulness that he saw thriving around him.[8]

German philosopher and historian Heinrich Niehues-Pröbsting describes cynicism as a form of social and cultural critique that emerged out of a particular historical situation, the disintegration of the ancient Greek polis (cf. 1988: 16), and by which the critic tried to preserve his individual integrity through a life of radical non-compliance. Now, all of this is far from providing an accurate picture of Trépagny. Although, like Diogenes of Sinope, Trépagny dreams of cabbages, he is far from being a critic and much more of a profiteer of French colonialism. If anything, Trépagny is a cynic in the modern sense of the word and unselfconsciously so: "A person to rail or find fault" (OED) – only that what he rails against and finds fault with is not a social or political system but an ecological one – the vastly exuberant boreal forests of North America. Like 'common' modern cynicism which, in its extreme, thinly veils its contempt for the lives of human Others, the ecological cynicism underlying the story of deforestation veils its destructiveness in the rhetoric of economic and social progress. And it captivates even those who, like René Sel and his descendants, sell their labor in the market place of extractive capitalism without profiting from the limitless exploitation of earth's material resources, but subscribe to the ideology that props up that system.

This becomes most apparent in a passage of the novel that contrasts René Sel's attitudes towards the forest with those of Mari, his Mi'kmaw wife. In spite of the fact that René's "relationship with Mari became a marriage of intelligences as well as bodies," they "stood opposed on the nature of the forest" (*Barkskins*: 50):

> To Mari it was a living entity, as vital as the waterways, filled with the gifts of medicine, food, shelter, tool material, which everyone discovered and remembered. One lived with it in harmony and gratitude. She believed the interminable chopping of every tree for the foolish purpose of "clearing the land" was bad. But that, thought René, was woman's talk. The forest was there, enormous and limitless. The task of men was to subdue its exuberance, to tame the land it grew on—useless land until cleared and planted with wheat and potatoes. It seemed both of them were subject to outside forces, powerless to object in matters of marriage or chopping. (50–51)

With this last sentence, Proulx addresses the limits of individuals to actuate change, and the indifference of deeply ingrained thoughts and ideas to social

---

[8] Diogenes is said to have claimed that "if you knew how to live on cabbage, you would not pay court to a tyrant" (cf. Goul 2019: 165), i.e. you would not be tempted to yield to the culinary pleasures or the politics of a tyrant.

and economic inequities. René Sel's position as an indentured servant disempowers the white, male European in ways not unlike those experienced by the Indigenous woman – they are both subjected to economic and social forces they do not control. Yet René's recognition of Mari as his equal does not translate into a shift in his intellectual habit of perceiving the forest as something other than a limitless resource for timber. The alternative of an ecologically mindful life in cooperation rather than in conflict with the forest remains unheeded, as does Mari's culinary, medicinal, and architectural knowledge. Mari, who thinks of "gardening" as "French foolishness" (29), is far superior in her 'mastery' of the forest not just as supplier of building material but also as pantry and pharmacy. When Trépagny's working animals, two oxen named Roi and Reine, suffer from the assault of flies and gnats, she "steeped tamarack bark in spring water and twice daily sluiced their burning eyes" (18). She builds her own *wikuom*, a bark house on Trépagny's clearing that shelters her and her children at night. Later, she shows René how to catch fish in the nearby river. And when Trépagny, who had sent Mari away to live at the nearby mission when he found a French bride, summons her back to cook his wedding dinner,

> Mari made several side forays to gather wild onions, mushrooms and green potherbs. She spent a long time searching along the river for something particular, and when she found it —tall plants with feathery leaves—she stripped off the seed heads and put them in a small separate bag. (40)

As readers, we never learn what those seeds are or what they are used for. But it is more than obvious that Mari's intimate knowledge of the forest ecology is far superior to that of the 'enlightened' Europeans. Passages like this reveal the racism inherent in modern practices of deforestation, for what is destroyed is not only an ecosystem but also Indigenous epistemologies and cultural practices such as those embodied by Mari. And they amplify the ecological cynicism that bolsters the history of colonialism and extractive capitalism. Part of that history is the marginalization of and violence against those who represent alternative interactions with forest environments. It may at times appear that *Barkskins* participates in that marginalization by not giving enough narrative space to First Nation/Indigenous actors. Yet it would be wrong to criticize the novel for simply repeating the history, or violence, of sidelining Indigenous uses of the forest. Quite the contrary, those uses appear in the novel's narrative structure as they exist in the modern imaginary more generally – as rudiments of cultural and epistemological traditions rooted in an environment that was literally steamrolled by modernity. Rather than fully appropriating an Indigenous perspective, *Barkskins* encourages the attentive reader to become an archeologist of sorts, someone who finds evidence of non-destructive, ecologically sustainable uses of the forest in a story filled with evidence of ecological prejudice and destruction.

One such alternative is suggested by the ways in which Mari interacts with the forest environment, as described above. Another presents itself in Proulx's treatment of sustainability, an idea and practice whose origin is commonly ascribed to the history of German forestry and associated with the name of Hans Carl von Carlowitz (1645–1714), but which, as environmental philosopher Jens Soentgen argues, can be traced back to the concept of *usus fructus* in Roman law (cf. Soentgen 2016). However important Soentgen's argument is historically, the exact intellectual history of sustainability is less significant for the purposes of Proulx's narrative project than its mythical presence in the popular imagination. For Mari's attitudes towards forests rhyme with those of Armenius Breitsprecher, the son of a German immigrant forester, one of the nineteenth-century characters in the novel and an employee of Duke & Sons, the lumber empire run by the descendants of Charles Duquet. Both Mari and Armenius are deeply affected by the arboreal destruction they witness, although for different reasons. Where Mari and her descendants mourn the destruction of an ecology that gave rise to their culture, Armenius laments the blindness of his own culture "where people spurned" (*Barkskins*: 475) the practice of sustainable forestry, believing that wood is a limitless, self-renewing resource.

Armenius' job is that of a "timberland looker" (361), someone who scouts woodland territories for new lumber resources. In the mid-nineteenth-century, the "glory days" (451) of the American lumber industry, Armenius is instrumental in opening up vast forests of the Michigan territory to his employers – even though he despises their ecologically ignorant, purely commercial approach to those yet unexploited woodlands. Exploring those territories with James Duke and Lennart Vogel, two members of the Duke family who perceive those forests as a "green gloom" and a space reminiscent of the "trackless immensity" (459) of the ocean, Armenius Breitsprecher becomes increasingly annoyed with the mindless ways of using up resources, both soil and wood, that "the forest took *tausend* years to make" (462). One evening, sitting at a camp fire with James and Lennart, Armenius Breitsprecher "gazed into the fire and said nothing" (466). Yet his complicity in the destruction and, ultimately, his ecological cynicism is revealed in a passage delivered in the mode of indirect thought:

> Not for the first time he saw the acquisitive hunger of Duke & Sons was so great they intended to clear the continent. And he was helping them. He hated the American clear-cut despoliation, the insane wastage of sound valuable wood, the destruction of the soil, the gullying and erosion, the ruin of the forest world with no thought for the future—the choppers considered the supplies to be endless—there was always another forest. Rapine

had been a force in the affairs of Duke & Sons since its beginnings, but with this find [in the Michigan territory] it would likely become the company's engine. (466)

For the longest time, Armenius witnesses, even participates in the "slaughter" (475) of America's boreal forests, but feels powerless to stop it. He shares with most Europeans and their American cousins the idea that the natural world exists for their benefit. But unlike the Dukes of this world, Armenius does not perceive this material and economic resource as limitless. His knowledge of "the age-old craft of forestry" (475), rudimentary as it may be – he knew it "only partially from books, his father's lectures and his own observations" (475) – creates in him an awareness that even "the fantastic complexity of the New World forest" (474) will not be resilient enough to withstand the onslaught of modernity's "acquisitive hunger" (466). Armenius' sense of frustration in light of his failure to convince his employers of the benefits of sustainable forestry eventually becomes an incentive for him to lure his German cousin, Dieter Breitsprecher, to the United States, where they establish their own lumber business built on the principles of sustainability. *Barkskins* puts the discourse of sustainability into play by associating Armenius and Dieter Breitsprecher with two of the most prominent proponents of sustainable forestry at the time, Hans Carl von Carlowitz and Johann Heinrich Cotta (1763–1844).

Armenius Breitsprecher, whose thinking was shaped by his father's fascination with the idea of using the forest and yet preserving it, often "moaned with envy" (474) when he read his cousin's letters. In one of them, Dieter, who "had studied privately with Heinrich von Cotta in Saxony" (474) and managed "a large forest" on the estate of a fictitious German aristocrat, provides his American cousin with a "description of his catalog of the forest's insects and how they affected the different species of trees, temperature diaries and rainfall measurement, boundary plantings, a coppice experiment" (474). Although Armenius is skeptical that "the fantastic complexity of the New World forest" (474) could ever be controlled or managed, he recognizes in Dieter a kindred spirit and decides to invite him "to come and see for himself the Michigan forest, a massive but innocent forest standing complete before the slaughter began" (475). Dieter accepts the invitation, relocates to America, and, together with Armenius, purchases woodland property, and starts Breitsprecher Seedlings, a tree nursery that will eventually transport the ideas of modern forestry into the twenty-first century. More on that later.

At this point it is important to note that Proulx's literary appreciation of the discourse of sustainability comes with a grain of salt – and with a pinch of sarcasm, if not cynicism. Hans Carl von Carlowitz, the man who entered the history books with his "innovative forestry manual" (Caradonna 2014: 35), *Sylvicultura oeconomica, oder haußwirthliche Nachricht und Naturmäßige Anweisung zur wilden Baum-Zucht* (1713), appears in the novel only as the name of Armenius Breitsprecher's "kurzhaar hunting dog" (*Barkskins*: 465). The historical Hans Carl von Carlowitz was a royal mining administrator in the German state of Saxony. Carlowitz did not want to protect Saxonian forests on ecological or aesthetic grounds but for economic and political purposes. Like Johann Heinrich Cotta, the founder of the Royal Saxon Academy of Forestry,[9] Carlowitz recognized that deforestation in Saxony was the result of the wide use of timber in mining operations and for fuel. Both men were pragmatists, who saw forests as an important tool to secure their state's economic security and political power. And both employed economic reasons and mathematical calculations to assess the value of a forest.[10] Proulx must have been aware of sustainable forestry's inability to escape its own entanglement in forms of ecological cynicism, and, ultimately, become an effective counterforce to practices of deforestation.

In *Forests: The Shadow of Civilization* (1992), Robert Pogue Harrison observes:

> modern forestry reduces forests to their most literal or "objective" status: timber. A new "forest mathematics" goes so far as to measure them in terms of their volume of disposable wood. Method thus conspires with the laws of economy to reappropriate forests under the general concept of "utility," even in those cases where utility is conceived in aesthetic terms: forests as recreational parks, for example, or as 'museums' of original nature. (108)

Harrison's historical narrative of modern forestry's tendency to submit forests to an anthropocentric regime of utility, sometimes in the neo-Romantic guise of preserving natural beauty and celebrating natural history, is a reason to critically assess the ecological efficacy of sustainability. Harrison's critical caution finds its literary equivalent in Proulx's tongue-in-cheek introduction of Hans Carl von Carlowitz as a dog. In *Barkskins*, the doyen of sustainability literally appears as a cynic – the *kyôn* of philosophical cynicism's Greek etymological origin. While Proulx conjures the ancient Greek tradition of performing a critical evaluation of the social, cultural, and political status quo (in *Barkskins* it is the status quo of modern capitalism's indifference towards the immediate and long-term effects of its extractive economy), and thus paying heed to sustainability's critical potential, she is also mindful of the concept's entrapment in practices that

---

9 The Royal Saxon Academy of Forestry, located in Tharandt near Dresden, was founded in 1816 and survived into the twenty-first century, existing today as part of the School of Environmental Science at the Technical University of Dresden.
10 For more detailed information on Carlowitz and Cotta see Caradonna 2014, Lowood 1990, Mauch 2014. http://ark.cdlib.org/ark:/13030/ft6d5nb455/.

keep non-sustainable forms of environmentalism well and alive. Proulx's treatment of the trope of sustainability relies on ecological cynicism's contradictory meanings: on the one hand, it is "ein Selbstbehauptungsphänomen" (Niehues-Pröbsting 1988: 367), a mode of self-affirmation, or perhaps more accurately, self-protection, which shields the cynic from becoming too vulnerable to his (or her) own powerlessness vis-à-vis "outside forces," while continuing to criticize those forces; on the other hand, sustainability can itself be understood as a form of cynical response to environmental degradation. For in the long historical perspective offered by the novel, the ideas and practices that had been around since their inception in the early modern era failed to prevent deforestation. *Barkskin*'s closing image drives home that point.

Beyond Images and Stories: Residues of Narrative Solace

In the scheme of *Barkskins*' historical narrative of environmental degradation, the ultimate culpability lies with extractive capitalism, represented by the Charles Duquets of this world. A man equipped with an "agile mind" (*Barkskins*: 68) and with an insatiable desire for "great and permanent wealth" (68), Charles "had come to New France hoping for quick riches and a return to Old France" (65). Soon after his arrival, he escapes his indentured servitude, spends time as a *voyageur*, a fur trader, and begins to "ceaselessly [work] over the question: what resource existed in this new world that was limitless, that had value, that could build a fortune?" (68). Before long he realizes that there is "one everlasting commodity that Europe lacked: the forest" (69). Accumulating enough seed capital by trading furs, Charles successfully builds the timber-producing company Duquet et Fils, which later becomes the American enterprise Duke & Sons. In the company's history, Duke & Sons moves beyond the business of logging and becomes involved in ship building, paper making, and, after the Great Depression, in the production of prefabricated houses. When Charles' great-great-granddaughter Lavinia becomes the head of the company, and the original name no longer seemed appropriate, Duke & Sons morphed into Duke Logging and Lumber. Later, after Lavinia's marriage to Dieter Breitsprecher, by that time himself a successful business man, the Dukes merge their business with the Breitsprechers, now operating under the name Duke and Breitsprecher, and eventually as Breitsprecher-Duke. Breitsprecher-Duke is finally sold to an international paper producing company as a measure to avoid a long legal battle over inheritance claims by members of a disconnected branch of the Duke family tree. "Only boxes of paper and several portraits remained of the old company. And a separate entity called Breitsprecher Seedlings" (678), the tree nursery originally founded by Armenius and Dieter Breitsprecher as a means to install the methods of sustainable forestry as the core of their lumber business.

In the narrative universe of Proulx's novel, the culprit – the Dukes lumber empire – does not survive. But neither does the forest. Yet there is a glimmer of hope in the moonlit darkness at *Barkskins*' end. It comes in the shape of Sapatisia Sel, a descendant of both René Sel and Charles Duquet, who, as a college undergraduate, develops a "burning interest in the plants and forests of the earth" (683), starts asking her Mi'kmaw grandparents "many questions about our people and old Sel stories" (684), and finally acquires a doctoral degree in plant ecology. Her ethnobotanical interest in the ecosystem of the forest and her work for a tree project connected with Breitsprecher Seedlings casts her as both the biological as well as the cultural heir of the two family histories. Proulx's narrative project symbolically culminates in the figure of Sapatisia. Metaphorically speaking, that project can be conceived as decoding modernity's genome. The double helix of its cultural DNA – with its two strands of economy and ecology – spirals around the shared axis of nature, metonymically represented in the novel as forest. The genetic information stored in this structure are the modes of thought, cultural habits, economic interests, ethical principles, political ideas, ideological preconceptions – all of which are on display to the reader, and only some of which could be made the subject of this essay. Using Sapatisia, the very embodiment of historical, cultural, and social hybridity, as a guide, Proulx takes her readers to an existential threshold. Talking to two Mi'kmaw students, Jeanne and Felix, who also turn out to be her distant cousins and who came to tap her knowledge about how to use "the old medicine plants" (696), Sapatisia telescopes more than five hundred years of environmental degradation in the Americas:

> Since the conquest the air has been filled with pesticides and chemical fertilizers, with exhaust particles and smoke. We have acid rain. The deep forests are gone and now the climate shifts. Can you figure out for yourselves that the old medicine plants grew in a different world? ... Those plants were surrounded by strong healthy trees, trees that no longer exist, trees replaced by weak and diseased specimens. We can only guess at the symbiotic relationships between those plants and the trees and shrubs of their time. (696)

As it turns out, for Sapatisia the existential threshold is a point of no return. Or is it? For in spite of her initial impatience with the students who want to tap into her knowledge of traditional medicinal plants, she invites them to join her in her project of reforestation, one that is supported by the Chicago Breitsprecher Tree Project. "My interests are overlapping ecosystems," she tells Jeanne and Felix, "the difficulties in understanding the fabric of the natural world" (697). Sapatisia has turned away from ethnobotany to ecosystems biology. As a descendant of both family lines, Sapatisia embodies the contemporary entanglement of economy and ecology, modern European and Indigenous American epistemological systems, and of the oscillation between hope and despair – despair that is created by the loss of precious botanical and ecological knowledge ("on badly degraded land we are not entirely sure what was there before the cut," 705), the violence that "forest restoration workers" (711) have to endure, by the experience "that any kind of interruption to the profitable destruction of forests invited reprisal" (711), and by seeing "the coming disappearance of a world believed immutable" (712). And yet, she does not give up the fight.

> It will take thousands of years for great ancient forests to return. None of us here will see the mature results of our work, but we must try, even if it is only one or two people with buckets of seedlings working to put forest pieces back together. It is terribly important to all of us humans—I can't find the words to say how important—to help the earth regain its vital diversity of tree cover. And the forests will help us. They are old hands at restoring themselves. (706)

Perhaps this is the ultimate expression of ecological cynicism: to know the truth about the destructive nature of modernity and continue the work of ecological restoration anyway; to acknowledge the ultimate ecological irrelevance of human work and insist on its cultural significance anyway. Ecological cynicism in this sense does not mean the self-abandonment of the human individual or of human society, but the self-abandonment of modernity and its false assumptions about the relationship between humans and earthly nature. In this sense, *Barkskins* is a perfect example of "bad environmentalism," a discursive mode detected by Nicole Seymour in "contemporary Western works that both identify and respond to the ... absurdities and ironies" of our current existence, "often *through* absurdity and irony" (2018: 4). Through irony, absurdity, and perhaps also through cynicism, these works "disrupt the binarized logic of despair/hope," and, even more importantly, they question "basic environmentalist assumptions: that reverence is required for ethical relations to the nonhuman, that knowledge" (or, one should perhaps say more precisely, scientific knowledge alone) "is key to fighting problems like climate change" (5).[11] *Barkskins* can easily fare as an ex-

---

11 Seymour's *Bad Environmentalism* is a response to a sense of despair and "emotional distress" (2) many people may experience in view of environmental crises, but also to "the negative public emotions" (shame, guilt, fear) "stoked by environmentalists" (2). As in so many other situations that evoke a sense of powerlessness, irony as a mode of (self-)distancing promises to prevent emotional as well as political and social inaction. In a similar spirit, yet without a

ample from the archive of "bad environmentalism": it is nonreverential, nonsentimental, nondidactic. And it relentlessly tells the story of deforestation as a story of ecological cynicism.

Works Cited

Arendt, Hannah. 1998. *The Human Condition*. 1958. Intro. Margaret Canovan. Chicago: The University of Chicago Press.
Arendt, Hannah. 1992. *Vita Activa oder Vom Tätigen Leben*. 1971. München: Piper.
Bringhurst, Robert and Jan Zwicky. 2018. *Learning to Die: Wisdom in the Age of Climate Crisis*. Saskatchewan: University of Regina Press.
Buell, Lawrence. 1995. *The Environmental Imagination: Thoreau, Nature Writing, and the Formation of American Culture*. Cambridge, MA: Harvard University Press, 1995.
Caradonna, Jeremy L. 2014. *Sustainability: A History*. Oxford: Oxford University Press.
Felski, Rita. 2015. *The Limits of Critique*. Chicago: The University of Chicago Press.
Glotfelty, Cheryll. 1996. "Introduction: Literary Studies in an Age of Environmental Crisis." In: Cheryll Glotfelty and Harold Fromm (eds.). *The Ecocriticism Reader: Landmarks in Literary Ecology*. Athens: The University of Georgia Press. xv–xxxvii.
Goul, Pauline. 2019. "The Pointless Ecology of Renaissance Cynicism." *The Comparatist* 43 (October 2019): 159–172.
Harrison, Robert Pogue. 1992. *Forests: The Shadow of Civilization*. Chicago: The University of Chicago Press.
Lowood, Henry E. 1990. "The Calculating Forester: Quantification, Cameral Science, and the Emergence of Scientific Forestry Management in Germany." In: Tore Frangsmyr, J. L. Heilbron and Robin E. Rider (eds.). *The Quantifying Spirit in the Eighteenth Century*. Berkeley: University of California Press.
Mauch, Christof. 2014. *Mensch und Umwelt: Nachhaltigkeit aus historischer Perspektive*. München: Oekom, 2014.
Miller, Ian M. 2020. *Fir and Empire: The Transformation of Forests in Early Modern China*. Seattle: University of Washington Press, 2020.
Niehues-Pröbsting, Heinrich. 1988. *Der Kynismus des Diogenes und der Begriff des Zynismus*. 1979. Frankfurt am Main: Suhrkamp.

---

sense for "absurdity and irony," Canadian poet Jan Zwicky writes: "To be aware that death is imminent is not to wallow in despair; it is precisely not that. … To wallow in despair that the natural world is dying is to fail to be aware that it is still, in many ways, very much alive. It is also to fail to understand that in precipitating drastic climate change and a sixth mass extinction, industrialized humans are not destroying everything. Being will be here. Beauty will be here" (Bringhurst and Zwicky 2018: 51). Zwicky's reflections do not completely avoid the risk of sounding blasé, given the inequality between those "humans" who, in one way or another, profit from environmental degradation and those who bear the physical, social, and economic brunt of such degradation. At the same time, however, she recasts "being" and "beauty" in decidedly non-anthropocentric terms.

Nixon, Rob. 2011. *Slow Violence and the Environmentalism of the Poor.* Cambridge, MA: Harvard University Press.

Proulx, Annie. 2016. *Barkskins.* 4th Estate: London.

The Letters of George Santayana, Book 2, 1910–1920. The Santayana Edition at Indiana University-Purdue University. <https://santayana.iupui.edu/wp-content/uploads/2018/12/LGS2.pdf>. [accessed 24 November 2021]

Rochester, Rachel. 2018. *Postcolonial Cli-Fi: Advocacy and the Novel Form in the Anthropocene.* Dissertation, University of Oregon. <https://scholarsbank.uoregon.edu/xmlui/bitstream/1794/23736/1/Rochester_oregon_0171A_12157.pdf>. [accessed 24 November 2021]

Rock, Lucy. 2016. "'I've had a life. I see how slippery things can be': Interview with Annie Proulx." *The Guardian*, June 5, 2016. <https://www.theguardian.com/books/2016/jun/05/annie-proulx-ive-had-a-life-i-see-how-slippery-things-can-be>. [accessed 24 November 2021]

Seymour, Nicole. 2018. *Bad Environmentalism: Irony and Irreverence in the Ecological Age.* Minneapolis: University of Minnesota Press.

Smith, Logan Pearsall. 1902, 2010. *Trivia.* Aeterna Publishing.

Soentgen, Jens. 2016. "Nachhaltigkeit als Nießbrauch: Das Römische Rechtsinstitut des *usus fructus* und seine systemantische Bedeutung für das Konzept der nachhaltigen Nutzung." *Gaia* 25:2 (2016): 117–125.

Vermeulen, Pieter. 2020. *Literature and the Anthropocene.* London: Routledge.

White, Jr., Lynn. 1967, 1996. "The Historical Roots of Our Ecological Crisis." In: Cheryll Glotfelty and Harold Fromm (eds.). *The Ecocriticism Reader: Landmarks in Literary Ecology.* Athens: The University of Georgia Press. 3–14.

Williams, Michael. 2003. *Deforesting the Earth: From Prehistory to Global Crisis.* Chicago: The University of Chicago Press.

Section Three: **Identity and the Poetics of Transgression**

Astrid Franke
Claudia Rankine's *Citizen: An American Lyric:* Fighting Microaggression, Loneliness, and Disconnection

Abstract: Through a close reading of several passages from Claudia Rankine's *Citizen*, this essay emphasizes the centrality of time in the volume. It is the reoccurrence and repetition of events that makes people realize slights as microaggression; it is the surprising timelessness of a severed hoodie that underlines how little progress may have been made in race relations, and it is the possibility to recognize history in a tennis game or soccer match that can defamiliarize the world of sports. Establishing relations through time to create insights into the mechanisms of racism is thus one of the functions of the anecdotes and artworks; the many failed communications, however, also create loneliness and a desire for connection with people.

Claudia Rankine's *Citizen: An American Lyric* reverberates with a number of current issues from 'outside' the world of poetry, such as state violence against Black persons, racism in the world of sports, and forms of microaggression amongst fairly educated and affluent people. It has thus been read and lauded as a political book, aligned to activism such as that of #blacklivesmatter (see Adams 2017 and Hill 2017). Its cover, however, already announces the importance of time and history in order to read and understand the present: It displays David Hammons' sculpture "In the Hood," depicting a severed part of a hoodie, the piece of clothing that became central to the case of Trayvon Martin, an unarmed Black teenager, who was fatally shot on February 26, 2012 because a private security guard found that he had looked suspicious while wearing it. Rankine's volume was published in 2014 and looks back at Martin's death; Hammons's artwork, however, was created in 1993. Similar to Spike Lee, who spliced scenes from his 1989 movie *Do the Right Thing* with video footage on Eric Garner's killing by a law enforcement officer on July 17, 2014, Rankine uses a loop of time to suggest that works of art containing a sensibility toward racism later seem prophetic (see Kopp 2020: 180–182). Hammons' artwork on the cover of a work remembering Martin stresses how little may have changed in the last twenty years; it also provides the comments on Martin's hoodie with a history and establishes a connection between the isolated, severed hoodie on the cover and its potentially numerous counterparts. An awareness of time, history, and its possible loops, as established through art, is crucial to understand the present situation of American citizens, the cover seems to suggest. I will therefore inquire into the role of time in *Citizen*, which I think is needed to fully grasp the notion of microaggression and the attempts in *Citizen* to (re-)connect instances and situations. What I hope to show is that the text registers often invisible social and individual costs of racism which may be understood as such only when taking time into account, individually and collectively. It also displays a desire for intimacy, a need to reconnect in order to fight feelings of self-alienation and loneliness.

Time and Microaggression

A distinctive mediation of temporal sequences is one of the recurring features of the volume. We encounter it as early as the first page of the text when we pay attention to "literary dynamics" (Perry 1979), that is, the sequence of meanings which emerge and then need to be revised: Rankine's *Citizen* begins in the lyrical mode of 'night thoughts.' Tiredness and nightfall suggest a fluid state of mind where thoughts flow freely through association in a kind of inner monologue. The second person personal pronoun, which is the predominant mode of address in the volume, is easily assimilated into this mode – it functions, at least initially, not as a form of specific address but as suggesting a state we may all know and identify with. This is why "You smell good" (*Citizen* 2014: 5) may at first be understood as part of that state and be interpreted as a statement of self-acceptance – after all, smell, as being tied to the limbic system in our brain is connected to who and what we feel attracted to or repelled by and also, as is known by literary scholars and neurologists alike, to memory. Not surprisingly, this statement is followed by a childhood memory: In elementary school, you help a little girl to cheat, this girl is white and says "you smell good and have features more like a white person" (ibid). The interpretation by the speaker is to "assume she thinks she is thanking you for letting her cheat and feels better cheating from an almost white person" (ibid). Because of the use of second person and the present tense, the phrase "you smell good" is now retrospectively reinterpreted as a white girl's phrase understood as embedded in a racist attitude. This taints the first occurrence of the phrase, suggesting that this encounter can work its way deeply into the psyche and thwart one's self-perception and self-acceptance. Later, this is explicitly formulated as an insight into human nature, "the body has a memory" (28), and the moment of disbelief at what people say is captured by "[t]he moment stinks" (9). The more immediate context of the anecdote in the volume, however, is a subsequent photograph by Michael David Murphy of a "Jim Crow Rd." in a suburban area with very white houses (6). It confirms and expands on the idea of racism as ingrained in everyday encounters between individuals and their environment. It also disambiguates the gist of the previous narrative, which left open whether the assumption about the white girl should be accepted as correct. Generally, these first two pages are characteristic of the larger part of the book which consists of miniature narratives and sometimes images set side by side, reinforcing and disambiguating each other; another section of the book switches into a different mode of essayistic writing. For the moment, however, I would like to stay with the anecdotal structure of parts I, III, IV, and VII.

In reviews and criticism of *Citizen*, the key term to describe the subject matter in these parts is 'microaggression', as discussed by Mary-Jean Chan, who praises Rankine for her "keen awareness of how linguistic injury caused by microaggression registers in the body" (2018: 1; see also Adams 2017: 63). The term has its origin in the field of psychology and therapy, and has since entered activist discourses, especially on university campuses. The references to microaggressions and to the victims of police violence anchor the volume in current discussions on racism and establish a continuum between a micro level of individual interactions and its reverberations in the individual psyche all the way to the macro level of state violence and systemic racism. Rankine does not actually use the term 'microaggression' in the volume, but she does use an important literary form the psychologists themselves have used to illustrate microaggression: the personal anecdote.

While the term dates back to the 1970s, is has been revived by Derald Wing Sue et al.'s "Racial Microaggressions in Everyday Life: Implications for Clinical Practice," published in 2007. The definition they offer is:

> Racial microaggressions are brief and commonplace daily verbal, behavioral, or environmental indignities, whether intentional or unintentional, that communicate hostile, derogatory, or negative racial slights and insults toward people of color. Perpetrators of microaggressions are often unaware that they engage in such communications when they interact with racial/ethnic minorities. [...] The power of racial microaggression lies in their invisibility to the perpetrator and, oftentimes, the recipient. (271)

The definition is, however, not complete since it leaves open how microaggression can be identified if it is so often invisible to both perpetrator and recipient. The answer is given by way of a personal anecdote, beginning with "I [Derald Wing Sue, the senior author, an Asian American] recently traveled with an African American colleague on a plane flying from New York to Boston" (1). Shortly before take-off, Sue and his colleague were asked to move to the back of the plane to distribute weight evenly. This seemed strange since three white men, also sitting in the front, had arrived after Sue and his colleague. At this point, the narrative is interrupted by a number of questions in direct speech but in the past tense, which both Sue and his colleague ask themselves, such as: "Were we being singled out because of our race?" The author then narrates his thoughts. Though he kept telling himself to drop the matter, he was unable to, and when the flight attendant approached next, he said: "Did you know that you asked two passengers of color to sit to the rear of the 'bus'?" with 'bus' in single quotes. The female flight attendant is taken aback and rejects the accusation of racism.

By focusing on the mind of the author, the anecdote is meant to primarily illustrate the painful consequences of the situation for the "victim," such as a temporary uncertainty whether his reality is more valid than hers, how to counter the perceived minimal harm of microaggression, the catch-22 of responding or not responding, both of which might make the matter worse for himself. But most unsettling is the "attributional ambiguity" suffered by Sue who is caught in a number of questions: "Did what I think happened, really happen? Was this a deliberate act or an unintentional slight? How should I respond? Sit and stew on it or confront the person? If I bring the topic up, how do I prove it? Is it really worth the effort? Should I just drop the matter?" (279).

Resuming the collective voice of the scientist in the remaining text (the anecdote is distinguished from it by a different font size), Sue et al. conclude that the flight attendant did not consciously intend to snub Sue. Statistical evidence supports the notion that there is, however, often a racial bias in supposedly well-intentioned white people that is unconscious and occurs partly due to their adherence to an ideology of so-called "colorblindness" – as may have been the case with the flight attendant. Sue reaches this conclusion because both he and his colleagues have experienced similar requests before and the situation is, for them, a non-random event. It is the accumulation of experiences that makes microaggression visible as such and thus the focus is necessarily on the mind of the victim. As Chester Pierce stated as early as 1974, "The subtle, cumulative miniassault is the substance of today's racism" (Pierce: 15).

The comparison to the scientific article sharpens our perception for some of Rankine's techniques and its effects: Like Sue, Rankine makes one side of the "perceptual clash" visible that is predominantly overlooked, namely the side of the victim. What *Citizen* can do much better than any scientific article is to focus precisely on what underlies the invisibility to the perpetrator and sometimes even to witnesses, namely the accumulation of experiences: "Almost all black-white racial interactions are characterized by white put-downs, done in an automatic, preconscious, or unconscious fashion. These mini-disasters accumulate." (Pierce: 13). A microaggression is, by definition, one in a series, and it is the accumulation of these interactions that makes a person "see" it. *Citizen* dramatizes the psychic mechanisms underlying the accumulation of experience and a gliding scale of racial aggression. To achieve the former, anecdote after anecdote together establish a mutually reinforcing context where the meanings of utterances can be disambiguated over time.

This disambiguation mainly concerns the attribution of race to victims, perpetrators and, as in some cases, witnesses. A child saying to her mother on a plane, "This is not what I expected" looking at three seats with "you" sitting in the window seat and the mother's reaction "I see, she says. I'll sit in the middle" (*Citizen*: 12) could be about all sorts of aspects of a person that a child may find unexpected and uncomfortable. Likewise, "When the waitress hands your friend the card she took from you, you laugh and ask what else her privilege gets her? Oh, my perfect life, she answers. Then you both are laughing so hard, everyone in the restaurant smiles" is not saying anything obvious about "you" and the waitress, only that the friend is somewhat privileged in a restaurant but not male. But we are led to assume that the anecdotes are all about race because of the mentioning of "Jim Crow" and "John Henryism" (11), because of unequivocal racist remarks or actions and, of course, the list of names of African Americans who have died "because white men can't / police their imagination" (135). If the anecdotes are meant to make the same point, then "you" is always a Black person, and in most cases clearly a woman; the friend is white and the waitress and child and mother also white. Or are they Latina? Or Asian? These are real possibilities, statistically speaking, but they hardly matter because the focus is, as in Sue's article, on the mind and psyche of the victim. In the scene at the restaurant, the relief of laughter follows the acknowledgment of white privilege, prompted by a poignant question and offered with graceful humor: the waitress' mistake is, after all, not the white woman's fault. More often, however, the aftermath of microaggression adds insult to injury: Not only is it painful to be overlooked, snubbed, or declassed, it is also painful not to be able to shrug it off and instead to internalize it, to ponder, and wonder: "Did this really happen?" "Who said that? She said what? What did he just do? Did she really just say that?" (63) "What did you say?" (41, 43) "Why do you feel comfortable saying this to me?" (10) "Hold up, did you just hear, did you just say, did you just see, did you just do that?" (55). We need to be reminded of this painful self-questioning because, as readers, we may not actually see and feel the ambiguity that much, as the cataloging of similar events makes them coalesce into a unifying picture. This creates a certain tension: After all, part of reading literature *as literature* is to be sensitive to, even actively searching for, ambiguity, polysemy, gaps, or incongruities. They exist in *Citizen*, too, but a number of literary means are employed to disambiguate the situations. This is the case with the most salient literary features of the anecdotes, the use of "you" and the present tense.

Contrary to what one might think, the use of "you" and the questions do not turn *Citizen* into a dialogic text: the questions are more like exclamations of disbelief and the desire for a witness. Indeed, one effect created by the second person combined with narratives in the present tense is the urge to imagine. "Imagine:" could be the introduction to each anecdote, explaining the choice of the second person singular and the present tense. In that sense, the "you" carries a function similar to that of the lyrical I in romantic poetry, such as Whitman's, in that it invites you to inhabit or 'assume' the experience depicted. Derald Wing Sue's specified "I," by contrast, only offers a personal experience as illustration of a concept and takes care not to invite readers too closely into this experience. This is in line with a skepticism as to whether understanding across ethnicity and race is possible or desirable. The article by Sue et al. is contradictory on this point: On the one hand, statements by white women, such as "As a woman, I know what you go through as a racial minority" or "I understand. As a woman I face discrimination also" are considered microaggressions by Sue et al. On the other hand, the authors suggest at the end of the article that "gender, sexual orientation, and disability microaggressions may have equally powerful and potentially detrimental effects on women, gay, lesbian, bisexual, and transgender individuals, and disability groups" (2007: 284). Remembering the confrontation of the white female flight attendant with two male scholars of color, one realizes that these intersections of race, gender, and other sources of status create ambiguous situations with regard to "who is heard/hurt" (Arghavan et al. 2019.).

Another trait of the pronoun in *Citizen* initially seems to confront this issue directly: It opens up the possibility that the experiencing person of color need not always be the same person, so that the anecdotes could be perceived as a collection of different voices. The genre of documentary has been invoked, not least by Rankine herself who said she collected these anecdotes. This opens up the possibility of "you" to be of different ethnicities, visible religions (turban, headscarf) and differently gendered – perhaps "you" in the window seat is a bulky man or a person with a disfigured face the child is scared of? But then, in addition to the references to African American history, we are introduced to the initial speaker as a Black female and are reminded of "you" as female in a number of anecdotes (5, 7, 41, 43, 45). Moreover, the genre of the lyric traditionally asks us to minimize the awareness that the speaker might be different from the author and this seems to fit when it comes to many of the socioeconomic settings: a Catholic school for girls, university campuses, travel with elite status on

United, therapy, a party at an expensive house in London. Most importantly, Rankine erases the markers of different voices to create a uniform style for all the anecdotes. It is marked by the frequency of short sentences, the absence of embellishment and any detail not immediately given significance, and a restraint with regard to judgment or closure, but clear hints as to what utterance is thoughtless and potentially a hurtful reminder of racial superiority: "A woman you do not know wants to join you for lunch. You are visiting her campus. In the café you both order the Caesar salad. This overlap is not the beginning of anything, because she immediately points out that she, her father, her grandfather, and you, all attended the same college" (*Citizen*: 13). As a result of the uniform style, the initial notion of an interior monologue and an autobiographical mode as in night thoughts is reinforced. The present tense as the usual tense for these two genres (cf. Cohn) supports this notion too, but the present tense has yet another function: as the tense used for statements about timeless truths or, if you prefer, for findings by scholars, scientists, or cultural critics, it facilitates the transition from narrative into essay. This transition is most effectively used in part II which analyses and interprets Serena Williams' verbal outbursts as an accumulation of experiences of racism on the tennis court. This essay begins with a discussion of the use of anger in Black art and then switches to "you" watching various tennis matches, beginning in 2009 and then in another time loop, going back to 2004, from where the "you" goes forward to explain Williams's open expression of anger in 2009. It is in this context we read, in the manner of statement and thus explication of the initial passages: "Yes, and the body has memory." The essay and its tense, like the image of "Jim Crow Rd.," affirms our earlier interpretations and in another loop, links the anecdotes to Serena's experience: We understand that the accumulation we have witnessed as readers and are now aware of is what is likely to have happened to Serena Williams as well.

The Accumulation of Collective Experience

The essay on Williams and the script for the Situation Video "October 10, 2006 / World Cup," as two texts about events in the world of sports, hold a special place in the volume because they are about visible reactions to accumulated racist incidents. While "you" in the anecdotes is remarkably composed and measured in her reactions even though her swallowing of anger and disbelief seems to make her sick, Williams and Zidane, as interpreted in the essay and script, finally react with righteous anger in a gendered way: Williams primarily through words and gestures, Zidane with an act of physical aggression that brings his opponent to the ground. But the script on Zidane is also important because it is central in connecting a present moment to history. Contemporary history is also present, of course, in the artwork on the cover as described above; the more distant past of slavery is alluded to in William Turner's *The Slave Ship* (*Citizen*: 160–161) and of the Jim Crow era in the lynching photograph with the Black body erased so you focus on the white crowd (91). The most challenging one, however, is the script on the encounter between Zinedine Zidane and Marco Materazzi in the final game of the world cup, France against Italy.

In 8x6 frames accompanied by a collage of quotes, the script charts the build-up to Zidane's famous headbutt, as a reaction to something Materazzi continued to say and that a number of lip readers have tried to reconstruct. What you see in very slow motion, or when looking very closely at the very small frames reproduced in the book, is that Zidane is initially walking away, pausing, then again trying to walk away before he suddenly turns around and butts the Italian. Above and below the strips of frames are quotes from, amongst others, Maurice Blanchot, Ralph Ellison, Frantz Fanon, William Shakespeare, James Baldwin, the lip readers who reconstructed the presumed defamatory words, and Zidane himself. These comments create a historical lineage of the situation which also, as a time loop, makes literature seem prophetic of the present situation on the soccer field because it actually records a timeless phenomenon – it is as old as Shakespeare's 17th century drama *Othello* whose protagonist is quoted as saying "Let him do his spite" in the (mistaken) belief that achievement may trump over racism. And it cannot only be found across time but also across space in Africa or America, where insulted men attempt to control their rage and the fantasies of revenge, as described by Fanon and Baldwin. While the assumed insult, as suggested by lip readers, is repeated, however, there comes a point where Zidane turns toward the Italian and this turning point is accompanied by Frederick Douglass's account of the moment where he turned from slave to man, as he put it: "But at this moment – from whence came the spirit I don't know – I resolved to fight; and, suiting my action to the resolution..." (*Citizen*: 128). The phrase turns the headbutt into a heroic act of demanding recognition as a man, one that Rankine sums up through a quote from James Baldwin: "This endless struggle to achieve and reveal and confirm a human identity, human authority, contains, for all its horror, something very beautiful" (128).

The present situation is filled with accumulated history: the agents before us are not just themselves but also representative of a collective history and pain. This, as one realizes only after having read the entire sequence, is the meaning of the initial quote by Maurice Blanchot: "Something is there before us that is neither the living person himself nor any sort of reality, neither the same as the one who is alive, nor another" (122). Earlier in the volume, the idea of a "historical self" (14) is brought up by one of the many friends mentioned in a short text that merges, through its employment of "you," the voice of the friend with that of our speaker so that the status of the thesis is held at arm's length. With this term and its enactment in the video on Zidane, the volume comes closest to the terminology by Pierre Bourdieu who would consider "micro-aggression" as a form of "symbolic violence" and hold that both perpetrator and victim are each locked into their interrelated habitus which persists through history. Like a dance, it is a form of interaction where both parties act according to a choreography none of them has invented, yet they recognize the prompts and cannot but react accordingly. As a "gentle violence, imperceptible and invisible even to its victims," it reminds both sides of the power relation between them, without the "intention" (as in conscious goal) of one and "consent" (as in conscious agreement) of the other (see Bourdieu 2001: 1; see also Buschendorf 2018).

The script expands upon much that has been said so far: The memory of the body transcends the individual and reaches back in time; the stored up anger and hurt may make you sick but also find a way out in different forms of achieving, revealing and confirming a human identity; in order to make visible the connections between individual experiences in one life or over the course of history, we need to reduce the complexity and diversity of each encounter, as I have shown above in a reconstruction of the reading process; likewise we are asked to accept that Zidane may have something in common with Frederick Douglass even though, surely, a soccer field is not a plantation. Or is it? The reason the script is challenging is that we either reduce Douglass to the quote about the resolution to fight – which makes the connection to Zidane easy to see – or we allow all our knowledge of Douglass into the picture and see in Zidane a "modern slave": In both cases, we have strongly reduced Douglass to "fit" Zidane. It highlights again the tension between the literariness of the text that (re-)produces the ambiguities and complexities of human encounters and the simultaneous urge to contain or constrain multiple possibilities, to flatten them so that the encounters, even over centuries, fit into recurrent patterns of racism and the fight against it. This way, the repetition of similar incidences in the volume can reveal a historical pattern of domination in which actors such as Zidane and Materazzi as well as "you" and everyone "you" encounter, act not only as individuals but as manifestations of dominated and dominator. Zidane, like Douglass before him, is caught in an interaction he does not fully intend, let alone control. This is also true for Sue with his verbal outburst on the plane, but also for the flight attendant and many other participants in the less spectacular interactions of *Citizen*. If we accept this as working not only through the history of colonizer and colonized or master and slave, but also through gender, age, religion, sexuality, or disability, we realize how most of our everyday interactions are navigations of power relations. Especially in diverse environments, such as

American university campuses, trains and airplanes, in restaurants or at parties, in the world of sports or art – the settings of *Citizen*'s anecdotes – we have to expect meeting people whose "historical self" (*Citizen*: 14) is prone to be hurt by something we might say or do – and vice versa. To be mindful of that, we seem to need a new form of communication. Commenting on microaggression at Harvard, Henry Louis Gates said: "We're talking about people in close contact who are experiencing the painful intersections of intimacy, [...] The next part of that is communication, and this is a new form of communication" (qtd. in Vega 2014: n. pag.). *Citizen* makes us painfully aware of that need which has not been met. For it is all very well to understand people as shaped by centuries of privilege or oppression and therefore downplaying conscious intent – but what is the meaning of an apology then? How can a socio-historical understanding of everyday racist interactions help people get along without assuming intention, agency, and accountability? "I am sorry," says the trauma therapist after a traumatic encounter based on her racist prejudice. "I am so sorry, so, so sorry" (*Citizen*: 18). As so often in the volume, this is followed by silence as an end of communication.

Alienation and Craving for Intimacy

The book conveys, effectively I think, how collective historical experience and individual experience over a life-span register and accumulate in the embodied psyche. Both body and psyche suffer: the suspicion of perhaps feeling too much leads to endless self-questioning and questioning of others which, in turn, leads to more questions and disappointing answers and this is, literally and metaphorically, sickening. Not only does it lead to an inability to relate to oneself lovingly, as in the episode on smell, it also hurts precisely because it endangers and often ends friendships and assumed intimacy across race. To counter these severed relations, Rankine also establishes surprising connections through, for instance, intertextuality. "Words work as release" (*Citizen*: 69) suggests the beginning of part V. In what seems perhaps an unexpected literary dialogue, the speaker in this part of the book repeatedly alludes to Robert Lowell, perhaps even addresses him: "Your ill-spirited, cooked, hell on Main Street, nobody's here, brokendown, first person could be one of many definitions of being to pass on" (72) talks to the Lowell-figure in "Skunk Hour" as the last poem in *Life Studies*: "I hear / my ill-spirit sob in each blood cell [...] I myself am hell; / nobody's here –" (Lowell: 90) and a couple of lines further down, "Listen, you, I was creating a life study of a monumental first person, a Brahmin first person" (*Citizen*: 73) might be Lowell as imagined by Rankine talking back to her. As artists, the two have more in common than one may think as they both feel the strain of living registering in their bodies and minds, they share symptoms of feeling cut off and lonely, and they both render their mental health problems as representative of a moment in history to which they constantly allude (cf. Franke 2019) – it is not the same history, though. Lowell, of course, uses the first person for his confessional mode, but "Drag that first person out of the social death of history, then we're kin" (72).

Intertextuality is but one instance of seeking, discovering, and re-establishing connections, even intimacy in odd moments, perhaps to make up for the many thwarted communications and friendships. That they involve white men – the group furthest away in the hierarchy of power from a Black woman – shows how much of an effort is behind the project of recording severed conversations but also of discovering surprising emotional relations in them: There is, for instance, the encounter with a stranger who referred to boisterous teenagers at Starbucks with a racist slur. In the ensuing exchange, you discover that "repeating this stranger's accusation in a voice usually reserved for your partner makes you smile" (16). Calling out someone's racism may create a sudden intimacy that is surprising. There is also "a novelist with the face of the English sky" at a party in London who becomes a new friend and prompts the important question "How difficult is it for one body to feel the injustice wheeled at another?" (116). In these passages, the text implies a careful optimism that readers may indeed feel the injustice of another and develop a kind of awareness, sensibility and reflexivity that the volume itself displays. The hope springs from a craving for intimacy which becomes valuable and rare when communication, especially with friends who so often fail to say something or say the wrong things, or look the wrong way, is so precarious. The pain of so many "mini-disasters" (Pierce: 13) emphasizes the need for people to connect, to share experiences, to feel kinship, to laugh together, to be included in a scope of caring "vigilance" (149) and to be loved. Love means, as the final interaction of the book suggests, to be embraced while telling one's story – literally and metaphorically.

Works Cited

Adams, Bella. 2017. "Black Lives/White Backgrounds: Claudia Rankine's *Citizen: An American Lyric* and Critical Race Theory." *Comparative American Studies: An International Journal*, 15.1–2: 54–71.

Arghavan, Mahmoud, Nicole Hirschfelder, Luvena Kopp and Katharina Motyl (eds.). 2019. *Who Can Speak and Who is Heard/Hurt: Facing Problems of Race, Racism, and Ethnic Diversity in the Humanities in Germany*. Bielefeld: transcript.

Bourdieu, Pierre. 2001. *Masculine Domination*. Trans. by Richard Nice. Stanford: Stanford University Press.

Buschendorf, Christa. 2018. "Introduction: Key Concepts of Relational Sociology as Tools of Hermeneutics." In: Christa Buschendorf (ed.). *Power Relations in Black Lives: Reading African American Literature and Culture with Bourdieu and Elias*. Bielefeld: transcript. 11–34.

Chan, Mary-Jean. 2018. "Towards a Poetics of Racial Trauma: Lyric Hybridity in Claudia Rankine's *Citizen*." *Journal of American Studies* 52.1: 1137–1163.

Cohn, Dorrit. 1978. *Transparent Minds. Narrative Modes for Presenting Consciousness in Fiction*. Princeton: Princeton University Press.

Franke, Astrid. 2019. "Revisiting Robert Lowell's Mental Hospital Poems." In: Thomas Austenfeld (ed.). *Robert Lowell in a New Century: European and American Perspectives*. Rochester: Camden House, 2019.

Hill, DaMaris. B. 2017. "Mirrors and Windows: Black Poetry in this Era." *American Studies* 55.4 / 56.1: 207–219.

Kopp, Luvena. 2020. "Towards a Black Prophetic Critique of Neoliberal State Violence: Spike Lee's *Do the Right Thing* and the Death of Eric Garner." In: Andrew Dix and Peter Templeton (eds.). *Violence from Slavery to #BlackLivesMatter: African American History and Representation*." New York: Routledge. 175–192.

Lowell, Robert. 1956. *Life Studies and For the Union Dead*. New York: Farrar, Straus & Giroux.

Perry, Menakhem. 1979. "Literary Dynamics: How the Order of a Text Creates Its Meanings [With an Analysis of Faulkner's 'A Rose for Emily']." *Poetics Today* 1.1–2: 35–64; 311–361.

Pierce, Chester. 1974. "Psychiatric Problems of the Black Minority." In: Silvanio Arieti (ed.). *American Handbook of Psychiatry*. Vol. II. New York: Basic Books. 512–523. <https://www.freepsychotherapybooks.org/ebook/psychiatric-problems-of-the-black-minority/>. [accessed 24 November 2021]

Rankine, Claudia. 2014. *Citizen: An American Lyric*. Minneapolis: Graywolf Press.

Sue D.W.; Capodilupo C.M.; Torino G.C.; Bucceri J.M.; Holder A.; Nadal K.L.; Esquilin M. 2007. "Racial microaggressions in everyday life: implications for clinical practice." *American Psychologist* 62: 271–286.

Vega, Tanzine. "Students See Many Slights as Racial 'Microaggression.'" *New York Times*, March 21, 2014. <https://www.nytimes.com/2014/03/22/us/as-diversity-increases-slights-get-subtler-but-still-sting.html>. [accessed 24 November 2021]

Andrew S. Gross
Ellen Hinsey: Poet of the Public Sphere

Abstract: This article explores how Ellen Hinsey moves from lyricism towards aphorism in her efforts to create a poetry of the public sphere. She is concerned with who we are but also, and perhaps more crucially, how we interact. Hinsey's last three books of poetry trace a journey of lyrical form (which is not the same as a lyrical journey) away from identity (considered as both personal selfhood and group membership), through passion in order to embrace a very public form of compassion. Passion is intimate. Compassion is a communal feeling. Aphorism, in Hinsey, becomes its voice.

In 1996 Ellen Hinsey won the Yale Series Award for her first collection of poems *Cities of Memory*, which in part commemorates the fall of the Berlin Wall and the Velvet Revolution in Prague. Since the "end of history," as the end of communism was then called, she has quietly published three volumes of poetry, a book on the rise of illiberalism in Eastern Europe, a long conversation-biography with the Lithuanian poet Thomas Venclova, along with translations of his poetry and other works into English. I say "quietly" because Hinsey's verse responds to a history that decidedly did *not* end, in ways that have caught critics unawares. There has been little discussion of her turn from the first-person conventions of confessional poetry towards what she describes as the "more generous I" of "shared human experience" (Hinsey 1998: 143). Nor has there been adequate recognition that this turn has a purpose. Hinsey has moved away from confessional lyricism in an attempt to find a verse form more congenial to the public sphere, which seemed to be expanding in the Europe of the 1990s, but has since shown signs of strain, fragmenting into smaller groups, including identity-based groups vulnerable to manipulation by illiberal autocrats (Hinsey 2017a: 14–15; Hinsey 2017b: 383). Hinsey's poetics, like her politics, affirm the importance of the public. She is concerned with who we are but also, and perhaps more crucially, how we interact. Her last three books of poetry trace a journey of lyrical form (which is not the same as a lyrical journey) away from identity (considered as both personal selfhood and group membership), through passion in order to embrace a very public form of compassion. Passion is intimate. Compassion, in Hinsey, is a communal feeling—not for the lover needing devotion, or the group demanding loyalty, but for the neighbor deserving justice or forgiveness. Hinsey's pluralistic poetry makes its emotionally compelling case for justice at a moment in history her most recent book of verse calls *The Illegal Age*.

Illegality poses a serious threat to any conception of justice. It also poses formal problems to compassionate verse. There is a sense, of course, in which illegality validates the lyric as a poetic form. This is because lyrical poetry testifies to passion, whether it be love or lament, and needs no laws but its own; its nomos is pathos. However, absent any legal framework that might provide an actionable basis for testimony, pathos does not bring about justice except in any but the most private, cathartic sense. Since private justice is not really justice at all, Hinsey approaches testimony compassionately, from the outside in, elaborating the social and civic structures that make selfhood possible before returning to the travails of the self. Her guides here are Hannah Arendt, who emphasizes the public context of personal action, and Simone Weil, who turns to aphorism as a compassionate literary form. In Hinsey, aphorism is to personhood what lyricism is to the personal; aphorism articulates the conditions that allow the "lyrical I" to speak. In what follows, I will explore the genesis and the significance of Hinsey's aphoristic style by showing how her poetry moves from confession to compassion in *The White Fire of Time* (2002), *Update on the Descent* (2009), and *The Illegal Age* (2018).

1 The Insomniac Ego

In 1998, Hinsey published "The Rise of Modern Doggerel," a critique of confessional-style lyricism, then in its fourth decade of popularity and still going strong. She argued that the self-absorption always evident in confessional verse was undermining the relevance of a younger generation of poets preoccupied with finding therapeutic means for coming to terms with personal suffering (141). While Hinsey has no qualms about treating poetry as therapy, she does see two problems with the confessional style: first, it is a style, and therefore not as personal as it seems; and second, it closes itself off to the outside world. She turns to Czesław Miłosz for support on both points, quoting his observation that certain poetic schools reflect an "automatism of opinions and beliefs" (140, 143). Her philosophical authority at this stage is Martin Buber: any "I" that does not include a "thou" reduces itself and others to objects (142). She also turns to Simone Weil, whose aphoristic style will ultimately prove as influential as her philosophical insights, to argue that affliction can be a "gift," linking us to others in our shared human condition (143). Poetry is a form of communication that can bring people in contact with each other, even when they are in pain. Hinsey thus advocates turning from confessional self-absorption to the more "generous 'I'" of "shared human experience" (143). The essay ends with Adrienne Rich's call in "In Those Years" to look up from the "I" and pay attention to the "birds of history" (144).

History will be linked to flight and transcendence in Hinsey's most optimistic poetry, though it becomes increasingly "reptant" in her subsequent books, slouching from catastrophe to catastrophe, until she remarks in the last line of *The Illegal Age* that "History, it has been reported, is tired" (112). In Hinsey's idiosyncratic usage, history is less a record of events than an index of compassion, measuring the ability of her speakers to overcome personal concerns and place themselves in relation to a plurality of others. Heinz Ickstadt emphasizes the rapt, ecstatic aspect of this compassion and its sensuous materiality: "Hinsey tries to avoid the trap of subjective speech by creating a voice that, although personal, is trans-subjective, a meditative voice bent in rapt contemplation on things in their sensuous existence, on consciousness and texts—religious, philosophical and psychological—that deal with ultimate matters: the body the passions, language, mortality and time" (2016: 201). The later poetry, I will argue, moves away from rapt contemplation towards a more measured look at the public sphere. It is this measured look that confronts the real possibility of public collapse. The "tiredness" of history, lamented in Hinsey's more recent work, marks a failure of the trans-subjective, a falling away from compassion into the traps of egotism, identity, and tribalism.

In *The White Fire of Time* (2002), the central image of verticality (the opposite of tiredness) is the "Celestial Ladder" in the prose poem and the section bearing its name. The significance of "The Dream of the Celestial Ladder" is reaffirmed by its position at the center of the book, which is structured bilaterally, with poems in the second half reiterating the themes and forms of those in the first (see Hinsey's final note to the volume [91]). The celestial ladder is anatomically the spine of a collection that stresses its materiality as a book – something I will return to in a moment. It is structured as a dialogue, which allows Hinsey to use a series of interrogative prompts to interject what is otherwise a rarity in her verse: a lyrical "I" answering questions posed by an interlocutor. This "I" stands almost alone in a book otherwise notable for its rejection of first-person pronouns, but it stands alone in order to disappear. The answers show the speaker climbing the rungs of the celestial ladder away from egotism, beyond violent passion to compassion, observing from her elevation "tiny human forms preparing their revenge, defiling the house of their brothers with their bloodshed" (61). This journey from passion to compassion will be repeated in all three books of poetry, as the speaker tries to achieve a heavenly vantage from where she can regard "the totality of history," and "hear the weight of things and be a thing among them" (ibid). Synesthesia – "hearing weight" – is a figure of sympathy in this poem. The speaker "speaks" through her material position in a sequence; her voice is a chime that reverberates with the gravity of the things surrounding it. The emotion they reverberate is fear (62).

The presence of fear in heaven suggests that it is not a place of eternal peace. This in turn indicates that the celestial ladder does not play a strictly religious role in Hinsey's verse (something she discusses in her exchange with Venclova about his use of "Jacob's ladder" in *Magnetic North* [380]). In her notes to *The White Fire of Time*, Hinsey points to the "many written and graphic depictions of the ascent of the Celestial Ladder," drawing particular attention "to the appearance of the ladder in the form of an inverted cross with numerous transecting beams, an ancient symbol of the soul's pilgrimage from earthly existence towards paradise" (90). In the next book this symbol will suggest not the ascent to heaven but the "descent from the cross, a moment understood in the context of this book as one of doubt and moral eclipse, or what the German critic Heinz Ickstadt has called 'the bottom of history'" (*Descent*: 89). In the unorthodox use Hinsey makes of this mystical symbol, these directions are not at all contradictory; transcendence involves an expanded awareness of the vulnerability that afflicts all people; an elevated perspective reveals the immanence of fear and grief. Thus, a poem about the patriarch Jacob, who dreamed his own dream of a celestial ladder, depicts his equally famous "Struggle with the Angel" as "the internal struggle of the self with consciousness," as Hinsey puts it in her notes (*White Fire*: 89–90). Jacob, presented as a kind of everyman, has to tear himself away from instrumental calculations like tallying grain to confront his personal anxieties (46). This existential rewriting of a religious story both secularizes spirituality and firmly locates selfhood in a welter of everyday, material concerns.

The materiality of this perspective launches Hinsey on a journey towards the body that is also a journey of lyrical form, moving away from the first-person preoccupation with consciousness and thought towards a recognition of the body and ultimately the plurality of bodies that constitute the public sphere. At first, the orientation is strictly corporeal: "thought, not body, is sin" (44). This pronouncement is from a poem "On the Story of Cain and Abel," which depicts "the mind, spite-harborer" as the ancient source of strife—hence the anachronistic use of kenning. Brother killing brother, like Jacob wrestling himself, is described as a "Temptation—to indulge in difference" (44). Even "temptation" turns out to be too weak a word since a few lines later, thinking and fratricide are compared to a cell splitting in two. Division is natural, and fear an indelible part of our fallen state, except that Hinsey pushes violence back into the Garden, before original sin. Knowing the difference between good and evil turns out to be an ancillary problem; the source of trouble is knowing (equating with *no*-ing or negating) anything at all. A poem about Adam naming the animals suggests that language, because it imposes differences between words and their objects, is intrinsically flawed; Adam turns his face from God's in shame "for he knew his swift / Tongue flawed and approximative—it alone / Lacked the precise, assured syntax of flight" (35). Adam naming the animals is like Jacob counting grain, and both are preludes to the killing of sons and brothers. Hinsey's biblical figures fall back to the horizontal the moment they think or speak. There is a sense in which humans were always fallen, and history tired before it could properly get started.

Nevertheless, Hinsey imagines a way beyond division that is also a way beyond egotism. The key is not to struggle with the self but to abandon it to erotic passion. In a programmatic "fragment" called "On the Origins of Consciousness," the "I" that "was unable to retain even one full instant of being" turns to "love's arbor" as the "only hope of fulfillment": "*Simply that*, the *I* argued—casting before it its long, thin shadow: the desire to lie down with *You* under its wild, forked lightening" (12). Another poem opposing body to thought, "On A Miniature from the Sacred Ark," is an aubade in which Eve addresses Adam; she praises his body, their passion, and the mutual "wish for eternity," which is the desire to "hide another / Night from knowledge" (37). Eternity here is not an infinite expanse of time; it only lasts until daybreak – the conventional problem in any aubade. Still, the ecstasy depicted in this, as in the other erotic poems of the collection, does transcend the limits of the self, establishing a bond of sympathy between cell and cell, *I* and *you*. "For that which the body loves, it wishes to make its own—and so between you, in the air, there rose bridges of sympathy, tying simple cell to cell and simple breath to breath" (74). Love thus provides a temporary solution to the violence of thought, revenge, and division. It also helps the poet escape "The prison of self-consciousness. Insomnia of the ego" (27). This is the erotic expression of the rapture Ickstadt mentions in his account of Hinsey's early poetry.

If *White Fire* culminated in love poems it would be a very different book. However, Hinsey is too wise to accept romantic love as a solution to isolation and division: "Wisdom is knowledge to which one has been forced to submit" (79). Her collection submits to the knowledge that love, which does not last, only forms one rung on a celestial ladder. In a poem entitled "From the Book on the Nature of Things," which contains the line on "the prison of self-consciousness," another entry entitled "*Maturity of Sorts*" enjoins readers to keep climbing: "To abandon simplicity and climb the tilted ladder of paradox" (29). Why is paradox tilted? Transcendence is not "simply" a matter of elevated passion, but a coefficient that moves up as it travels along a lateral axis of corporeality and grief. Grief, as Hinsey learns from Weil, can open the self to others, and it interpolates a horizontal element of suffering into the heavenly aspirations of the more mystical poems. In "Commentary: On the 13 Rungs of Sorrow," the ascent or descent of the rungs (the direction is unclear) involves some unnamed crime and trial. This poem is important enough to contain the phrase that names the entire collection, and it poses a challenge to erotic passion in its description of what happens after nightfall: "Courage is lost in the wild dark hours when chaos swirls, and face to face with the abyss, you near the white fire of time" (79). "The white fire of time" lights up the dark night of the soul, involving a different kind of passion and demanding another kind of bodily response, one attributed to another *you* standing in for another personal *I:* "You learn that the body in grief is privileged, and called to enter, in its rags, the immaculate garden of compassion" (79). The "immaculate garden of compassion" is not Adam and Eve in the bower, nor is it the prize for wrestling with the angel. The verse is pointing somewhere else, and it seems to be coming from a different place as well. An unnamed tragedy lies behind much of Hinsey's poetry, motivating its flight from passion to an awareness of common travail. Even the love lyrics contain elements of grief.

The similarly named "Thirteen Aphorisms on the Nature of Evil" addresses the transformation involved in moving from grief to compassion, here explored through a similar contrast between thought and action. The key metaphor is a material object that also helps explain the shift in poetic form – from lyric to aphorism – announced in the title: "The brave make a place at their table for Evil. For only first-hand knowledge of evil can transform meditation into action" (49). Why a table? In her notes Hinsey explains that *White Fire* is modeled on a concept proposed by Hannah Arendt in *The Human Condition:* the Vita Contemplativa (91; see Arendt 1998: 304). Arendt's preferred image for the public sphere in that book is the table, which holds people together by keeping them apart. The table is the material instantiation of a pattern of human interaction.[1] By assigning evil a place setting, the poem moves from Vita Contemplativa to Vita Activa, contemplation to action, shifting its focus from personal reflection to the material relations that define the presence of evil in a community. The other aphorisms provide an etiology of personified evil, which "loves its own innocence" and "the shape of the human hand;" they also stress the materiality of evil, its operation in actual human environments. Hinsey's other material metaphors, including the ladder, move in the same direction — away from abstraction and

---

[1] "To live together in the world means essentially that a world of things is between those who have it in common, as a table is located between those who sit around it; the world, like every in-between, relates and separates men at the same time. The public realm, as the common world, gathers us together and yet prevents our falling over each other, so to speak." (Arendt 1998: 52)

self-absorption, towards human activities and relations. Her subsequent books will replace these concrete images with even more concrete historical case studies. However, the urge towards concrete renditions of the public sphere is there from the very beginning, manifesting itself, for instance, in the material organization of her books, which are difficult to describe or reproduce through citation because of the way they use the layout of the codex as a bound and spatially organized *thing*. The books are more than collections: the interplay of section titles, poem titles, and poetic forms draws attention to a tangibility that in turn evokes something tangible about the public sphere. Sections bear titles like Commentary, Dialogue, Notebook, Correspondence, Chronicle, Annals, Internal Report, Investigation File, and Confidential Documents, which are classifications of how texts circulate, or are prevented from circulating, in the public sphere.[2] These are pointedly not terms of art like sonnet or sestina that refer to established literary forms. Like the concrete images and later the case studies, they reflect on the materiality of human interaction, including the materiality of evil, in order to turn Hinsey's writing into a vehicle for public voice. Lyrical poetry, modeled on the soliloquy and often described as "speech overheard," is *always* confessional insofar as it involves a public demonstration of privacy. Aphorism strives to put words in everyone's mouth. If lyrical poetry is the "first-hand knowledge" that has a seat at the table, aphorism is the table as sounding board.

2 *Descent* – Into the Human Element

Evil is inhuman but not unhuman. Man is the wolf to man. Hinsey's next book traces the origins of inhumanity through "Our everyday descent into the human element" (*Descent*: 28). The poem "Preparation for the Descent" invokes a journey metaphor to take us along a "rugged incline that was once said to lead up to Paradise" (27–28). The path no longer goes up like a ladder, and this book has all but abandoned the transcendent notion of history. The reference is to *The Divine Comedy*, but Hinsey finds Dante's pilgrimage to be immaterial to salvation: "But, you have read this before. From the start, you have known you can always just turn the page" (28). The book metaphor is both a reflection on Hinsey's carefully organized collections and a rejection of the eschatological story arc. Hinsey urges us to confront the human and material rather than the religious aspects of

---

[2] Michael Warner, building on Arendt and other theorists of the public sphere, argues that "the social imaginary of publics" tends to take the form of "a relation among strangers projected from private readings of circulating texts" (2002: 116).

evil ("The real journey is stranger"). By "descent" Hinsey does not mean to imply that she has abandoned the celestial ladder for negative theology: she does not represent life as unmitigated hell or attempt to approach the divine through its opposite. Rather, she questions the usefulness of the *celestial* aspect of the ladder for understanding moral categories. "Evil," as she points out in an interview, "is an entirely human affair, and is an ethical rather than a theological category. If we, as human beings, choose to carry out atrocities, then these acts are a reflection of our own nature" ("Interview").

What, then, is human nature in *Update on the Descent?* The title hints at Darwin and perhaps an instinctual source of violence; but Hinsey's account of humanity has less to do with the theory of evolution than with the politics of how human beings make and unmake their world. The concept of world-making comes from Arendt. Hinsey provides a concise version of Arendtian world making in an aphorism whose tone stands out in this largely pessimistic book: "Optimistic Postulate: Despite its homelessness, the Self can find sanctuary in the eternal *Now*—the ever-renewing instant of *world* and *other*" (47). If *White Fire* seeks rapturous solutions to the problem of suffering, *Update on the Descent* turns to politics, and more specifically to the basic political distinction between the public and the natural world. Arendt characterizes the natural world as cyclical, seasonal, repetitive, and governed by cause and effect (1998: 19). Humans liberate themselves from causality when they gather into publics, creating a space for free activity that did not exist before (Arendt 1998: 175–178). This freedom is self-generating – a collective pulling up by the bootstraps – but it is not spiritual, meaning it has nothing to do with a personal relation to the divine. People gather into publics in order to bear witness to memorable words and deeds, thereby creating the space in which such deeds can be performed (Arendt 1998: 54–58; 176–178). Arendt's formulation, like Hinsey's aphorism, is classical in its emphasis on recognition: there is no virtue without a witness.

Violence is also uniquely human, but it transforms spectators into props: people are no longer called upon to bear witness to memorable deeds – or to perform them – but are degraded into means to achieving someone else's ends (Arendt 1998: 151, 156, 199–207; Arendt 1972: 141). Violence is instrumental, which means it is causal but not natural, and it transforms the public sphere in ways that can require a great deal of criminal ingenuity. Hinsey follows the route of violence through the human collectivities it negates, insisting, all the time, that violence is human in its ability to destroy the free space of interaction: "Instinct is as puzzled as the rest of us about the existence of secret military prisons and mass graves" (*Update*: 26).[3] Violence might try to justify itself by appealing to human nature, but this is mythology; it is really a goal-driven application of force that exploits human connections in order to turn people into things. In "An Intimate History of the Hand," which builds on a remark about Evil's predilection for the hand in "Thirteen Aphorisms" (*White Fire*: 48), Hinsey looks to the uniquely human appendage as the metaphor – and means – of dehumanization. The first line subtly recalls Auden's remark about suffering in the "Musée des Beaux Art":

> 1. Condition
> About the Hand, nothing has changed. When its moment comes, it is deferential and compliant.
> ...
> 8. Comment
> The Hand's logic has always been fed by suspect mythologies.
> 9. Means
> The Hand appreciates convenience: a stone or club fits nicely.
> 10. Intention
> But the Hand loves best the close, direct blow. There it can witness the blood rise, and the eyes close.
> ...
> (6–7)

The role of "suspect mythologies" in this etiology of the blow emphasizes the difference between violence and nature, red in tooth and claw. Violence can be motivated by stories and is itself a perverse mode of storytelling – a way of using people as raw material. Tribal violence follows the same symbolic "logic," though there are limits to the stories that can be told using other people's bodies: "The Tribe is ever surprised before the *other's* broken body—by the eternal *sameness* of its blood" (45). Violence does not constitute a public but moves through publics; the story it tells transforms human relationships into relations between things.

In a poem entitled "Transcript," which is paired with "Hand" through the structural organization of the book, an interlocutor relates this story through a catalogue of unmaking – destroyed houses, towns, fields, wells, and bodies – before asking, "*Who said to shoot without mercy? Because the hand remembers, knows it must face the soul*" (35). The answer is a non-sequitur that indicates there is no "because" – no explanation for violence except the perverse desire *not* to explain. The next poem, called "Inventory," explains how the roles people

---

[3] Another poem does link violence to the "animal [that] prowls in our veins," but it also stresses the way violence isolates victims from other people in order to make them "more lowly" (20–21).

play in each other's presence are rendered deliberately obsolete by mass murder: "Here, lined up head to head, and foot to foot, is life's inventory. / *This one was a husband. This one was a brother*" (39). This book of poetry devotes some of its most detailed descriptions to cataloguing the evidence of historical Evil (here in phrasing borrowed from Eliot): "you have seen them all already – / ... / Have seen the torturer's notes, the scattered identity papers, / Have seen the shallow graves, by the roadside, so near to the / Churches, near to the mosques..." (60).

The central case study in *Update on the Descent* is the former Yugoslavia. The cover photograph depicts a grim scene of deportation or resettlement, described in the credits as Kosovar Serbs descending from a train in the snow (a photo from Kosovo also adorns the cover of her next book). The documentary poem "Testimony on What Is Important," as central to this book as "Celestial Ladder" was to the previous one, places readers in the gallery of a court hearing on war crimes committed in Kosovo. In her notes Hinsey describes the poem in this way: "Fragments of testimony presented in this poem, composed in *coblas unissonans*, come from a witness session at the International Criminal Tribunal for the Former Yugoslavia in The Hague, February 2001" (88). The archaic verse structure shapes testimony that is contemporary and sounds verbatim. The interlocutor is a prosecutor or judge who is more interested in entering evidence into the record than in acknowledging what the victim feels to be significant:

> "The court questioned him, said, "*We are only interested in the facts.*"
> He said, "But, I have something to add—"
> "*Something important.*" He said he knew the torturer. He knew the man."

The witness repeats twice more that he knew the man who tortured him – knew him well enough to ask him, "*Do you know what you are doing?*" (49). This is what is important, he insists, more important than the gruesome details of the crime, which are included in painful detail. The witness asked to be forgiven for describing the obscenities he was subjected to (48). The need for forgiveness is also "something important," and it is related to the man's compulsion to explain what it means when somebody who knows you begins to hurt you. Evil is obscene in the way it transforms the possibility of human intimacy – in this case the abstract intimacy of casual acquaintance – into an instrument of violence. Justice must include some kind of forgiveness if it is to restore the possibility of positive human interaction.

The witness does not ask the court to forgive his torturer. This would compromise the foundation of justice, which must assign punishments that fit the crimes – something Arendt notes to be nearly impossible when dealing with crimes in which "the international order, and mankind in its entirety, might have been grievously hurt and endangered" (Arendt 1992: 276). Rather, the witness asks to be forgiven for his testimony, as if his words are somehow complicit in the atrocities they relate. This problem of witnessing is related to survivor's guilt; it is also a problem of poetic representation. The witness here stands for the poet, not as a fellow sufferer – there is no lyrical identification in this poem – but as someone struggling to represent evil in a way that does not perpetuate it. An epigraph to the next book again stresses this point: "Forgive me for what I'm telling you" (*Illegal Age*: n.pag.). The line comes from Osip Mandelstam, a poet who was one of Stalin's victims, but it could be this book of poems talking about itself.

In *Update on the Descent*, Hinsey confronts the problem of forgiveness by shifting her register of allusions from the biblical to the classical, abandoning images of transcendence, such as the celestial ladder or Dante's journey, for concrete situations of conflict and revenge. Instructive here are two references to the *Iliad* that frame the book: the prose poem "A Natural History of Compassion" and a collection of aphorisms called "Interdiction." Together, they offer a retelling of the *Iliad* from the perspective of Simone Weil. In her famous essay "The Iliad, or the Poem of Force," Weil describes how violence "obliterates anybody who feels its touch" (Weil: 17). Force transforms subjects into objects; it also takes on a momentum of its own: an eye for an eye, a tooth for a tooth, until violence leads to an interminable cycle of revenge. (In *The Illegal Age*, Hinsey demonstrates how so-called justice can miscarry by comparing a revenge-lynching to the dragging of Hector's body around the walls of Troy [107]). Weil finds a moment of respite from this cycle when Priam visits Achilles to beg him, his son's murderer, for his son's corpse. Each man has allowed himself to become an instrument of violence in this war of retribution, but they most resemble each other in the grief they feel for their dead. Hinsey emphasizes the "compassion" between the two men and their "commonality," deliberately adopting an external point of view that mimics Weil's own theoretical distance (12). The third-person prose rendition allows her writing to resist the undertow that eventually capsizes the epic: "under each [compassionate] word the ceaseless river of revenge flowed" (*Descent* 11: 87). Hinsey, like Weil, knows that language – even the language of justice – can become a medium of the violence it represents. "Interdiction" states the problem succinctly: "We have become afraid of them, the old words, as if at last we / Could escape punishment if, for once and for all, they were forbidden / Utterance in the public squares" (76). However, as this poem makes clear, simply forbidding words is not an option. Like Priam, so the poet: "But here, under the blackened sun, there are things, in the trammeled, / The ruined, the old words, which must still be said" (77).

3 The Road to *The Illegal Age*

What must be said? The epigraphs to *The Illegal Age* (there are three of them) provide a hint in the way they link forgiveness to justice, carrying forward some of the major themes of the previous volume, and pointing to Hinsey's most important formal innovation: the impersonal voice of compassion. I have already mentioned the epigraph from Mandelstam asking forgiveness for the evidence he has to present. Another is from Arendt's *The Origins of Totalitarianism:* "The first essential step on the road to total domination is to kill the juridical person in man" (*Illegal Age*: n.pag.; Arendt 1994: 447). This sentence occurs near the end of the book, where Arendt takes up the awful task of describing the death camps. Her argument is that the Nazis destroyed people in order to kill personhood. From a totalitarian perspective, "individuality, anything indeed that distinguishes one man from another, is intolerable" (457). Their approach was systematic. The Nazis began by revoking legal rights; then murdered "the moral person in man" by placing people in situations where there was no right way to act. After destroying juridical and moral personhood, the next step involved "the preparation of living corpses" through starvation and maltreatment. The step-by-step process – really an assembly-line approach to mass murder – was designed to make the actual deaths of individuals seem superfluous (452–455). Once individuality or personhood is killed, mortality is just a statistic. Arendt is clear about the aim and the consequences of this system, which she does not hesitate to call "radical evil": "They have corrupted all human solidarity. Here the night has fallen on the future. When no witnesses are left, there can be no testimony" (451, 459).

Arendt's grim prognosis is Hinsey's starting point as she moves into the dark future of *The Illegal Age*. She sets herself the poetic task of turning dehumanized objects back into subjects in an age that has unfortunately conformed to Arendt's dire predictions: "The eternal prison is still in operation"; "Like those who will come after, we will now inhabit the windy, disinherited house of the present" (78). The disinherited house, a metaphor for the decayed public sphere, is a place where testimony does, indeed *must* take place. Hinsey invokes this testimony to "explor[e] the continuity and variations of the autocratic experience," as the notes to the volume put it, but also to recuperate the abstract personhood put at risk by the systematic attack on human community (119). The poems in this book expand the range but also fill in emotional details of witnesses who speak in historically compelling, but not verbatim language to describe atrocities committed in Nazi Germany, the Soviet Union, the former Yugoslavia, and elsewhere. Emblematic here is the "evidence" presented in "Carved Into

Bark," a poem commemorating those deported to the Gulag Archipelago in the early 1950s. Messages scratched on bark are not likely to survive. The poem is thus forced to invent evidence that no longer exists: "If you cannot fully remember, then you must invent: until pure invention recalls the forbidden truths" (52). The evidence comes in the form of aphorisms rather than first-hand accounts: "Virtue too can be muddied like a fist; but even in imperfection, it brings a scrap of forgiveness to the table" (53). The aphoristic form is linked to the forgiveness that is here brought to the table, perhaps displacing the evil that once had its own place setting.

To understand how aphorism is linked to forgiveness, it is essential to note a change that has occurred in Hinsey's attitude towards history. At the turn of the millennium, she still hoped for historical transcendence and rapture, but personal grief, which led to an increased sensitivity to the pain of others, forced her to recognize how history rolls over victims on its way to questionable ends (see also "On the Progress of History" in *The Illegal Age*: 111). The eponymous poem sets out to pinpoint where "decency stumbled" in order to "erect / There a monument: to the advent of the *Illegal Age*" (15). Decency has stumbled so often that Hinsey needs an entire book to map out the missteps. *The Illegal Age* provides this map, but it also choreographs the fall. This particular poem shows Hinsey pushing her syntax over the cliff-edges of the line endings, creating awkward breaks between "erect/There" and more suggestive ones like "just/Mercy" (13). This has the effect of leading us step by step through the numbing process of learning "To not suffer the pain of others," while isolating words that have a special meaning in Hinsey's lexicon, such as "tables" (13).

In "The Illegal Age (Reprise)," a tandem poem near the end of the book, the speaker assumes that though we cannot mark exactly when or where the illegal age began, we are in it: "A way forward has been made for the hour without mercy" (103). After what we have read, after what we have seen, we are all implicated in illegality: "Don't think your compliance is not being observed" (104). The poem urges its readers to salvage something from the destruction that has already occurred, here referencing the way prisoners were singled out for execution during the French Terror:

> But by then, all the doors will have been marked in/ yellow chalk.
> Still, let us not pass each other this final time, without/ recognition, without looking each other in the eye.
> Remember: in the ink-light of testimony, a record may/still be kept. (104)

The line endings, which I have marked here with a slash, are probably not intended as line-breaks in this poem. Hinsey deconstructs her prosody at strategic moments, as in this effort to find words for that "for which we have no name" (103). Still, the final lines, quoted above, are neither completely prosaic nor completely hopeless. The speaker turns to traditional devices like apostrophe to insist on the importance of recognition and record keeping. Indeed, the "ink-light of testimony" brings recognition and record-keeping together in a catachresis that inscribes what is spoken in the space where it is said. Ink becomes a metaphor for the way records bleed into relations as the poem takes us across the text-space threshold, into the public sphere.

The effect could hardly be farther from that of confessional poetry, and it prepares the way for Hinsey's idiosyncratic use of the aphorism as the voice of the public sphere. Elsewhere I have explored the tendency of confessional poets to identify with the victims and even perpetrators of atrocity (*Pound Reaction*; "Snodgrass"). The most widely recognized example is Sylvia Plath, who identifies with Jewish victims of the Holocaust and calls her father a Nazi in "Daddy," a poem that projects family drama onto the world historical stage. This technique can easily lead to accusations of misappropriation. Confessional poetry, even when it expresses authentic emotions, runs the risk of trivializing evil and treating mass murder as a metaphor for personal unhappiness. In the extreme example of Plath's "Daddy," personal pain seems linked to the desire to strike out. Even if most confessional poems avoid this extreme, they hardly ever ask for forgiveness.

Hinsey avoids this trap by gauging the public impacts of illegality before making her way back to the private. She insists on both forgiveness and justice by separating testimony from the "lyrical I," and by otherwise depersonalizing her poetry. I have argued that aphorism is crucial here, but many devices work towards this end, including apostrophe and personification. "A Concise Biography of Tyranny," for instance, provides a synopsis of political oppression in its account of how capital-T Tyranny starts small and dreams big. Personification lives and dies through a poet's ability to breathe life into an abstraction. Hinsey manages this in an understated way, providing comic relief in the depiction of Tyranny's "awkward adolescence," and mordant irony in the observation that Tyranny's grave is never bereft of flowers (56). The portrait of Power in *The Illegal Age* works in a similar way: "Power hopes that the People will eventually come to love it, or if not, cease to exist" (65).

There is a sense in which personified abstraction is a correlative of aphorism. The one is impersonality as a figure, the other impersonality in voice. If confessional poetry moves from the personal to the historical, Hinsey moves in the opposite direction, from the public to the private. Her verse conveys a great deal of personal suffering, but it strives to bring something else to the table, namely the table or the public sphere. Another way to put this is that Hinsey returns to the person through personhood, which is constituted through a series of relations that exceed the psychological, spatial, and temporal boundaries of the self: "To praise the virtues of the private life: beside the bedside lamp quietly cultivate a private relationship with the Facts" (99). The basic fact that she recalls, even in her most private moments, is the fact of our communal existence.

Works Cited

Arendt, Hannah. 1972. "On Violence." *Crises of the Republic*. New York: Harvest/Harcourt.
Arendt, Hannah. 1992. *Eichmann in Jerusalem: A Report on the Banality of Evil*. New York: Penguin.
Arendt, Hannah. 1994. *The Origins of Totalitarianism*. New York: Harvest/Harcourt.
Arendt, Hannah. 1998. *The Human Condition*, 2nd ed. Chicago: University of Chicago Press.
Gross, Andrew S. 2015. *The Pound Reaction: Liberalism and Lyricism in Midcentury American Literature*. Heidelberg: Universitätsverlag Winter.
Gross, Andrew S. 2017. "W.D. Snodgrass' The Fuehrer Bunker: Confession, Memory, and the Personification of History." In: Marius Henderson and Julia Lange (eds.). *Entangled Memories*. Heidelberg: Universitätsverlag Winter. 69–96.
Hinsey, Ellen. 1998. "The Rise of Modern Doggerel." *New England Review* 19.2: 138–145.
Hinsey, Ellen. 2002. *The White Fire of Time*. Highgreen, UK: Bloodaxe Books.
Hinsey, Ellen. 2009. *Update on the Descent*. Highgreen, UK: Bloodaxe Books.
Hinsey, Ellen. 2017a. *Mastering the Past: Contemporary Central and Eastern Europe and the Rise of Illiberalism*. Candor, NY: Telos Press Publishing.
Hinsey, Ellen. 2017b. *Magnetic North:* Conversations with Tomas Venclova. Rochester, NY: University of Rochester Press.
Hinsey, Ellen. 2018. *The Illegal Age*. Todmorden, UK: Arc Publications.
Ickstadt, Heinz. 2016. "Verbal Abstraction and the Democratic Promise of Natural Speech." In: Susanne Rohr, Peter Schneck, Sabine Sielke (eds.). *Aesthetic Innovation and the Democratic Principle*. Heidelberg: Universitätsverlag Winter. 179–204.
Warner, Michael. 2002. *Publics and Counterpublics*. New York: Zone Books.
Weil, Simone. 1965. "The Iliad, or the Poem of Force." *Chicago Review* 18.2: 5–30.
Wheatley, Susan. 2009. "An Interview with Ellen Hinsey." 03 October 2009. <https://pionline.wordpress.com/2009/10/03/an-interview-with-ellen-hinsey-2009/>. [accessed 25 November 2021]

Kai Hopen
"In Part, Absolutely": Language, Form, and Potential in Ben Lerner's *The Topeka School*

Abstract: Ben Lerner's *The Topeka School* (2019) is an extremely ambitious, loosely autofictional 'novel' about language and politics in the U.S. from the 1990s to the present, specifically in relation to the seething white masculine reaction that is understood to have made possible the rise of Donald Trump to the Presidency. The book reflects on how to combat the contemporary U.S.-American right wing. This essay attempts to take seriously the dizzying array of *Topeka*'s reflections on language – what it is, how it relates to character, and how it relates to history – and lays out the emphatically formalistic structure of the book's progression. It argues that *Topeka*'s ambiguities, linguisticism, formalism, and didacticism lead it away from the political, regardless of its (somewhat) rousing ending, although the same features do present occasions for reflection on the nature of literature and politics, on their intersections, and on their ultimate divergence.

There is something sinister about Ben Lerner's *The Topeka School* (2019) today, a few years after the potential to which it was attuned came to its as yet unsatisfying eruption. "Constructive" readings have made way for "suspicious" readings, or have become awkwardly enmeshed with them. This essay is the product of that tumult, an attempt to grapple with *Topeka*'s intricate mappings and their place in a world.

Topeka is the story of Adam Gordon. Adam is Ben Lerner's fictional alter-ego whom readers may remember from *Leaving the Atocha Station* (2011), the first of what has been declared retroactively, although not wholly convincingly, a trilogy of Lernerian 'novels'. The plot of *The Topeka School* acts both as prequel and crescendo to Lerner's in-medias-res autofiction in *Atocha* and *10:04* (2014), even though the protagonist in the latter book is named Ben instead of Adam. In *Topeka*, in 1996/1997, the reader encounters a high-school senior named Adam Gordon as seen from the perspective of Adam in 2019 – this much is par for the Lernerian autofictional course – but is also introduced to Adam's parents, Jonathan and Jane, who get to share their own perspectives and histories in alternating chapters, as well as to Darren Eberheart, a bullying victim of Adam's who scans as a budding school shooter and who grows up to be a

Trump supporter.[1] Darren also has an unspecified intellectual disability; in this essay, I will steer clear from comprehensive critique of the book's depiction of "Trumpism as, essentially, mental disorder," as Rumaan Alam put it in his review for *The New Republic*, though it does deserve critical attention. Instead, I want to follow how *The Topeka School* alternates between characters as it tells its 'prehistory of the present' both of Adam Gordon and of a Trumpian America. The novel traces a decline in 'public speech' and suggests, in final scenes sentimental and grandiose, strategies for the rejuvenation of that speech. In this essay, then, I want to come to an understanding of *The Topeka School* on its own terms: I trace what it positively claims it is doing and how it realizes and reflects on these tasks, and moreover I intend to question their exigency. I will argue that *The Topeka School* trades in a symptomatic valuing of didacticism and formal architecture over evaluative content – specifically in light of the values of life and freedom.[2] This is not to question the novel's literary value: instead, it is to observe and think about a more or less political literature that is explicitly grappling with language, art, and their overlap. What remains of the political among Lerner's linguistic and aestheticist fireworks?

Claims

Before I proceed to explain what *Topeka* tells its reader it is doing, a caveat: a feature of Lerner's oeuvre that is particularly present in *Topeka* is a set of profound ambiguities with regard to the scope and power it attributes to literature and language. Two distinct but overlapping ambiguities are present in *Topeka*. The first is that the book sets out to explain both the character of Adam and the development of U.S.-American society since the 1990s – its scope is both individual and societal, micro- and macro-historical. Second, the book's ambitions at both levels, on the one hand, seem grandiose and revolutionary, but are also continually downplayed, with emphasis on the book's humility, perspectival limits, and experimental parameters. In its cover blurb, the book promises to be both a "riveting story about the challenges of raising a good son in a culture of toxic masculinity" and "a startling prehistory of the present" in broadly defined American public life, which will explain "the collapse of public speech,

---

[1] The book opens on a scene of Darren Eberheart in a police interrogation room: as *Washington Post* reviewer Ron Charles, of all people, has also noted, Darren's story "read[s] like a recipe for making a school shooter" (Charles 2019).
[2] This essay marks an attempt to practice literary criticism in light of the values of the "democratic socialism" articulated by Martin Hägglund in *This Life* (2019).

the tyranny of trolls and the new right, and the ongoing crisis of identity among white men" (Lerner 2019). Putting a finer point on it, Lerner has rearticulated his diagnosis in an NPR interview, saying, "I think we live in a moment of total regression to fascistic unreason in our political speech." In further promotional interviews surrounding the book's publication, both Lerner's profilers and the man himself helpfully assure readers that his autofictional body of work is a project of "radical imaginative humility" (Giles 2019), that "radically mocks" Adam Gordon/Ben Lerner's stupid-white-boy character (Shapiro 2019; cf. Barnett 2019). In the same interviews, however, Lerner also points to moments in the novel "where we re-encounter the miracle of language as such and the possibility of building a new language out of the limits of this one," a project of revolutionary reconstruction for which the book "offer[s] some countermodels" (Shapiro 2019) – at which point that humility seems to have been repressed. These puzzling ambivalences have also come to haunt this essay's attempt to understand them, so that particularities from *Topeka* seem to come to stand for the state of language, literature, and the world and vice versa.

A number of metaphors overlap regarding the question of what *Topeka* is, but they all have roughly the same upshot: the book is a progressive inventory of the character of Adam Gordon and/or of America at the end of history, which culminates in a number of 'ways forward' for Adam and/or for America at the restart of history.[3] The book's most explicit self-description occurs halfway through, when 2019 Adam (fictional writer/compiler and narrator of the book) says of 1997 Adam that he "will go on, when history resumes, to [...] attempt this genealogy of his speech, its theaters and extremes" (*Topeka*: 142). The book thus promises to uncover where Adam's "speech" comes from. As I will show, most of *Topeka* is dedicated to charting the lineage of Adam and his speech, between his parents and the character who is his negative, and through a number of 'theaters and extremes.' It does this to such an extent that the book's action does not properly start until the final chapter when the then fully-realized character of Adam translates into action the input he theretofore has received. This understanding is affirmed by *Topeka*'s title: we are reading Adam's schooling more than we are reading his life. The reading – *The Topeka School* as a development of Adam becoming Adam, and then at the end doing things as Adam – is unsettled by a strange moment in the book's final scenes, where a question is interjected in brackets: "(why does it feel dangerous to fictionalize my daughter's names?)" (265). Whereas all of the preceding chap-

---

[3] The notion of the "end of history" refers to Francis Fukuyama's by now clichéd declaration of the same in 1992, which appears as a motif in *Topeka* – more on this later in the essay.

ters can be read within the fictional frame (Adam is writing about past Adam), we here have Lerner stepping into the narrative, reminding his reader that he wrote this book with a purpose and that he decided to "fictionalize" it. This declaration is reiterated twenty pages later in the "acknowledgments" section. Lerner explains that *Topeka* features Duccio's painting, *Madonna and Child*, as an "anachronistic appearance [...] [that] can stand for the unstable mixture of fact and fiction" (285).[4] *Topeka*'s school is thus transposed, however unstably: from Adam's learning from his past, to the reader learning from Lerner.

The Topeka School sets out to 'school' its reader – or, at least, along the lines of radical humility, tries to paint a particular picture, make particular suggestions, hint at particular avenues of possibility. Lerner's conceptions of his art suggest as much, that this is what literature might do. In his MacArthur Fellowship-laureate interview, he praises 'the novel' for being a "curatorial form" that is "elastic" in that it "can absorb other modes" (MacArthur 2015) – like poetry, like essays, like debating, rap, therapy. *Topeka* is emphatically a work of inventory in this sense, curating Adam's language and its precedents. It is also an inventory of moments of poetic possibility. In his one academic monograph, *The Hatred of Poetry* (2016), Lerner argues that actual poetry must always be hated (perfectly, or "with a perfect contempt for it," as quoted from Marianne Moore's poem "Poetry" (Lerner 2016: 3)) because it stands in negative relation to "the utopian ideal of Poetry" (76). While *Hatred*, like *Topeka*, is more inventorial than straightforwardly argumentative, it does give a positive definition of this ideal, or what it means to approach it.

> I remember my feeling that I possessed only part of the meaning of the word, like one of those fragmented friendship necklaces, and I had to find the other half in the social world of speech. [...] To derive your understanding of a word by watching others adjust to your use of it: Do you remember the feeling that sense was provisional and that two people could build around an utterance a world in which any usage signified? I think that's poetry. And when I felt I finally mastered a word, when I could slide it into a sentence with a satisfying click, that wasn't poetry anymore—that was something else, something functional within the world, not the liquefaction but its limits. (79)

Among the slippery language of this definition, Lerner recycles, abstracts, and purifies familiar ideas about poetry: its sense is provisional, emptied of determinacy, and filled with possibility. Language here is a bare object or form. Poetry's

---

[4] It is always hard to know whether paratexts should be numbered in line with the 'actual' literary text. *Topeka* does include its acknowledgments in its table of contents, listing page 285 – striking both for the fact that there is a table of contents at all and for its inclusion of this section.

utopian ideal is 'pure possibility' in language; it is a type of freedom, however we might think of our ability to achieve other freedoms elsewhere.

Topeka trades in inventory, specifically genealogy, and Lerner's conception of the novel trades in inventory, specifically curation: so is *Topeka* definitively a novel? We may assume that just about everyone involved in its production thinks it is. Praise quotes from Rachel Kushner, Maggie Nelson, and Sally Rooney, included in the British Granta-published paperback, use the classification. The American cover of the book prints "A Novel" in the same font and size, though not the same opacity, as title and author name. The "Note About the Author" in the same edition mentioned above refers to *Leaving the Atocha Station* and *10:04* as novels. Questions may arise, however, as to whether we accept the identification of, first, inventory and, second, autofiction within the form of the novel. With regard to the former, the work may fail a test of narrativity: can a novel enumerate, or, as we will see, build linguistic or poetic forms, rather than worlds based on plot? With regard to the latter, the work may fail a test of fictionality: can a novel be non-fictional? And, regardless of the ontological and/or epistemological minefield that shades that question, what are we to do with the repeated emphasis *Topeka* places on its own non-fictionality, or its "unstable mixture" (*Topeka*: 285)? My answer to the latter question would follow a similar line of agnosticism or equivocation to the caveat introduced above: this ambiguity is simply present, to be taken, depending on the temperament of the reader, either as 'productive' or as another prevarication. In answer to the former question, it could be exciting to call *Topeka* a long manifesto-poem, or a poetic inventory-manifesto in defense of manifestation. In general, however, accepting the malleability (or equivocation) of form regarding the category of the novel will, in turn, allow for more sustained attention to be paid to questions of (political) literature (about politics or political literature) and its power or lack of it.

Topeka and Defining Language

If the novel is generally a curation of linguistic modes, and Lerner's *Topeka*, in particular, is a genealogical account of speech ('theaters and extremes'), it is worth asking what language itself is. *Topeka* delivers ample definitions for the idea of language, although it does so in the manner of enumeration, inventorying rather than classifying. These definitions can be mapped on to Roman Jakobson's classic division of the six functions of language, which structure the event of linguistic communication. Thankfully, this will make my account of the dizzying book that *Topeka* is that much more legible. Jakobson explains that

> [t]he Addresser sends a Message to the Addressee. To be operative the message requires a Context referred to [...] graspable by the addressee, and either verbal or capable of being verbalized; a Code fully, or at least partially, common to the addresser and addressee [...] and finally, a Contact, a physical channel and psychological connection between the addresser and the addressee. (1960: 1147)

In relation to language, *Topeka* is in control of all its faculties, and so it stands to reason that it would feature accounts of the nature and present state of language from all these different dimensions.

To begin the discussion of *Topeka*'s descriptions of language, I turn to one of the forms of language's extremes that the book promotes: purification. Breaking the heuristic as soon as it has been established, it appears that language can be purified towards Jakobson's Code and Contact, but that purification towards Message poses problems. When marveling at the fact of his participation in a "cipher," an underground rap practice appropriated (*embarrassingly*, as emphasized both in the book and in interviews with Lerner) by Adam and his friends in Topeka, Kansas, Adam names language "the fundamental medium of sociality," and explains that in this particular cipher, "what mattered was that language [...] was being displayed in its abstract capacity, and that he would catch a glimpse, however fleeting, of grammar as pure possibility" (*Topeka*: 256). Language thus becomes both pure "medium" (pure linkage; pure Contact), and the totality of language, grammar, becomes "pure possibility" (pure potential; pure Code). There is also some acknowledgment of the fact that these accounts of language are "abstract" – that they guide away from what we might expect language to be: a conveyor of meaning, an inventory of tools for building communication. Or more specifically: language here becomes a purified conveyor and a purified inventory, but seems strictly speaking to lack meaning or communication. A more emphatic example of this problem is Adam's transcendence in policy debate: his "experience of prosody" (25).

> He began to feel less like he was delivering a speech and more like a speech was delivering him, that the rhythm and intonation of his presentation were beginning to dictate its content, that he no longer had to organize his arguments so much as let them flow through him [...]. If the language coursing through him was about the supposedly catastrophic effects of ending the government's Stingray program [...] he was nevertheless more in the realm of poetry than of prose, his speech stretched by speed and intensity until he felt its referential meaning dissolve into pure form. (25)

Although Adam's speech is still understood by its interlocutors – i.e. it is still a Message – his experience of its purification is a development *away from* meaning. Purification towards Message is explicitly not purification towards meaning;

it is the opposite, purification towards letters and words regarded as a formal affair, abstracted away from the meaning they are attributed in different contexts. Meaning appears as a problem: where is it, if not in language?

Meaning, for *Topeka*, is an event of unification (between Addresser and Addressee, in Jakobson's terms). This understanding is suggested by the notion of "weak spells." In relation to the character of Darren and his uneasy relationship with reality (he is often caught in lies), the narrator asserts that "*a spell is valued not by its truth but by its power*" (150; emphasis in the original – all chapters focusing on Darren are italicized in full). Language means when it *does* something – when someone does something with it. Often, it should do something to other people. Adam, whose defining characteristic is his virtuoso control of language, is good at doing things to other people with language. His main skill is public speaking, which he uses in rap battles, scholastic debating, and poetry, as well as more properly non-linguistic activities, such as "[c]unnilingus, cunning linguist" (253). Just before he has to give the most important speech of his adolescent life, the reader learns that "Americans consistently report that their greatest fear is public speaking" (225). Why?

> Because it's a linguistic primal scene, Klaus's voice in the dark. The assembled, the community, demand that the speaker be at once individual (your speech must be original to be prized) and utterly social (your speech must be intelligible to the tribe). Through the individual mouth we must hear *the public speaking*. (225; emphasis in the original)

Klaus is an old German psychoanalyst, friend, and colleague of Jonathan and Jane Gordon, Adam's parents. Successful speech – again described formally, so that we might question if 'meaning' is what is actually happening here – exists at the meeting-point of the speaker and the spoken-to, where the speaker says what the spoken-to want to hear *and* what they did not quite expect to hear. Drawing on Jacques Rancière's "two ideas of the avant-garde" (2004: 29), the speaker at the same time appears as, idea number 1, a leader to the audience, pulling them along into before unknown territories of meaning, *and*, idea number 2, as the perfect panderer, anticipating what the audience will want to hear before they know it themselves. Regardless of the direction, the upshot is that Addresser and Addressee 'meet' in the Message.

The Addressee of linguistic meaning need not be someone else than the Addresser, however. *Topeka* handily has a word or a phrase to epitomize each of its insights (tidbits that become poetic through their recurrence, as in Lerner's definition in *Hatred*; see, for instance, "public speaking" and "weak spells" above – and note that more are on the way), and the word for coming to linguistic self-understanding is "processing." As in public speaking, Adam also shines in the realm of processing, albeit in a less poetically transcendent way. He has recurring fits of rage that force his parents to send him to research psychologist Dr. Kenneth Erwood, "a pioneer in biofeedback" (*Topeka*: 31) – who is, incidentally, a colleague of Jane and Jonathan's, themselves psychotherapists, also working at 'the Foundation' in Topeka. Adam's "intensity, [his parents] said, was out of control, how quick he was to rage, even if he was relatively quick to cool" (28). The slightest provocation elicits "an overwhelming barrage of ridiculous but somehow irrefutable arguments," shouting, slammed doors, and "twice he punched holes in his bedroom wall" (28–29). "His parents were, in addition to being exasperated, worried, but not that worried [...]. As long as there was language, there was processing" (29). Elsewhere, Jonathan reflects about one of his patients that "if he had the language he wouldn't be acting out with symptoms" (56). In language, *Topeka*'s characters thus come to understand themselves and to be understood; when they do not 'have the language,' their behavior is symptomatic and they become a patient.

Enter, stage left, more problems. *Topeka* complicates the problem of public and private meaning with wrinkles in Jakobson's "Context." The "spread," combined with the possibility of the breakdown of "processing" under high intensity, obstructs beneficent meaning-making both for individuals alone and for society collectively. "Spreading" is a portmanteau of 'speed reading' (a fact not mentioned in *Topeka*). It refers to the practice in competitive debating where debaters "make more arguments [...] than the other team can respond to in the allotted time, the rule among serious debaters being that a 'dropped argument,' no matter its quality [...] is conceded" (22). Because this is allowed, debaters speak as fast as possible, "at the far edge of intelligibility" (213), incomprehensible to the uninitiated. *Topeka* goes on to use the spread to refer to proliferation in general, and specifically to the overload of information in contemporary society: "Americans," were "getting 'spread' in their daily lives" (24). First by "financial institutions and health-insurance companies" and later by "the twenty-four-hour news cycle, Twitter storms, algorithmic trading, spreadsheets, the DDOS attack": Americans are besieged by "types of disclosure [...] designed to conceal" (24).

What happens at the extreme end ('theaters and extremes') of the linguistic spread? Language breaks down into nonsense. *Topeka* introduces this latter idea with the "speech shadowing" experiment that Jonathan uses in his doctoral research, "in which a subject repeats speech immediately after hearing it" (44). When he speeds up the tape, he finds that "the subjects would, past a certain threshold, begin to drivel, thinking all the while that they were repeating the recorded passage clearly" – a descent or ascent "into glossolalia, although without any apparent ecstasy" (44). The images of the spread and the linguistic breakdown of the speech shadowing experiment thus bring together 1) the notions of information overload and the impossibility of 'processing' that information overload, and 2) the concurrent possibilities of language that intentionally obscures by disclosing, and language that attempts to – and believes that it does – disclose, while in fact obscuring. The recurring words and phrases that were poetic tidbits just a paragraph ago, now come to embody *Topeka*'s own spread – a spread that, rest assured, can lead to breakdown.

(In the background, listen to an NPR interviewer asking Ben Lerner, "Are you saying that our political failures are failures of speech?" Lerner gets slightly flustered, stumbling before answering, "in part, absolutely" (Shapiro 2019). The same interview features Lerner's diagnosis that "we live in a moment of total regression to fascistic unreason in our political speech.")

Adam in Language

It is in these conditions, then, that we can begin to investigate Adam's speech more properly. As I have begun to suggest, Adam thrives on the centrality of language in *Topeka*'s America. Given the largely maleficent role that the spread is assigned, it is striking how the character of Adam wields it, thrives among it, and comes to embody it. Adam's success in life is based entirely on his talent for speech, and especially his use of the spread, which surfaces in each of his linguistic activities. He is a nationally competitive debater and a future national champion in extemporaneous speaking, a budding poet, and a freestyle rapper at his high school house parties. In competitive debate, the spread appears in its original definition. The competitive format of extemporaneous speaking, or "extemp," "emphasized improvisation: a competitor draws three questions at random and chooses one, then has thirty minutes to prepare a five- to seven-minute speech delivered without notes" (*Topeka*: 134) – it "was officially about developing such a command of current affairs that one could speak confidently on a range of topics, but it was of course as much about the opposite," i.e. how to fake confidence and range (135). The spread in extemp takes on the form of an all-encompassing diversity of speech in order to pander to the largest possible audience – the spread as the individualized "*public speaking*" (225), using the slippage found in the Klaus-quote above. Poetry is "shaped sound unmaking and remaking sense that inflicted and repelled violence and made you renowned, or made you renowned for being erased, and could have other effects on bodies" (126). It thus features the spread of possibility, as poetry is language as an imaginative object, potentially open to meanings but not meaningful itself already: the spread as an ever-growing avalanche of language and of meanings ("how it's made and unmade" (227)). Adam's freestyling in ciphers and rap battles ("the most shameful of all the poses [...] a small group of privileged crackers often arrhythmically recycling the genre's dominant and to them totally inapplicable clichés" (127)), which "transmuted his prowess as a public speaker and an aspiring poet into something cool" (127), is the result of a positive reframing of his other linguistic spreading activities. Finally, Adam spreads even in his fits of rage, as noted above. Adam thus successfully navigates a world that seems to be a sequence of linguistic theaters, by processing and wielding the spread that bombards him and everyone else better than everyone else.

There are limits to Adam's linguistic prowess, but they never turn into real problems: rigorous training, luxurious healthcare, and well-rationed chemical aids reduce potential obstructions to "workable tensions" (127). Adam's debating coach Peter Evanson tells Adam that his speeches are good, but not good enough: they are too liberal, he is too much a capital-D Democrat. Evanson tells Adam to "imagine you're running for President and now you're in a swing state [...] What you have in your favor is Kansas [...] I want quick swerves into the folksy" (206). Adam is thus being trained to cover his ideological bases: pandering in order to become, as an individual, the most collective voice possible. In a debate, he realizes this through complete control over his communication to both his opposition and the one-man jury. He offers reassurances to his opponent debater, "knowing it will sound like politeness to the judge, and to his opponent, infuriating condescension" (19). At another point, "he realizes that [...] he might have just made a feminist argument; his pivot is without detectable hesitation" (21). Evanson's influence becomes (yet) more nefarious when he wants to complete his purification of Adam's individualized collectivity by eliminating a tic that he has when speaking – "the bouncing your head thing" (209). "[It] has to stop," Evanson says (209). Jane, who narrates this episode, is reminded of "Glenn Gould's humming in *The Goldberg Variations* [...] a sign that the artist was alongside an art that exceeded him" (209). Evanson's training thus comes to stand for the total cynical repression of Adam's individuality.

Adam is made to feel the tension of his characterization as the Renaissance man of millennial American English – his constant toggling between the aggression of debating and freestyle rap and the quiet sensitivity of poetry, between the nerdiness of debating and poetry and the coolness of freestyle, and between his liberal upbringing and conservative (or regressive) Topeka (i.e. his Democrat and Republican selves). Beyond his fits of argumentative rage, these "workable tensions" also manifest physically, in the form of "[h]is disastrous tonsorial compromise" and "[h]is migraines" (127). The former refers to Adam's "hair [...] drawn into a ponytail while the sides of his head are shaved," accommodating both "the lefty household of his parents and the red state in which he was raised" (27); the latter refers to Adam's intense episodes of migraine, "periodic full-bodied involuntary confessions that he was soft, a poser" (31) – or, perhaps, reminders that he does, in fact, retain the physical dimension of a body, that he is not just the range of American language. Adam's being sent to Kenneth Erwood, a body- rather than language-focused therapeutic psychiatrist, is thus fitting. After an intense and magical-seeming episode in a sensory deprivation room, Erwood notes the tension in Adam's shoulders: "Why don't you try talking, since you're such a great talker, to those muscles? Ask them—with a lot of kindness, with a lot of humility—to relax" (34). Ultimately, however, even this treatment at the forefront of psychotherapy needs to be supplemented by chemicals for Adam to complete his national-championship-final extemp speech: Jane gives him one of her pills, "Valium. Or lorazepam" (215). Whether the pill allows Adam to repress "the bouncing your head thing" is left to the reader's imagination – *Topeka* does not (or cannot) describe his winning speech, the distillate of 1997 America.

Genealogy: The Making and Limits of Adam

It is finally time to return more explicitly to the concept of genealogy. Adam's speech is not just molded in theaters and extremes: it is also formed in relation to other characters. Contrasting Lerner's earlier work, *Topeka* seems to feature four rather than just the one character. It is divided into fifteen chapters, of which seven are *fully italicized* vignettes describing episodes from Darren Eberheart's life, two are monological reminiscences by Jonathan Gordon, two are largely monological interviews of Jane Gordon by Adam, and the remaining four are focused on Adam. As I have noted, all are ultimately written by Adam within the fiction (which is why I hedge and say the book *seems to* feature four characters), barring the unsettling interjection about the daughter's fictional names and the insistence on the mixture of fact and fiction in the acknowledgments – Lerner's work. As presented in a convenient table of contents at the beginning of the book, the chapters are interwoven so that they are formally reminiscent of a sonnet (rhyme scheme: ABAC ADAB ACAD AB B, followed by "Acknowledgments" on page 285). Of course, at fifteen lines, it overflows the sonnet's fourteen: this can stand for the book's tightly choreographed formalism, which it attempts to transcend, or must necessarily overflow, at its crescendo. Before getting to a discussion of that crescendo, however, I first continue to lay out this map of *Topeka*. Adam's parents, Jonathan and Jane, appear linguistically as avatars, respectively, of the ability to passively accommodate language, and the ability to actively use it, to act upon the world with it – abilities that in Adam are synthesized, naturally, as he is their child, the best of both of their worlds. Simultaneously, Adam's all-encompassing linguistic capacities are contrasted by the character of Darren Eberheart, who is both Adam's parallel and his inverse, living just beyond his reach.

Once you start noticing it, the extent and thoroughness of Jonathan and Jane's inverse characterizations – listener and speaker, passive and active, conforming and transgressing, rule-abiding and distinction-blurring – becomes extreme: we might need to ask whether they can still be understood as characters, or if they are theses in a loosely dialectical argument. Jonathan, who, in his passivity, would never describe himself, is instead characterized by his brother (member of "the nascent Weather Underground," "who would prefer to be left out of a novel" (*Topeka*: 43)), when he says, "You're great at making fascists feel heard" (51). Jonathan confirms that "this was what my practice was based on, finding a way to get people, especially reticent Midwestern boys and men, to talk" (ibid): it is, moreover, "what Jane insisted was my gift" (57).

> I wasn't interested in extracting latent content, making manifest some deeper truth motivating Jacob's speech; my goal was to make the kid *feel heard*. I didn't mind the cliché; in fact, I admired the phrase, its rightness of fit, a mixture of the somatic and the semantic; maybe it explained the desire for heavy metal that registered as touch as much as sound. (58; emphasis in the original)

Jonathan repeats his brother's phrase, happily accommodating the tradition of clichés and admiring the way the phrase 'fits': the way it too accommodates pre-existing realities. Moreover, Jonathan *does not* want to do or create anything: he refuses to extract or to make.

Jonathan resists creativity even in his creative endeavors. His doctoral research on speech shadowing, described above, centers on accommodation and its limits, and he proves unable to make meaning with his striking findings: he reminisces, "My theory was that, under conditions of information overload, the speech mechanisms collapse—but, as Jane was quick to point out, this was more a basic description of the driveling than its explanation" (44). Another episode has Jonathan starting "a tiny 'film and video department' [...] with the stated purpose of investigating and eventually producing instructional films about therapeutic topics and techniques" (53–54) – that goal never comes to fruition, instead developing mainly into his "own version of activity therapy," another environment for making people feel heard, feel accepted. He does also produce a short film based on Herman Hesse's story "A Man by the Name of Ziegler." Despite the assertive act of filmmaking, the narration stresses Jonathan's inability to create novelty – his passivity even in creation. The film is a straightforward adaptation of Hesse's short story, and it is narrated both in terms of its story and in terms of its production: for example, "This is the City

Museum in Berlin, circa 1909; this is the Nelson Atkins Museum in Kansas, circa 1983. Cue title sequence. The tall man, who might have met Hesse in Basel, is and is not acting" (63). In this excerpt, the different levels of reality in the film's production coexist: its referent setting and its actual set, its cues, and the actor, Klaus, who represents the Germany to which the story refers both in real life and in the film. It is the type of postmodernist flattening that Jonathan's (literally) meaningless accommodative characterization calls for.

Jane, in contrast, is nothing but meaningful, acting upon and attempting to change the world. Her therapeutic practice is based in her ability to speak: "I believed that I could help a lot of people by describing triangles or sibling dynamics as clearly as possible and that the translation of those concepts into practical advice was my strength as a therapist," she asserts (102) – clearly not requiring a more radical brother to characterize her, as Jonathan did. Her activity is moreover not limited to one-on-one relationships: she is a famous and contentiously feminist author, she has been "on *Oprah*" (89). As Jonathan turns creation into accommodation, so Jane turns (non-)accommodation into action. This is evidenced by her handling of "The Men," embodiments of "fragile masculinity" who call the Gordons' landline phone and sometimes even come up to her in public. On the phone, they ask for Dr. Gordon, and then "the voice would drop into a whisper or a hiss; then—almost without fail—I'd hear the word 'cunt'" (90), followed by related insults and threats. Jane develops a characteristic manner of fielding the calls: "I would pretend that I couldn't hear," which makes the men first repeat themselves in louder voices, and ultimately hang up in shame (91). Jane's active refusal to accommodate, a better-executed version of *"Bounces off me sticks to you"* (37; emphasis in the original), unsettles the man on the other end of the phone, and neutralizes his threat. The mode of active non-listening reappears in a scene in which Adam is at university, away from Kansas, and calls his parents in a panic because his girlfriend has just dumped him. Jane uses her technique therapeutically, letting Adam snap out of his rising frenzy. As narrator Jonathan concludes at the end of the chapter, "Jane had talked us down" (183).

Jane's voice also takes over *Topeka*'s narration. Whereas Jonathan's chapters are squarely descriptive, a de-emphasized or neutralized first-person perspective, and Adam's are emphatically written from the perspective of present-day Adam, Jane's contain intermittent reminders of their status as interview transcriptions (Jane is speaking, in monologue, to present-day Adam, who sometimes reacts), as well as being engaged in their own meaning making. Recall Jonathan's inability to draw out the significance of the breakdown of speech due to information overload; contrast Jane who, in the section that first describes "The Men," begins with a reflection on how landline phones strengthened the bonds between children and extended family more so than modern-day mobile phones, an idea that introduces The Men, their landline phone calls, and thus their contact with Adam. She then presents two situations that exemplify the ways Adam was negatively impacted by this "toxic masculinity" (94). Finally, she comes to the episode where Adam really "did experience a trauma," a severe concussion that gives him memory loss and causes him to forget who his parents are (96). Jane's narrative voice thus realizes her characterization, translating concepts into practical understanding about the relations between different events.

As an obstacle to her assertive voice, however, Jane finds that actions can have diverse and unintended consequences, or 'paradoxical effects.' In medicine, a paradoxical effect is an unexpected and contradictory effect of a drug, like the stressful effect of a benzodiazepine Jane experiences when she takes one at Adam's championship speech (227–228). Benzodiazepine is the usually-calming drug most associated with paradoxical effects. The 'paradoxical effects' at the center of the eponymous chapter, however, are the effects Jane worries her parenting decisions may or may not have had on Adam. Adam's behavior is a through-line in the chapter. He first appears as Topekan in the derogatory sense, toxically male: in response to his behavior at a restaurant, talking over his girlfriend, Jane consciously focuses on "trying to think of my bully of a son as a vulnerable young man passing through a complicated social and hormonal stage" (196). Later, at an event where Jane has been asked to speak, there are also Christian fundamentalist protestors from the Phelps family and the Westboro Baptist Church – "Adam, maybe showing off for Amber [his girlfriend], snapped back at them, told them to shut the fuck up" (198). Jane reflects that "[m]aybe I'd offered my boy up to the wrong tutelage, the Brain [Jane's nickname with the Phelps crowd] had offered him to the Men, thinking he would somehow know better. And now he was a graduate of the Topeka School" (209). Ultimately, though, Jane finds that Adam "was eclectic, after all, despite his training," when he argues in favor of a universal basic income during a debate. He is, of course, nothing if not eclectic, acting and accommodating, working the tension between violent Topeka and cranial East Coast cities, the ultimate Presidential candidate in a swing state, the public speaking through his individual mouth.

Darren Eberheart is Adam's negative: he remains mute and outside of Adam's social group, despite their similarities. His adolescence climaxes not with glorious public speaking victory and "cunnilingus" (253), but with extreme frustration and an eruption of violence, when he throws a cue ball from a pool table at "Mandy Owen's face [...] it strikes her three inches below the temple, shattering the jaw in several places, dislodging multiple teeth, knocking her unconscious, forever altering her speech" (258). This ending is inevitable from his introduction in the first pages of *Topeka* onwards. The book opens on Darren fantasizing about violence in a police interrogation room. He sees a poster that reads "*KNOW YOUR RIGHTS, then fine print he couldn't read,*" thinks back on high school scenes where he has zoned out and failed to hear the teacher calling on him ("*'Earth to Darren'*"), and, when he begins to answer a police officer's question, he is swiftly interrupted by the other officer, "*albeit gently [...] we need you to start at the beginning,*" (3–4; emphasis in the original here and in following quotes). "*What Darren could not make them understand was that he would never have thrown it except he always had*" (4); this time it is not a police officer but narration intervening. In these, the opening scene's references to language, the reasons for Darren's violent explosion are explained in terms of linguistic exclusion. He cannot read well, in part because of the "fine print" that the book will go on to identify as a type of spread, perpetrated by "financial institutions and health-insurance companies" (24). He cannot hear, or forgets to listen. And he is not allowed to speak, which, even if it was possible, would be futile because he does not have the language to explain his predetermined life, cannot summon or even fathom its beginning or causes. Adam, our author, contributes to this, a fact that is emphasized in this opening scene by his narratorial intervention – his social capital drowns Darren out, makes that the reader can only 'know' Darren through Adam.

So what does Adam tell us regarding Darren's development? To an extent he empathizes; to an extent he pathologizes. Darren has an intellectual or developmental disability – "*think nine- or ten-year-old in a teenage body*" (72) – but the condition is not specified beyond the recurring reference to his relative 'real' and 'bodily' ages (37, 72, 112–113, 188). He might need "the medicalized pastoral of in-treatment" (118–119), but "(who would pay?)" (118). Darren's single mother, a nurse who cares for Adam when he has his migraines, is "*powerless [...] so far from being able to afford the few special programs that she did not retain the details [...] insurance covered none of it*" (188). Darren lacks the ability to give a socially understandable and thus acceptable account of himself – or, better, although *Topeka* does not make this point explicitly (recalling the questions mentioned at the top of this essay about "Trumpism as [...] mental disorder"), society lacks the means, or will, to provide him the accommodative space and opportunity to give such an account of himself. His "*style was a little off, non-native: the thin beige braided belt he wore [...] somehow constituted less a single bad decision than a deep incomprehension of the language game in which he was attempting to feign fluency*" (187) – close, but yet so far. Darren's make-work job bagging groceries is also complicated by problems with language, when he is asked to look up the price of a product. Unable to "*define a border between what costs this, costs that*" and finding that the "*letters and numbers [...] go ants running across the pavement twigs floating away on water,*" he panics and flees (72). He goes to a place that does accommodate him: the military "*Surplus where he can sit far in the back latching and unlatching a .50-caliber ammo can*" (72–73). The point being made here is driven home when Darren is described as representing, to the seniors of the class of '97, "the bad surplus" (117). Darren is "the perverted form of the empire's privileged subject" (118). When his peers – ex-classmates since Darren dropped out of high school at sixteen – leave him in the woods after a night of partying during which he had finally been included again, Jason's joke to Adam is, "Milieu therapy" (118). The only community into which Darren fits, according to Adam and his friends, is that of exclusion: loneliness in the woods, or the shop literally called, with psychoanalytic resonance, "the Surplus." From the latter, moreover, the transition to a site where he is *included*, "wearing the red baseball cap, holding his sign in silence" – a Trump rally – is easily made (275).

It is profoundly unclear what can be done with the figure of Darren Eberheart, in the same way that it is profoundly unclear what can be done with *The Topeka School*. Darren's frustration – as well as, crucially, cue alarm bells, his *disability* – is historicized and empathized with in some ways, but it is also posited as a type of irreducible otherness. Darren is, quite overtly and explicitly within *Topeka*'s own narration, a reminder that "aesthetic totality is always not-all" (Edelman 2019: 24). Adam's social world seems all-encompassing, but Darren's otherness is irreducible to it, and attempts to integrate him can only fail: "Each attempt to name it *mis*names it by turning its nothing into something" (Edelman 2019: 18; emphasis original). But, clearly, such radical and *irreducible* otherness or beyondness to the coherence of respectable American society that Darren represents is really just a fiction: the coherence of respectable American society is a fiction, and Darren's radical disjunction is a disjunction from the fiction, rather than from the formal organization of society. Darren's inability to receive a social role that will not lead to the ultimate eruption of violence has been manufactured by systems that are not part of the coherent fiction of American society: the radical liberalization of the American and global imperially-administered economy and, flowing from this, the elimination of the state's and society's ability to care for the people living in it. Darren's place in the socio-economic order is a feature of it, a place created by its design, regardless of intention – even if it is radically other to the coherent fiction by/in/through which Adam and friends live. But it also is not radically other to that fiction: *Topeka* remarks on socio-historical developments and its formalized set-up is so heavy-handedly self-aware it approaches parody. As it implies with the strange classification as "genealogy," *Topeka* cannot make up its mind whether it is analytical or narrative history, dealing with abstract and ontological divisions or concrete and causally related events – or, instead, it claims that it is both, or perhaps neither. The problem is exacerbated at the book's crescendo, when *Topeka*'s historical structure is inverted outwards into poetical manifesto.

The Restart of History: or, "Countermodels"

The first twelve, or possibly fourteen, chapters of *Topeka* take place during or are broadly narrated from what Francis Fukuyama has called "the end of history" (Fukuyama: 1992). At the end of chapter twelve, "Paradoxical Effects," narrated by Jane, Adam stands on the stage for the final of the national championship in extemporaneous speaking, "motionless, as if he's holding my gaze, waiting for me to start his time" (*Topeka*: 228) – so this may be where history is about to restart. Of 1969, in a reader-flattering elliptical contrast, Jonathan remembers "we felt that history was alive" (43). Adam and his debating coach Evanson are said to be training "in a largely empty school eight years after history has ended" (143). The "Muzak" that links "the Mall of America and the Summerset Home and Rolling Hills and the Hypermart and the Foundation and the Dillon's on Huntoon" is "[t]he white noise at the end of history" (227). As it turns out, however, these diagnoses were premature: on a drive through his hometown, present-day Adam reminisces about his youth in Topeka, when "history [was] not over but paused" (271). Before the book's late (re)start, its narration seems to place itself in the concurrently empty (of meaning, an 'empty school') and overloaded (with 'white noise') end of history, even if it recalls events from before that time, or proleptically refers to later events. The last pages are thus especially interesting in that they might give an image of what the post-90s era does, should, or could look like, in Adam Gordon's America – as well as in Ben Lerner's.

The last two chapters of *Topeka* have a chiastic structure, hinging on the partial reprint of Duccio's *Madonna with Child* (*Topeka*: 259). In 1997, as I will elaborate below, Adam uses individualized language to succeed and to shut out the evils of the world – History, what hurts – but finds those evils, and thus History, to be obstinate. History's obstinacy and according meaning or meaninglessness are then epitomized in the reprint of the bottom quarter of the *Madonna*. Then, in 2019, Adam first finds individualized language to be largely futile, but collective language to anticipate the birth of a new American public.

First, fresh off his extemporaneous speaking championship, Adam and his parents go to visit his maternal grandfather, the one who abused Jane. The grandfather is now catatonic in his dying days at a nursing home. The grandfather lets out a "groan or croak—deep, hoarse" that haunts Adam (*Topeka*: 236). At home, he asks to listen to a recording of the old man's voice to forget the strange noise, which they do, until "[h]is mom stopped the tape abruptly," unable to bear the patriarchal voice of the terrible man anymore (241). To eradicate the echoing voice in the silence that follows, Adam repeats the line from the poem "The Purple Cow" that he has always stubbornly refused to learn, in a game in which he repeats the wrong line so that his mother has to correct him: "'I hope to never see one'" instead of "'I never hope to see one,'" which, "his split infinitive, that broken little future . . . their ritual refusal of repetition across the generations," removes the specter of his grandfather and of "the Men, however briefly," from the room (241–242).

In the second scene of this chapter, Adam processes an intense fight between his parents, regarding Jonathan's adultery, by taking fragments of their speech, and fragments of his mother's writing, and putting them in poetic experiments typed on his mother's computer:

> There was some kind of special power involved in repurposing language, redistributing the voices, changing the principle of patterning, faint sparks of alternative meaning in the shadow of the original sense, the narrative. The power was both real and very weak, a distant signal. (247–248)

The gesture of sheltering oneself in language is necessarily a weak one. As if to double down in his weakness, Adam moves on to look up some early edition internet porn. A sudden movement behind him scares him and he abruptly turns the computer off because he thinks he is being watched. After this, he finds himself fearing that his browsing history will be published everywhere: "The obstinacy of history" (249).

History becomes most obstinate in this chapter's final scene: the party with Darren's violent outburst. Adam and Amber enter the party (at Sima's, Jason's mother's, house) and share a sex scene in the master bedroom (Adam's workable tension returning in his "Cunnilingus, cunning linguist [...] a joke that might have been made for him, he who tried to cover the body in speech" (253)). When the Olde English, a malt liquor, takes hold, things begin to derail: first there is a cipher, in which Adam "enter[s] a zone in which sentences unfolded at a speed he could not consciously control" (256), and then finally "everyone is in position in the crowded basement" (257). Adam had been in total control in personal (linguistic-social) relations – he could reject the toxicity of historical masculinity, process the tensions of familial strife, mine it for possibility, and he was near the top of the social pyramid. Nonetheless, he loses control and history intrudes, obstinately, materially, critically. He cannot prevent Darren's violence and Mandy's injury.

"In Part, Absolutely" — **247**

In the final chapter, present-day Adam, circa 2019, is the husband of a wife, Natalia, and father to two daughters, Luna and Amaya (even if "it feel[s] dangerous to fictionalize my daughters' names" (265)).

In the first of three scenes, the young family are leaving the apartment of Doña Alana, Natalia's Puerto Rican great-grandmother, to take the daughters to a playground in Manhattan (263–265). At the playground, they encounter a bully – a boy who will not share the slide ("these girls are stupid, these girls are ugly, no stupid ugly girls allowed" (267)). Adam confronts the boy's father, who is similarly obtuse and refuses to intervene ("Let the kids figure it out" (270)), which Adam refuses to accept ("what the kids will 'figure out' is repetition" (270)). In the course of the conversation, Adam goes from trying "to channel my own father's voice, a voice that somehow disarmed other men," to trying to "weaponize my father's empathy" (268–269), while at the same time invoking the specter of President Donald Trump as an interpretive frame for the boy's behavior: "it's about pussy grabbing; it's about my fears regarding the world into which I've brought them" (270). Finally, he knocks the other father's phone out of his hands – a futile gesture to end a futile conversation in which Adam proves unable to enact change.

In the second scene of this chapter, Adam and the family return to Topeka for a poetry reading he is giving at the university. Adam drives around Topeka, taking in memories among the actuality of the town that has aged two decades: he first passes the Foundation building that has been abandoned and desecrated by vandals, possibly Darren, ("'In my 29 years as a law enforcement officer, I don't know that I've ever seen a building attacked this savagely'" (272)), and then goes by Amber's old house and his grandfather's nursing home, before returning for the reading, where protestors have come out "not because I was a 'well-known poet,' but because I was the Brain's [Jane's] son" (275). In an ominous ending to the episode, Darren is among the protestors, "heavier than the last time you saw him, bearded, almost certainly armed, although no printing is visible in the photograph; he is wearing the red baseball cap, holding his sign in silence" (275).

In the last scene of the book, Adam, Natalia, and Luna join a sit-in protest at the offices of Immigrations and Customs Enforcement, ICE, in Manhattan. When Luna gets scared by the intensity of the protest, Adam leaves with her; outside, Luna joins another kid drawing with chalk on the sidewalk, and Adam gets into a menacing confrontation with a police officer about the defacement of government property and the question of the policeman's authority, before all finally join a human microphone, "wherein those gathered around a speaker repeat what the speaker says in order to amplify a voice without permit-requiring equipment" (282). Whereas Adam's individual gestures of resistance through linguistic communication, talking to the other father and the police officer, and perhaps also reading poetry in Topeka in the presence of Darren's silent protest, thus appear as relatively futile, as both men, and Darren, are stone-faced in their rejection, the human microphone is presented as the recovery of a lost ability to transmit ideas, with its distinctive feature being collectivity rather than individuality: "a public learning how to speak again, in the middle of the spread" (282).

Reasons and Reading Models

Topeka can help to teach what language is and what literature is, and it shows how a book might function internally, but it feels like something is lost in the conflagration of literary theory and forms. Didacticism and formalism, inventorization and mobilization, they repress something. Recognizing the chiastic structure of the book's ending may be a good way to get at this frustration. To the extent that Adam's participation in the human microphone is an inversion of his national championship speech, I am left wondering whether the glory of that last sentence is a celebration of a particular politics, or if it is a celebration of a particular rhetorical device. More suspiciously, we might also ask why Adam remains on the side of respectability in this final scene, and what we can say about the end of Darren's character arc, and perhaps why language remains not just accepted but celebrated at all, after the book has mobilized so much evidence for its *total unmooring* from value. In some of those interviews, mentioned at the start of this essay, Lerner has argued that *Topeka* features moments of "glitches in the voice" of its narration – these, he says, are to be found in the voices of the three non-Adam characters, and once more emphasize the (fictional) writer's humility, the extent to which his voice-throwing acts fail. As a reader, I do not recognize the glitches, rifts in the literary fourth wall, in the places where Lerner would have them. I would assign the comment about the fictionalization of Adam's daughters' names the status of rift. Another moment that jumps out as a rift is one that can help to indicate what *Topeka*'s focus on language and literature represses. It arrives just before the book's final – apparent – celebration of the form of linguistic transmission (Jakobson's "Contact") that is the human microphone. Adam, Natalia, and Luna are inside the ICE headquarters together with the other protestors. Luna is scared at the intensity of the moment; Natalia wants to get her to participate in the activism; Adam is drawing parallels between the Nazis' "World Ice Theory" and America's ICE (really). At the bottom of the page, the protestors' chant erupts into capitalization: "FAMILIES AND CHILDREN [...] DESERVE TO BE SAFE" (279). It is as though a hole is momentarily torn in Adam's absurd musings, as though he is finally being drowned out by the collective understanding and expression of the basis of value: fragile human life. On the other hand – not to upend my own reading – the capitalization of this fragment also works simply to counterbalance the capitalization of ICE, so maybe Adam, and Lerner, are once more building little parallel forms, even here.

If *Topeka* is about (political) literature to the detriment of its politics, it is not a huge problem to the extent that the reader retains ultimate control. I round out this exhaustive/-ing essay with a sampling of reading models suggested by the book, options for our literary and political understanding.

Topeka's last chapter is called "Thematic Apperception." The psychotherapeutic concept is explained early in the book, surrounding a picture of Adam after an early preliminary round in his road to the debating championship, standing next to Senator and future Presidential candidate Bob Dole.

> Now I am going to show you a picture and I'd like you to make up a story about it. We call the Thematic Apperception Test, or TAT. A story with a beginning, a middle, and an end. It's a black-and-white photograph that appeared on the front page of *The Topeka Capital-Journal* [...] What are the people in this picture thinking? Feeling? Start by telling me what led up to this scene. (27)

It returns at the end, in the snapshot of Darren standing among Topekan Trump supporters.

> Now I am going to show you a picture of one of the protesters. Darren is heavier than the last time you saw him, bearded, almost certainly armed, although no printing is visible in the photograph; he is wearing the red baseball cap, holding his sign in silence. If your eyes were to meet, only the little mimic spasms would indicate recognition. What is happening in this moment? What are the characters thinking and feeling? Tell me what led up to this scene. (275)

The book is commenting on the changed view we might have of Darren, perhaps; it is absolving itself of having to say anything directly about Trump supporters, perhaps. This act of interpretation is moreover precisely the point: reading *Topeka* is a thematic apperception test, too, the artwork an intransigent entity, occasioning an exercise in reflection. It is here, moreover, where *Topeka* decides for itself that it is not political: it is offered up as an object for free consideration, never as directional. At the same time, I would want to leave open the option that there are absolute sources of value in human life, as suggested by the Abolish ICE protesters, which a work of literature might do more to open up rather than repress.

Extended analogies to the experience of reading can be found in the first scene of the first Adam-oriented chapter, which reads like the book's 'real' start after an initial vignette starring Darren. The scene opens with Adam in a boat with his girlfriend Amber. There are no immediate clues that the reader should be imagining sound: it seems to be quiet on the lake, a quiet that is disrupted, and thereby seems confirmed, when Adam "hear[s] the scrape of her lighter," and that then is retroactively unmade, disappeared in a puff of smoke, in the first paragraph's last line: "For a long time he had been speaking" (7). Then, "[w]hen [Adam] turned to see what effect his speech had had, [Amber] was gone" (7). Leaving aside the formulation drawing attention to the effects of linguistic utterance, Amber's disappearance is cause for concern. Adam, not a boater, clumsily starts the boat to go look for her and somehow manages to dock it before walking into the house that he thinks is Amber's family's, but turns out not to be: having noted the difference only after entering the third floor bathroom because they are so architecturally similar, he feels that "[i]n a single shudder of retrospection his impressions of the house were changed" (10) – much like a reader attentive to the first paragraph's retroactive sound engineering. He also gets "a sense, because of the houses' sameness, that he was in all the houses around the lake at once; the sublime of identical layouts" and, even better, "[h]e was in all the houses but, precisely because he was no longer bound to a discrete body, he could also float above them [...] then he could toggle rapidly between these perspectives, these scales, in a relay that unfixed him from his body" (10–11). Similar sublimes of identity echo through the rest of the book, for example in relation to rows of products in Topeka's Hypermart USA (130).

After Adam flees the wrong McMansion and finds his way back to Amber's house, she tells him a story of having to listen to her father's seemingly endless monologues about "Ross Perot and China" (14), and how she once slipped under a table and fled the dining room without him noticing, while he was still droning on. Present-day Adam's narration intervenes to help those not attuned to the satirical comparison: "It would take Adam twenty years to grasp the analogy between her slipping from the chair and from the boat" (15). White male monologues, then, are difficult to escape, even if Amber has her techniques. Case in point, in fact, is Adam's narrative intervention – we might ask: what shields *Topeka* from being just another monologue? (Should the reader slip away under the table?) Literary distribution is monological: a speech directed to a group. *Topeka*'s counter-proposal might be that literature has the collectivizing potential of the human microphone. Participants engage and even reproduce, reconstruct, co-create, a text with which they are not familiar ahead of time. The effect may be one of defamiliarization ("It embarrassed me"), but it may also seem to hold the potential to create an experience of genuine constructive collectivity ("a public learning slowly how to speak again"). Reading as contextualizing a picture, exploring a familiar but strange house, (not) listening to a droning speech, or taking part in a public speaking. Whichever we prefer (the McMansion reading of reading is my favorite), it is clear that the magic here is ultimately a weak spell. Genuine politics prefers to be left out of a book, even if the values it seeks to manifest – life and mutually sustaining freedom – must from time to time intrude.

Works Cited

Alam, Rumaan. "The MAGA Plot." *The New Republic*, 20 September 2019. <https://newrepublic.com/article/154963/ben-lerner-topeka-school-novel-review-trump-fiction> [accessed 28 February 2021].

Barnett, Catherine. "Ben Lerner on Writing and Magic Pills." *The Yale Review*, [n.d.]. <https://yalereview.yale.edu/ben-lerner-writing-and-magic-pills> [accessed 28 February 2021].

Charles, Ron. "Ben Lerner's Brilliant New Novel, *The Topeka School*, Captures America's Brutal Divisions." *The Washington Post*, 7 October 2019. <https://www.washingtonpost.com/entertainment/books/ben-lerners-brilliant-new-novel-the-topeka-school-captures-americas-brutal-divisions/2019/10/07/20286d50-e911-11e9-9c6d-436a0df4f31d_story.html> [accessed 28 February 2021].

Edelman, Lee. 2019. "Queerness, Afro-Pessimism, and the Return of the Aesthetic." *REAL: Yearbook of Research in English and American Literature* 35: 11–26.

Hägglund, Martin. 2019 [2020]. *This Life: Secular Faith and Spiritual Freedom*. New York, NY: Anchor Books.

Harvey, Giles. "To Decode White Male Rage, First He Had to Write in His Mother's Voice." *The New York Times Magazine*, 8 October 2019. <https://www.nytimes.com/interactive/2019/10/08/magazine/ben-lerner-topeka-school.html> [accessed 28 February 2021].

Jakobson, Roman. 1960 [2010]. "*From* Linguistics and Poetics." In: Vincent B. Leitch (ed.). *The Norton Anthology of Theory and Criticism*. Second edition. New York, NY: W.W. Norton and Company. 1144–1152.

Lerner, Ben. 2011. *Leaving the Atocha Station*. Minneapolis, MN: Coffee House Press.

Lerner, Ben. 2014. *10:04*. New York, NY: Picador.

Lerner, Ben. 2016. *The Hatred of Poetry*. New York, NY: Farrar, Straus & Giroux.

Lerner, Ben. 2019. *The Topeka School*. London: Granta Publications.

MacArthur Foundation. 2015. "Ben Lerner: Writer – Class of 2015." *MacArthur Fellows Program – MacArthur Foundation*. <https://www.macfound.org/fellows/class-of-2015/ben-lerner> [accessed 28 February 2021].

Rancière, Jacques. 2004 [2011]. "The Distribution of the Sensible." *The Politics of Aesthetics: The Distribution of the Sensible*. Transl. Gabriel Rockhill. London: Continuum International Publishing Group. 7–45.

Shapiro, Ari. "How High School Debate in 1990s Kansas Explains the Present: A Novel Argument." *All Things Considered* [radio show]. *NPR*, 8 October 2019. <https://www.npr.org/2019/10/08/768356577/how-high-school-debate-in-1990s-kansas-ex plains-the-pre sent-a-novel-argument> [accessed 24 July 2020].

Laura Bieger
The 1619 Project as Aesthetic and Social Practice; or, the Art of the Essay in the Digital Age

Abstract: In August 2019, *The New York Times* launched The 1619 Project, a multimedia initiative to commemorate the arrival of the first enslaved Africans on the shore of the land that would become the United States and to reckon with the impact of slavery on U.S. culture and society. This essay seeks to examine The 1619 Project. I argue that The 1619 Project draws on the tradition of the essay – for Frankfurt School thinker Theodor Adorno "the critical form *par excellence*" (1988: 166) – and adapts it to our continually evolving media environment in ways that revamp its form and reinforce its aesthetic, critical, and political potential. Assessing this claim from the perspective of the reading public, I ask: what are some of the strategic advantages of the essay form when it comes to engaging readers as publics?

In August 1619, the first enslaved Africans arrived on the shore of the land that would become the United States. Four hundred years later, in August 2019, *The New York Times* launched The 1619 Project, a multimedia initiative to commemorate this fateful event and reckon with the impact of slavery on U.S. culture and society. Its declared goal is "to re-frame American history" (Silverstein 2019: n. pag.), and in an effort to achieve this goal, *The New York Times* has published textual, visual and audio content by predominantly Black American journalists, scholars, and artists addressing the many ways in which slavery continues to shape virtually all aspects of life in the U.S. Premature as it is to determine the outcome of this ongoing initiative, it is safe to say that The 1619 Project made one of the most powerful interventions in public discourse on race and racism in the U.S. in recent years. This essay seeks to examine the form of this intervention. More concretely, I argue that, in its attempt to reframe U.S. history, The 1619 Project draws on the tradition of the essay – for Frankfurt School thinker Theodor Adorno "the critical form *par excellence*" (1988: 166) – and adapts it to our continually evolving media environment in ways that revamp its form and reinforce its aesthetic, critical, and political potential.

In considering the form of The 1619 Project, this essay seeks to assess the critical affordances of a new, activist journalism of which it is emblematic – a "more personal" journalism, driven by "reporters more willing to speak what

https://doi.org/10.1515/9783110771350-016

they see as the truth without worrying about alienating conservatives," some even going so far as dismissing "'objectivity'-obsessed, both-sides journalism" as "a failed experiment (Smith 2020: n. pag.). But if pleas to "moral clarity" have become a war cry in the ongoing battle over journalism's social and political responsibilities, it is important to note that the term elect lends moral legitimacy to partisanship in the domain of news media (the famous "Fourth Estate" in the political architecture of democratic societies); and that the development of which it is emblematic bears the risk of further polarizing an already polarized country. I will return to this issue at the end of this essay. For now, suffice it to say that insiders agree that the new journalism, which gained traction in response to the unrest erupting in Ferguson after the killing of Michael Brown by a police officer in August 2014, has caused a "shift in mainstream American media" that "now feels irreversible" (ibid). Indeed, this shift is further solidifying in the face of the mass protests sweeping the country in response to the murder of George Floyd by yet another police officer – protests fuelled by frustration about the toxic conjunction of structural racism and social inequality that the Covid-19 pandemic had so ruthlessly exposed in the disproportionately high infections and deaths among Black Americans by the time the video of Floyd's killing went viral.[1] The 1619 Project is not only part of this shift; it crystallizes it. Moreover, and crucially, its use of the essay is indicative of how the new journalism seeks to intervene in public discourse and shape public opinion.

My interest in The 1619 Project and its use of the essay is tied to my larger interest in the reading public as a political actor, which is indispensable to modern democracies (see Bieger 2018, 2019b, 2020). Aligning The 1619 Project with the tradition of the essay allows me to consider it as a work of "engaged literature," which I understand as a social practice that is firmly committed to the transformative potential of a literary aesthetics, and that aims to impact society at large.[2] Reading The 1619 Project along these lines employs a praxeological un-

---

[1] The battle over journalism's social and political responsibility came to a powerful eruption when the Opinion editor of *The New York Times* James Bennett resigned on June 7, 2020 under the pressure of staff members protesting the publication of an op-ed piece by Senator Tom Cotton that called for using the military against antiracism protests. For a lucid discussion of the shift in mainstream news media, see Smith (2020). Smith points out that the development is driven by a new generation of journalists, most of them young, many of them Black, and all of them complementing their journalistic work with articulating their personal views via Twitter.
[2] I should note that this alignment goes against Adorno's rejection of the idea of a socially engaged literature, which was popularized by Jean-Paul Sartre in the aftermath of World War II. See Adorno (1992) and Sartre (1988). For Adorno, the essay's transformative power resides in an object-oriented aesthetic. From this point of view, social engagement must be rejected at all cost as it threatens the very foundations of the essay's transformative potential: its art-like

derstanding of literature to trace and explore the political agency of the reading public which it summons into being. A claim recently made about practices is that they are the very stuff out of which the social world is made – with literature being one of these practices.³ So, who are the actors conjointly engaged in the practice of literature, and what brings them together? What structures their interactions, and how do these interactions intersect with other, non-literary practices? These kinds of questions inform my approach to The 1619 Project as a social and aesthetic practice whose power for public engagement both stems from and reinvigorates the essay form.

In U.S. literary culture, the personal essay has often served as a vehicle for public engagement, and the African American essay tradition – powered by writers such as Richard Wright, James Baldwin, Ralph Ellison, Angela Davis, Audre Lorde, and, more recently, Ta-Nehisi Coates and Imani Perry – has been exemplary in mobilizing the essay's critical and political potential to support the struggle for (Black) civil rights.⁴ So yes, The 1619 Project stands on the shoulders of giants, and like them, it draws on the personal essay's capacity for public engagement by creating "a sense of intimacy and concern with someone we have never met" (Fiedler 1958: xi). But to understand The 1619 Project's creative use of the essay in a vastly changed media environment, the tradition of the personal essay is not enough. Rather, gaining a grasp on how The 1619 Project breaks new ground for the essay's capacity for public engagement requires examining the realignment of the essay's aesthetic and political dimensions in and through its expansive multimedial form. Hence it makes sense to commence with an inventory of the main components (and media sites) of this form; and start by noting that The 1619 Project is such a rewarding object of study for the purpose of

---

autonomy. From the view of Sartre's reception-oriented aesthetics, however, social engagement is not the product of a fixed political agenda inscribed into a text. Rather, it is the result of an interactive process, in which the literary work is co-created by the reader in the act of reading, existing only as long as it is being read, but potentially extendable through a media network that reaches beyond the printed book. It is in this latter sense that I consider The 1619 Project – through its use of the essay form – as a work of 'engaged literature'. For a comprehensive discussion of my praxeological and reception-oriented understanding of 'engaged literature', see Bieger 2019b.

3 For an introduction to what is often referred to as a "practice turn" in critical theory, see Schatzki (2001). For scholarship on the praxeological dimension of literature, see the body of work produced by the Cluster of Excellence 2020 *Temporal Communities: Doing Literature in a Global Perspective* at Freie Universität Berlin.

4 On the tradition of the personal essay in general and in U.S. literary culture in particular, see Fiedler (1958) and Lopate (1994). On the African American essay tradition, see Wall (2018) and Junker (2010).

assessing the critical und political affordances of the essay in the present age because most of its content was not published as part of the regular newspaper, and is thus especially free to endorse the aesthetic strategies of the essay and capitalize on their potential for public engagement.

At the heart of The 1619 Project is the one-hundred-page thick 1619 issue of *The New York Times Magazine*, published on August 18, 2019, which contains essays, photographs, historical sketches, and literary and visual art by predominantly Black American journalists, scholars, and artists. Contributions address topics ranging from U.S. democracy and capitalism to health care and diet to pop music, mass incarceration, and rush hour traffic. The magazine was published in tandem with a broadsheet: a photo essay on the history of slavery, created in collaboration with the Smithsonian Museum for African American History and Culture, flanked by an essay on the shortcomings of teaching this history. These print publications are featured in nearly full length on a website with an unusually elaborate and flashy design. The website has at least three functions: it makes the magazine and the broadsheet available free of charge to an online mass readership, and it serves as a digital archive, as well as a hub to publicize and interlink the various parts of the project – among them an education initiative with the Pulitzer Center, a public symposium at the Smithsonian, a forum for sharing stories and photographs of enslaved ancestors, and a podcast hosted by The 1619 Project's initiator and *New York Times* staff writer Nikole Hannah-Jones and first published by *The Daily* (a *New York Times* news podcast with over 2 million subscribers). The podcast consists of five episodes, released between August 23 and October 11, 2019, which re-use and expand on the journalistic and literary work produced for the magazine, and are available on demand and free of charge via major podcast distributors. Like the website, the podcast expands The 1619 Project's public outreach. But in its shift from reading and viewing to listening, usually alone, with headphones – and this receptive mode sets the podcast distinctly apart from its historical predecessor, the radio (see Soltani 2018) – the 1619 podcast makes engagement with the assembled material more personal and intimate. We hear the host and her guests "speaking, quite literally, between our ears, adding a certain reality to the phrase 'getting inside someone's head'" (McDougall 2011: 722). It also makes engagement more seamless and coherent; no flipping, scrolling or clicking though pages, no mental combining of texts and images but one continuous, evenly flowing, "mobile narrative track" (McDougall 2011: 715; see also Soltani 2018). So, the aesthetic effect of these mutually reinforcing affordances of the podcast is to make The 1619 Project more accessible, and create stronger affective bonds with an increasingly "consumerist public" (Lombardo 2008: 219) – an issue that I will address in more detail later.

Powered by the reputation and resources of *The New York Times*, the launch of The 1619 Project was a calculated media event. Information about the initiative was disseminated over the internet prior to launch, including via the project's own website, which went public on August 14, four days before the Sunday paper with the 1619 magazine and broadsheet appeared. When the paper did come out on August 18, people stood in line to get a copy, some allegedly stealing the magazine and the broadsheet from the pricy Sunday paper. News media bolstered enthusiasm by covering both The 1619 Project and the craze around it, and *The Times* further fuelled the craze by distributing hundreds of thousands of extra copies of the magazine and the broadsheet (printed with money from private and public donors including pop musician John Legend and the N.A.A.C.P.) at libraries, schools, and museums. The activist move of "taking it to the streets" was key to securing public attention, and in the following months a heated debate ensued across the political spectrum and broad coverage in the mainstream media. The debate reached a peak last December, when a handful of well-known historians (many of them close to or past retirement age) questioned the accuracy of the story told by The 1619 Project in an open letter to the editor, prompting a passionate defense of The 1619 Project on behalf of *The Times* (and providing an occasion for an online publication of the Editor's Note, which explains the design and the goals of the initiative but had not previously been part of the website).[5]

The debate has helped more than harmed, keeping public engagement high and prompting follow-up projects including a book series that expands on the magazine issue and a graphic novel for young readers, both commissioned by Random House and to be realized in close cooperation with *The New York Times* staff. (And I would not be surprised to learn that Netflix had acquired the rights and hired a director of the caliber of Ava DuVernay or Barry Jenkins, who wrote a piece of short fiction for the magazine issue, to produce a mini-

---

[5] Conservative critics include Newt Gingrich and Erik Erickson. But The 1619 Project has also drawn stark opposition from *The World Socialist Website* as well as from Black community leaders such as Bob Woodson, who has voiced concern that the Project's reiteration of the victimization narratives endemic to the insistence on structural racism forwarded by Afropessimist critics stifles Black agency. The letter to the New York Times editor A. G. Sulzberger was initiated by Sean Wilentz, professor of history at Princeton, and signed by James McPherson, Gordon Wood, Victoria Bynum, and James Oakes, all leading scholars in their fields. The perhaps most striking thing about the dispute among historians is that most of those who do not fully agree with the story told by The 1619 Project were unwilling to sign the letter out of disagreement with the harshness of its critique, many adding that they found the debate about the legacy of slavery timely and useful. For a comprehensive summary of the debate and its peak in the letter to the editor, see Sewer (2019).

series.) Which is to say: The 1619 Project's form is open both in the sense of reaching across different media, audiences, and public arenas (and one might think of the social impact that this openness affords as spatial), and it is open in the sense of being open-ended and evolving (and one might think the social impact of this openness as temporal). This openness, which is a key feature of the essay form, makes it difficult to measure the impact of The 1619 Project's intervention in public discourse on race and racism in the U.S. at the present stage. But the sheer fact that this newspaper-based publication sparked a substantial debate gives occasion to think about the lasting significance and shifting shape of the reading public in the digital age, and how this shape is affected by the current shift toward an activist journalism in U.S. mainstream media. And even though The 1619 Project is clearly a work of journalism, its use of the essay raises fundamental questions about the political functions and uses of literature today.

I have mentioned that this essay is part of a larger effort to trace how reading in general and reading literature in particular are involved in the constitution of publics as political actors – which is arguably literature's primary political function and use in modern democratic societies. Reading The 1619 Project as an essay aims to link this effort with current concerns about the social implications of form (see especially Levine 2015) while adding to them a transmedial and transnational dimension.[6] Specifically, I draw on the German intellectual tradition which, spanning from Georg Lukács to Max Bense (and Robert Musil) to Theodor Adorno, has been marked by a shared desire to theorize the essay as a distinctive literary form (see also Hohendahl 1997; Huhn 1999; Alter and Corrigan 2017). And while views of this form and its merits differ, thinkers of this tradition agree that the essay has a distinctly hybrid form – part art, part science or philosophy – and that this hybridity is the source of its critical and political potential. My own understanding of the essay and its capacity for public engagement is firmly rooted in this idea. But in my attempts to read The 1619 Project as an essay – and by this I mean not individual pieces of it but its expansive web of textual, visual, and audio content – the work of film scholars has been extremely helpful. I have learned a lot from their nuanced approaches to understanding the essay film as the transmedial and transnational adaptation of a literary genre, which they trace from early photo essays to the beginnings of the essay film in prewar European avant-garde cinema to present-day multi-screen museum in-

---

[6] See also the "Theories and Methodologies" section in *PMLA* 132.5 (October 2017) on Levine's book.

stallations and videographic essays disseminated over the internet.[7] From them I take as my guiding principle the essay's "capacity to adapt and morph, to be flexible and open, both sponge and probe" (Elsaesser 2017: 247), and especially its ability to communicate among and across different genres, media, and modes of address in an open-ended critical engagement (Papazian and Aedes 2016: 2). Moreover, and crucially, I take inspiration from a recent tendency in film scholarship to view the essay as both a form and an act (or practice): from Tim Corrigan's understanding of the essayistic as a "tactic" that thinks through and assimilates other (narrative, rhetorical) forms with the effect of "inflecting" them (2016: 15–17; see also 2011). And from Rick Warner, who mobilizes an understanding of the essay as an extended act of essaying – "a diachronic affair that spins a web of reflection across the essayist's expanding oeuvre over time" (2018: 7) – to push beyond received understandings of the essay as a unified form. The 1619 Project does not have a unified form. In fact, the form of the project – possibly *the* artistic and/or creative form of our age[8] – requires that we push even further and think of the essay's form as a set of carefully planned and professionally administered acts of essaying, unified by a shared goal, unfolding unevenly in and across different genres and media, intersecting with and playing off of each other, with the potential effect of broadening and deepening each other's aesthetic and social impact.

"To essay" shares a semantic field with words such as "to attempt," "to test" or "weigh," suggesting an open-ended, evaluative search. For Adorno, "*essay* is a word in which thought's utopia of hitting the bull's eye unites with the consciousness of its own fallibility and provisional nature" (1988: 164). Using the term for a distinct form of writing goes back to the sixteenth-century social critic and philosopher Michel de Montaigne, who used his *Essais* (1580) to test ideas – "Of Sadness or Sorrow" (on the passing of a dear friend), "Of Sleep," "Of Vanity," "Of Drunkenness," "Of one Defect in our Government;" in short, of (his own) selfhood and subjectivity, and of society. The idea tested by The 1619 Project is to ground the founding narrative of the U.S. not in declaring independence, but in the collective practice of enslaving fellow human beings and the implications of this practice for the emerging social structures. In the words of magazine editor-in-chief Jake Silverstein (2019):

---

[7] The essay film has received broad attention in film scholarship. Two recent edited volumes that capture the state of the art are Papazian and Aedes (2016) and Alter and Corrigan (2017).
[8] I owe this thought to my colleague Kathryn Roberts, who deals with the project as an artistic/creative form in the context of her work on writers' residences, collective creativity, and contemporary literary production.

> Out of slavery—and the anti-black racism it required—grew nearly everything that has truly made America exceptional: its economic might, its industrial power, its electoral system, its diet and popular music, the inequities of its public health and education, its astonishing penchant for violence, its income inequality, the example it sets for the world as a land of freedom and equality, its slang, its legal system and the endemic racial fears and hatreds that continue to plague it to this day. The seeds of all that were planted long before our official birth date, in 1776, when the men known as our founders formally declared independence from Britain. (n. pag.)

Backed by this sweeping inventory of slavery's social and cultural legacy, Silverstein declares: "The goal of The 1619 Project is to reframe American history by considering what it would mean to regard 1619 as our nation's birth year" (n. pag.). Note how achieving this goal is bound to *considering* – spelling out, trying out, weighing – the implications of this thought experiment for U.S. American self-understanding (and in this sense The 1619 Project is indeed involved in thinking about both selfhood and society in a Montaignian vein). Note further how the idea of considering aligns the goal of The 1619 Project with the speculative mode of essay, of which Lukács writes: "two essays can never contradict each other: each creates a different world" (1971: 11). Which is to say: The essay owes its world-making capacity to its literariness, to the ability of creating "as if" scenarios in and through narrative, which it shares with literary fiction.

In the world of The 1619 Project, the act of testing, weighing, essaying "requires us to put the consequences of slavery and the contributions of black Americans at the center of the story that we tell ourselves about who we are as a country" (Silverstein 2019) (and Silverstein's use of the unifying "us" and "we" is a fixture of the personal essay's repertoire of public engagement).[9] Turning the arrival of the first enslaved Africans into an occasion for raising fundamental questions about U.S. society and its self-understanding resonates with Georg Lukács's claim that the essay takes a concrete topic as a "starting-point, a springboard" to consider the idea behind it. "A question is thrown up and extended so far in depth that it becomes the question of all questions, but after that everything remains open; something comes from outside ... and interrupts everything" (1971: 14). Which also means: the essay digresses and circles around an idea without bringing it to a scientifically rigorous conclusion. And despite all claims to historical rigor, The 1619 Project is no exception. The springboard of 1619 is used to explore, in a series of powerfully narrated essays, how Black Americans fought to make true U.S. democracy's corrupted founding ideals;

---

9 On the "pronominal tact" of the personal essay and how it moves from "you" and "I" to "we," see Lopate (1994: xl–xli; here xl).

how the brutality of American capitalism was bred at the plantation; how stealing from Black music is such a common practice because this music has been the sound of freedom for centuries; how segregation jams traffic in present-day Atlanta, and the list goes on.

And yes, all of these essays are personal in one way or another. Hannah-Jones begins her lead essay on U.S. democracy's corrupted founding ideals by telling her readers (whom she frequently addresses as "you") how, as a child, she did not understand why her father would fly the flag of a country that clearly did not love him, and ends by returning to her childhood self to claim that flag as rightfully hers after a historical tour-de-force that shows how these ideals were realized through the struggle of Black people. Wesley Morris, *The New York Times* music critic at large, sets his essay in the kitchen of a friend, where the two men cook dinner while listening to a Yacht Rock station. Matthew Desmond, a professor of sociology at Princeton, links the cotton plantation to the workplace of his readers ("Perhaps you are reading this at work") to drive home his point that the plantation was not a site of a pre-modern agrarianism but "America's first big business" and the capstone in a global economy, where output was carefully monitored and quotas ruthlessly enforced. The reader, whom he imagines being at work "at a multinational corporation that runs like a soft-purring engine," thus becomes linked to another multinational enterprise, in which "the poor slaves immediately feel the effects" of "price ris[ing] in the English market" in being "harder driven" and "the whip [being] kept more constantly going."[10] The podcast shrewdly enhances the essay's capacity for creating personal bonds, for instance when Hannah-Jones and Desmond, in the episode based on Desmond's essay, talk about how their student jobs had required them both to meet quotas, an experience that many listeners can to relate to, and that, for Desmond, is the linchpin of the capitalist work regime that started at the plantation. Or when Hannah-Jones opens said episode by telling a story about how her Great-Aunt Charlotte, who grew up in Greenwood, Mississippi ("Cotton Capital of the World"), finally talked about their haunted family history as the two women stood on the bank of the Yazoo River, which runs through Greenwood, prompting the host to reminisce: "the stories were in the land and in the water, in the Tallahatchie that flowed to the Yazoo, and the Yazoo that flowed to the Mississippi ... And that river created soils that were so rich that they led to the expansion of cotton unlike anything that the world had seen."

---

10 Unless marked otherwise all works of The 1619 Project are quoted from the website of *The New York Times Magazine.* <https://www.nytimes.com/interactive/2019/08/14/magazine/1619-america-slavery.html.> The quote above passage begins at 5:15 min.

(And I find it remarkable how the podcast uses the women's return to the land of their ancestors as a springboard to recount the story about the brutality of U.S. capitalism told by one of the few white contributors to the magazine.)

So yes, the majority of the text produced for The 1619 Project consists of a series of sweeping, powerfully narrated, and often personal essays, and these essays also provide most of the script for the podcast. But there is also writing in other genres, and what it adds to The 1619 Project goes beyond the personal in ways that enhance its aesthetic repertoire along with the critical potential that it affords. Historical sketches on topics such as "The Limits of Banking Regulations" or "How Slavery Made Wall Street" by well-known scholars add historical depth and scientific authority to the sweeping storytelling that drives the essays (and these two sketches add depth and rigor to Desmond's essay on capitalism).[11] Moreover, and crucially for the form of The 1619 Project, the sketches disrupt the narrative flow of the individual essays. Both in the magazine and on the website they are embedded in the main body of the text in ways that both augments and fractures it. The result is a digressive argument and a polyvocal, multi-layered form – which brings to mind Adorno's observation that, in an essay, "thoughts do not progress in a single direction; rather, the aspects of the argument are interwoven as in a carpet. The fruitfulness of the thoughts depends on the density of the texture" (1988: 160). Literary art adds further threads to this tapestry. Each of the sixteen commissioned works explores a date along a timeline: Jusef Komunyaka's poem about March 5, 1770 commemorates Crispus Attucks, the first American casualty in the Revolutionary War, in a Whitmanesque list of attributes:

> African & Natick blood-born
> known along paths up & down
> Boston Harbor, escaped slave
> harpooner & rope maker.

And Jesmyn Ward's piece of short fiction about January 1, 1808, the day that ended slave imports to the United States, imagines how an increasing domestic trade ("They always came before dawn") tormented the lives of the enslaved ("We felt it for the terrible dying it was"). Other works deal with planned slave rebellions, the beginning of hip-hop, medical experiments with and police brutality against Black Americans. What all of these works have in common is that, in animating forgotten or misrepresented historical figures and moments

---

11 The sketch on banking regulations is written by Mehrsa Baradaran, who is a professor of law at UC Irvine, the one on Wall Street by Tiya Miles, who is a professor of history at Harvard.

through the aesthetic prowess of fiction and poetry, they engage in an alternative historiography. In the words of Hayden White, their shared effort "to come to terms with the past involve[s] not only the uncovering of what [has] been ignored, suppressed, repressed or otherwise hidden from view." It also entails thinking

> about the utility, the worth or value, the advantages and disadvantages of the kind of knowledge of the past produced by the new cadres of professional historians that had been established in the late nineteenth century for service to the European nation-state but which, also, laid claim to the status of a "science" (Wissenschaft) and authorized to determine what kinds of questions could be asked by the present of the past, what kind of evidence could be adduced in any effort to ask the proper questions, what constituted properly "historical" answers to those questions, and where the line was to be drawn for distinguishing between a proper and an improper use of historical "knowledge" in any effort to clarify or illuminate contemporary efforts to answer central question of moral and societal concern: what Kant called the "practical" (by which he meant the ethical) question: what should I (we) do? (White 2010)[12]

And if this is indeed an apt description of the counter-historiography practiced and endorsed by The 1916 Project, bringing literature into this practice amplifies its force, for literature is even freer than the essay to displace the "historical past" with a "practical past" – which is, for White, a past of "memory, dream, and desire as much as it is of problem-solving, strategy and tactics of living, both personal and communal."[13]

The podcast further increases the power of literature to decenter the "historical past" by thematically pairing essays and literary works. Ward's piece on the slave trade, introduced and read by the author herself, brings the podcast episode on capitalism to an especially powerful end by bringing to life how the enslaved (may have) experienced the dehumanizing brutality of this economic regime. And Jacqueline Woodson's piece on Isaac Woodard, a decorated World War II veteran who lost his eyesight as a result of being beaten by the police on his way home from the battlefield, is picked up and fleshed out by Hannah-Jones in the democracy podcast episode to support her claim that

---

12 The quote is taken from the manuscript of a lecture which Hayden White gave at the John F. Kennedy Institute on May 6, 2010. I am grateful for his generosity to share it with me.

13 Drawing on Michael Oakeshott, who coined the term, White argues that the "practical past" departs from the "historical past" of professional historiography by referring to "those notions of the past which all of us carry around with us in our daily lives and which we draw upon ... for information, ideas, models, and strategies for solving all the practical problems—from personal affairs to grand political programs—met with in whatever we conceive to be our present 'situation'" (White 2010). See also Oakeshott (1999: 1–48).

Black Americans like Woodard – whose case was taken up by the N.A.A.C.P. and is now commonly viewed as "one of the sparks of the modern civil rights movement" – were essential in realizing the country's democratic ideals.[14] Neither the magazine (where literary works are interspersed with historical sketches, yet with no clear connection to the texts surrounding them), nor the website (where the literary works form a section of their own) creates this enticing call-and-response effect between and across different genres and media.

Yet even in the seamlessly flowing narrative track of the podcast, the texture remains heterogeneous, patch-worked – essayistic. For Adorno, building on Lukács, the essay "thinks in fragments ... and gains its unity by moving through the fissures, rather than by smoothing them over" (1988: 164). In doing so, it "corrects the isolated and accidental aspects of its insights by allowing them to multiply, confirm, and restrict themselves—whether in the essay's proper progress or in its mosaic-like relation to other essays" (ibid). In other words, and this is indeed key to The 1619 Project's critical practice: The disjointed, digressive form of the essay enables an open-ended and dialogic mode of reflection, whose networking operations reach beyond the confines of individual essays. This also means that individual acts of essaying, in intersecting with other such acts, are part of a larger, interconnected effort of public engagement. Moreover, and crucially for The 1619 Project's investment in the essay form, in its expansive media environment the dynamics of multiplication and confirmation that fuel this practice proliferate, not least because much of the same material is featured in print, online, and on the podcast, changing its shape due to the particular restrictions of each medium while consolidating insight – and intensifying impact – through repetition.

Morris' essay on Black music is a good example of this. The springboard to his story of how Black music is the foundation of U.S. popular culture is the scene described above in which the writer and a friend are listening to Yacht Rock (perhaps the most conspicuously non-Black music) while chopping vegetables. When the friend goes on an errand, Morris ("alone, just me, with the vegetables and the Yacht Rock") is (like the podcast user) free to immerse himself in the listening experience. The web version of the essay hyperlinks each musical reference to a YouTube clip, which is certainly a great advantage of the digital format. However, using the links to listen to the songs (and watch the clips) disrupts the reading process; in other words, the storytelling is far more powerful in the magazine than on the website. On the podcast music and storytelling are

---

14 See <https://www.nytimes.com/2019/08/23/podcasts/1619-slavery-anniversary.html.> Last visited: February 16, 2019. Hannah-Jones's account of Woodard's story starts at 32:20 min.

fully integrated. In the absence of text and image, the act of listening to Yacht Rock prompts an intimate conversation between Morris and the music itself, including Morris singing along to some of the tunes. The transcript of the podcast (which is freely available on the website) gives a good sense of this dialogic structure:

Wesley Morris
    There is something jazz-like in the syncopated music of something like Steely Dan.
Archived Recording
    [MUSIC – STEELY DAN, "DO IT AGAIN"]
Wesley Morris
    You can hear in somebody like Michael McDonald—
Archived Recording
    [MUSIC – THE DOOBIE BROTHERS, "WHAT A FOOL BELIEVES"]
Wesley Morris
    Ah, ah, ah, ah, ah-ah.
    That is, like, a gospel breakdown.
Archived Recording
    [MUSIC – THE DOOBIE BROTHERS, "WHAT A FOOL BELIEVES"]
Wesley Morris
    What I'm hearing in all of these songs is, basically, blackness.[15]

The transcript gives a good sense of the quick and upbeat pace of the dialogue. What it does not capture, however, is the syncopated simultaneity of soundtrack and narrative track, where the music often sets in right before Wesley shares his thoughts about it, thus increasing the listener's engagement by creating the impression that the music is driving the argument. So yes, the podcast is immensely powerful in telling the story of Black music as the foundation of American popular culture. But the act of sheer listening makes it impossible to keep track of artist names and song titles, which is why the podcast may also direct listeners (back) to the website or the magazine. In short: the essay on Black music as the foundation of American popular culture shows how the densely networked and recursive act of essaying afforded by the multi- and transmedial design of The 1619 Project – in anticipating feedback loops, capitalizing on media restrictions, and incentivizing repetitions – adds new dimensions to the openness of the essay form.

---

15 See <https://www.nytimes.com/2019/09/06/podcasts/1619-black-american-music-appropriation.html?action=click&module=audio-series-bar&region=header&pgtype=Article.> Last visited: February 16, 2019. The quoted passage begins at 4:05 min.

Adorno has described this openness as "not vaguely one of feeling and mood" but as one that "obtains its contour from its content" (1988: 165). The 1619 Project's carefully planned and administered effort of considering the legacy of slavery gives special force to the suturing, networking operation of closing gaps within a disjointed texture. In doing so, it reinforces the essay's inner drive toward open-ended reflection and dialogue. In Lukács's words: "The essay is a judgment, but the essential, the value-determining thing about it is not the verdict ... but the process of judging" (1971: 18). But if the iconic image for openness and (re)interpretation is that of the horizon, this image gains an uncanny twist (or undercurrent) in The 1619 Project. The cover photograph shows a horizon, and from the paragraph below we learn that it is the horizon off the coast of Hampton, Virginia, on which "a ship appeared" in August 1619 that "carried more than 20 enslaved Africans, who were sold to the colonists" (figure 1). This is the horizon of the Black Atlantic, grave of countless enslaved Africans who drowned in its waters in the infamous Middle Passage. Encountering it on the magazine cover, we may let our gaze wonder from the horizon in the background across the vast deep blue in the middle to the carefully composed rose-colored text in the foreground, written in an elegant serif font reminiscent of old-fashioned storybooks. And as we read and look, we might imagine the ship with its fateful cargo appearing on that horizon; and further imagine what it must have felt like for those onboard that ship, torn from everything they knew and loved, and about to be sold into bondage.

The magazine cover renders this space of historical horror as a space of critical revaluation, drawing us into this space, placing us (together with all of the other readers of the magazine) in the open water, with no solid ground beneath our feet.[16] We may also encounter the photograph on the home screen of the website, where the middle ground is filled with writing and the font is much larger – so large that we have to scroll down to read the entire opening paragraph, and are pulled into the depths of exploring the implications of the ship's arrival in the interactive and hyperlinked feed of texts and images animated by our own physical movements (figure 2). The podcast (which uses a miniature of the photograph for its icon) opens at the same historical site, where, engulfed in the melodic chant of seagulls and surf, the host and one of the producers are conversing:

---

[16] Among the profoundest insights of Michael Warner's work on discursive publicness of the type that sustains the critical potential of The 1619 Project is that its ability to bring forth political agency depends on its capacity to create relations among strangers who many have nothing in common but reading the same printed texts. See Warner (2002: 65–66).

Nikole Hannah-Jones
> It's quiet out here. There're seagulls. The sun is warm, but it's not too humid. It's actually kind of a great day for fishing, which is why it stinks.

Adizah Eghan
> What does it smell like?

Nikole Hannah-Jones
> It smells like dead fish. It smells like the water.

Adizah Eghan
> What is going through your head right now?

Nikole Hannah-Jones
> I don't know, thinking about what they went through.
> I don't know. I just wonder a lot what it was, what it was like.[17]

Note how the dialogue between the two women rehearses the imaginary and interpretative work inscribed into the cover photograph. When engaging with this work through the podcast, the voices of the two speakers (voices in our head, heard with great immediacy) add a powerful sense of physical presence, which gains a grainy, visceral intimacy in the sniffs or hawks that Hannah-Jones makes when envisioning what happened here. That the conversation goes on for almost four minutes before the podcast is properly introduced adds to the sense of being drawn into a personal relation, and over the course of listening to the podcast the feeling grows, as if one is becoming friends with the host and her guests.

But while consumability increases from magazine to website to podcast hand in hand with the enhanced stimulation of affective bonds, the form itself remains open. An aesthetics of playfulness and experimentation secures this openness, which is rooted in a journalistic format – magazine journalism – with a long tradition of producing readily consumable content.[18] Magazines such as *Leslie's Weekly* (1855), *Harper's Weekly* (1857), *Ladies Home Journal* (1883), *Cosmopolitan* (1886), *Vogue* (1892), and *McClure's* (1893) revolutionized the publication of periodicals in the nineteenth century with an extraordinary will to experiment – with styles and genres, texts and images, fonts and colors. This new magazine culture is the cradle of the essayistic, narrative-driven journalism perfected by *The New Yorker* and *Esquire* in the twentieth century and that is a staple of public discourse in the U.S. today. Moreover, and crucially, it is a viable resource for the more personal and activist journalism of which The 1619 Project and its use of the essay form are emblematic. And this brings

---

[17] See <https://www.nytimes.com/2019/08/23/podcasts/1619-slavery-anniversary.html.> Last visited: February 16, 2019. The quoted passage is the very beginning of the podcast.
[18] Only one article, on the topic of ownership in professional basketball, was published in the pages of the regular newspaper.

to mind a third thinker of the German intellectual tradition, Max Bense, for whom experimentation and configuration – the artistic practices at the heart of magazine journalism – define the essay's form. For Bense, essayistic writing is *writing while experimenting*, turning one's object this way and that, questioning it, feeling it, testing it, attacking it from different angles, collecting in one's mind's eye what one sees, and making it visible in what Bense calls a "literary 'ars combinatoria'" (2017: 57).[19] In The 1619 Project an experimental aesthetics of making something visible about its object of thought qua (re)configuration characterizes not only the writings but also the design. For instance, when the opening pages of the magazine fill the water-and-horizon space of the magazine cover with four gigantic white ciphers and a full stop glaring at us from a black page: an aesthetic effect that suggests that the writing is on the wall (figure 3).

The page design condenses the Editor's Note to the size of a footnote by the sheer weight of the date while the sans-serif font amplifies its programmatic tone. This (modernist) aesthetics of playfulness and experimentation shapes the engagement with the published material of The 1619 Project throughout its expansive multimedial form. And this brings me to one of Adorno's most evocative points about the aesthetic dimension of the essay. Whether flipping through the magazine, clicking through the webpage, listening to the podcast, or doing a combination of these activities, we engage with a form made up of "elements that crystallize as a configuration through their motion. The constellation is a force field, just as every intellectual structure is necessarily transformed into a force field by the essay's gaze" (1988: 161). The debate among historians about the accuracy of the story told by The 1619 Project is a case in point, and it reminds us that the essay's transformative power – its power to change the

---

[19] In Bense's words: "He who writes essayistically; who composes something experimentally; who turns his subject this way and that, questions, touches, inspects, and reflects upon it thoroughly; who approaches it from different angles, and collects what he sees in his mind's eye, and formulates in words what his topic reveals under the conditions established by writing" (2017: 52). And: "The transformation of a configuration, in which the object is located, is the point of the experiment, and the goal of the essay is less the revelation of the object's definition than is the sum of factors, the sum of configurations, in which it becomes possible. That is also of scientific value, because the circumstance, the atmosphere, in which something flourishes wants to be recognized and, after all, reveals something. Therefore, configuration is an epistemological category that cannot be achieved through axiomatic deduction, but rather through a literary 'ars combinatoria,' in which imagination has replaced pure knowledge" (57). Among literary scholars, Bense's work on the essay is much lesser known than that of Lukács and Adorno (who cites it affirmatively in "The Essay as Form"), while film scholars and makers value it for its emphasis of the artistic and critical merits of configuration, which is essential to the genre of the essay film.

world by putting thought against itself – resides in this form, no matter how unbound it becomes. In fact, The 1619 Project shows how an extended non-unified, multi- and transmedial update of the essay's generic openness becomes a powerful tool of critique.

Emerging from this reading of The 1619 Project's use of the essay form, we may say that it creates an opening in the discursive and epistemic fabric of public life. How this opening is closed again is not the job of the essay; it is the job of the social actors and institutions that have been mobilized by its gaze. In the case of the opening in public discourse on race and racism in the U.S. created by The 1619 Project, this work revolves around national self-understanding and identity, and the success of this work depends on reconciling the partisanship that drives the activist journalism of which The 1619 Project is emblematic with the need for coalition building around the aching and polarizing subject of race and racism in an achingly polarized country. This also means that The 1619 Project crystallizes one of the most urgent and serious questions about the new journalism: Is it is an agent of polarization or coalition building – or both? And how does the essay form contribute to shaping its agency in this regard?

Johannes Voelz makes a lucid point about the political logic of polarization when noting that it "gives rise to a perverted form of politicization," one that is not invested in "open[ing] up what is being politicized for democratic debate" but in "build[ing] up and consolidat[ing] the identities of 'us' and 'them.'" Which basically means that all politics have become identity politics: "Not the type of identity politics that pushes for the recognition of marginalized groups, but one in which taking sides in political struggles is a matter of people's identity as liberals or conservatives, or better: Democrats of Republicans" (Voelz 2020). For the politicized, activist journalism of the kind crystallized by The 1619 Project this means an almost default participation in identitarian block building – and the risk of becoming an agent in foreclosing democratic debate. So yes, within the sectarian logic of polarization that has come to dominate, and indeed pervert, political life in the U.S., a politicized journalism is pulled into the game of building and consolidating "us" vs. "them" identities. (And the polarizing force of the claim that some journalists work in the service of "moral clarity" while others cling to the "failed project" of "'objectivity'-obsessed, both-sidedness" [Smith 2020] is a powerful token of the partisan logic pinpointed by Voelz). So yes, it is apt to say that the activist journalism crystalized by The 1619 Project is an agent of polarization. And yet, within the game of identitatian block-building which has come to dominate not only politics but also public discourse in the U.S. – and which an activist journalism endorses and enforces rather than resists – the political potential of The 1619 Project lies in building a coalition of social actors with the power to revise the liberal script of national belonging in ways that might broaden its identitarian base. And my point about The 1619 Project's use of the essay form is that this potential stems to a significant degree from its use of the essay form.

But is this not a blunt exaggeration of the political agency afforded by this form? And is this form even as open as I have claimed? Does The 1619 Project not focus on establishing 'race' as the question of all questions (and the answer, too)? And does its declared goal to reframe U.S. history not amount to an attempt to establish a new founding narrative, one that makes use of a playful, transmedial aesthetics to replace the old premise of 'liberal democracy' with that of 'slavery' and the anti-black racism that it requires, all with the aim of building a new liberal identity based on the new narrative? In other words: how open is The 1619 Project ideologically? Does it, for instance, question its own assumptions about history writing? Or does it subscribe to and promote an educational goal that is exempt from its expansive acts of considering, testing, weighing? And if this were the case would it not make its form substantially less searching, and indeed rather clearly committed to realizing a concrete and pre-set political goal? And linked back to the question about the political affordances of its form that drives this inquiry: how much room does the playful and experimental aesthetics of The 1619 Project leave for the kind of multi-directional irritation that in Adorno's, Lukacs', and Bense's view is the basis for the essay's capacity to engage its recipients in an open-ended process of reflection? These are all valid questions about the political agency of The 1619 Project and its use of the essay form, for sure. And the first thing one may hold against them is a certain skepticism about the ideal of radical openness endorsed by the 'old world' thinkers. Was their essayistic practice really as free from the desire to show that some things are better or truer or more just than others as their theorizations imply? Be that as it may, the political agency that lies in the essayistic practice endorsed by The 1619 Project resides in an openness that is relative rather than radical – yet open nonetheless. In my strong reading of this relative openness, the critical and political affordance of The 1619 Project's use of the essay form lies in its capacity to unsettle and disrupt the liberal democratic founding narrative through its expansive act of considering an alternative narrative based on slavery and the anti-black racism that it requires – not to replace the old founding narrative with new one, but to open up an intellectual and imaginative space for the possibility of revision and renewal through the essay's expansive capacity for self-reflection and public engagement. Tied back to the question of The 1619 Project as an agent of coalition building, this means that its efforts in this regard are geared less toward consolidating a new liberal identity based on a new founding narrative, and more toward achieving a broad and solid consensus within the liberal camp that the old founding narrative must be revised in ways that reckon with the legacy of slavery with unprecedented rigor and sincerity.

So, at best The 1619 Project has the critical and political potential to expose the need to revise the liberal script of national belonging and broaden the base of those identifying with it. But it must be stressed that this transformative power is not radical. It is confined to the bourgeois and educated clientele of *The New York Times* – which may, in turn, hope to strengthen the ties with its readers. Indeed, if the shift toward an activist journalism "is driven in equal parts by politics, the culture and journalism's business model, relying increasingly on passionate readers willing to pay for content" (Smith 2020), The 1619 Project makes *Times* subscribers active participants (and potential activists) in the ongoing struggle over "who we are as a country" (Silverstein 2019). Moreover, and crucially, The 1619 Project can help *The New York Times* to correct its image and practice of racially biased reporting.[20] This practice was recently spotlighted by concept artist Alexandra Bell in a series of works that stage and expose how mainstream "quality" media marginalize Black experience in the U.S. to this day by showing how headlines, choice and placement of photographs and articles, and a racially biased language perpetuate racist assumptions and stereotypes (figure 4). In a prominent work of the series, Bell exposes how *The New York Times* front page of August 25, 2014 uses racist stereotypes to pit the lives of a white and a Black man from Ferguson against each other. In step (and picture) one, problematic passages are highlighted with red ink and a text marker, in step (and picture) two these passages are blackened out (with the result of blackening the entire article), and in step (and picture) three, a new page is offered: the black boy, described in the original article as "A Teenager Grappling with Problems and Promise," is shown in a graduation gown in a picture that fills the entire page, complemented with a new heading, describing him as "A Teenager with Promise."

Both Bell's artworks (in which *The Times* is indeed a main target) and The 1619 Project are interventions in public discourse on race and racism, for sure. And they are politically motivated and even activist in similar ways (Bell also

---

[20] Ironically, *The Times*' decision to abstain from calling Trump a racist led to an internal town-hall meeting in the week prior to The 1619 Project launch, in which one staffer asked whether *The Times* was not inviting "even more criticism from people who are like, 'OK, well you're saying this, and you're producing this big project about this. But are you guys actually considering this in your daily reporting?'" A recording of the meeting was transcribed and published by *Slate*, with the effect of intensifying the debate about *The Times*'s policy on racism and the status of The 1619 Project; see <https://slate.com/news-and-politics/2019/08/new-york-times-meeting-transcript.html>.

took her work to the street, pasting it on walls in her Brooklyn neighborhood). But unlike Bell's works, The 1619 Project is not a work of art but a work of journalism, powered not by the prestige and the consecrated display space of art institutions (Bell's work was shown at the 2019 Whitney Biennale when The 1619 Project was launched), but by the reputation and resources of one of the country's leading newspapers. And this brings me back one last time to Adorno, whose elaborations on the essay have been a such prominent guide to my reading of The 1619 Project's critical and political potential as aesthetically grounded. For Adorno, the aesthetic dimension of the essay protects it against reification, making it autonomous, art-like. The 1619 Project contradicts (or dare I say, *inflects*) this line of thought and the intellectual structure – Frankfurt School commodity criticism – of which Adorno's view of the essay is emblematic. The 1619 Project is a work of journalism that follows the logic of the cultural commodity. Its playful aesthetics is indeed at times so commercial that it is difficult to distinguish journalistic content from the advertisements surrounding it.

But this commodity aesthetics neither questions nor dwarfs The 1619 Project's ambition to change public discourse – a discourse powered by an imperative need for attention that in the U.S. developed, in the absence of a publicly funded media system, *under the conditions of capitalist mass media*. This commodity aesthetics does not diminish The 1619 Project's political zeal. But it reminds us that the aesthetic practice that is the driving force behind the essay's critical potential does not follow the logic of art, which may best be described as the logic of the "socially symbolic act" (Jameson 1981). The aesthetic practice driving the essay follows the logic of social reform through reconfiguration. The 1619 Project renews this practice in and through its extended multimedia form.

Figure 1: Cover of the 1619 issue of The New York Times Magazine.

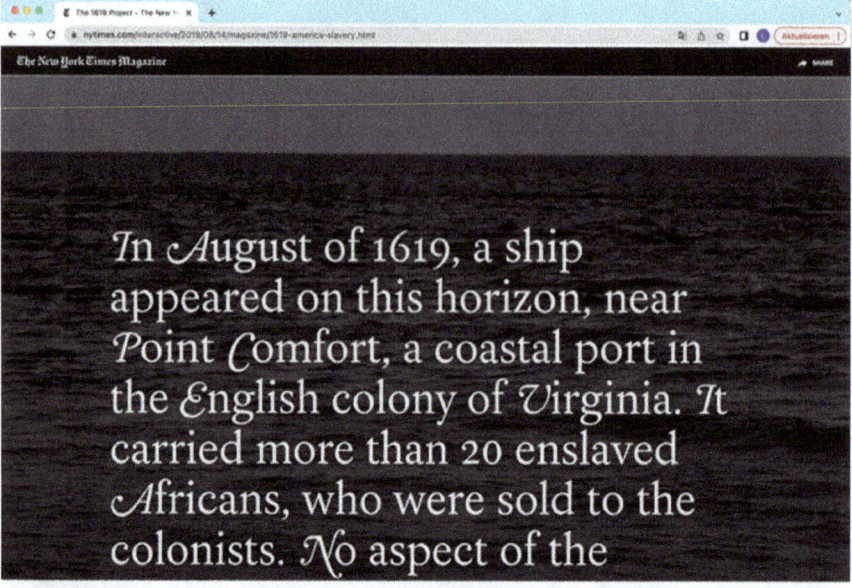

Figure 2: Home screen of The 1619 Project's website.

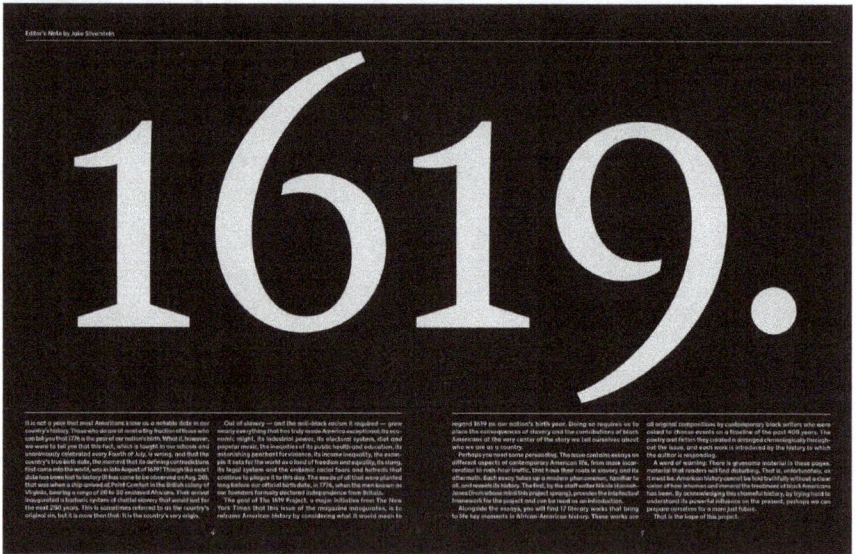

Figure 3: Double spread with Editors' Note in the 1619 issue of The New York Times Magazine.

Figure 4: Alexandra Bell, Teenager With Promise.

Works Cited

Adorno, Theodor W. 1984. "The Essay as Form" [1958]. *New German Critique* 32 (Spring – Summer): 151–171.

Adorno, Theodor W. 1993. "Commitment." [1992]. Trans. Shierry Weber Nicolson. *Notes to Literature* Vol. 2. New York: Columbia University Press. 76–94.

Alter, Nora, and Timothy Corrigan. 2017. "Introduction." In: Nora Alter and Timothy Corrigan (eds.). *Essays on the Essay Film*. New York: Columbia University Press. 1–18.

Bense, Max. 2017. "The Essay and Its Prose" [1948]. Trans. Margit Grieb. In: Nora Alter and Timothy Corrigan (eds.). *Essays on the Essay Film*. New York: Columbia University Press. 51–59.

Bieger, Laura. 2020. "What Dewey Knew. The Public as Problem, Practice, and Art." Special Issue "Truth or Post-Truth? Philosophy, American Studies, and Current Perspectives on Pragmatism and Hermeneutics." *European Journal of American Studies* 15 (1).

Bieger, Laura. 2019a. "Jean-Paul Sartre, Richard Wright, and the Relational Art of Literary Engagement." In: Winfried Fluck, Johannes Voelz and Rieke Jordan (eds.). *The Return of the Aesthetic in American Studies. REAL Yearbook of Research in English and American Literature* 35. 169–88.

Bieger, Laura. 2019b. "Learning from Hannah Arendt; or, the Public Sphere as a Space of Appearance and the Fundamental Opacity of the Face-to-Face." In: Ulla Haselstein, Frank Kelleter, Alexander Starre and Birte Wege. *American Counter/Publics*. Heidelberg: Winter. 37–52

Bieger, Laura. "Reading for Democracy." 2018. In: Donald E. Pease (ed.). *Democratic Cultures and Populist Imaginaries. REAL Yearbook of Research in English and American Literature* 34. 203–219.

Corrigan, Timothy. 2016. "Essayism and Contemporary Film Narrative." In: Elizabeth A. Papazian and Caroline Aedes (eds.). *The Essay Film: Dialogue, Politics, Utopia*. New York: Columbia University Press. 15–27.

Corrigan, Timothy. 2011. *The Essay Film: From Montaigne, After Maker*. Oxford and New York: Oxford University Press.

Desmond, Matthew. 2019. "In order to understand the brutality of American capitalism, you have to start on the plantation." *The New York Times Magazine*, August 14, 2019. <https://www.nytimes.com/interactive/2019/08/14/magazine/slavery-capitalism.html.> [accessed 25 November 2021]

Elsaesser, Thomas. 2017. "The Essay Film: From Film Festival Favorite to Flexible Commodity Form?" In: Nora Alter and Timothy Corrigan (eds.). *Essays on the Essay Film*. New York: Columbia University Press. 240–258.

Feinberg, Ashley. 2019. "The New York Times Unites vs. Twitter." *Slate*, August 15, 2019. <https://slate.com/news-and-politics/2019/08/new-york-times-meeting-transcript.html.> [accessed 25 November 2021]

Fielder, Leslie. 1958. *The Art of the Essay*. New York: Thomas Y. Crowell Company.

Gray, John. 1996. *Post-Liberalism: Studies in Political Thought*. London: Routledge.

Hannah-Jones, Nikole. 2019. "Our democracy's founding ideals were false when they were written. Black Americans have fought to make them true." *The New York Times Magazine*, August 14, 2019. <https://www.nytimes.com/interactive/2019/08/14/magazine/black-history-american-democracy.html>. [accessed 25 November 2021]

Huhn, Tom. 1999. "Lukács and the Essay Form." *New German Critique* 78, Special Issue on German Media Studies (Fall): 183–192.

Hohendahl, Peter Uwe. 1997. "The Scholar, the Intellectual, and the Essay: Weber, Lukács, Adorno, and Postwar Germany." *The German Quarterly* 70 (3): 217–232.

Jameson, Frederic. 1981. *The Political Unconscious: Narrative as Socially Symbolic Act*. London: Methuen & Co.

Junker, Carsten. 2010. *Frames of Friction: Black Genealogies, White Hegemony, and the Essay as Critical Intervention*. Frankfurt/M.: Campus

Levine, Caroline. 2015. *Forms: Whole. Rhythm, Hierarchy, Network*. Princeton, NJ: Princeton University Press.

Lopate, Philip. 1994. *The Art of the Personal Essay: An Anthology from the Classical Era to the Present*. New York: Anchor Books/Doubleday.

Lukács, Georg. 1971. "The Nature and Form of the Essay. A Letter to Leo Popper" [1910]. In *Soul and Form*. Transl. Anna Bostock. Cambridge, MA: MIT Press. 1–18.

Lombardo, Mark. 2008. "Is the Podcast a Public Sphere Institution?" *ipod and philosophy: iCon of an ePoch*. Eds. D. E. Wittkower. Peru: Carus Publishing. 215–228.

MacDougall, Robert C. 2011. "Podcasting and Political Life." *American Behavioral Scientist* 55 (6): 714–732.

Morris, Wesley. 2019. "For centuries black music, forged in bondage, has been the sound of complete artistic freedom. No wonder everybody is always stealing from it." *The New York Times Magazine*, August 14, 2019. <https://www.nytimes.com/interactive/2019/08/14/magazine/music-black-culture-appropriation.html>. [accessed 25 November 2021]

Oakeshott, Michael. 1999. "Present, Future and Past." In: *On History and Other Essays*. Indianapolis: Liberty Fund. 1–48.

Papazian, Elizabeth A. and Caroline Aedes. 2016. "Introduction: Dialogue, Politics, Utopia." In: Elizabeth A. Papazian and Caroline Aedes (eds.). *The Essay Film: Dialogue, Politics, Utopia*. New York: Columbia University Press. 1–11.

Sartre, Jean-Paul. 1988. *What is Literature? and Other Essays*. Trans. Bernhard Frechtmann. Cambridge, MA: Harvard University Press.

Schatzki, Theodore R., 2001. "Introduction: Practice Theory." In: Theodore R. Schatzki, Karin Knorr Cetina and Eike von Savigny (eds.). *The Practice Turn in Contemporary Theory*. London and New York: Routledge. 1–14.

Serwer, Adam. 2019. "The Fight over The 1619 Project is Not About the Facts." *The Atlantic*, December 23, 2019. <https://www.theatlantic.com/ideas/archive/2019/12/historians-clash-1619-project/604093/>. [accessed 25 November 2021]

Silverstein, Jake. 2019. "Editor's Note." *The New York Times Magazine*, August 18, 2019. Republished as "Why We Published The 1619 Project," December 20, 2019. <https://www.nytimes.com/interactive/2019/12/20/magazine/1619-intro.html>. [accessed 25 November 2021]

Soltani, Farokh. 2018. "Inner Ears and Distant Worlds: Podcast Dramaturgy and the *Theatre of the Mind*." In: D. Llinares, N. Fox, and R. Berry (eds.). *Podcasting*. London: Palgrave Macmillan. 189–208.

Smith, Ben. 2020. "Inside the Revolts Erupting in America's Big Newsrooms." *The New York Times*, June 9, 2020. <https://www.nytimes.com/2020/06/07/business/media/new-york-times-washington-post-protests.html>. [accessed 25 November 2021]

Voelz, Johannes. 2020. "The Post-Liberal Aesthetic; Or, How Can Literary Criticism Help Unsettle America's Polarization?" *American Literary History* (forthcoming).

Wall, Cheryl A. 2018. *On Freedom and the Will to Adorn: The Art of the African American Essay*. Chapel Hill: University of North Carolina Press.

Warner, Michael. 2002. "Publics and Counterpublics." *Public Culture* 14 (1): 49–90.

Warner, Rick. 2018. *Godard and the Essay Film: A Form That Thinks*. Evanston: Northwestern University Press.

White, Hayden. 2010. "The Practical Past." Talk at Freie Universität Berlin, May 6.

Notes on Contributors

Laura Bieger is Professor of American Studies, Political Theory and Culture at the University of Groningen, where she co-directs the Research Center for Democratic Culture and Politics. She is the author of *Belonging and Narrative* (transcript 2018), which considers the need to belong as a driving force of literary production and the novel as a primary place and homemaking agent. In another book, *Ästhetik der Immersion* (transcript 2007), she examines public spaces from Washington DC to Las Vegas that turn world-image-relations into immersive spectacles. Her essays have appeared in *New Literary History, Narrative, Studies in American Naturalism, Amerikastudien/American Studies* and *ZAA*. Her current research explores the reading public as a democratic institution and 'engaged literature' as a tool for social change.

Astrid Böger is Professor of North American Literature and Culture at University of Hamburg. She is the author of three monographs to date, *Documenting Lives: James Agee's and Walker Evans's 'Let Us Now Praise Famous Men'* (1994), *People's Lives, Public Images: The New Deal Documentary Aesthetic* (2001), and *Envisioning the Nation: The Early American World's Fairs and the Formation of Culture* (2010). In addition to several co-edited volumes on gender studies and transnational visual culture, she has published numerous scholarly articles on diverse topics in contemporary U.S.-American culture. A new collection of essays, on U.S.-American popular culture (co-edited with Florian Sedlmeier), is slated to appear in 2022. Böger is a member of a DFG-funded research network on Theme Park Studies and contributor to the forthcoming volume on *Key Concepts in Theme Park Studies* emerging from it.

Christa Buschendorf was Professor and Chair of American Literature and Culture at Goethe University Frankfurt from 1998 to 2015; in summer 2019, she was Harris Distinguished Professor at Dartmouth College. She published on the American reception of Schopenhauer, on the afterlife of antiquity in the U.S., and on ancient myths in American poetry. Currently, she is exploring the approach of relational sociology in (African) American Studies. Among her recent publications on Black literature and culture are articles on Edward P. Jones, W.E.B. Du Bois, Shirley Graham Du Bois, and Frederick Douglass; she edited conversations with Cornel West on *Black Prophetic Fire* (2014) and *Power Relations in Black Lives: Reading African Literature and Culture with Bourdieu and Elias* (2018).

Thomas Claviez is Professor for Literary Theory at the University of Bern. He is the author of *Grenzfälle: Mythos – Ideologie – American Studies* (1998) and *Aesthetics & Ethics: Moral Imagination from Aristotle to Levinas and from* Uncle Tom's Cabin *to* House Made of Dawn (2008). He has co-edited numerous volumes, most recently, with Kornelia Imesch and Britta Sweers, the collection *Critique of Authenticity*, published 2019 with Vernon Press. He is the single editor of the collections *The Conditions of Hospitality: Ethics, Aesthetics and Politics at the Threshold of the Possible* and *The Common Growl: Towards a Poetics of Precarious Community*, both published with Fordham UP in 2014 and 2017. Forthcoming, also with Fordham UP, is the collection *Throwing the Moral Dice: Ethics and Contingency* (2021). He is currently working on a monograph with the title *A Metonymic Community? Towards a New Poetics of*

Contingency. He has published widely on topics such as literature and ethics, populism, 19th and 20th century U.S.-American Literature, Native Americans, and eco-criticism.

Astrid Franke is Professor of American Studies at Tübingen University. Her publications include *Keys to Controversies: Stereotypes in Modern American Novels* (1999), *"Pursue the Illusion": Problems of Public Poetry in America* (2010), and various articles on the conjunction of literature and (social) justice. She is about to wrap up a long-term project on the persistence of the racial order in the U.S. within the Collaborative Research Center "Threatened Orders."

Catrin Gersdorf is Professor and Chair of American Studies at the University of Würzburg, and a past Executive Director of the German Association for American Studies. The author of *The Poetics and Politics of the Desert: Landscape and the Construction of America* (2009), her published work includes essays and edited volumes on ecocriticism, the intersection of ecology and (American) democracy, and on individual writers, thinkers, and artists such as Benjamin Franklin, Thomas Jefferson, Henry David Thoreau, Walter Benjamin, Angela Carter, Nathanael West, Ana Mendieta, and Toni Morrison. Her current research focuses on literary and cultural responses to the challenges of the Anthropocene.

Andrew S. Gross is Professor of North American Studies at the University of Göttingen since 2015. He previously held positions at the University of Erlangen-Nürnberg, at the John F. Kennedy Institute, Free University of Berlin, and at the University of California, Davis. The author of *The Pound Reaction: Liberalism and Lyricism in Mid-Century American Literature* (2015) and *Comedy, Avant-Garde, Scandal: Remembering the Holocaust after the End of History* (with Susanne Rohr, 2010), his published work includes essays and edited volumes on poetry and politics, the reading public, notions of authenticity, and on writers including W.D. Snodgrass, Rivka Galchen, and Joseph O'Neill.

Marius Henderson studied English and American Studies as well as Gender Studies at the University of Hamburg and Johns Hopkins University. His dissertation (Hamburg, 2019) deals with modes of rendering suffering in contemporary experimental North American poetry. Currently, he is Postdoctoral Researcher and Lecturer at the Chair of American Studies: Culture and Literature, at Friedrich-Alexander University Erlangen-Nuremberg and a member of the *Global Sentimentality Project*. His research interests include: affect theory, abstraction and abjection, African American studies, Afropessimism, modernisms, and artistic research.

One of his recent publications is the text "Passing Tone/Note," which deals with issues of racialized "passing," and which is an experimental poetic contribution to the volume *Who Can Speak and Who Is Heard/Hurt?: Facing Problems of Race, Racism, and Ethnic Diversity in the Humanities in Germany*, edited by Mahmoud Arghavan, Nicole Hirschfelder, Luvena Kopp, and Katharina Motyl (transcript 2019). Marius regularly cooperates with other scholars, writers and artists and is interested in collaboratively exploring and bridging gaps between scholarly and artistic practices. Marius's current research project investigates the paradigmatic function and intertwinement of dynamics of abstraction and abjection in North American modernisms.

Kai Hopen is Adjunct Lecturer at the University of Groningen's department of American Studies. His PhD project examines the role of the MacArthur Fellowship Program, or "Genius Grant," in the production of contemporary U.S.-American literature. His research interests are centered around contemporary U.S.-American literature and the question of "what is to be done?"

Heinz Ickstadt was Professor of American Literature at the Kennedy Institute of American Studies, FU Berlin and has been Emeritus since 2003. He is the author of numerous publications on modern poetry (Hart Crane, William Carlos Williams, Ezra Pound) and on modern and postmodern U.S.-American fiction (John Dos Passos, William Faulkner, Thomas Pynchon, Robert Coover, Don DeLillo). His most recent collection of essays is *Aesthetic Innovation and the Democratic Principle* (edited with Susanne Rohr, Peter Schneck, and Sabine Sielke; Winter 2016). He was president of the German (1990–1993) and the European Associations of American Studies (1996–2000).

Jan D. Kucharzewski has held positions as an assistant and associate professor for American Studies at the universities of Düsseldorf, Hamburg, and Mannheim. He received his PhD at the University of Düsseldorf for a thesis on the relationship between literature and science, focusing on the works of the contemporary American novelist Richard Powers. The dissertation was awarded with a publication grant by the German Research Foundation. He has published papers and co-edited volumes on contemporary American film and literature, the frontier, network theory, neorealism, postmodern subjectivity, masculinity studies, American hunting texts, and on American modernism. His current research project examines the connection between masculinity, liminality, and exceptionalist ideologies in American film and literature from 1800 to the present.

Julia Lange studied English and American Studies as well as Law at the University of Hamburg and Oxford University. Her dissertation (Hamburg, 2021) examines German American memory politics and its interrelation with the Holocaust discourse on both sides of the Atlantic. She currently works as a journalist with Der SPIEGEL specializing in U.S. politics and transatlantic relations. She continues to hold seminars in American Studies at University of Hamburg. Her publications include a monograph: *Herman the German: Das Hermann Monument in der deutsch-amerikanischen Erinnerungskultur* (Münster: LIT 2013). She recently also edited two collected volumes: *Entangled Memories: Remembering the Holocaust in a Global Age*, co-edited with Marius Henderson (Heidelberg: Winter 2017); *Was denkt das Denkmal? Eine Anthologie zur Denkmalkultur*, co-edited with Tanja Schult (Köln: Böhlau 2021).

Jolene Mathieson is Lecturer in the Department of British Studies at the University of Leipzig. Her many research interests include ekphrastic poetry, digital poetry, aesthetics, ecology, and oceanic literature. She is currently completing a project on the metaphysics of ekphrasis in Germany, England, and the U.S. during the eighteenth and nineteenth centuries, and has published articles on digital poetry in *Poetics Today* (2018), China Miéville's *The Scar* in *Spaces and Fictions of the Weird and the Fantastic* (Palgrave 2019) and the Blue Humanities in *Cultivating Sustainability in Language and Literature Pedagogy* (Routledge 2021).

Prof Dr. Ulfried Reichardt holds the Chair of North American Literature and Culture at the University of Mannheim. He studied at the University of Heidelberg, Cornell University, and the Free University of Berlin, was assistant professor at the University of Hamburg, visiting professor at the University of Cologne as well as visiting scholar at Columbia University, the University of Toronto and the University of British Columbia, Vancouver, York University and the

University of California at Santa Cruz and Santa Barbara. He received his Ph.D. at the Free University of Berlin in 1988 (*Postmodernity Seen from Inside*, 1991) and his Habilitation at the University of Hamburg in 1998 (*Alterity and History: Functions of the Representation of Slavery in the American Novel*, 2001). He has edited *Time and the African American Experience* (2000) and *Mapping Globalization* (2008), co-edited *Engendering Men* (1998) and *Network Theory and American Studies* (2015). Further publications include *Globalization: Literatures and Cultures of the Global* (2010) as well as essays on the dimension of time in literature and culture, on American Pragmatism, on music in America, on diaspora culture, and U.S.-American authors of the 19th, 20th and 21st centuries. He was founder and speaker of the graduate program "Formations of the Global" (2004–2009) and principal investigator (with Regina Schober) of the research project "Probing the Limits of the Quantified Self" funded by the German Research Foundation (2015–2018).

Joseph C. Schöpp is Professor emeritus of American Literature and History of Culture at the University of Hamburg. He is the author of *Allen Tate: Tradition als Bauprinzip dualistischen Dichtens* (1975) and *Ausbruch aus der Mimesis: Der amerikanische Roman im Zeichen der Postmoderne* (1989). He has co-edited *Die Postmoderne – Ende der Avantgarde oder Neubeginn?* (1989) and *Transatlantic Modernism* (2001). His current research focuses on American Transcendentalism.

Sabine Sielke is Chair of North American Literature and Culture and Director of the North American Studies Program and the German-Canadian Centre at the University of Bonn. Her publications include *Reading Rape* (Princeton 2002) and *Fashioning the Female Subject* (Ann Arbor 1997), the series *Transcription*, and 20 (co-)edited books, most recently *Nostalgia: Imagined Time-Spaces in Global Media Cultures* (2017), *Knowledge Landscapes North America (2016)*, *New York, New York! Urban Spaces, Dreamscapes, Contested Territories* (2015), and *American Studies Today: New Research Agendas* (2014), as well as more than 140 essays on poetry, (post-)modern literature and culture, literary and cultural theory, gender and African American studies, popular culture, and the interfaces of cultural studies and the sciences.

Hubert Zapf is an Americanist and Co-Director of Environmental Humanities at the University of Augsburg, Germany. His main areas of research are Anglo-American and Comparative Literature, Cultural Ecology, Literary Theory and History, and the Environmental Humanities. His publications include *Literature and Science,* ed., Anglia 2015; *Handbook of Ecocriticism and Cultural Ecology,* ed., De Gruyter, 2016; *Literature as Cultural Ecology: Sustainable Texts*, Bloomsbury, 2016; *Ecological Thought in German Literature and Culture,* co-ed., 2017; "Ecological Thought in Europe and Germany," *Global History of Literature and Environment*, Cambridge UP 2017: 269–285; "Literature, Sustainability, and Survival," *The Value of Literature,* eds. Vera and Ansgar Nünning, REAL 36 (2020): 261–274; *Environmental Humanities. Geistes- und sozialwissenschaftliche Beiträge zur Umweltforschung,* eds. Matthias Schmidt and Hubert Zapf, Göttingen: V&R Academic, 2021.

Index

Actor-Network-Theory   167
Adorno, Theodor W.   7, 13, 17–19, 56, 253–272
Aesthetics   2–3, 6–7, 11–13, 17, 19, 28–29, 35–46, 50–61, 85, 93, 106, 111–125, 129–143, 161, 167, 172, 181, 193, 244, 253–275
African American Writers => Black Culture
Anderson, Sherwood   113
Anthropocene   9, 11, 147–157, 159–177, 179–197
Anti-facticity => Post-factual
Arendt, Hannah   58–62, 179, 184, 214–224
Aristotle   10, 37, 88, 131–133, 139–143
Atwood, Margaret   147
Authenticity   1, 5–6, 52, 58, 105, 143, 173

Baldwin, James   208, 255
Barnes, Julian   8, 49, 51–53, 57–62
Barth, John   19, 39, 73, 105, 173
Beethoven   17–18
Benjamin, Walter   8, 9, 71–82
Bense, Max   13, 258, 268–270
Bieger, Laura   6, 13, 25–27, 254–255
Birkerts, Sven   1–3
Black Culture   8–9, 12–13, 71–82, 85–106, 201–211, 253–275
Boyle, T.C.   40
Buschendorf, Christa   9, 104, 209

Capitalism   3, 20–22, 104, 117, 124, 187–194, 256, 261–263,
Carver, Raymond   1, 2
Cavendish, Margaret   42
Chabon, Michael   111
Claviez, Thomas   6, 10, 129, 130, 139, 142
Cole, Teju   6, 8, 71–82
Colonialism   9, 21, 71, 112–115, 180–190
Confessional Poetry   12, 211, 213–226
Contingency   10, 20, 50, 55, 63, 114, 129–143
Coover, Robert   17, 19, 28–32

Covid-19 Pandemic   13, 124, 254
Cultural Ecology   6–8, 37

Danielewski, Mark Z.   111
DeLillo, Don   2, 7, 17–32, 39, 49, 77
De Man, Paul   79, 131, 136–141
Democracy   3, 13, 49–50, 102, 114–116, 123, 230, 254–270
DeWitt, Helen   2
Dickinson, Emily   39
Digital Culture   2–3, 21–24, 28, 171, 256, 258, 264
Dos Passos, John   18, 113
Dreiser, Theodore   116
Du Bois, W. E. B.   9, 85–106

Ecocritical => Ecocriticism
Ecocriticism   21, 159–161, 179–185
Egan, Jennifer   4, 11, 111, 114, 125, 173
Eggers, Dave   111–124
Ellis, Bret Easton   115
Emerson, Ralph Waldo   160–161, 166, 174
Essay Form   253–275
Ethics   8, 12–13, 44, 51, 62–66, 89–104, 130, 143, 150–151, 166, 213–227, 254
Everett, Percival   9, 85–88, 101–106
Eugenides, Jeffrey   11

Faulkner, William   18
Federman, Raymond   39
Fitzgerald, F. Scott   113
Forest Ecology   182–197
Frankfurter Schule   3
Franzen, Jonathan   2, 4, 9, 10, 11, 111–125, 131, 140–143, 147–154, 173
Frost, Robert   174

Global Novel   71
Globalization   3, 71, 111–113, 118, 121

Hegel, G. W. F.   10, 132–133, 139–143
Hemingway, Ernest   1, 2, 18
Hempel, Amy   2

Hinsey, Ellen   12, 213–227
Howells, William Dean   2, 17, 116, 118
Hustvedt, Siri   2, 4, 6–8, 35–46, 111, 125

Ickstadt, Heinz   4, 7, 21, 24, 29, 215, 216, 217
Indigenous   180–190, 196
Irony   4–5, 8–10, 22, 49–52, 60–61, 67, 105, 117, 120–122, 142, 196–197, 226

Jakobson, Roman   129–141, 233–248
James, Henry   17–18, 116, 140, 173

Kant, Immanuel   10, 143, 161, 175, 263
Krauss, Nicole   4, 173
Kucharzewski, Jan D.   4, 11, 165, 167, 174

Latour, Bruno   40, 167–168, 172
Lerner, Ben   12, 229–251
Lukács, Georg   13, 162, 258–270
Lyotard, Jean-François   3–4

Mann, Thomas   45
Melville, Herman   19, 39, 118, 165
Metaphor   10, 27, 32, 37, 46, 64, 113, 129–143, 152, 163–167, 175, 181, 185, 188, 204, 210, 211, 218, 219, 221, 224, 226, 231
Metonymy   10, 11, 129–143, 162, 174–176, 195
Modernism   3, 7–11, 18–19, 39, 56, 113, 130–143, 268
Modernity   11, 179–197
Morals => Ethics
Morrison, Toni   2, 93, 117
Music   8, 17–19, 22, 45, 49–67, 72, 74, 180, 256, 257, 260–265
Musician => Music
Myth   9, 29–31, 42–46, 85–106, 131, 137–139, 221
Mythology => Myth

Neorealism   1–14, 111–125, 129–143
New Sincerity   5, 51, 121
New York Times, The   6, 13, 73, 76, 152, 164, 253–275

Norris, Frank   17, 118
Nostalgia   22, 112, 116

Plato   37–38, 53, 131, 139, 183
Poe, Edgar Allan   39
Postcritical => Postcritique
Postcritique   5–6, 11, 179
Post-factual   3–5, 12
Postmodernism   1–10, 17–33, 39, 50–61, 71, 105, 111, 122–125, 140, 172–173, 241
Postmodernity => Postmodernism
Postmillennial   1–9, 51, 88, 105–106
Powers, Richard   4, 8, 11, 40, 49, 51, 53–57, 66–67, 117–118, 159–176
Proulx, Annie   11, 179–197
Public Mind   1–14, 111–125, 167, 213–227, 229–251, 253–275
Pynchon, Thomas   2, 3–4, 7, 17–23, 29, 39, 173

Racism   3, 12–13, 75, 92, 103–105, 182, 190, 201–211, 253–272
Rankine, Claudia   6, 12, 201–211
Reading Public => Public Mind
Realism   1–13, 16, 39, 111–125, 129–143, 172–175
Reichardt, Ulfried   8, 119
Rohr, Susanne   9, 112–113, 118, 141
Romanticism   38–39, 133, 142–143, 181, 193, 206
Romantic => Romanticism
Rorty, Richard   120, 174
Rowson, Susanna   117

Said, Edward   7, 17–19, 25, 32, 79
Science   3, 7–8, 23–24, 35–46, 155, 164–168, 184–185, 192–194, 258, 263
Science Fiction   39, 42, 170
Sebald, W. G.   8, 71–82
Shelley, Percy Bysshe   38
Shostakovich, Dimitri   8, 49–67
Sidney, Sir Philip   38
Sielke, Sabine   5, 9–10, 116–118
Sinclair, Upton   117
Slavery   9, 76–78, 89–94, 104, 208–210, 253–275

Stein, Gertrude 18, 174
Steinbeck, John 122–123
Stephenson, Neal 39
Stevens, Wallace 184
Stowe, Harriett Beecher 117, 168
Surveillance 3, 8, 49–67, 124

Thoreau, Henry David 166
Totalitarianism 8, 49–67, 113–117, 224
Twain, Mark 29, 32, 113, 116

VanderMeer, Jeff 147
Vollmann, William T. 8, 49–51, 62–67

Wallace, David Foster 4, 51, 60, 71, 111, 173
Ward, Jesmyn 9, 84, 87, 94–101, 105–106
Wharton, Edith 117, 118
Whitehead, Colson 2
Whitman, Walt 2, 206, 262
Williams, John 112
Wolfe, Tom 117

Yates, Richard 112

Zapf, Hubert 7–8, 37
Zink, Nell 11, 147, 148, 150, 152–156

www.ingramcontent.com/pod-product-compliance
Lightning Source LLC
Chambersburg PA
CBHW050517170426
43201CB00013B/1994